Crime of 1873

The Comstock Connection

Robert R. Van Ryzin

Published by

700 East State St., Iola, WI 54990-0001
715-445-2214
www.krause.com

Please, call or write us for our free catalog of antiques and collectibles publications.
To place an order or receive our free catalog, call 800-258-0929. For editorial comment and further information, use our regular business telephone at (715) 445-2214

Library of Congress Catalog Number: 00-110087
ISBN: 0-87341-873-5

Printed in the United States of America

TABLE OF CONTENTS

ACKNOWLEDGMENTS

This study of the Crime of 1873 began in the 1980s as part of fulfilling my master's requirements for the University of Wisconsin-Oshkosh. Additional study has brought it to the state of completion you see before you. Along the way, I have been aided, assisted and directed by a host of truly talented, caring and helpful scholars and professionals, as well as devoted family and friends, without all of whom, I could not have arrived at this point.

In particular, at the scholastic level, I am indebted to the members of my thesis committee—Dr. Watson Parker, Dr. Frederick Schapsmeier and Dr. George Sieber of the University of Wisconsin-Oshkosh history department—all of whom lent their support to my initial research and in completion of my thesis, "The Tainted History of the Crime of 1873," portions of which survive unaltered in this work.

For much of the initial research, in the 1980s, I sifted through hundreds of rare books and articles related to the Free Silver Movement and the Crime of 1873. Much of this material I would not have been able to obtain without the help of librarian Erin Czech, a member of the Forrest Polk Library staff at the University of Wisconsin-Oshkosh, who tirelessly hunted down material, from around the country, on my behalf.

In the last year or so, in preparation of this text, I have been aided similarly by other gifted librarians, including Stephanie Thomas of the Waupaca Public Library, Waupaca, Wis., who was able to obtain several reels of microfilm from the *Alta California, Virginia City Territorial Enterprise* and the *San Francisco Chronicle,* as well as hard-to-find books, which helped greatly in the chapters relating to the history of the Comstock Lode and the activities of William C. Ralston and the Bank of California.

Also to be credited for her tireless work in locating and photocopying the invaluable letters of Henry R. Linderman to William C. Ralston (as well as scarce documents relating to the Trade dollar's history) is Naomi Schultz of the staff of the Bancroft Library in Berkeley, Calif. Thanks also to Bancroft Library Director Susan Snyder, who graciously granted permission to quote from the Ralston Correspondence and assisted with obtaining photographs from the library's vast collection of western history prints.

For the bulk of the photographs of Virginia City and the Comstock Lode, I have Robert Nylen, curator of the Nevada State Museum, Carson City, Nev., to thank. Without his help, this work would be largely barren of such illustrations. Others, who have graciously aided in supplying photographs or manuscripts, include Joe Curtis of Mark Twain's Book Store, Virginia City, Nev.; Ellen Harding of the California State Library, Sacramento, Calif.; Stephen Bobbitt of the American Numismatic Association, Colorado Springs, Colo; Francis D. Campbell of the American Numismatic Society, New York, N.Y.; Michael Edmonds of the State Historical Society of Wisconsin Library, Madison, Wis.; Randy Miller of Chief Coin Supply, Oshkosh, Wis.; and Kerry Schaefer of Banta Digital Group, Menasha, Wis.

Many people within the various departments at Krause Publications also assisted greatly in this work. My thanks to Tracy Schmidt, book department editor, who was assigned the task of bringing all aspects of this book into its final form; Tom Michael, of the catalog department, who provided invaluable suggestions, beginning with the initial book proposal and continuing through the completion of this project; Merna Dudley, of the catalog department, who reformatted the data base to provide the Morgan and Trade dollar prices found within; and Ross Hubbard, of the photography department, and his staff, for help with photographing material. Fred Borgmann and George Cuhaj, both of the catalog department, and David C. Harper, editor of *Numismatic News,* also provided worthy assistance in this project.

Thanks also to the entire Krause Publications book department, headed by Pat Klug, for accepting this work for publication and for their efforts in layout and design.

No work of this nature could be completed without the encouragement and support of a loving family. Thanks to my parents, who have never flagged in their encouragement, and to my wife, Sharon Van Ryzin. A talented writer, Sharon spent several hours at her "second job," pouring over each chapter, making key changes to the rough text prior the manuscript's submission.

Finally, a special thanks to Dr. Watson Parker, a friend, mentor, and tireless head of my thesis committee. A gifted and noted author, his constant guidance was an inspiration to all who had the good fortune to have studied under him, including myself. If there is anything within this work that is worthy of praise, it is because of his efforts in that regard.

Robert R. Van Ryzin
October, 2000

PROLOGUE

"You shall not press down upon the brow of labor this crown of thorns, you shall not crucify mankind upon a cross of gold."

—William Jennings Bryan, July 8, 1896, Democratic National Convention, Chicago.

On a sweltering San Francisco afternoon in late August 1875, more than two years after the so-called Crime of 1873 had been committed, a perspiring, portly, middle-aged man went for his regular swim at San Francisco's North Beach, thrashing out toward Alcatraz Island. Playfully alternating between diving and floating on his back, the man swam out yards further than most of the Neptune Bath House's regular patrons. Yet this was not unusual. He had done so many times before, as it no doubt helped to shed the day's tensions. Only this day would be different, much different. This was no ordinary man; this would be no ordinary swim.

William Chapman Ralston, once the most powerful, influential and ambitious man in California, a man who some credit with building the Golden State, and who coin collectors, economists and historians need to recognize for his great impact on 19th century U.S. coinage laws and the nation's economy, died that day.

Some said he drowned. Some said the day's overbearing heat, combined with great personal stress and exertion, hurried the failure of an already fragile heart. Others, looking to read into the tragedy an element of human foible, eagerly pointed to Ralston's recently decimated personal fortunes, the collapse of his beloved Bank of California and his forced resignation as its president, only a few short hours prior to his death, to suggest he committed suicide. He drank a vial of poison before entering the water, gasped the worst of San Francisco's scandal-mongering early tabloids.

In the grand scope of things, however, it matters not a whit how he died. Either way, one of California's most influential was lost. Either way, it was the beginning of the end of an era in which great personal and business fortunes were quickly amassed and just as quickly lost in battles waged over control of the nation's mineral wealth. It was the end of a time characterized by ill-advised commercial ventures, questionable management decisions and overextended credit that led a once powerful institution and its popular leader to financial ruin. For, even before Ralston's motionless body was reclaimed from the chilly waters of San Francisco Bay, the tide had turned against this man and his untethered ambitions.

The world was changing. The way it viewed and handled money was changing. Ralston's place in it was all but gone. Yet aftershocks of this early empire builder's far-reaching influence would reverberate through the remainder of the century, manifested in the emotion-laden Free Silver Movement, which enjoyed great political success with its popular cry for the free coinage of silver, and in the millions of largely unwanted, unneeded, uncirculated silver dollars the movement produced and then cast aside.

This, therefore, is the story of Nevada's Comstock Lode, of Ralston (who through the Bank of California once masterfully manipulated most of its mines, mills and miners), and of the silver coins that were his and the Comstock's glittering legacy—Morgan dollars, Trade dollars, and Seated Liberty coins. It's a tale richly splattered with references to famous minting facilities (Carson City, San Francisco, New Orleans and Philadelphia), shaded in with details of scarce pattern coinages and experimental alloys (coiled and flowing hair $4 Stellas, Metric and Standard Silver pieces), serving as apt illustrations of what might have been, perhaps what should have been. It's also a story broadly painted with the wide strokes of a history liberally slathered with political ambition and corruption, and forever tinted, tainted and stained by the machinations of a host of so-called champions of the common man, those who bombastically waved the banner of free silver until it was finally, thankfully, frayed beyond recognition.

It is only through such a complete look at the events that surrounded this period—which encompassed the recodification of the nation's coinage laws in 1873 and ended in an insipid whimper with William Jennings Bryan's unsuccessful bid for the presidency in 1896—that we can truly understand the history of this tumultuous period in American history and appreciate the significance of the coins that now hold revered places in museums and numismatic collections, and in hoards of coins passed down from generation to generation. In coming to such an understanding, one encounters fascinating stories of great fortunes made and lost, of unfortunate deaths, of great tragedy, and of greed, manipulation and bribery, stretching from California's frock-coated elite to the highest echelons of the Treasury Department in Washington, D.C., that serve to illustrate the real, and as yet untold, story of the Crime of 1873.

We will trace the history of the U.S. silver dollar; track the ups and downs of the gold and silver trade; explore the depths and inherent dangers of Nevada's wondrous Comstock Lode; delve into the history of the Carson City Mint and its famous CC-mint-marked coinage; scrutinize the not-so-lily-white biographies of those most responsible for the Coinage Act of 1873 (those who, it might justly be said, actually perpetrated the Crime of 1873); follow the ill-fated U.S. Trade dollar on its exotic Far Eastern sojourn; and pause for a moment to talk of the lofty attempts of the day to bring about a unified international currency, much like today's euro. Along the way, we will also visit with free silverites who forced through coinage of the Morgan silver dollar, examine this popular collectible's history, and take a brief look at the series of Bryan Money that blatantly lampooned the fanatical fringe that was the Free Silver Movement.

This is the true story of the Crime of 1873 as illustrated by previously unpublished contemporary letters that tend to blur the line between free silver myth and reality and present a clearer picture of what really led to the change to a gold standard, the omission of the standard silver dollar from the Coinage Act of 1873, and, ultimately, to charges of conspiracy that fired imaginations through the late 19th century.

First, however, we must return to a time when an opportunistic yet, some say, dunderheaded prospector whose name would be forever linked with the Big Bonanza, stumbled upon great riches to become the temporary toast of Nevada's Washoe Mountains. It was, for hapless Henry T.P. Comstock, his 15 minutes of fame and, for the world, a wake-up call that changes were on the horizon. Silver would soon become too plentiful; gold too dear. Fortunes could and would be lost overnight; economies ruined.

Chapter 1

RUSH TO WASHOE

Nestled more than a mile above sea level within the expansive shadows of the Virginia Range's highest peak, Mount Davidson, lies Virginia City, home to the fabled silver-rich Comstock Lode. Its main thoroughfare—C Street—looks today much as it did in the 1800s when it teemed with freight wagons, horses and mules and reverberated with the sounds of the nearby mines, as millions of dollars in gold and silver were extracted from the surrounding hills or from man-made caverns deep below the town itself. Gone, however, are most of the miners who once toiled thousands of feet below the city, most of its merchants who once hawked everything from flour to foodstuffs to frilly frocks, and most of its town folk who ran the gamut from respectable citizens to rowdies, ruffians and red light-district prostitutes. Still it is a grand and glorious old mining town, one that during its heyday was graciously clothed in all of the amenities of any refined Eastern city—opera houses, millionaires' mansions and clubs, schools and churches, a railroad connection to Reno and points beyond, and, of course, saloons, plenty of saloons.

Today, with most of the gold and silver gone or flooded under, they mine tourists on the lode, by the millions. During the summer months, legions of sightseers flock to the city made famous in the 1960s by the television show *Bonanza*, filling its still plentiful saloons to capacity with those hankering for a taste of the gun-toting old west. Yet, what many of these tourists do not realize until they arrive, is that Virginia City was cut from a different bolt of cloth than other western towns. It was not a cowboy town as is often thought. It was a mining town. It was not flat, as on the TV western. It was tilted severely. In fact, if gold and silver had not been discovered there, it is hard to imagine that this town, or any town, clinging as it does to the mountain's steep, rocky flanks and surrounded by hills on all horizons, could ever have been conceived, much less inhabited. And it may have remained that way if it had not been for a bit of happenstance that led to the lode's discovery in 1859.

Thousands of the unsuspecting had passed this way in the years prior, among them explorers, fur trappers, and those who plodded by as part of the trail-weary wave of humanity heading west with the California Gold Rush—all of whom remained unaware that gold lay nearby. Having followed the old Emigrant Trail across expansive wastelands and

Virginia City's famed C Street as it looks today. Virginia City's grandest hotel, the International, which burned to the ground in 1914, stood next to the first building on the left.

Mount Davidson looms in the background of this decrepit remnant of Virginia City's past.

sagebrush prairies through rugged mountains toward the eastern slope of the Sierra Nevada, most had only paused in the fertile valley of the Carson River. There they sought a welcome respite for themselves and their animals before attempting the slow, exhausting, and often dangerous passage through the majestic upheaval of the Sierra Nevada range, nature's imposing snow-capped barrier to the promised riches of the Pacific coast.

Few found reason to dally longer than necessary in this valley. Not only was California an alluring temptress, but the mountain crossing, still some 25 miles to the west, had to be made with the utmost caution. Parties who waited too long risked a frozen death, trapped in the unforgiving fall snowstorms and blizzards that inevitably blanketed the mountains. Those who broke camp too soon, before the thaw, might find grass for livestock in short supply and their progress stalled by still impenetrable passes.

In May 1850, however, this all changed. The never-ending flow of passersby was interrupted when a wagon train of California-bound Mormons, following this same path, rested momentarily in the Carson River Valley. There, an ambitious one of their number, William Prouse, wiled away the time by panning in a snow-fed stream to the east of their camp, freeing a few flecks of gold before his party made a failed attempt at reaching California. Finding the Sierra passes still snow-covered, members of Prouse's party returned to the region, spending the next few weeks scouring the various sandbars and gravel banks of the long shallow gulch they had nicknamed Gold Canyon, gathering what gold they could before their mountain avenue cleared and California again beckoned.[1]

With most of the gold and silver gone (or flooded under), it took a television western, Bonanza, to bring Virginia City back into the spotlight. Memories of Ben, Little Joe, Adam and Hoss Cartwright attract droves of tourists to Virginia City and the distant ranch, where much of the filming was done.

Word of their find would spread, and soon other, better-equipped prospectors tramped by. By 1851 the ragtag community numbered around 100. Establishing a shantytown, dubbed Johntown, bedecking a plateau about four miles north of the Carson River, the loosely organized community of miners continued to sift and dig their way up the canyon with limited success—a lack of water restricting their work to periods in which mother nature doled out sufficient rain or melting snow with which to sift away the worthless sand and rock, revealing the specks of free gold. It was not until the winter and spring months of 1852 and 1853, when their numbers swelled at times to more than 200, that the area had a permanent population—most of whom continued to claw what gold they could from the earth's surface, unaware of the region's rich, native silver deposits.[2]

For two of these early residents, however, the story was a bit different. Allen and Hosea Grosh (or Grosch), had been drawn west as part of the great gold rush. In the early 1850s they crossed the Sierra Nevada and began prospecting in Gold Canyon.[3] Unlike the others working the gulch and its branches, the Grosh brothers had experience recognizing silver in its native state. By March 1856, they had become convinced of the existence of a large body of silver around what would become Silver City. In letters to their father, they detailed the discovery of four veins, one of which they described as "a perfect monster."[4]

"The show of metallic silver produced by exploding it in damp gunpowder is very promising," they wrote home, "...the rock is iron, and its colors are violet-blue, indigo-blue, blue-black, and greenish-black."[5]

By August 1857 the Grosh brothers had obtained assays of the silver from their workings in the American Ravine that suggested one of their veins would yield $3,500 to the ton, "by hurried assay," and another vein, $200 per ton, by a more careful assay. They wrote to their father that they were "very sanguine of ultimate success," but, for the Grosh brothers, fate was against them, as both would soon meet with tragic ends.[6] On Aug.19 Hosea accidentally struck his foot with a pick ax. Gangrene set in, and he died. Allen continued to tend their claim, delaying his return to California in order to settle his brother's affairs. It was November before he and a traveling companion set out, too late for a safe ascent of the mountains.

Today not much remains of the original mining equipment, except at museums. These relics—an old ore car and shaft—stand outside of the Chollar mine, which continues to give tours.

Caught in a fierce blizzard, Allen died in the mining camp Last Chance, shortly after being rescued.

The Grosh brothers' secret went with them to their graves, partly because, as Dan De Quille wrote in *The Big Bonanza*, silver was so little on the minds of early miners, they "were all working in blissful ignorance of silver existing anywhere in the country."[7] Most also cared little about what lay very far below the surface. When the gold that could be caught by washing in their pans or trapped in the riffles of their rockers and sluices was exhausted, they packed up their few belongings and followed the scent of the next strike to the next hopeful camp. It was a scenario that had played out since the days of the forty-niners and would be repeated from rush to rush.

Within a few years of the Grosh brothers' demise, the traces of pay dirt that had once supported a small community of prospectors were largely depleted. Average returns dropped from $4 to $5 per day to just $2.[8] Only the most stubborn hung on. The winter months of 1858-1859, however, brought heartening news to those who had toughed it out. James Finney (known as "Old Virginny") and Henry T. P. Comstock (nicknamed "Old Pancake"), along with a mishmash of other experienced Johntown prospectors, began working the canyon's head on Mount Davidson's southern slope, where Finney, an old hand at spotting good ground, stumbled on a small rise of yellowish quartz that proved to be especially rich in gold. Unwittingly, Finney had also fallen upon the southern outcropping of the Comstock. Hundreds of feet below its gold-specked surface, lay the yet undisturbed ore bodies of some of the lode's most valuable mines—the Belcher, Crown Point, Yellow Jacket, Imperial, Empire, Kentuck and others.[9] Aptly christened Gold Hill, Finney's find quickly became a beehive of activity, as miners from neighboring regions abandoned their claims and moved to Gold Hill.

For some time, on the northern slope, other prospectors had been working up a similar ravine, known as Six Mile Canyon. Joining them were Peter O'Riley and Patrick McLaughlin, who had ambled over from crowded Gold Hill. Working at the canyon's head, they chanced upon the lode's northern outcropping, at a point where Gold Canyon and Six Mile Canyon close to within a little more than a mile of each other.

Like the find at Gold Hill, the discovery at the northern end of Six Mile Canyon was largely a matter of chance. Finding water for prospecting

Henry T.P. Comstock. After selling off his interests in the lode, Comstock spent much of the remainder of his days in pursuit of a new strike. Most accounts say he took his own life in 1870.

scarce, McLaughlin and O'Riley had set about digging a reservoir a few feet up from where they were working in order to pool a trickle of water from the mountainside. About four feet down, they struck a strange looking layer of blue-black sand, which, when washed, revealed an abundance of pale yellow gold and, unbeknownst to them, the northern end of the Comstock Lode. All that was left was for a lanky, some say lazy, and certainly loudmouthed, prospector to lay claim to the site and secure his indelible spot in history.

Like most placer miners who scurried from camp to camp in search of gold, Henry T. P. Comstock had tried his luck first in California. Gravitating to Nevada in 1856, he bounded aimlessly from claim to claim. Riding into McLaughlin and O'Riley's camp on the evening of their discovery, Comstock spied the gold and with a quick wittedness that belies his rumored diminished mental capacity, preposterously announced to the Irishmen tending their claim that he had already posted the surrounding 160 acres of miserably steep, rocky hillside for a ranch. With perhaps a bit more substance than bluff, he also argued that, besides being guilty of working his claim, McLaughlin and O'Riley had been using water rightfully belonging to him and his partner, Emanuel Penrod. Penrod, it seems, had previously purchased rights to the spring from which the trickle of water originated.[10] Deciding not to contest Comstock's claims, McLaughlin and O'Riley agreed to take the pair on as equal partners. Staking out the area as a quartz claim, each of the four miners received 300 feet and Comstock and Penrod an additional 100 feet as the original locators.

The area was indeed rich in gold, and news of their discovery echoed loudly through neighboring mining communities. Where during the prior season most Washoe miners had barely eked out an existence, Comstock and his partners were now pulling hundreds of dollars of the precious metal—in pounds, not ounces—from the odd-colored sand.[11] Elated by their good fortune, they were, at first, only slightly bothered by the unusual bluish, black sand that clogged their rockers—the gold yield was high and waste material easily cast aside. But as they dug deeper, this decomposed top layer gave way to an only partially decomposed substratum and, ulti-

After its rough and tumble beginnings, Virginia City blossomed into a refined city, boasting several opera houses and mansions. The International Hotel stood before Piper's Opera House. It was destroyed by fire on Dec. 12, 1914. Courtesy of the Nevada State Museum Photograph Collection.

mately, to a solid vein of stubborn rock that could not be worked in their cradles until it had been reduced by repeated blows of sledgehammers and picks. With the help of two arrastras (rock-crushing devices that could slowly reduce the quartz to pulp), obtained from Joseph A. Osborn and John D. Winters in exchange for a portion of their claim, more gold could be amalgamated and the partners' profits grew.[12]

It was not, however, until an enterprising rancher transported samples of the growing pile of cast-aside rock to the well-established quartz mining regions of Grass Valley and Nevada City, California, in late June 1859, that reputable assays confirmed that the Comstock ore was rich not just in gold but in silver as well and worth in excess of $3,000 per ton.[13] By the next morning's light the rush to Washoe was on. Leading the way was Grass Valley judge and mining speculator James Walsh, who had been privy to the assay results of the prior evening. He arose early and before daybreak was riding pell-mell toward the western slopes of the Sierras with others to take up claims in Washoe. By the time they arrived, however, the Comstock ledge was already dotted with stakes and notices for miles to the north and south, forcing the judge, his partner Joseph Woodworth, and others to enter into negotiations with the original locators to secure good ground ahead of the thousands of California prospectors who would surely be following close on their heels.

A severe winter slowed the assault on the Comstock, but by the first wisp of spring of 1860, a humbug driven sea of hopefuls choked the main passage through the Sierras, south of Lake Tahoe, emerging from a tapestry of colorfully named California mining towns—Old Dry Diggins, Mad Mule Gulch, Ophir, Rough and Ready, Whiskytown and others—to take up a precarious residence along the Comstock ledge, nearby Gold Hill diggings, and the barren foothills of the Virginia Range. From the west, along the 100 miles to Washoe, came veteran California placer miners. From the northwest, arrived those who went bust following the disappointing trail of gold to the Fraser River in British Columbia in 1858. From the east, debarked a hodgepodge of newly minted prospectors, entrepreneurs, merchants, and various forms of the footloose who had become part and parcel of prior rushes.

Where Washoe Indians once peacefully hunted and fished, a legion of wide-eyed gold and silver seekers now arrived by mule, horseback, or on foot. "Old men and young, waifs from many nations, who had drifted during ten years to the Californian gold fields, with every variety of dress and equipment, mounted and on foot, driving pack-mules, burros, horses, and oxen—dusty, muddy, tired and foot-sore—this oddly-assorted company was knit together by the bond of a common purpose," Eliot Lord wrote.[14] Hurriedly they staked off the area for 20 to 30 miles until "even the Desert was pegged, like the sole of a boot, with stakes designating claims."[15]

"Every foot of the canon was claimed, and gangs of miners were at work all along the road, digging and delving into the earth like so many infatuated gophers," gifted scribe James Ross Browne related of what he witnessed in the spring of 1860, upon passing through Devil's Gate en route from Carson City.[16] At Gold Hill, the "excitement was quite pitiable to behold," Browne wrote. "Those who were not at work burrowing holes into the mountain were gathered in gangs around the whisky saloons, pouring liquid fire down their throats, and swearing all the time in a manner so utterly reckless as to satisfy me they had long since bid farewell to hope."[17]

Original settlers, though few in number, soon found themselves strangers in their own land as an unending stream of prospectors poured into the region, staking claims on all quartz outcroppings and in every crevice throughout the barren hills for miles around.[18] Lacking suitable roads, food, water and, importantly, lumber for building (and mining), these were tough times for all who tempted to make a go of it in Washoe.

"If a city was to be built on the line of the lode, it must be a foreign creation," Lord wrote. "Water must be made to flow from the rocks or conducted from distant lakes; roads must be cut and blasted through the cañons and along the edge of mountain precipices; the frame-work of the houses and the timber used in the mines must be cut from the trees of the Sierras and dragged up to the mountain camp; food, clothing, tools, and supplies of all kinds must be transported by slow and costly methods from the Pacific sea-board."[19]

Thus, at first, housing of a conventional style was nonexistent. Many simply burrowed deep into the hillside or dug straight into the ground—

a telltale stream of smoke from their stoves in some cases the only visible evidence of their meager earthly existence. The rash of unkempt humanity made a misbegotten sight that even the well-traveled Browne found distressing:

> Frame shanties, pitched together as if by accident; tents of canvas, of blankets, of brush, of potato-sacks and old shirts, with empty whisky-barrels for chimneys; smoky hovels of mud and stone; coyote holes in the mountain side forcibly seized and held by men; pits and shafts with smoke issuing from every crevice; piles of goods and rubbish on craggy points, in the hollows, on the rocks, in the mud, in the snow, every where, scattered broadcast in pell-mell confusion, as if the clouds had suddenly burst overhead and rained down the dregs of all the flimsy, rickety, filthy little hovels and rubbish of merchandise that had ever undergone the process of evaporation from the earth since the days of Noah. The intervals of space, which may or may not have been streets, were dotted over with human beings of such sort, variety, and numbers, that the famous ant-hills of Africa were as nothing in the comparison. To say that they were rough, muddy, unkempt and unwashed, would be but faintly expressive of their actual appearance; they were all this by reason of exposure to the weather; but they seemed to have caught the very diabolical tint and grime of the whole place. Here and there, to be sure, a San Francisco dandy of the 'boiled shirt' and 'stove-pipe' pattern loomed up in proud consciousness of the triumphs of art under adverse circumstances, but they were merely peacocks in the barn-yard.[20]

Despite the often-unbearable living conditions, Washoe prospectors were true to the spirit of the rush. They were unflagging in their optimism. Hope did not spring eternal for just a few unflappable souls, but was free flowing for everyone. The big strike was always within reach. Every one of them thought they could get rich, would get rich. Every one of them knew it would happen soon. "Nobody had any credit, yet every body bought thousands of feet of glittering ore," Browne wrote. "Sales were made in the Mammoth, the Lady Bryant, the Sacramento, the Winnebunk, and the innumerable other 'outside claims,' at the most astounding figures, but not a dime passed hands. All was silver underground, and deeds and mortgages on top; silver, silver every where, but scarce a dollar in coin."[21]

Sadly though, it quickly became apparent that these early prospectors, although great in spirit, were of a different breed than what would be needed to exploit the Comstock's mineral wealth. They were not equipped, financially or otherwise, for the requisite hard rock mining. So, understandably, and lamentably, most of the original locators disposed of their valuable claims for a mere pittance of what even a foot of the same ground would be worth only a few years later. By the spring of 1860 many of the original claimants to the Comstock had sold out. The good judge from Grass Valley purchased Comstock's claim for $100 down with the promise of $10,900 to follow. McLaughlin got just $3,500 from George Hearst, who would later father publishing magnate William Randolph Hearst. O'Riley held out the longest, receiving nearly $50,000 through the sale of his claim and back dividends. Penrod let go for $8,500 to Judge Walsh, and Osborn sold his claim for $7,000. Though all had been blessed to participate in the greatest silver strike in U.S. history, local legend has it that, almost to a man, they later drifted inexorably into poverty, despair and even insanity.

With his money, Comstock opened supply stores in Carson City and Silver City. Both failed. For a number of years his wanderlust drove him from one mining camp to the next, much of his time spent in unsuccessful Idaho and Montana ventures. In 1870, most tellers say, the once brazen and well-known "Old Pancake" became distraught and sought permanent relief with a fatal bullet to his head.

McLaughlin's $3,500 went quickly. He spent the remainder of his life doing odd jobs in various California mining camps, often serving as the camp cook. O'Riley squandered his nearly $50,000 on a hotel in Virginia City and on some bad stock investments. Paying undo heed to persistent voices in his head, he was soon found burrowing deeper and deeper into the Sierras near Genoa, reassured by his constant cranial companions that a new Comstock lay just ahead. In time, the voices did irreparable damage. A broken and delusional figure, he spent the last years of his shattered life in a private asylum for the insane in Woodbridge, Calif.

James "Old Virginny" Finney, who some claim gave his name to the city of silver that sprang up around the Comstock, sold off his interests in the Gold Hill claims for an undisclosed sum. A colorful, well-liked figure, with a weakness for drink, he fell from a horse in 1861, fracturing his skull.

It seems, if these oft-retold stories bear even a hint of truth, that finding precious metals is one thing, profiting from it another, and the odds of living beyond the discovery in comfort next to nil.

Two views of Virginia City taken from similar angles. The top is a vintage photograph of the Comstock during the 19th century. Note the International Hotel near the center. Courtesy of the Nevada State Museum Photograph Collection. The bottom is a later 20th century view. The mine workings and many of the buildings are gone.

Chapter 2

HEADY TIMES

Among the early arrivals on the Comstock, making the passage in mid-1859 before the mad rush, were a number of savvy California capitalists, including the good judge from Grass Valley. Having talked Comstock into selling, Judge James Walsh momentarily laid claim to a part of the lode before he too succumbed to the temptation of quick money. His partner, Joseph Woodworth, however, hung on and, with others, formed the Ophir Silver Mining Company the following year. Future Bank of California president William C. Ralston would serve as its treasurer.

George Hearst was another who made the trek in 1859. A storekeeper-turned-quartz-mining speculator, Hearst set aside work on a promising vein in the Nevada City region to follow Walsh to the new strike. Once there, he made a deal with Patrick McLaughlin to acquire the Irishman's one-sixth interest in the Ophir for $3,000. Hearst then withdrew to California in order to raise the necessary capital to complete the transaction and, in the process, lay the framework for his family's future fortune.

In August 1859, the first ore, 3,151 pounds, was transported to San Francisco by Walsh, Comstock and Hearst, where it sold for $1.50 a pound.[1] Encouraged by the profits, the Ophir owners rushed to beat the winter snows, shipping 38 tons of the most promising ore to Joseph Mosheimer's San Francisco smelting works by fall. The yield was an impressive $112,000, averaging just shy of $3,000 a ton. Even with the high cost of transportation, $140 per ton, and a $412-per-ton charge for reduction, the owners enjoyed a profit in excess of $90,000.[2] When the freshly poured bars of silver—an usual sight in this city built on gold—were carried

The Hale & Norcross works. To the left is the train trestle to the dumps. Stock prices soared in 1868 at this mine, jumping from $1,300 a foot to $2,200 in just two days. The same mine later served as a fulcrum for the bonanza crowd to wrest control of the Comstock away from William C. Ralston and the Bank of California. Courtesy of the Nevada State Museum Photograph Collection.

This 1870s photograph shows the inside of one of the Comstock's processing mills (possibly the California Pan Mill in Six Mile Canyon). Courtesy of Joe Curtis, Mark Twain's Book Store, Virginia City, Nev.

through the streets of San Francisco, an excited crowd gathered. A throng of miners and the curious gawked for hours through the windows of Alsop & Co. bankers, where the bars were placed on prominent display. If there had been lingering doubt of the richness of the Washoe strike, it was quashed, and the excitement spread from mouth to mouth, newspaper to newspaper, town to town, and, rapidly, from west to east.

Back on the Comstock, not much additional work was done for the remainder of 1859, the winter of 1859-1860 being one of the severest on record. Like the Ophir, the neighboring Central shipped ore to San Francisco that year—more than 20 tons, grossing $50,000.[3] Both mines employed a small number of men working what, at first, were just large open pits.

Unlike California, where much of the gold could be taken with relative ease near the surface, the Comstock ore bodies were spread out in cavernous pockets sometimes several thousand feet below the earth. Encasing the gold and silver were large masses of unstable barren rock, composed of sheets of clay and partially decomposed porphyry. As the Ophir pit deepened, the use of heavy machinery became mandatory. Buckets and ropes were out. Steam-powered hoists were needed to haul the ore car and men up from the depths. Pumps were required to remove the ever-increasing amounts of water that threatened, hampered, and soaked most Comstock operations.

By December 1860, the Ophir was about 180 feet deep, and the ore body had expanded to approximately 45 feet in width.[4] Normal methods of working a mine, using a cap and post timbering system to support the mine walls (consisting of two vertical posts surmounted by another post laid horizontally on top, much like a doorway), would not suffice. The caverns became too tall for available lumber without splicing. Nor could the timbers withstand the tremendous weight of such a wide body of ore—one that by nature swelled when exposed to air.

So, in November 1860, the Ophir's owners sent for Philipp Deidesheimer, a German-born-and-trained mining engineer who had been managing an El Dorado County, California, mine since 1851. Arriving in November, Deidesheimer set to work developing a new timbering system. Resembling a honeycomb, thick, squared timbers of four to six feet in length were mortised and tenoned at the ends, so they could be fit together to create hollow cubes that could be interlocked, side by side or on top of each other, bracing the lode in several directions. In cubes not located near workable ore, waste rock was piled to the ceiling to provide additional support. Deidesheimer's revolutionary square-set system would become standard throughout the lode, and, though not foolproof, it opened the mines for deeper and deeper exploration.

The next major hurdle mine owners faced was finding an economical and efficient means of locally reducing the ore to retrieve the precious metals. In the Comstock's early days, it was not uncommon for mine owners to pack up what was deemed to be the best yielding ore and ship it, via San Francisco, to England for reduction. However, smelting was expensive and transportation costs high. This would only work with the ore that promised the highest return per ton, and much of the Comstock ore was not of that quality. It would await development of local mills and new processes, before its silver could be profitably extracted.

Methods of freeing the silver and gold from surrounding less valuable minerals had been pioneered more than a century before in Mexico and Peru, but these time-consuming processes were of use only on a small scale. What was needed was a faster, mechanized system of reduction to fit the scope of the tons of Comstock ore that awaited crushing. One of those credited with modernizing amalgamation of precious metals from pulverized rock was California mill owner Almarin B. Paul. Paul, who bought claims in the Washoe district and, in March 1860, formed the Washoe Gold and Silver Mining Company No. 1, opened the first mill in the area, beating another worthy for that honor by only a few short hours. Soon the region would be over-bloated with hundreds of mills, competing for the Comstock's often-scarce ore for survival.

Aided by the use of 24 deafening ore-pounding stamps, Paul's mill, located in Gold Canyon below Devil's Gate, became a standard that the others would follow. An advancement on earlier methods, the heavy metal stamps replaced horse-, mule- or water-driven arrastras while large steam-heated pans, which could amalgamate the silver in six hours, replaced the four- to six-week Mexican patio process.

As part of Paul's special process, into the steam-heated pans was introduced a recipe of quicksilver, salt and copper sulphate. Heavy mullers mixed the brew, inadvertently introducing a key ingredient in the amalgamation process, iron filings added by friction of the grinding process.[5] From the pans, the mix went to a system of settling basins to extract the silver amalgam and quicksilver, following which the quicksilver was evaporated off. By the end of 1862, Paul's Washoe pan process had replaced a variety of "secret brews," ranging from one that employed the locally prevalent sagebrush to one using bark stripped from indigenous cedar trees.[6]

Even with the new process, mill extractions were not perfect. An average of 60 to 65 percent of the assayed value could be recovered before any special treatments. With time, another 20 percent could be realized. But the additional profit did not go back to the mines. Rather, it regularly padded the pockets of the mill owners or those who had worked out lucrative deals to provide the mills with the ore to keep running.[7]

Also relatively new to the Comstock was the method of mine ownership. In the early 1850s, the majority of California mines had been owned by partnerships, but with the Comstock Lode, the most popular method of setting up a mine or a mill became the establishment of a corporation, which diffused the risk by issuing large bodies of stock, pooling the money received and leveling assessments to cover costs.[8] *The First Directory of Nevada Territory*, published in 1862, showed the aggregate capital of 1860 incorporations (which ranged from the Ophir, with $5,040,000, to Coso G. and S. Mining Co., with $30,000) to be in excess of $30 million.[9] By 1863, more than 4,000 such companies were incorporated for the purposes of issuing stock.[10] Investment in mining stock also mushroomed with the growth of the Comstock. Of the 17,000 claims "located" on the Comstock, only a few ever paid dividends, yet most sold "stock at astounding prices to a gullible and speculative public," Ira Cross wrote.[11]

It was during this early period on the Comstock, long before Virginia City blossomed into a refined city, that a young Samuel Clemens (Mark Twain) accepted an offer, in 1862, to work on the *Virginia City Territorial Enterprise*. There he honed his writing skills, while learning firsthand of the Comstock's seemingly endless riches. Years later, in *Roughing It*, Twain wrote fancifully of the early speculative stock fever surrounding the Comstock:

> The great 'Gould and Curry' mine was held at three or four hundred dollars a foot when we arrived; but in two months it had sprung up to eight hundred. The 'Ophir' had been worth only a mere trifle, a year gone by, and now it was selling at nearly four thousand dollars a foot! Not a mine could be named that had not experienced an astonishing advance in value within a short time. Everybody was talking about these marvels. Go where you would, you heard nothing else, from morning till far into the night. Tom So-and-So had sold out of the 'Amanda Smith' for $40,000—hadn't a cent when he 'took up' the ledge six months ago. John Jones had sold half his interest in the 'Bald Eagle and Mary Ann' for $65,000, gold coin, and gone to the States for his family. The widow Brewster had 'struck it rich' in the 'Golden Fleece' and sold ten feet for $18,000—hadn't money enough to buy a crape bonnet when Sing-Sing Tommy killed her husband at Baldy Johnson's wake last spring.[12]

Well-versed in the realm of mining speculations, many a prominent California citizen became a director of a mining or milling company on the Comstock and "every community was contributing a sum, monthly to pay the assessments."[13] Each day, California and Nevada newspapers dutifully reported the stock prices and the latest intelligence gleaned from the day's activities at each important mine throughout the region. By late 1862, the first of several stock exchanges operating during the Comstock's heyday, the San Francisco Stock and Exchange Board, opened for business in San Francisco.

Mining stocks were attractive to all, and the lode yielded its share of success stories among those astute enough, or lucky enough, to buy into the proper mine during times of borrasca (barren ground) and sell during periods of bonanza. As Joseph L. King observed in his history of the board: If a speculator had purchased 100 shares of the Consolidated Virginia at $8 per share in 1871, by 1875 (with subsequent capital stock issues and mine acquisitions) he would have controlled 1,600 shares of stock—1,000 in the Consolidated Virginia and 600 of the California. With both stocks selling at $800 per share in early 1875, his initial $800 investment would have grown to a staggering $1.28 million.[14] Yet that first $800 was no small sum of money in 1871, and for the most part those in the best position to profit were not those who dabbled in the market but investors with the ready capital and the insider knowledge to manipulate it. This fell often to the mine owners, who, when not actively involved in attempts to artificially bull or bear the market, were also the first to know when their mine encountered a promising body of ore and, therefore, able to best benefit from the news.

It did not always matter, however, whether the strike ever materialized. Timing, though, was critical. Dan De Quille likened Comstock market

The $40,000 Shave

The number of seats on the San Francisco Stock and Exchange Board, where brokers could quickly make or lose fortunes, rose as did their value in the years following the exchange's formation. According to Joseph L. King, who served as a board chairman and detailed its history in 1910, when seats were first offered, in 1862, they could be had for $100. In the board's biggest year, 1875, the often profitable and in-demand seats were going for $43,000.

King delighted in relating anecdotes about the board during the Comstock's boom period. For instance, according to King, broker Wayman C. Budd partook of a break one day to sit down for what he would thereafter refer to as his $40,000 shave. The year was 1873, and Budd, a longtime board member, having learned that a discovery of ore had been made at the Ophir, amassed 2,500 shares of the mine between the price of $16 and $82. As the market advanced, he disposed of 1,500 shares, leaving him with 1,000 shares now valued at $82 a share. During the recess in the day's trading, Budd settled in for a shave at a local barber shop and drifted off to sleep. By the time he awoke and dashed back to the exchange, the Ophir had been called and the market had broken, its shares were now worth only $40 each.[1]

In dull trading periods, King relates, William C. Ralston's business associate, William Sharon, would give his broker, B.F. Sherwood, a large sell order termed a "settler." Such a sale of 2,000 shares of six or seven principal stocks would break prices across the board and bring buyers into the market. A break of $3 to $10 on such mines as Ophir, Chollar, Belcher, Crown Point, Yellow Jacket, Savage and Overman, King said, "would turn the whole street into buyers..." Prices would thereby rise again and all shares could then be sold at a profit.[2]

booms and busts to a bricklayer piling bricks one atop the other, until the entire column tumbles to the ground.[15] The trick was to sell your stock before that unmortered paper wall came crashing down around you. Yet this was no easy task, as stock prices could be very erratic, rising or falling not only through good or bad fortune but also through market manipulation. Eighteen-sixty-three, for example, was a boom year on the market, as hundreds of new companies opened and began trading their stock, forcing prices, at least temporarily, to dizzying heights. The Ophir sold for $6,300 a foot, the Savage for $4,000, and the Hale & Norcross at $2,100.[16] By year's end, the fever had subsided and stock values dropped. In November 1870, the Crown Point mine at Gold Hill struck promising ore at the 1,100-foot level. In seven months, its stock soared from $3 to an amazing $6,000 per share, only to fall to $1,825 by May 1872.[17]

The slightest mention of a strike was, at times, all that was needed to spark an all-out market frenzy. In 1872, shares in the Savage, selling for $30 in January, were driven up to $725 by April on a rumor of a strike, apparently started to bull the market. Other stocks followed suit. The hectic market broke in May 1872, cutting stock values by about one-third.[18]

The California, a bonanza mine organized in December 1873, is another good example. In November 1874, its stock could be had for $90 a share. By January of the following year, the same stock was worth $790. One month later, it fell to $55. During the same period, prices at the neighboring Consolidated Virginia, which tapped into the Comstock's biggest bonanza in mid-1873, jumped from $160 to $790, only to slump dismally to $40 by the end of February 1875.[19]

Because making a profit in the market most often depended on quick response and inside knowledge, a popular method employed by Comstock mine owners to maintain secrecy was to entomb miners who were following the course of a promising vein. The practice began early in the lode's history and by 1868 had become commonplace.[20] When a strike was anticipated (and sometimes when stimulating the market was the sole goal), a group of miners were made to eat, sleep and live at their subterranean work stations for days, or even weeks, leaving those on the surface to wonder what, if anything, their explorations had uncovered.

It could be quite an effective tactic or a useless ploy. In January 1868, miners on the 930-foot level of the Hale & Norcross became willing prisoners in return for triple pay of $12 per day. Upon their release, on Jan. 10, the discovery of rich ore was reported, and Hale & Norcross stock, which had been trading at $1,300 a foot two days prior, shot to $2,200 in heavy buying.[21]

In its "Mining Intelligence" column, the Tuesday, Feb. 16, 1869, issue of the *Virginia City Territorial Enterprise* reported that workers cutting the ledge in the Imperial-Empire, having just "passed through the east clay wall," generally considered a good place to find ore, had been "shut up in the bowels of the earth" since the prior Friday.[22] Two days later, beds were furnished to the overnighting miners.

"Nothing is known of the nature of the developments being made below by outsiders upon the surface," the *Territorial Enterprise* tendered, though we "venture to guess that the Imperial drift, on the 1,000-foot level, is about 10 feet in the vein, and that very good looking quartz has been found."[23]

After seven days of captivity, the miners were released. The Feb. 20, 1869, *Territorial Enterprise* reported: "No startling developments have been made. The 1,000-foot station drift has penetrated the ledge about 15 feet, encountering a body of barren white quartz carrying no streaks of ore at all." Still, the newspaper related, those associated with the mine remained confident that good ore would be found within a few weeks. Stockbrokers and buyers were not impressed. In fact, Imperial-Empire shares sagged by nearly one-third during the period in which the miners were entombed.[24]

In 1872, this practice came into utter disrepute. A rumor that the Ophir was forcing four miners to remain in the mine led to threats of law suits, causing Ophir values to drop, and other mines to abandon this tactic.[25]

Despite the various market manipulations and best efforts of those who kept a keen eye on mining news, in the end only a few mines paid dividends (the money having been absorbed by operating costs and often in time-consuming, expensive claim litigation). Likewise, only a few investors ever made a fortune in the market.[26] Figures show that from 1859 to 1882 some mines—like the Bullion, Utah, Best & Belcher, Knickerbocker, Rock Island, Baltimore and a handful of others—yielded no paying ore.[27]

Still these were heady times. The West was free and open for those with nerve, know-how, capital and the vision to exploit it. Men here who amassed great fortunes and dreamed big dreams were looked upon as visionaries and empire builders. William C. Ralston, cashier and real leader of the Bank of California, was

Some mines never produced any paying ore. One of these was the Utah. Courtesy of the Nevada State Museum Photograph Collection.

one such man. Early in the lode's history, against the advice of others, he invested his own and the bank's money freely in the Comstock, stuck with it through its periods of bust, and amassed a fortune in the process.

Yet, on the Comstock, making money was a game anyone could play, not just wealthy California bankers like Ralston. Its allure knew no social, religious or economic boundaries. Even if you could not own a mine, you could own a piece of it. For the miners who daily descended into the Comstock's harsh, pitch-black environs—as some of the more grizzly tales in the following chapters evince—it was a high stakes gamble on which they risked not just money but their very lives. Making money on the Comstock was not for the faint of heart. It required a kind of fortitude, and bravery, that reached to the very soul of every Comstock miner.

Chapter 3

DANGERS BELOW

On the morning of July 5, 1882, Comstock miner William F. Grant was riding the cage up the hoisting shaft of the Chollar-Norcross-Savage mine when he became faint, lost his balance and fell. The startled miners riding with Grant signaled the hoist engineer to lower them to the bottom of the shaft. There they recovered Grant's mutilated remains. When Grant fell, he became unmercifully pinned between the cage and the mine shaft's wall plates, where his right hip was horribly crushed and mangled, nearly cutting his body in two before he plummeted to his death.[1]

Slightly more than one month later, Thomas Veale, a car man at the 2,400-foot level of the same mine, fell from the cage 280 feet to his death into a pool of scalding water. Veale had climbed aboard the cage to go to the surface in order to pick up tools and parts with which to fix a malfunctioning hydraulic pump. The cage traveled only four feet before he signaled the engineer to stop it. A witness to the accident, who had been at work in a nearby drift, heard a noise and ran to the shaft only to find a newly emptied cage. Several miners then descended to the bottom of the shaft, where they spent a number of hours, working with grappling hooks, before they were able to drag Veale's badly deformed body from the sump.[2]

As gruesome as these deaths were, they were a fairly common occurrence in the Comstock mines. Between 1863 and 1880, according to Eliot Lord, nearly 300 miners were killed and another 600 injured in various mine-related accidents.[3] The unstable nature of the lode, as well as the extreme temperatures encountered as the shafts plunged deeper and deeper into the earth's core, combined to create, as historian T.H. Watkins described it, "a catalog of hor-

The Chollar-Norcross-Savage joint shaft. Courtesy of the Nevada State Museum Photograph Collection.

rors to challenge Dante's tour through the Inferno."[4] Besides falling down a mine shaft, miners could be torn to shreds by premature explosions of blasting materials, roasted in underground fires, hit by falling equipment, or crushed by a runaway ore car.

Leading such horrors was the always prevalent danger of a cave-in, which could occur without much warning, entombing or crushing the unfortunates in its path. Unlike other mines, the ore bodies of the Comstock did not always run in veins, but were spread out, as Bonanza King John Mackay put it, "like plums in a charity pudding."[5] This formation included walls of worthless rock generally known among miners as "horse," composed of crushed quartz, clay and bits of porphyry that were at best unstable and made mining the ore difficult and extremely dangerous. It was not until Philipp Deidesheimer developed his square-set system of timbering, in 1860, that successful deep mining of the Comstock became possible. But even so, it could not completely alleviate the problems of cave-ins, as the walls of the Comstock were often made of thick sheets of clay that swelled when exposed to air.

Interestingly, the constant threat of cave-ins is why a strange bond of friendship formed between the miners working the Comstock and the rats that infested it. New miners were sometimes tempted to kill the freeloading vermin, who were regular lunchtime companions, but were quickly informed by old-timers of the rodents' uncanny ability to forecast impending doom. The rats, it seems, were able to sense the pressure of the settling ground, even before the cracking timbers could be heard, and would scurry about, giving miners fair warning.

Comstock rats were also revered as a sign that a new body of ore would soon be discovered. One such case occurred in November 1882, when a rat was sighted in a new crosscut at the 2,700-foot level of the Sierra Nevada mine. The *Virginia City Territorial Enterprise* reported:

> There is much talk among the miners about the coming of this rat, and the men in the new crosscut are very proud of it, and have high hopes on account of its presence. Woe unto the man who shall intentionally kill that Sierra Nevada rat![6]

The introduction of Philipp Deidesheimer's square-set system of timbering helped to alleviate cave-ins. Courtesy of the Nevada State Museum Photograph Collection.

A Comstock miner (circa 1867-1868) at work at a stope in the Savage mine. Photograph by Timothy O'Sullivan, for the Department of the Army's Geological Exploration of the 40th Parallel (or King Survey), with the use of the glare of burning magnesium to provide light. Courtesy of the Still Pictures Branch, National Archives, College Park, Md.

With a few notable exceptions, such as the Consolidated Virginia and its neighbor, the California, most of the major ore bodies on the Comstock Lode were discovered a few hundred feet below the surface, and by the 1880s, those deposits had been mined out, forcing the miners to begin working on the nominal ore bodies 1,000 to 3,000 feet below the surface, where about all that was regularly encountered was extreme heat from underground hot water springs that, in some cases, raised temperatures to a life-threatening 140-160 degrees Fahrenheit.

The stifling heat encountered at the lower levels also required miners to consume tremendous quantities of water and ice. Three gallons of water and 95 pounds of ice were allotted every day for each miner.[7] The *Territorial Enterprise* wrote that, "If there are to be found anywhere in the world a set of human salamanders we may claim credit of having them here on the Comstock." It added, "no ice water is too cold to be swallowed with a relish."[8]

In such intense heat, miners could work only 15 minutes before they needed a half-hour rest break. However, the visit to the cooling-off station could be an irritation of its own. According to the *Territorial Enterprise:*

> In a place where the temperature is ninety the man will feel so cold as to shiver. Often at the cooling off station, where the temperature is 100 degrees, the perspiration will cease and the man will begin to feel very uncomfortable. On leaving and going back to where the temperature is from 115 to 120, as the perspiration begins to start, there is for a minute or two an intolerable itching over the whole body.[9]

If the miner survived the perils of the heat at the Comstock's lower levels, he still had to worry about his ascent to the surface. The rapid temperature change a miner experienced while riding a fast moving cage could cause him to feel nauseated and dizzy, lose his balance, and plummet to his death. But even if he kept his wits, he still had to worry whether or not the cage would stop at the collar of the shaft or shoot right on by, throwing its passengers violently from it. The cage's movements were controlled by a hoist engineer who, by watching a large dial, could determine its exact position at any time. Using a system based on the number of times a bell sounded, the miner could tell the engineer when and where he wanted the cage to start and stop. Because a moment's indecision could be disastrous, the hoist engineer's job was generally given to a competent person. Still, tragic misunderstandings could and did occur.

Pierce Powell, a tour guide at the Chollar mine, explains the mine's workings while crouched in a section of the mine supported by the cap and post system of timbering. The Chollar was opened in 1861.

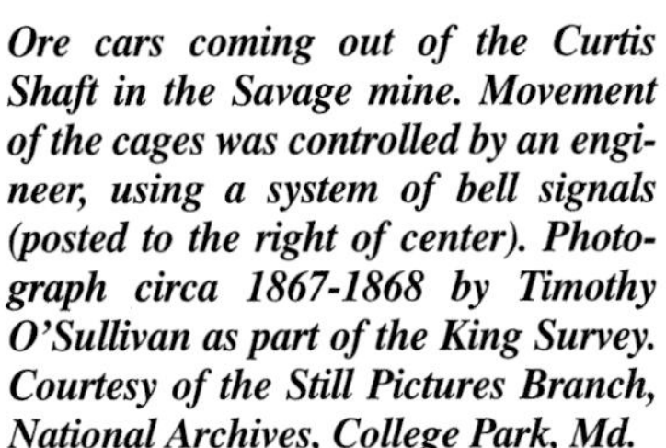

Ore cars coming out of the Curtis Shaft in the Savage mine. Movement of the cages was controlled by an engineer, using a system of bell signals (posted to the right of center). Photograph circa 1867-1868 by Timothy O'Sullivan as part of the King Survey. Courtesy of the Still Pictures Branch, National Archives, College Park, Md.

In February 1882, Dennis Callahan was riding the cage up the hoist shaft of the Alta mine when he was forced to leap off the cage, saving himself by grabbing onto the boards of the gallows frame just before an inattentive engineer rocketed the cage through the top of the frame. The next day saw a new engineer on the job.[10] Workers in the Union mine shaft, in December 1879, faced a similar situation. Their engineer pulled the wrong lever, smashing their cage through the frame. The cage's 17 passengers were strewn over the hoist house floor. Two of the miners were killed and seven others seriously injured.

In January 1874, four miners were setting charges at the 1,700-foot level of the Ophir mine when disaster struck. Having drilled four holes and set charges in each, they gave the signal to the hoist engineer—five bells. Five bells called for the cage to be lowered, which it was. The miners then lit their fuses, climbed aboard the cage, and pulled on the bell rope one time—the signal to raise the cage. But nothing happened. With no way of stopping the explosion, three of the miners escaped injury by climbing up the surrounding timbers and securing themselves against the walls of the shaft. However, the fourth miner, paralyzed by fear, remained near the cage and was killed by a rock let loose by the explosion. Later, it was determined that engineer was not at fault, the 1,700-foot long rope, which should have signaled the hoist operator to lift the cage, had fouled on a timber.[11]

Dennis Callahan, who survived the extra ride given him by the careless hoist engineer in February 1882, died four months later in one of the Comstock's most terrifying accidents. On May 31, 1882, the main water pump column in the Alta mine broke. Fearing that a recently constructed bulkhead might give way, shift foreman Richard Bennett set out to warn the miners of the danger, but before he could reach them, the bulkhead burst, sending a torrent of water through the mine's lower levels, trapping Bennett and six others. The main water pump was immediately repaired, and rescuers began pumping out the flooded mine. Meanwhile the air compressor used to supply air to the hydraulic drills and to ventilate the mine was kept running in case the trapped miners had discovered a pocket of air and were able to tap into one of its pipes.

At first little hope was entertained that the miners were still alive, and the *Territorial Enterprise's* headline for June 1, 1882, read: "Seven Miners Drowned and Cooked on the 2150 level of the Alta Mine." By the following day it had become apparent that someone was making use of the compressor's air supply, and work was begun on constructing a boat small enough to navigate the narrow opening at the top of the drift.

Callahan and William Bennett volunteered for the dangerous mission, but were advised to wait until the mine could be ventilated. The next day, however, the two would-be rescuers became impatient and set out on their journey. Overcome by gases, which pervaded the drift, they died before reaching their destination. Their bodies were discovered by Arthur Van Dusen, who was also able to reach the seven missing miners by wearing a

The tombstone of one of the heroes of the Alta mining disaster. William Bennett (shown here as Bennetts) and Dennis Callahan died trying to save seven trapped miners.

homemade gas mask. All of the men were found to be alive and well. They had been trapped for 65 hours and stayed alive by taking refuge in a cooling-off station located at the west end of the drift.

The San Francisco Stock and Exchange Board presented Van Dusen with a gold medal inscribed "Greater Love Hath No Man Than This, That A Man Lay Down His Life For His Friends." They also filled a tin box with gold and silver coins to be given to Callahan's niece.[12]

Bulkheads, such as the one that gave way in the Alta mine, were constructed anytime exploratory drilling with a diamond drill revealed a hidden body of water. The diamond drill was employed as a safety precaution against the accidental blasting of a wall, in a drift, that held back tons of water. The June 2, 1882, *Territorial Enterprise* reported:

> The great use of the diamond drill is now acknowledged to be not in hunting for ore, but in guarding against water. When the drill has been run ahead and the ground to be passed probed for a distance of 150 to 250 feet, the miners feel perfectly safe in banging right along on a drift.[13]

Tragically, it also gained the sobriquet "widow maker" because the fine spray of silica dust that it produced would lodge in the miner's throat and, over time, led to death from tuberculosis.

With the mines reaching such a great depth, it became extremely dangerous pushing into unexplored ground. "Bodies of water are liable to be reached that stand under such pressure that the whole face of the drift may be forced in and a torrent of scalding water poured out," the *Territorial Enterprise* wrote. "In the event of such an accident occurring the men could only run for their lives to the nearest shaft or winze. In not a few situations loss of life would be almost inevitable."[14]

In 1877, a hot water spring was uncorked in the Savage mine that shot out scalding 160 degree water. According to Lord, the men who worked in that drift were "forced to breathe this suffocating vapor till they often staggered forth from the station half blinded and bent over by agonizing cramps."[15]

By the 1880s most of the Comstock mines were experiencing trouble with flooding—so much flooding that it became unprofitable to continue mining the ore at the lower levels. The high cost of pumping, the frequent shut-downs and the constant refilling of the mine shafts by new underground springs—combined with the realization that no major ore bodies were discovered below the 2,000-foot level—showcased the futility of trying to make additional money deep mining the Comstock.

Between 1859 and 1882 the Comstock mines yielded $320 million from ore and tailings, and the mines paid out $147 million in dividends, but when the assessments and expenditures (most of which were incurred during deep mining) are subtracted, the total profit for 20 years of hard labor

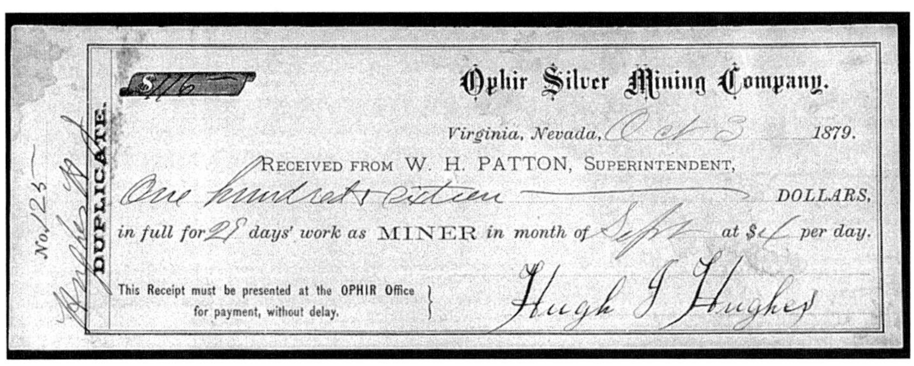

No 125

$116

DUPLICATE.

Ophir Silver Mining Company.

Virginia, Nevada, Oct 3 1879.

Received from W. H. Patton, Superintendent,

One hundred & sixteen DOLLARS,

in full for 29 days' work as MINER in month of Sept at $4 per day.

This Receipt must be presented at the OPHIR Office for payment, without delay.

Hugh J Hughes

In general, miners earned $4 a day. Left: An Oct. 3, 1879, receipt for 29 days of work in September by miner H.J. Hughes at the Ophir. Below: On May 3, 1871, the Gould & Curry Mining Company paid Paul Duncan $135 for his work as a miner. Author's collection.

was a mere $55 million. From its peak at $300 million in 1875, the value of the Comstock mining stocks sunk to a dismal $7 million by 1881, and thus, the bonanza period of the Comstock Lode was over.[16] Yet no one wanted to admit it.

The miners regularly descended into the mines, not just because of the high wages, often $4 a day, but, like those who invaded the California gold fields in search of a new El Dorado, they dreamed of striking it rich. The major difference being, California placer miners hoped to find ore of their own, whereas, the Comstock miners searched for ore they did not own in order to drive up the value of mining stocks they did own. With few exceptions, Comstock miners sank all of their savings into the stock market hoping to get rich quickly. They then eagerly swarmed around the new day's posting of the stock quotations, which were always tacked up at the heads of the mine shafts. As Grant Smith observed, "Not infrequently a miner noting a big rise in his stocks would throw his lunch bucket in the air, exulting 'To hell with work!' But it would not be long before he was back asking for a job."[17]

They did not want to admit that the source of their dreams was at an end. Rather, they kept praying that just a few more feet would bring never-ending wealth. It is easy to understand, therefore, why miners in the Sierra Nevada mine put so much faith in their good luck rat—they had staked their lives, hopes and dreams on it.

For those trapped in one of the Comstock's worst mining disasters, however, all such hope was lost one early morning in April 1869 when fire broke out in the Gold Hill mines on the Comstock. Their deaths would serve to draw additional attention to the dangers of working the Comstock and give force to the ideas of one of the Comstock's biggest schemers—Adolph Sutro.

Miners at a cooling-off station at the Hale & Norcross. Courtesy of the Nevada State Museum Photograph Collection.

Chapter 4

AWFUL CALAMITY

Fire! Fire in the Gold Hill mines! was likely the cry that rang out through the Comstock mining towns of Gold Hill and Virginia City during the morning of Wednesday, April 7, 1869. In the next few harrowing hours, as rescuers desperately fought dense smoke and overpowering gases, the full scope of the "greatest mining calamity that has ever occurred on the Pacific Coast or in any mines in the United States" became clear.[1] Devoured were the Yellow Jacket, Crown Point and Kentuck mines. Trapped below were first-shift miners from all three mines. Desperately clinging to hope aboveground were distraught wives and weeping children gathered at the mine shafts to begin an agonizingly long vigil.

Never before had the Comstock witnessed such a calamity. In the decade since Henry T. P. Comstock and others had clambered up the sides of Mount Davidson in search of gold, a number of miners had lost their lives working on the Comstock through accidents common to all mines, but nothing up to this date could compare. The events of that Wednesday morning overshadowed all, bringing a pall over a community that in the past decade had become as accustomed as humanly possible to the costly toll mining exacted on its husbands, fathers, sons and uncles.

"By far the most terrible calamity that has ever occurred in our mines will be found recorded in our local columns of this morning," the April 8, 1869, edition of the *Virginia City Territorial Enterprise* began its terrifying coverage of the fire. "It is appalling almost beyond description, and the communities of Virginia and Gold Hill are shrouded in gloom at the ghastly occurrence. This time the story is not of a singular man precipitated down a shaft, or crushed by a falling mass of earth. It is a whole chapter of fire and suffocation—of mangled and blackened bodies—of two score of strong men desperately struggling for life, and finally perishing by fire, smoke and poisonous gases, hundreds of feet under ground."[2]

Though, by some reports, the fire may have been smoldering for several hours, it was not discovered until 7 a.m., by which time most of the first shift of all three mines had descended to their workstations, nearly 1,000 feet down. Within a few anxious moments of the first encounter with the fire, at the 800-foot level of the Yellow Jacket, the three mines—interconnected by drifts and chambers—were consumed by choking fumes, overcoming almost all in its path.

"A rush was made for the cages, and the hoisting signal given," the *Territorial Enterprise* reported. "But few could be raised at one time, and therefore but few escaped to the surface with their lives."[3] At the Crown Point, a terrified miner pleaded to be allowed to board an already dangerously overloaded cage. "One man unable to find room to stand upright, crawled upon the cage, and thrusting his head between our informant's legs, begged to be allowed to remain there and go up," the *Territorial Enterprise* wrote. "He was allowed to remain and his life was saved."[4] As the cage ascended, those left behind were heard to throw themselves into the shaft while others slumped to the floor unconscious. Another miner told the *Territorial Enterprise* that as he rushed for a cage, it occurred to him that he might fall into the shaft. So he got down on his hands and knees to feel his way, but while crawling along, three or four others ran past and "pitched headlong into the shaft."[5]

Disasters usually bring out the best in men, and the fire at the Gold Hill mines was no exception. At one cage lowering, a rescuer, realizing that one of the miners he encountered below was ready to collapse, risked his life by giving up his place on the cage. Fate was on this hero's side. The courageous miner rode safely to the surface on a subsequent cage lowering.

John James, second shift foreman at the Crown Point, was another of the fire's list of notables. James took a cage down to the 600-foot level, where he begged 10 men he found there to climb on board with him. Only one did. There being little smoke in the drift at that time, the others regrettably chose to try an escape through the Kentuck, "but upon breaking down a partition which stood in their way, were met by the smoke, which rushed in upon them."[6] None survived.

Others later credited by the *Territorial Enterprise* with acts of heroism in battling the fire included Charley Merrow, who led the search for survivors; James Rosvere, "who almost equally risked his life;" James Reynolds; Riff Williams; Thomas Quirk; Jack Doble; Nick Andrews; William Gibson, chief of the Gold Hill Fire Department; William Lee; W.C. Joice; Frank Kellog; John Leonard; A.A. Stoddard; and John Percival Jones, superintendent of the Crown Point mine.[7]

Upon arriving at the mine from Virginia City, Yellow Jacket superintendent John D. Winters sounded an alarm bringing fire companies from Gold Hill and Virginia City to the scene. However, the rescuers were hampered by the raising and lowering of the cages, which created a draft and helped fill the mines with smoke. It soon became too dangerous to send anyone down on the cages. Instead, empty cages continued to be lowered into the pitch black, but "no hand was laid upon them."[8]

About 9 a.m., with nearly 40 miners still missing, the smoke began to clear at the Kentuck allowing Thomas Smith and another miner to descend to the 700-foot level, where they recovered the bodies of Anthony Toy and Patrick E. Quinn. At about the same time, two of three Bickle brothers employed in the Gold Hill mines, Richard and George, were attempting to escape the fire's fury on one of the lowered cages at the Crown Point, when Richard was overcome by the gases and sank down in the cage. As the cage ascended, "his head was caught between the cage and the timbers and nearly torn off."[9] Richard died as a result. So did his brother, who, despite making it safely to the surface, collapsed from the gases and passed away a day later. The third brother, John, also lost his life in the blaze.

John Percival Jones, a hero of the Gold Hill fire. Jones was later a Nevada State Senator. He is known to coin collectors for the proposal that led to the issuance of the U.S. 20-cent piece, minted from 1875-1878.

With rescue hopes still not entirely dimmed, at about 11 a.m., a cage was sent down to the 1,000-foot level of the Crown Point, where it was known that a number of men were huddled below the fire near a fresh air blower. On board was a lighted lantern, a small box of candles, and a dispatch from mine superintendent Jones reading:

> We are fast subduing and doing the fire. It is death to attempt to come up from where you are. We will get to you soon. The gas in the shaft is terrible, and produces sure and speedy death. Write a word to us, and send it up on the cage, and let us know how you are.[10]

No answer came back. Ventilators, which poured fresh air down to the miners, were kept open, but by noon, with 28 miners still missing and no one boarding the empty cages as they journeyed eerily up and down the shafts, there was little doubt as to the fate of these miners.

"No person who stood at the mouth of either of these shafts but experienced the choking effect of the smoke and gases issuing from below, or could for a moment entertain the slightest hope that any one of those in the mine could be alive, yet wives and relatives would still hope against everything, and in every direction almost superhuman exertions were made to extinguish the fire," the *Territorial Enterprise* tragically recorded.[11]

The fire could have been squelched by sealing the openings to the various shafts and forcing steam down into the mines, but to do so would have been to admit that all hope was lost. While the smoke and gases still bellowed from the other mines, at the Yellow Jacket, firemen were able to run a water hose down to the 800-foot level and make slow advances. In places where the timbers looked insecure, the water would be turned off, while miners moved forward to shore up the walls. The battle with the fire could then continue. In many places, even after the timbers had been extinguished, it was necessary to fall back. The rock walls being superheated, they had to first be cooled by a stream of water. In other places, boiling water covered the tunnel floors to two to three inches in depth.

Firemen battled the blaze late into the evening. At about 9 p.m., when the fire began to rise again, another water hose was lowered into the mine, to the 700-foot level. By midnight the firefighters had made enough headway that workmen were able to retrieve 11 bodies and locate nine others at the 800-foot level. The sickening task of recovering the dead continued through the early morning hours. Some were retrieved from the bottom of the Crown Point shaft where they had fallen. Others, likely those with whom Superintendent Jones had tried to communicate, were discovered at the 1,000-foot level, "lying in all sorts of despairing positions, just as they sunk down...under the effects of the foul smoke strongly charged with the pungent and deadly carbonic acid gas."[12]

By Thursday afternoon, the number of bodies recovered had risen to 23. Some of these miners worked in the Kentuck and Yellow Jacket, but had apparently sought exit through a drift connecting to the Crown Point, where they were caught near the shaft by an explosion "so great as to throw quite a body of chips, dirt and refuse in the shaft."[13] Another of the dead was found between the 800- and 900-foot levels of the Crown Point, still clinging tightly to the ladder on which he had desperately sought escape.

By late Friday morning, two full days after its discovery, the fire was still raging. Further recoveries being impossible, the decision was made to seal up the shafts of the Gold Hill mines involved. Planks, wet blankets, and moist earth were used to plug the entrances to the mines. An hour later, with the aid of heavy iron piping run from boilers, steam was sent down through the large pipe of the blower to the 800- and 900-foot levels where it would travel through other parts of the mines to help suffocate the fire.[14] But the fire proved more stubborn than most thought, and the mines remained sealed for days to come. Many months later, it continued to smolder.

Despite initial reports that third-shift miners had smelled smoke as early as 3 a.m. on the morning of the fire, others came to believe that the deadly blaze did not start until an hour before the first shift came on duty, at the time when only car men remained in the mine. These miners theorized that the fire originated on the 800-foot level of the Yellow Jacket mine, at a point 300 feet to the south of the main shaft, where a winze shaft connected to the 900-foot level. A lit candle in a nearby wooden candle box was thought to be the most likely culprit. Slightly more than one month earlier, on March 6, 1869, the candle box at the same location caught on fire. The fire quickly spread, but was discovered in time and successfully suffocated with nearby old coats and clothes.

On April 7, 1869, the same winze had last been used by a car man about an hour before the fire's discovery. The miners believed that the fire started when the lit candle tumbled in the box. The fire then spread, burning the timbers in the winze shaft to such an extent that they caved-in, filling the shaft with debris. Trapped gases within the shaft then caused an explosion, spreading the fire.[15]

The Yellow Jacket, source of the original fire, was reopened with "great volumes of gaseous smoke" pouring out on April 17.[16] Three more bodies having been raised to the surface during a prior opening of the mines, the number of dead stood at 33, with likely five more bodies to be recovered.[17] The cage being lowered, it was found, however, that the timbers had swollen so badly that they had to be carefully trimmed before it could pass. Despite optimistic reports from the mine owners that the mines would resume operations soon, shoring up the caved walls and trimming away burnt timbers proved dangerous and time consuming. Another workman lost his life in the process. It would be weeks, not days, before the mines were ready to be worked.

The effect of the devastating fire was lost on California stock speculators, some of whom, by virtue of distance and a starkly coldhearted nature, cared more about how their Comstock shares were doing than the fate of the miners. In San Francisco, a malicious rumor was spread that the fire had been purposely set to bear the stock market, so those who started the blaze could benefit from the lowered stock prices. Less than a week after the fire, the *Territorial Enterprise* reprinted a piece from the *Gold Hill News*, relating these charges:

> H.C. Bennett, a gentleman connected publicly and privately with the press in San Francisco, has sent us a letter stating that there were rumors on the streets of that city regarding the origin of the fire in our mines last Wednesday, to the effect that the conflagration was intentionally started by persons interested in the mines, expecting to "bear" the stock of the mines. Such rumors sound so infernally and so damnably malicious—and bearing upon their face the stamp and conception of some incendiary scoundrels—that it hardly seems necessary to notice them. But lest that silence on our part—as we live near, and were among the earliest

at the mines when the fire was discovered, and know what we state—and as we have been advised of the street reports in San Francisco—might be misconstrued, we take the liberty [to] state that there is not the least ground for supposing that the fire was anything but accidental, or culpable carelessness on the part of one of the workmen, who himself narrowly escaped from a horrid death. To attribute sinister motives to General Winters, the Superintendent of the Yellow Jacket, to Governor Jones, of the Crown Point and Kentuck, or to any of the hard-working and honest foremen under them, or even to any of the miners, is doing an act of such gross injustice, that the parties originating and circulating such reports had better not come to Gold Hill and repeat them. Our brawny-armed miners who escaped from the dread calamity would not rest easy under such imputations—and woe to the foul-mouthed villains who had the temerity to whisper such reports in this community. Mr. Bennett states that the reports have it that cans of benzine, shavings, and other inflammable materials were used to start the conflagration. Horrible and villainous thought![18]

On July 19, 1869, the annual meeting of stockholders of the Yellow Jacket Silver Mining Company was held at the company's office in Gold Hill for the election of officers. Named trustees were J.D. Winters, William Sharon, D. Driscoll, T.G. Taylor and T.B. Storer. The trustees in turn elected Winters president and superintendent, Taylor vice president, F.E. Osbiston secretary, and the Bank of California treasurer. The retiring board levied a $10-per-share assessment against stockholders, payable to the secretary at Gold Hill or to William C. Ralston at the Bank of California.

"But for the great fire in the mines it would not have been necessary to levy this assessment. It will probably be the last that stockholders will be called upon to pay in some time," the *Territorial Enterprise's* reporter assured.[19] Nevertheless, the town was shaken. Something needed to be done to make the mines safe. Adolph Sutro, who had been tirelessly searching for support for his plan to ram a tunnel through Mount Davidson, draining and venting the Comstock, found the disaster the perfect opportunity to turn public sentiment toward his ambitious, costly and controversial plan.

Gold Hill shortly before the devastating fire. King Survey photograph (circa 1867-1868). Courtesy of the Still Pictures Branch, National Archives, College Park, Md.

Chapter 5

SUTRO'S TUNNEL

To German-born Adolph Sutro, who in the early 1860s was operating a prospering stamp mill along the Carson River below the Comstock, his plan was a simple, time-proven one that could not possibly generate opposition. He would bore a tunnel, commencing to the southeast of Virginia City, through the mountains some four miles, piercing the Comstock at a depth of several thousand feet. Once completed, his tunnel would be of tremendous value to the mining community by providing drainage for the water-soaked Comstock mines, badly needed ventilation for the oppressively hot mines, and additional means of escape in case of a fire, cave-in or other mining disaster.

In return, Sutro and his company would be well compensated by the mines for every ton of ore removed and would earn additional fees for hauling men, machinery, supplies and waste rock through the tunnel. As far as Sutro was concerned, once his tunnel was in service, there would also be little need for the now-flourishing towns of Gold Hill and Virginia City. Instead, the citizens of these prosperous mining communities would take up residence in a grand new town, ultimately named Sutro, near the tunnel's mouth. There, he would make sure to have plenty of his own mills at the ready to process the Comstock's ore.

Though ambitious and shaded in the grandiose, Sutro's drainage scheme was not the first of its kind. Others had proposed similar methods of ridding the Comstock of its excess water. The Virginia Tunnel and Mining Company began construction of a tunnel in the summer of the Comstock boom year of 1863. Starting about a mile below Gold Hill, its tunnel would have cut through the Comstock at a depth of about 800 feet.[1] But this project failed the following year in the face of a major mining slump. In Europe, tun-

Adolph Sutro's tunnel was completed too late to be of much service to the mines. Courtesy of the Nevada State Museum Photograph Collection.

nels were already being employed for reclaiming problem mines.[2] The Harz Mines, in the Harz Mountains in Germany, utilized three different drainage tunnels, constructed from the 1500s up to the 1860s, cut at ever increasing depths. One of these tunnels ran 14 miles, more than three times the proposed length of the Sutro Tunnel.

Besides pointing to its practicality and obvious advantages, there was one more important factor Sutro stressed in making his plea for support of his tunnel scheme—the citizens of the Comstock and all of Nevada had no real choice in the matter. If it was not done, he told a Virginia City audience, the entire state was in jeopardy. Like dominos readied for a fall, all businesses, not just on the Comstock but throughout Nevada, would begin to topple. As Sutro told the likely stunned gathering:

> Your dwelling-houses would be deserted; your stores without tenants; your real estate valueless; your mills would be idle; no more lumber would be required; your farmers and gardeners would no longer have a market; your State Government would commence to totter; the assessor would find his assessment roll grow gradually less; the treasurer would see his cash account diminish in the same proportion; your State credit would be sadly shaken; the people in the mining districts of the eastern portion of Nevada would have to bear the whole burdens of taxation to support the Government and to pay the interest on the State debt, and bankruptcy, ruin and desolation would be brought upon a once flourishing country.[3]

This morbid scenario could, of course, be avoided and the Comstock saved, if Nevada's residents, particularly those who depended on the Comstock for their livelihood, pledged financial support to his tunnel, estimated in 1869 to cost \$4 to \$5 million to complete.[4]

In fairness, Sutro's plan did have merits that surmounted its proposer's obvious gift for the dramatic—merits that at first endeared his tunnel scheme to the mine owners, the community, and the state. Several of the mines had already endured prolonged work stoppages due to excesses of water. The Ophir was all but shut down from 1865 to 1867 because of flooding. The Belcher, Overman, Crown Point, Yellow Jacket and several others had suffered a similar plight in the years prior.[5] If a tunnel could dry out the Comstock, it would be a godsend to the mines and the surrounding communities. Yet, Sutro's tunnel was a business proposition, not a humanitarian cause—a factor not lost on those who would come to oppose it.

On Feb. 4, 1865, Sutro won an important franchise from the newly formed Nevada State Legislature granting him exclusive rights to build and operate the tunnel for the next 50 years. Five months later, he incorporated the Sutro Tunnel Company with prominent Comstock lawyer-turned-state-senator William Stewart as its president. With this substantial backing and his relentless appeals, Sutro was also able to convince owners of 23 of the leading mines, including the Ophir, Central, Gould & Curry, Yellow Jacket, Belcher, and Crown Point, to sign contracts with his tunnel company. Under the terms of the contracts, in order to use the tunnel, mine owners would begin paying \$2 per ton of ore extracted from their mines once the tunnel and its various drifts reached their mines. For additional fees, they could also employ the convenient underground passageway as an avenue for transporting materials, supplies and waste rock. Sutro, in turn, agreed to raise \$3 million by August 1867, one year later, and begin work immediately.

In June 1866, he arrived in Washington, D.C., where by July 25, 1866, he secured from Congress an act granting his company rights to construct the tunnel over federal lands and ownership of any mines discovered within 2,000 feet of each side of the tunnel, "commencing at the mouth of the tunnel and

Adolph Sutro. Courtesy of the California History Room, California State Library, Sacramento, Calif.

running through Mount Davidson into Washoe Valley, a distance of seven miles, excepting such mines as were already owned at the date of the grant."[6]

Sutro then set off for New York with a pamphlet in hand outlining the merits of his proposal. There he hoped to receive not only the warm reception afforded him in Washington but financial support from Eastern bankers and capitalists, including the likes of Cornelius Vanderbilt and William B. Astor. However, the leading banking houses and businessmen he contacted were wary. They resisted putting money into any untested scheme, particularly one that did not already show substantial financial backing from the West.[7] A number of them did, however, add their signatures to an Oct. 5, 1866, letter suggesting that, if Comstock mining companies pledged $400,000 to $500,000, the rest of the money could be raised in the East.

A still-hopeful Sutro pressed for home, where he was able to obtain a memorial from the Nevada State Legislature asking Congress to grant a $5 million loan to the tunnel company. He also raised $600,000 of the $3 million he needed in pledges from 11 of the original 23 mines that had signed on with the tunnel company, and gained a one-year contract extension from these same mines. But clouds of opposition had already begun to form. In June 1867, the trustees of the Crown Point mine, which was controlled by the Bank of California, failed to ratify the mine's earlier $75,000 subscription to the project. It was the first of several crushing setbacks Sutro would endure over the next few years and would blame on the Bank of California and its cohorts. The conspiracy, Sutro said, began upon his return from the Pacific coast in 1867, just as he was about to be "crowned with success." It was then that the California bank crowd stepped in, according to Sutro. In a secret session held the day prior to the June 7, 1867, annual election of trustees at the Crown Point mine, Sutro said, the bank decided to put its plan to squash him and his tunnel scheme into effect by taking control of the following day's meeting and voting against lending financial support to the tunnel company. Sutro told an audience of prospective investors in 1869:

> I saw at a glance what was up. The Bank which up to that time had warmly supported me, had now turned against me, and I knew quite well that none of the subscriptions already made by the mining companies would be ratified at their stockholders' meetings. Nearly all the persons who had previously stood by me deserted me; they shunned me on the streets and avoided me as if I had an infectious disease; every miserable cur and hireling of that Bank turned the cold shoulder to me—actually afraid their masters might be displeased at seeing them talk to me—and for the first time I commenced to feel and appreciate the immense, overwhelming and reunified power that concern wields. Men knew, as if by magic, that the bank was now against me; it seemed as if they all had been informed of it at once, and through some invisible power had received their instructions.[8]

Other companies did back out, arguing that Sutro had failed to live up to his end of the contract. He had not raised the $3 million he agreed upon when the contracts were signed. Nor had he begun construction of the tunnel as promised.[9] Sutro suffered an additional blow when Sen. Stewart, who had lent an air of credibility to the tunnel company as its nominal head, resigned.

Whether or not there was a conspiracy headed by the bank crowd, as Sutro charged, has never been proven. William C. Ralston and the Bank of California actively pursued an expanding control over most money-making ventures through the bank's often aggressive acquisitions of mills, mines and other Comstock operations and held critical trustee positions in most of the mines. They likely looked upon Sutro's scheme as competition to their own plans. It is unlikely, however, they ever viewed Sutro as much of a threat to their operation as he thought they were to his.

Besides any monopolistic tendencies the bank crowd exhibited, there were some legitimate concerns beginning to tilt opinion against Sutro's tunnel. By 1867, the $2 per ton Sutro proposed charging the mines for their ore production began to be viewed by most mine owners as an exorbitant tax on their businesses. The tunnel would only be of real benefit to the mines if its main attraction—drainage—could be achieved at a significantly lower rate than traditional means. However, advances in the efficiency of pumping equipment had by this time successfully checked problems at some of the mines with the worst flooding, including the Ophir, making a tunnel that would not be ready for use for years to come seem more of a wasteful extravagance than a necessity. Justified or not, many mine owners also believed that their flooding concerns would lessen the deeper their shafts progressed, and by the time Sutro's tunnel reached them, they would be working in dry ground. Sutro did not help matters, either. His actions raised concerns over his ability to complete the project, and his bombastic claims that the tunnel would depopulate the surrounding towns were offensive not only to the bank crowd but also to the residents of Virginia City and Gold Hill.

For the bank crowd, the formation of the Union Mill and Mining Company in June 1867 was another concern. Sutro's tunnel would be in direct competition. The new milling company, the brainchild of the bank's Virginia City agent, William Sharon, was an amalgamation of various mills the Bank of California had acquired through foreclosure. Under Sharon's plan, investors from San Francisco would provide the initial capital for the new company, which would haul most of the equipment from the former mills down the steep grade to the Carson River, where plentiful water would mean reduced operating costs.[10] If the milling company also purchased the Yellow Jacket and Crown Point, which were already under the bank's control, and additional mines when they became available, it could have what every mill needed to survive—a never ending source of ore, even during the inevitable mining slumps. The mill owners enjoyed an added bonus, as they were also the mine owners and could make lucrative contracts with themselves, pocketing the additional profit accrued from the processing charges.[11]

Sutro was determined to fight the bank crowd, but still needed funds to begin his tunnel. So he returned to the East to seek financial commitments. By July 1867, he was back in New York where again he had little success, this time attributing his failure to the contract rejections he was facing on the Pacific coast. According to Sutro, on July 16, 1867, the day after the Savage mine held its annual stockholders meeting, a damaging telegraph arrived in New York. A placard reproducing its destructive contents, Sutro said, was stuck up in the offices of Lees & Waller, the New York agency of the Bank of California, which read: "That the stockholders of the Savage Company, at their annual meeting, had refused to ratify the subscription made by their Trustees of $150,000 to the stock of the Sutro Tunnel Company, and that the same was utterly null and void."[12]

The news spoiled chances that he could find backing in the East, so he left for Washington to press Congress for aid. However, by the time he arrived, Congress had adjourned. So Sutro sailed for Europe, carrying with him favorable letters of introduction he had obtained from California bankers prior to his first trip to the East. Included among these was a warm letter from Bank of California cashier Ralston, now one of his avowed enemies, recommending Sutro and his well-traveled tunnel scheme. Penned in May 1866, the letter, which Sutro ultimately decided not to use, was written to the Oriental Bank Corporation of London (the London agent for the Bank of California) and demonstrated how quickly the Bank of California's position had turned from one of tacit support to active opposition.

Sutro visited Ireland, England, France, Belgium, Holland, Prussia, Austria, Poland, Hungary, Bavaria, Switzerland and Italy, where he met with many of Europe's financial, political and scientific leaders. He also toured its deepest mines, becoming convinced that, "in order to work mines rationally and profitably, wherever the topography of the country allows it, great district or main tunnels, which serve as highways under the mountains, must be constructed."[13] He was not, however, able to obtain any pledges of money.

Departing by ship from Liverpool on Dec. 1, he resolved to be successful with a new appeal in Washington when Congress reconvened. There he was again warmly welcomed by the nation's leaders but was soon confronted by a disturbing flood of telegrams of opposition from home. Chief among these, Sutro said, was one dated Jan. 15, 1868, linked by its first signature (that of William Sharon) to the bank crowd. Others who signed the telegram urging Nevada Sens. Stewart, former tunnel company president, and James W. Nye, former Nevada territorial governor, to defeat the tunnel project if possible were: Charles Bonner, superintendent of Savage Company; B.F. Sherwood, president of the Central Company; John D. Winters, president of the Yellow Jacket Company; John P. Jones, superintendent of the Kentuck Company; John W. Mackay, superintendent of the Bullion Company; and Thomas G. Taylor, president of the Alpha and superintendent of the Crown Point and Best & Belcher Companies. Additional letters condemning his project arrived on Jan. 17 from a number of mining presidents in San Francisco, "nearly all well-known tools and flunkeys of the Bank," Sutro said.[14]

Undeterred, Sutro pressed on. To support his project, he published a 250-page book espousing the advantages of his tunnel would afford the Comstock and the nation. One thousand of these were distributed to members of Congress, business leaders and the press. In the end, Sutro's untiring resolve led the House Committee on Mines and Mining to agree to recommend a measure to the full House approving a $5 million loan. But just as Sutro was again ready, as he put it, to be "crowned with success," impeachment proceedings began against President Andrew Johnson. By the time the lengthy impeachment process had ended, it was too late in the session for the funding measure to be brought up.[15]

Frustrated, Sutro retreated to California, where he would remain for a few months awaiting the new congressional session. Late that same year he headed back to Washington, where his measure failed to come up and died with the close of the 40th Congress. He would try again with the new Congress the following year but was, again, unsuccessful.

In April 1869, just as all seemed the darkest for Sutro, the suffocating fire at Gold Hill breathed new life into his project. On Sept. 20, 1869, he addressed a large crowd, composed primarily of miners, at Piper's Opera House in Virginia City, gruesomely showing lantern slides of burning mines and dying miners to illustrate the importance of his tunnel to the miners' safety.[16]

Early in his speech, Sutro outlined the 10 primary benefits his tunnel would afford the mines and its miners, including: (1.) the ability to dispense with pumping machinery; (2.) increased ventilation, "giving health and vigor to the miners;" (3.) the ability to work the mines to greater depths, as much as 2,900 feet; (4.) the ability to further explore mines that had so far proved unproductive; (5.) increased ore extraction, up from the current $12 million to $16 million annually to as high as $50 million; (6.) the ability to dispense with hoisting engines, because the bulky ore would no longer need to be raised to the surface for transportation by wagons or railroad to the mills on the Carson River—rather, it could be dropped to the tunnel level and moved to the mills at 20 cents per ton by means of a railroad he would build inside the tunnel; (7.) extra money, freed through the elimination of hoisting and pumping equipment, could now go toward working the large bodies of low-grade ore that otherwise would remain in the earth, some $500 million worth; (8.) hydraulic engines or turbines placed at tunnel level that would aid in working the shafts to lower levels; (9.) increased employment, up from 2,000 to 10,000 men, made affordable because mining costs could be reduced so much that "those mines which now barely pay expenses would be enabled to pay regular dividends, and allow liberal wages to the men employed;" and (10.) a sound future to the country, increased property values and restored confidence.[17]

Next, Sutro launched into his attack on his enemies. Terming the bank crowd a "hydra-headed monster," which had grown to such gigantic proportions that it now threatened to devour the entire Pacific coast, Sutro used the recent Gold Hill mining disaster to condemn the Bank of California and all of its supporters:

> Fellow citizens! Let me enlighten you. Allow me to pierce that darkness and let in a ray of daylight; let me explain to you why these men so bitterly oppose a work which in them, the ostensible owners of the Comstock lode, should find the strongest advocates; let me show to you why they have turned to be the guardians of the treasury at Washington; let me tell you why they tremble with fear lest work on the Tunnel be started; let me explain to you why they make you work in a foul atmosphere, which sends half of you to your graves in the prime of manhood; let me show you why they have allowed forty-two of your miners to be foully murdered at the fire of the Gold Hill mines for want of an exit through the Tunnel; and let me show them to you in their true colors, and then hold them up to the shame, contempt, and ignominy they so richly deserve.[18]

Frustrated also by the ability of the bank crowd to obtain financial support from the public and the mines for the building of the Virginia and Truckee Railroad, Sutro charged that the bank crowd's railroad was a direct attempt to kill the tunnel project by providing transportation of ore to the mills that would otherwise be handled by his tunnel. Completion of the tunnel, Sutro claimed, would destroy the bank crowd's monopoly, as the tunnel was the key to the mountain. This was something, Sutro said, the bank crowd was determined to prevent. For if his tunnel was completed, "they could then no longer bull and bear stock, manipulate the mines and mills, and their railroad would be of but little use."[19]

Imploring the miners to band together to "shake off the [bank crowd's] yoke of slavery" and to assert their manhood, Sutro played on the miners' instinctive distrust of bankers, cautioning that there would be no Andrew Jackson to fight off the oppressive bank that had stripped away their liberties, as there had been in Jackson's 1830s battle with the Bank of the United States. They would have to do so themselves. Plus, if they banded together, the cost to the individual miner would be minimal and the benefits great. Of course, they could also buy stock, at $5 per share. The dividends from a few thousand invested now "may give you an income to support you the balance of your life…and probably that of your children," Sutro pitched.[20]

Though Sutro's impassioned pleas were embraced by many and garnered a pledge of $50,000 from the Miners' Union, the local press was not sympathetic. *The Gold Hill News* launched an attack on Sutro and his tunnel while the *Virginia City Territorial Enterprise* observed that it was not surprising that Sutro would meet with opposition since he did not begin the tunnel project with the sole aim of benefiting the mine owners or adding to the state's coffers. Rather, it was a business proposition from the start, aimed at enriching all of those concerned with it, including Sutro. This, the *Territorial Enterprise* said, could be clearly demonstrated by Sutro's very favorable contracts with the mines. The newspaper then scolded Sutro for his open attacks on his competition (i.e., the bank crowd), reminding him that the whole affair was a private matter not a public one. Therefore, Sutro should refer to his opponents with less feeling and less of a tendency for personal abuse. "Besides[,] disappointments are quite common, and Mr. Sutro should learn to bear his with more philosophy," the *Territorial Enterprise* admonished. "He admits that the tunnel, if completed, would be immensely profitable. The admission, without regard to the necessity of the tunnel, deprives him of the privileges of martyrdom, and of all apology for a denunciation of those who do not find it profitable to favor his undertakings."[21]

With the funds he obtained from the Miners' Union, Sutro broke ground for the tunnel on Oct. 19, 1869. A grand barbecue (for which two oxen were spit-roasted and six to eight hogs baked) was held featuring speeches, a flag raising and a gun salute. Despite the hoopla, progress on the tunnel was slow, and by 1870 the project was nearly dead. It would take the bonanza strike at the Crown Point to breathe new life into the tunnel scheme. With the increased production on the lode, Sutro was able to obtain substantial subscriptions from England in September 1871, totaling more than $1.45 million.[22]

Additional aid from Europe would help complete the tunnel in 1879. However, its completion came much too late. It did not connect to its first mine on the Comstock until nine years after it was started, by which time most of the mines had already reached their maximum depth, well below the tunnel's intersection at approximately 1,700 feet.[23] The wet tunnel also failed to provide the promised ventilation, nor did it ever offer any service in hauling ore to the mills. The loans were not repaid, and the company failed. It was sold on foreclosure in 1879, the same year it was completed.[24]

As for Sutro, he disposed of his stock in 1878 and moved to San Francisco, where he helped develop that city and made a fortune in real estate investments. Ever the seeming defender of the common man, he ran a successful campaign for San Francisco mayor on the Populist ticket in the early 1890s, supporting the free and unlimited coinage of silver. He served in that post from 1894 to 1896. Two years later, the great Comstock tunnel builder died a rich man.

Large pumps were used to extract water from the often water-soaked Comstock mines. The engineer leaning against the engine at this pumping station in the Utah gives a good indication of the scale of the pumping equipment. Adoph Sutro argued that his tunnel through the Comstock would eliminate the need for this costly and cumbersome method of getting rid of the water. Courtesy of the Nevada State Museum Photograph Collection.

Chapter 6

THE CROOKEDEST ROAD

While Adolph Sutro scampered from coast to coast in search of money for his tunnel project, William Sharon stayed at home, finding most of the cash he needed to lay track for the Virginia and Truckee Railroad readily available from two local counties and the Comstock mine owners. Unlike Sutro's tunnel, which would require years of blasting and drilling to complete, Sharon's railroad could be pushed through quickly, aided by the support of the Bank of California, while offering a range of services to the community well beyond ore hauling.

Like Sutro and his tunnel idea, Sharon was not the first to champion the merits of a railroad on the Comstock. Several previous charters had been awarded, beginning in Nevada's territorial days, but all of these had failed. By 1867, however, Sharon had taken up the challenge, promoting a railroad as a means of lowering freight costs to the Union Mill and Mining Company on the Carson River.[1] The bank-controlled mills could reduce ore at about half the cost of steam-driven mills because of their ready supply of water. However, the high expense of hauling the ore in a steep descent more than 1,000 feet down to the Carson by horse-drawn wagon and the hazards of roads often rendered impassible by winter snows and spring rains made finding a cheaper, more efficient method of moving the ore to mills of importance.[2]

Prior to the opening of the Virginia and Truckee Railroad, in 1869, ore was hauled to the processing mills by teamster wagons. King Survey photograph of the Savage works (circa 1867-1868). Courtesy of the Still Pictures Branch, National Archives, College Park, Md.

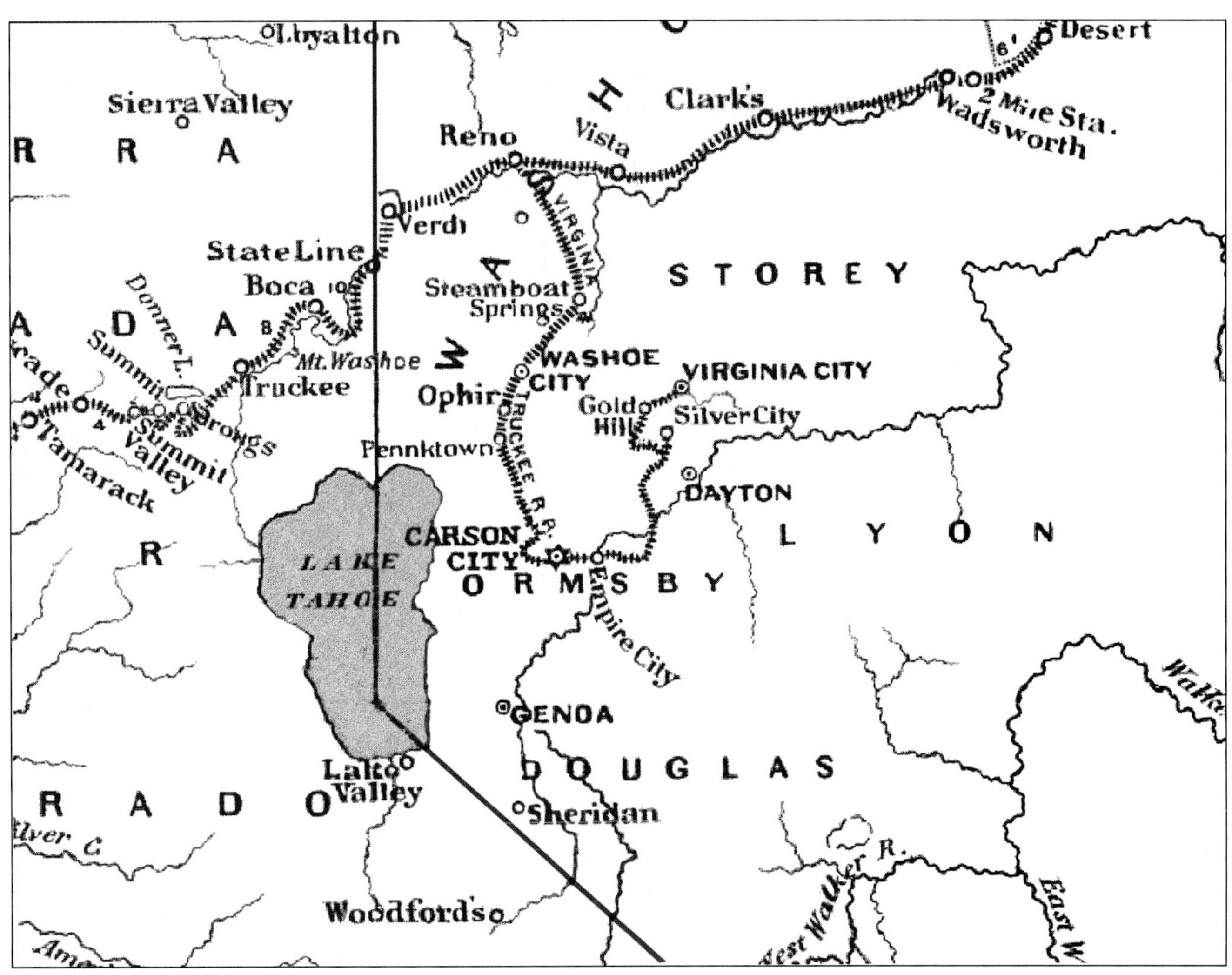

The Virginia and Truckee Railroad ran from Virginia City, through Gold Hill, Silver City, and Carson City. In 1872, the connection was made to Reno and the Central Pacific.

Unlike Sutro's tunnel plan, which was met with lukewarm endorsement and scant financing, Sharon's railroad scheme was embraced by the community, which anticipated the significant benefits of a railroad link between their isolated towns and the outside world. In order to assure that the road ran through their communities, the counties of Ormsby, with Carson City as its seat, and Storey, of which Virginia City was the seat, made gifts in the form of bond issues amounting to $500,000, while the Comstock mines contributed $700,000 to the project. On Feb. 26, 1868, a meeting held at the Bank of California offices in Virginia City set in motion the incorporation of the Truckee Railroad Company with William C. Ralston, Thomas Bell, Charles Bonner, Thomas Sunderland, W.E. Barron, A.W. Baldwin, F.A. Tritle, J.D. Fry and D.O. Mills as its directors.[3]

Isaac E. James, who had made his mark surveying most of the important mines on the Comstock, was called in by Sharon to cut the road, which would run from Virginia City, 1,600 feet down to the Carson River. Along its route, the line would service Virginia City, Gold Hill, Carson City and, eventually, connect to the Central Pacific and the transcontinental railroad at Reno.

Ground for the new railroad was broken at 3 p.m. on Feb. 18, 1869, with no great ceremonies—"The few gentlemen present took a nip or two of old Bourbon, and with a few words, more in the shape of toasts than speeches, the thing was done."[4] Work then began at the head of American Ravine, with the blasting of one of six tunnels along the line.

In September 1869, railroad superintendent H.M. Yerrington drove a silver spike laying the first rail at Carson City, just a block from the site of the Carson City Mint then under construction, and by early November the leg to Carson City had been completed, allowing the first locomotive to come chugging up to Gold Hill. As the Gold Hill band triumphantly played on, town dignitaries anxiously waited at rail side to warmly greet the jubilant

Virginia and Truckee Railroad workers pose on an ore-ladened train stopped on a trestle. The bank crowd's railroad cut the cost of hauling ore from the mines to its waiting mills on the Carson River. Courtesy of the Nevada State Museum Photograph Collection.

Sharon, who was on board for the inaugural run.[5] From San Francisco, Bank of California President D.O. Mills and cashier Ralston telegraphed their congratulations.[6] The Virginia and Truckee Railroad was open for business.

Though its main line ran only 52 miles when connected to Reno in 1872, the Virginia and Truckee Railroad was an engineering miracle, described by Dan De Quille as "the crookedest road in the United States—probably the crookedest in world." Traveling southwest from Virginia City to Carson City, a V&T rail passenger wound through enough curves to go around in a circle a dizzying 17 times. Yet upon arriving at Steamboat Springs, halfway between Carson City and Reno, the same passenger had journeyed 40 miles by rail around Mount Davidson but was only 5 1/2 miles from where he started in Virginia City.[7]

Despite later complaints from citizens of Ormsby and Storey counties, who felt overburdened by their bond issues when promised additional taxes did not come through, the Virginia and Truckee Railroad was generally judged a success. With the Comstock in a depression, the quality of ore lessening, and only a few mines paying dividends to shareholders, the railroad was viewed by many as a necessity, no matter what the cost or who ultimately profited. This was true not only on the Comstock but also to the east and west of it, where there were mines capable of yielding great quantities of ore that were not being utilized because of the high cost of mining and reduction. The *Virginia City Territorial Enterprise,* arguing in favor of community support for the railroad, wrote in its Oct. 19, 1869, issue:

> The completion of the railroad, which will reduce the rates of transportation between Virginia and Carson nearly two-thirds, will throw open to labor these exhaustless stores of wealth; more mills will be required; labor will be in demand; real estate will advance in price; the development of abandoned mines will be resumed, and an era of renewed prosperity will again dawn upon Western Nevada. This is what the Virginia and Truckee Railroad will do for us; and no matter who may be profited by the subsidies granted to the enterprise, every dollar advanced by the people of Storey County will be returned to them thousand fold.[8]

By almost completely supplanting the laborious and dangerous hauling of ore down to the mill via teamsters' wagons, transportation costs were lowered enough that low-grade ore could now be profitably dispatched to the mills. A network of spur lines branching out to the various mines made it easy to haul ore to the hungry mills, while the cost of transporting ore from the mines to the Carson River mills dropped to $2 per ton and the amount of ore being delivered on a daily basis spiked dramatically. Where before teamsters could carry, on average, 25 tons to the mills on the Carson each trip, the railroad far exceeded those totals, by the early 1870s surpassing 400,000 pounds.

Prices for cordwood delivered to Virginia City, necessary for operating steam-driven machines, fell from $15 to $11.50, or $9 on contract. The effect on transporting other supplies from outlying regions, including machinery for the mines, was also dramatic. Soon 30 to 45 trains a day were winding their way between Virginia City and Carson City, loaded with ore, passengers, and an array of goods that enriched daily life on the Comstock and made the Virginia and Truckee the most famous short line in the world. Over these same lines, silver and gold would soon be transported to the Carson City Mint, where it could be turned into CC-mintmarked gold double eagles, eagles, and half eagles as well as silver dollars, half dollars, quarter dollars, 20-cent pieces, and dimes, all from the riches of the Comstock.

Chapter 7

EMPIRE BUILDER

William Chapman Ralston, who battled with Adolph Sutro over control of the ore hauling on the Comstock (and a few years later played a key role in reshaping the nation's coinage laws), was born Jan. 12, 1826, to Robert Ralston and Mary Chapman Ralston, on a farm near Plymouth, Ohio. His father having been engaged in the river trade on the Ohio and, later, building riverboats and steamers, it was only natural that as a youth Ralston would show similar leanings. Leaving school at age 14, young Ralston did a stint in a grocery store before taking to the river aboard one of the growing number of steamers plying the nation's teaming network of inland waterways. It was there, serving as a clerk, charged with overseeing the ship's manifest, keeping the books, supervising the loading and unloading of cargo, and assuring that his vessel was amply supplied with fuel and other ship-board necessities, that Ralston learned elements of the domestic and international shipping trade that would serve him well in later years.

Steaming up and down the busy Mississippi, he also formed lasting friendships that would prove seminal to his later career in banking. Among these were two veteran riverboat captains 17 years his senior, Cornelius Kingsland Garrison, captain of the side-wheeler *Convoy*, one of the Mississippi steamboats on which Ralston clerked, and Ralph Stover Fretz, captain of a rival vessel. When, in 1849, both Garrison and Fretz abandoned the overcrowded river trade for the promise of more lucrative ventures in California, Ralston eagerly followed.

On July 3, 1849, he boarded the bark *Madonna* bound for California. Like the thousands before and after him drawn west by gold fever—some 80,000 in 1849 alone—Ralston was faced with the decision of whether to go by land or sea. Traveling by land, the anxious emigrants generally hooked up with an organized company for safety and support on the expansive American frontier. Departing from various jump-off points along the Missouri River, they would traverse the continent in prairie schooners, on horseback or foot along a number of well-worn trails west.

William C. Ralston was drawn west by the California gold rush. After a stint in Panama City, he moved to California, where he built an empire.

The most popular pathway was the old Emigrant Trail, which traced along the Platte and Sweetwater to South Pass, then around Great Salt Lake. There those wedded to this course faced the most harrowing part of the journey—crossing an unforgiving barren stretch of miserable land known as Forty Mile Desert, which stretched from the Humboldt Sink to the Carson River before depositing weary travelers safely on the other side of the Sierra Nevada. Along the way, they squared-off against everything from cholera outbreaks to skirmishes with Indians in order to reach the already overcrowded gold fields.

Going by sea, the forty-niners faced no fewer perils. Sailing first along the Atlantic coast of

North and South America, they could either chance the treacherous waters, rounding Cape Horn, and then sail northwest, up the Pacific to California (an 18,000-mile trip that could take six to eight tedious months to complete), or travel a shorter route, disembarking, most often, at a port on the Chagres River to cross the Isthmus of Panama. Those who chose the latter route then negotiated a portion of the way by canoe and the rest by mule through mosquito infested jungles, where malaria and cholera reigned, to arrive at the decrepit walled coastal city of Panama. There they found lodging scarce and bookings on California-bound vessels often even scarcer.

In the early days of the rush, only a few vessels regularly serviced the Pacific coast (mail carriers granted government subsidies). So the backlog of stranded gold seekers created a new trade for those adventurous enough, brave enough, or plain foolish enough to remain on in Panama City. By the time Ralston arrived in Panama, Garrison and Fretz had recognized the opportunities and opened a currency exchange from which their business expanded into providing transportation services to the gold fields for California-bound arrivals.

With his years of experience on the Mississippi River, Ralston, then in his early 20s, was an immediate asset to the prospering firm. He would soon be making regular trips for the company between the Isthmus and the United States, handling booking arrangements with ships' captains, relocating people and goods from Panama to San Francisco or vice versa, and working with the firm's overland transportation service to Panama City. Through its mule train service, Garrison & Fretz could offer complete travel arrangements from the docking at Chagres to California, eventually providing insured passage for eastern-bound bullion across the Isthmus—hauling as much as $1.5 million in gold in a single shipment through the dense jungle to waiting ships.[1]

Two years after his arrival in Panama City, Ralston made his first visit to San Francisco, the city he would help build. In September 1851, the captain of the *New Orleans*, one of the company's charters, died of cholera the night prior to the steamer's departure for the scheduled Panama to California run. Though he had never served as a steamer pilot, Ralston was assigned to captain the vessel. He did so with ease, bringing its 200 passengers safely to port in San Francisco's busy ship-littered harbor.

In March 1852, this time as a passenger aboard the *New Orleans*, he again sailed for California, assigned to look into a scheme to build a railroad between San Francisco and San Jose at the behest of powerful shipping magnate Commodore Cornelius Vanderbilt, a sometimes associate and other times business rival of firm partner Cornelius Garrison in the ocean steamer trade.

With Garrison & Fretz flourishing amid a sea of anxious argonauts, who daily arrived from eastern ports, Ralston's value to the company grew. In May 1852, he was named a junior partner.[2] Less than a year later, with Garrison's removal to San Francisco to work for Vanderbilt, Ralston was named a full partner. The firm's name was changed, slightly, to Garrison, Fretz & Company, to reflect his new status.

Ralston would again sail for California, this time to stay, in March 1853. There he and Fretz served as agents for Vanderbilt's new Independent Opposition Steamship Company, offering round-trip steamer service between the nation's coasts. Unfortunately, by the time Fretz & Ralston began operations in San Francisco, the rush to California had begun to wane. Competition for ocean traffic had grown fierce. Agents were forced to cut round-trip prices and recklessly push steamer captains to attain greater speed in order to remain competitive.[3]

In the years prior to Ralston's 1853 arrival in San Francisco, several steamers had gone down, torn apart in heavy storms, hurricanes, or lost through errant piloting. In the years following, even more would meet with tragic ends. Often the cost in human lives was high. Many of these vessels also carried golden cargoes, the salvage of which would have to be left to treasure hunters.

On Sept. 30, 1854, Ralston was on hand for the departure from San Francisco's Jackson Street Wharf of the *Yankee Blade*, en route for New York. On board were 800 passengers. Stacked in the ship's hold was approximately $153,000 in gold consigned by Page, Bacon & Company, one of California's leading exchange and express services.[4] The following afternoon, terrible news arrived. The *Yankee Blade* had struck a reef off Point Arguello, west of Santa Barbara, and was hung up. The ship's captain, Henry T. Randall, had misjudged the shoreline in his race to Panama. Eventually, the ship broke apart and sank. Reports of the number of deaths varied, but at least 30 people died as a result of the tragedy. Some of the unfortunates drowned in desperate attempts to gain the shore in lifeboats. Others, according to newspaper accounts, were robbed, murdered and tossed overboard by marauding passengers and crew who, after the captain abandoned ship, ruled the *Yankee Blade* during the sleepless night before the ill-fated vessel sank.

Fortunately for those who survived the lawlessness, the southbound *Goliath* happened by the next morning and picked up the nearly 600 passengers still on board, carrying most on to San Diego. It then retrieved the 200 or so who had made it to the shore, depositing them in San Francisco. Meanwhile, Fretz & Ralston chartered the *Brother Jonathan* to bring those who had been transferred to San Diego back to San Francisco.[5]

With no lodging, food, or way to complete their journey to the East, the harried and still white-knuckled passengers demanded refunds on their tickets. Fretz & Ralston refused, referring the disgruntled to seek out the ship's owner for compensation. On Oct. 15, angry passengers held a meeting in which they denounced Fretz & Ralston for pressing the captain of the *Yankee Blade* to gain speed, running too close to shore, and Capt. Randall's abandonment of the ship, which, it was said, cost some passengers their lives. Of more immediate concern to the irate passengers was the company's failure to issue refunds or provide for their stay in San Francisco.

As the mob grew more and more restless, Fretz & Ralston offered no solution. On the one hand, they did not have the funds to pay back the passengers if they wanted. On the other hand, the ship was in the midst of an ownership transfer when it steamed out of San Francisco, and neither Vanderbilt or Garrison, the ship's new owner, wanted responsibility. Ralston was forced to call in the police to handle the menacing mob that gathered at his firm's doors. In the end, Garrison, who was scheduled to take over the *Yankee Blade* from Vanderbilt when it docked in Panama City, issued partial refunds, likely to no one's satisfaction.

The tragedy marked the end for Fretz & Ralston. Vanderbilt's decision to sell off the *Yankee Blade* and his other Atlantic and Pacific steamers to the Nicaragua Transit Company, now controlled by Garrison and Charles Morgan, brought a close to this chapter in Ralston's life. After shutting down their remaining business interests on the Isthmus, Fretz and Ralston accepted an offer to join Garrison in forming a new banking venture based in San Francisco. Garrison, Morgan, Fretz & Ralston was organized on Jan. 1, 1856, with a capital of $700,000. Morgan would run the firm's New York office as Charles Morgan & Company, with Garrison, Morgan, Fretz & Ralston operating out of a building on the southwest corner of Montgomery and Clay streets in San Francisco. The new partnership lasted only a little over a year, dissolving in July 1857, when Garrison and Morgan withdrew. Fretz and Ralston continued on, with their bank located at the corner of Washington and Battery streets, and were immediately successful.

In 1861, looking to expand its capital base, the firm of Fretz & Ralston was dissolved, the partners teaming with successful dry goods merchants Eugene Kelly and Joseph A. Donohoe to form a new banking venture. Kelly took over the eastern business under the name Eugene Kelly & Company, while Donohoe joined with Ralston and Fretz, forming Donohoe, Ralston & Company, on June 1, conducting transactions out of the same San Francisco location as had Fretz & Ralston.

Organized during a period in which there was a severe shortage of banking houses in California, Donohoe, Ralston & Company was an immediate success. At one point the firm handled more gold and silver than any other Pacific coast banking firm. Ralston biographer David Lavender notes that each morning Ralston would oversee the sorting and weighing of boxes of gold dust, gold ingots, and crude amalgam delivered by express companies. Some of the gold was dispatched to private refiners and some to the nearby San Francisco Mint for coinage. Along with the bullion came silver and gold coins, which had to be sorted, counted, stacked and placed in the vault, or be boxed, along with some of the bullion, for shipment east.[6]

Despite their immediate success, friction between the partners soon erupted. Allegedly, Kelly, from his New York base, objected to too much of the bank's money being loaned to western enterprises. Others said Donohoe had concerns over the propriety of some of the loans authorized by Ralston. Either way, Ralston began secretly organizing a new bank through the sale of stock. The formal end of the partnership came on June 30, 1864, with Donohoe and Kelly leaving to form Donohoe, Kelly & Company on the West Coast and Kelly & Company on the East Coast. The former name of Fretz & Ralston was reused by the remaining partners until July 5, 1864, when the heavily funded Bank of California swung open its doors at the former location of Donohoe, Ralston & Company. A couple of years later, the successful new bank would occupy an imposing building commanding the northwest corner of California and Sansome streets, along what came to be known as the Wall Street of the West.[7]

The Bank of California was a novelty in California, which up to this point had shunned banking corporations. It was incorporated on June 15, 1864, with $2 million in capital, each of its prominent

William C. Ralston was a major backer of the Comstock, investing his own and the Bank of California's money at times when most others shied away from the lode. The bank eventually controlled most of the major industries on the Comstock. Courtesy of the Nevada State Museum Photograph Collection.

investors having paid $100 per share to participate. All of the investors were leading citizens and brought with them a diverse range of business interests and expertise, running the gamut from shipping and import to mining and express companies. The certificate of incorporation was sworn on May 12, 1864, with the last signature affixed on June 14.

Officers of the new Bank of California were Darius Ogden Mills, president; William C. Ralston, cashier; and Stephen H. Franklin, secretary. James Lees, a longtime friend and business associate from Ralston's days in Panama, would handle the eastern business through his New York banking house, Lees & Waller. The Oriental Banking Corporation of London served as its British representative, and agencies were soon opened in Virginia City and Gold Hill, reflecting Ralston's growing investments in Nevada's mining industry.

While Mills, who had been a prominent and respected banker in Sacramento, was generally considered conservative, Ralston was the antithesis. His grandiose visions for California led him to place his own and the bank's money in a wide range of risky ventures, some of which, like the Comstock, at first proved quite profitable. Even before the Bank of California opened, Ralston had already aligned himself with the lode's key operations, becoming treasurer of several of its mines, including the Ophir. Along with William Sharon, the Bank of California's Comstock agent, Ralston and his associates, collectively known as the "bank ring" or "bank crowd," would build a monopoly over the Comstock that, at its height, controlled (through placement of allies in key trustee positions) or owned most of the major ore producing mines, processing mills, lumber supplies, water and the important railroad link, provided by the Virginia and Truckee Railroad. In the process, they would skim millions of dollars in profits from the hurried exploitation of Nevada's vast mineral wealth.

One of the keys to this success was the opening of the Virginia City office in September 1864, which, under Sharon's guidance, began undercutting competitors by offering loans to area mines and mills at 2 percent instead of the standard 5 percent. The bank's loans were particularly attractive to the processing mills. Many of these extravagant operations, which sprang up during the lode's early boom days, had cost between $30,000 to $70,000 to erect—some with ornate landscaping and facades that belied their stark industrial purpose. Now that the lode had fallen on hard times, there was not enough ore to go around. To keep their mills from deteriorating, mill owners jumped at the chance to take the low interest loans, only to regret it later when the stubborn Comstock continued to withhold its best ore.[8]

The first mill to fall into the bank's hands through foreclosure was the large, 40-stamp, steam-driven Swansea, located in Gold Canyon, which it obtained in May 1866. By the following year, the bank owned seven or eight such properties, all of which were worthless unless they remained in operation. So Mills and Ralston, in consultation with Sharon, decided to form the Union Mill and Mining Company, sell stock in the venture, and relocate what equipment they could to the Carson River.[9]

The bank, which had already enjoyed good fortune with the Yellow Jacket mine, acquired by Sharon shortly after his arrival on the lode, began an aggressive pursuit of additional mines with which to ensure that the Union Mill and Mining Company's stamping mills could feast on a steady diet of the richest in Comstock ore. Among these were the Chollar-Potosi, Bullion, Kentuck and the Hale & Norcross.[10]

To cut competition, the bank either foreclosed or purchased other mills. If a mill resisted, the bank could choke off its supply of ore until it came into compliance. By this process, the bank soon owned not only most of the mines but most of the major mills throughout the surrounding counties—everything from small, 10-stamp operations to more substantial businesses with 40 or more of the noisy ore pounders.

By the late 1860s, Ralston's investments, which expanded well beyond the Comstock, had made him one of the wealthiest and most influential men

The Ponderosa Saloon & Mine (which offers tours of the Best & Belcher) now occupies the building that served as the Virginia City Agency of the Bank of California.

William Sharon served as the Bank of California's agent on the Comstock. With his help, the Bank of California was able to acquire most of the processing mills on the lode as well as many of its important mines. Following Ralston's death, in 1875, he took over Ralston's home, Belmont, and reorganized the Bank of California. Courtesy of the Bancroft Library, University of California, Berkeley.

of his day—able to enjoy an array of luxuries befitting a member of the nation's growing fraternity of self-made elite. Not one to shirk the good life, Ralston spent his money freely, building one of the finest stables of thoroughbred horses in the West while continually expanding his palatial mansion, Belmont, acquired in 1864 from an Italian count.

It was at Belmont, located some 22 miles from the hustle and bustle of San Francisco, that Ralston became famous for playing the ever-gracious host to a staggering list of world's elite. U.S. presidents, congressmen, foreign dignitaries, ambassadors, and social leaders all vied for invitations to dine with Ralston under Belmont's gas-lit crystal chandeliers, dance the evening away in its mirrored ballroom to the sounds of Ralston's hand-cranked French piano, or casually lounge above, observing the swirling dancers from a specially designed balcony surrounding the ballroom floor. Those so inclined could also relax away the day's tensions in the estate's Turkish bathhouse or enjoy Ralston's private bowling alley before retiring for the evening to the mansion's richly appointed guestrooms.

Among those prominent guests who came under Belmont's spell was Anson Burlingame, first U.S. minister to China. Ralston, as well as most Californians, had long been interested in opening up trade with the Orient. During the Civil War, Ralston chaired the Committee on Steam Communication with China as a member of San Francisco's Chamber of Commerce. On Aug. 18, 1861, the committee's report, signed by Ralston, announced that "events of such a grave and all engrossing character have occurred, and are transpiring in the Eastern States of the Union" that the committee felt it was an inopportune time to press Congress on its wishes for steam communication with China, "even important as we feel this subject is to local California interests, and in, a secondary degree, to the commerce of the United States." Instead, Ralston and his committee urged that each member of the chamber collect "informative statistics" on the subject of steam communication to be placed in the organization's records that "will enable us to make adequate preparations for the successful presentation of such data to Congress, through our Senators and Representatives in Washington."[11]

Ralston's interest in the Far East lay not only in China but also Japan, both of which he saw as ripe for investment. In January 1872, while the bill that would become the Coinage Act of 1873 was still before Congress, Ralston entertained Japan's prime minister Sinu Tomomi Iwakara along with a trade commission of 105 diplomats and students from Tokyo traveling through the United States and Europe to investigate western life as part of Japan's new Meiji Restoration government. Prior to a visit by a portion of the delegation to Belmont, on Jan. 25, 1872, Ralston took his Japanese guests on a tour of San Francisco, with stops at the San Francisco Mint and the bank-controlled San Francisco Assaying and Refining Company.[12]

Among the Meiji government's reforms were sweeping changes to Japan's archaic coinage system. The new Meiji Restoration government had taken over from the Tokugawa shogunate in late 1867. Hoping to revamp Japan's complex monetary system, the new government purchased mint equipment from the British mint in Hong Kong.

With consultation from the British, the Meiji government at first planned to use its abundant supply of silver to establish a silver standard but were advised otherwise by Japanese statesman Hirobumi Ito. Ito, while on tour of the United States, had a chance to study the mint bill that would become the Coinage Act of 1873, recommending instead that his nation switch to the gold standard, as the United States was planning, and adopt a decimal system of coinage. Thus, the yen was born, and a coinage of silver trade dollars planned to provide competition with the Mexican silver dollar, then prevalent in foreign trade.[13]

Problems with purity had plagued the Japanese coinage system, and the Japanese appealed to Ralston to take their old rectangular gold two-bu coins, melt them and refine them to the proper purity at the San Francisco Assaying and Refining Company. In return, the bank would receive, as partial payment, the silver from melting the coins, which, depending on when the coins were issued, ranged from a little over 40 percent to nearly 80 percent of the total weight. The contract was signed on Jan. 30, 1872.[14]

Later that same year, when Ralston met with Dr. Henry R. Linderman, the co-author of the Coinage Act of 1873, they discussed plans to avert problems with the December 1871 German demonetization of silver, including the release of a U.S. trade dollar they both hoped would gain acceptance in Japan and China. Linderman viewed the standard U.S. silver dollar as a useless coin, having been set by the nation's founding fathers at too light a weight to be of use in world trade. It was true, the path of the silver dollar had been a tumultuous one from its beginning. Ever since the founding of the U.S. Mint in 1792 and the first coinage of the dollar in 1794, the silver dollar had failed to live up to expectations, being hoarded or exported as soon as it was released.

To Linderman, Ralston and John Jay Knox, all of whom would play important roles in the formulation of the Coinage Act of 1873, this coin would prove expendable. The nation's coinage system, which since 1792 had been based on bimetallism (in which both gold and silver served as equal full legal tender representatives of the unit of value) had proved to have some serious flaws. Any time one metal rose in value against the other, the more valuable metal would disappear from circulation. Congressional patches applied in 1834, 1837 and 1853 had failed to solve the problem, all of which came to a head with the new mint bill and a growing worldwide trend toward monometallism.

Japan's new Meiji Restoration government at first considered adopting a silver standard. However, after viewing a version of the bill that became the Coinage Act of 1873, Japanese statesman Hirobumi Ito recommended that his country convert to a gold standard, as the United States was planning. The new system was based on the gold yen, first minted in 1871. At left is a gold one yen. At right is a two-bu coin from the Japanese coinage system prior to reform.

Chapter 8

ORIGINS OF A CRIME

In the late 1860s, vast increases in the nation's supply of precious metals led to the construction of new mint buildings in Carson City and San Francisco and to the realization that, in order to adequately manage the U.S. Mint's expanding number of facilities and responsibilities, a reworking of the government's outdated coinage laws and a rethinking of the ways in which the mints were administered was essential. Out of this was born the Coinage Act of 1873, which, because it switched the monetary standard to one based on gold and eliminated the standard silver dollar, came to be known by later generations as the Crime of 1873.

This one act set a course for the introduction of the popular Morgan silver dollar and the often maligned but highly collectible Trade dollar. The economic events that engendered the change to the gold standard also set the tone for other U.S. coinage, including the weight revisions in 1873 that created the popular "with arrows" varieties of U.S. dimes, quarters and half dollars, and bore a direct link to metric pat-

By the late 1860s, the growth in the nation's precious metal supplies, along with plans for a new mint in Carson City, led Treasury Secretary George S. Boutwell to call for a restructuring of the nation's coinage laws. The Carson City Mint, shown here, opened in January 1870 and began striking coins shortly thereafter.

terns of the period and the unusual but attractive gold $4 Stella.

In order to retrace the history of this much-condemned coinage act, we return to 1869 when the Grant administration's newly appointed Treasury secretary, George S. Boutwell, set the wheels of change in motion, writing in his first annual report to Congress of the need for a centralized mint bureau, which would be located in Washington, D.C., under the direct oversight of the Treasury Department.[1] Up until that point, the country's mints and assay offices had been nominally under the control of the Treasury Department, Boutwell told Congress, however, with the increase in mining and coining of precious metals, there was an urgent need for an officer within the department who would have knowledge of all mint activities and could report back to the Treasury secretary.

In making his call for a new mint bureau and recodification of the outdated minting laws, Boutwell relied upon the investigations and suggestions made by Deputy Comptroller of the Currency John Jay Knox, outlined in a report attached to the mint bill. Knox's knowledge of problems with supervision of the nation's mints and assay offices came from first-hand experience. In 1866, he had been sent, on orders from Treasury Secretary Hugh McCulloch, to conduct a thorough investigation of the San Francisco Mint. Large losses totalling nearly a quarter of a million dollars, had occurred in the office of the melter and refiner and had raised concerns.[2] Knox's investigation uncovered considerable differences between the accounts of the chief coiner and the mint's treasurer, which, he reported, could "have easily been traced to the responsible party if the different officers of the mint had been required in their transfers of bullion to take and receive the ordinary receipts required in business transactions."[3]

Again, in 1869, but this time under order from Boutwell, Knox, along with Dr. Henry R. Linderman, engaged in an investigation of the individual mints and assay offices, including the already troublesome San Francisco Mint and the New York Assay Office. At the New York Assay Office, Knox was surprised to discover gross irregularities, which included large losses to the government as well as an illegal bullion lending and cash loan operation. He claimed that many of these problems could have been avoided if periodic inspections had been conducted by a competent person. Examinations, he said, showed that for many years vouchers had been paid by various treasurers without first requiring signature approval from the officers who ordered the supplies. Also, when these vouchers were submitted to the accounting officers at the Treasury, the accounting officers apparently did not consider it part of their duty to determine whether or not the vouchers met the regulations of the parent mint at Philadelphia. Knox reported that as far as he could ascertain, there had never been an official examination of the New York Assay Office by a Mint director, and he lamented that it was only with great "difficulty that a copy of the regulations of the mint for the transaction of business could be found."[4]

The first U.S. silver dollar was minted in 1794. By the time of the introduction of the mint bill, in 1870, the coin had gone through design, weight and fineness changes, none of which helped to keep it in circulation.

An international coinage bill introduced by Rep. William D. Kelley in February 1870 would have required U.S. coins metrically oriented to a German gold coin of 10 grams. To do so, Kelley's bill called for the U.S. gold dollar to be reduced in weight from 1.62 grams to 1.5 grams. Kelley's plan would have required only a miniscule adjustment to future U.S. gold coins and was favored by John Jay Knox.

Based on the nation's growing interest in precious metals brought on by the California gold discoveries and the more recent silver and gold strike in Nevada, along with the evident disarray in the reports and supervision of the branch mints, Boutwell determined that it was time not only to create a new mint bureau but that a complete revision of the mint regulations, in force since 1837, was also necessary. As Knox was obviously the man most familiar with past mint operations, Boutwell commissioned him to prepare a bill revising the laws on mints and assay offices.

Knox was well suited for the task, and having received his commission in January 1870, he worked quickly, thus allowing Boutwell to submit the final version of the new mint bill to Congress by April 25, 1870. In constructing the final draft of the proposed mint bill, Knox submitted a tentative draft, with wide margins for comment, to more than 30 mint and coinage experts and incorporated their views into the final draft he sent to Boutwell. Knox gratefully acknowledged the help he had received in formulating the mint bill, granting:

> In preparation of the bill I have been greatly indebted to Robert Patterson, Franklin Peale, and J. Ross Snowden, of Philadelphia; L.A. Garnett and John Hewston, jr., of San Francisco; E.B. Elliott, of the Treasury Department, and to the officers of the different mints and assay offices for notes and suggestions, and particularly to Hon. H.R. Linderman, late Director of the Mint, who has been associated with me by your direction in the final revision as now presented.[5]

In its final form, Knox's mint bill consisted of 71 sections of which the most important revisions were the establishment of a mint bureau at the Treasury Department, the elimination of the office of the treasurer of the mint, the repeal of the coinage charge for transforming depositor's bullion into coins, a reduction in the amount of wastage and tolerance in the manufacture of coins, making the subsidiary coinage subject to government account, and the discontinuance of the silver dollar. The last of these revisions, the dropping of the silver dollar, was to become the burning issue of later debate over the so-called Crime of 1873.

By the time Knox presented the final version of the mint bill to Boutwell, the Seated Liberty silver dollar was trading at a premium of about three cents over its face value, precluding its active circulation in the United States. Since the foundation of the U.S. Mint in 1792, the nation's lawmakers had been constantly faced with inherent problems of bimetallism, as fluctuations in metal prices regularly led to the exportation or hoarding of one metal or the other. By 1870, the failure of the silver dollar to remain in circulation, along with a prevalent world trend toward monometallism, raised the question as to whether or not this coin served a useful purpose as part of the nation's monetary system. Due to changes in the legally adopted mint ratio for gold and silver (i.e., the number of ounces of silver equivalent in value to one ounce of gold) and price movements of precious metals in the world's bullion markets, the United States had been on a *de facto* gold standard for quite some time.

In an attempt to keep the nation's half dollars, quarter dollars, dimes and half dimes and silver three-cent pieces in circulation, they had all been reduced in weight in 1853 to 384 grains to the dollar, and were receivable in payments of government obligations only up to $5, while the silver dollar had remained at 412 1/2 grains and maintained a full legal tender status. With the popularity of international coinage schemes then being bandied about, all of which called for the adoption of a gold standard, and a worldwide movement toward a single standard, most of those who responded to Knox's request for comments on the mint bill favored a switch to monometallism by either reducing the silver dollar to the 384-grain level employed for other U.S. silver coins or its removal from the list of coins being produced at the U.S. Mint.

One of the first to reply to Knox in favor of the gold standard was Linderman. Dr. Henry R. Linderman had served as Philadelphia Mint director by appointment of President Andrew Johnson in April

1867, a post he held until May 1869 when he was replaced by the Grant administration, after which he was appointed by Boutwell as a commissioner for the government to the Pacific coast. Sometime later (as acknowledged by Knox), Linderman had been asked by Boutwell to assist in the final revision of the mint bill. A leading advocate of conversion to a gold standard, by the time of his 1867 *Report of the Director of the Mint*, Linderman had already observed the general worldwide trend toward adoption of an exclusive standard based on gold and began recommending the same for the United States. He would be aided in this regard by a rash of international coinage proposals that sprang up during the period and gained considerable lip service in the United States. In his 1867 report, Linderman explained that, if an international coinage system—one which would allow all coinages to be readily accepted across international boundaries—such as that proposed at the Paris International Monetary Conference in mid-1867 were to succeed, conversion to a gold standard was essential.

Linderman also expressed his belief that eventually most countries would turn to gold, stating:

> In regard to a grand and comprehensive scheme of international coinage, it is of course not necessary for me to say a word as to the desirableness of its accomplishment. I shall simply offer a few words as to the most feasible plan.
>
> The first great difficulty that meets us is the fact that in some commercial countries gold is the principal medium of trade; in others silver. To maintain these at a steady relation, may be given up as an impossibility. We must, therefore, calculate, or assume, that, as the world grows richer, one nation after another will fall into the wake of those which have taken the lead in adopting gold as the standard, using silver only for subsidiary purposes.[6]

The 1867 International Monetary Conference, attended by delegates from 19 nations, was to be the most successful of four attempts at bringing about a unified coinage. The others, held in 1878, 1891, and 1892, broke up in disagreement. This first conference, however, resulted in the almost unanimous adoption of five major resolutions, which called for:

> 1. A single monetary standard, exclusively of gold, nine tenths fine.
> 2. Coins of equal weight and diameter.
> 3. Of equal quality.
> 4. The unit to consist of the weight of the existing five-franc gold coin with its multiples.
> 5. The coins of each nation to bear the names and emblems preferred by each, and to be a legal tender in all for public and private debts.[7]

While the support given to the international coinage at the Paris conference did not translate into an overwhelming acceptance in the United States, it did lead to a flurry of international coinage bill submissions over the next several years by key players in the later debate over the Coinage Act of 1873, including Sen. John Sherman, chairman of the Senate Finance Committee during the mint bill's time in the Senate, and Reps. William D. Kelley and Samuel Hooper, both of whom were at points charged with the bill's direction in the House of Representatives. Though none of these measures passed, their influence on Knox in his preparation of the mint bill is evident by his inclusion, in his report

This 1868 U.S. Mint pattern for a $5 gold coin equivalent to 25 French francs was produced in response to the 1867 Paris International Monetary Conference. Conference members had voted 13 to 2 in favor of using the French five-franc gold coin as the basis for an international coinage and suggested that countries coin gold pieces of 25 francs for use in international trade.

Most nations favored basing any international coinage system on the French gold five-franc. Along with his mint bill, Knox provided suggestions for adjusting U.S. silver coinage to the French five-franc silver coin. In 1872, the bill was amended to raise the weight of the subsidiary silver coins to accomplish this. The 1870 coin shown here is a silver five-franc. The 1860 coin is a gold five-franc.

accompanying the bill, of a chart detailing weight revisions to U.S. coins that would be necessary should the United States agree to such a coinage. Recommending that, if it did so, it accept Kelley's so-called "German scheme," which would have required coins metrically oriented to a German States gold crown of 10 grams, he wrote:

> The United States would undoubtedly agree to any system of international coinage having simple relations to some acknowledged unit of weight, first agreed upon by England and France, in order to simplify the present absurd system of calculating exchange; but if it is proposed to lead the way in such a system, then the metric system presents advantages over any other proposed. It is probable that the larger portion of our gold coins (to-day) in circulation would, if weighed together, fall short of their original weight (arising chiefly from abrasion) more than three dollars on the thousand dollars, which is the difference between the values of the metric coins proposed and of the existing coins, so that if the existing coinage of the country were to be exchanged weight for weight for the proposed metric coins there would probably be very little difference.[8]

In reference to the other popular international coinage scheme, supported by Sherman and Hooper, in which the French five-franc gold coin would be the pattern for the unit of value, Knox also presented conversions to adapt U.S. silver coinage to a relationship with the silver five-franc piece. Of the suggested modifications, Knox wrote:

> The double eagle here proposed is the exact equivalent, both as to weight and fineness, of the German Union crown, the only *gold* coin having exact and simple relations to the metric unit of weight yet issued by any country. It is smaller than the standard double eagle now authorized by about three-tenths of one per cent., (more exactly by 3.088-parts in one thousand). The other gold coins specified are in proportion. Two of the *silver* half-dollar pieces here described constitute in weight and fineness an exact equivalent to the silver five-franc piece of France; and the other silver coins are of proportionate weight and fineness.[9]

Writing to Knox on Jan. 25, 1870, in response to Knox's rough draft of the mint bill, Linderman made no direct reference to an international coinage, but took the opportunity, as he had three years earlier when he termed the change in monetary standards essential to the success of any such scheme, to again press for the adoption of a gold standard. In doing so, he felt that it was important to drop the silver dollar from the bill rather than reduce its weight as proposed in Knox's rough draft. Linderman wrote of Knox's call for a subsidiary dollar:

> Section 11 reduces the weight of the silver dollar from 412 1/2 grains to 384 grains. I can see no good reason for the proposed reduction in the weight of this coin. It would be better, in my opinion, to discontinue its issue altogether. The gold dollar is really the legal unit and measure of value. Having a higher value as bullion than its nominal value, the silver dollar long ago ceased to be a coin of circulation; and, being of no practical use whatever, its issue should be discontinued.[10]

Another of Knox's correspondents who favored a gold-based currency was James Pollock, director of the Philadelphia Mint. Pollock was an experienced mint official, having served as Philadelphia Mint director from the spring of 1861 through the fall of 1866. He again took over that post, replacing Linderman, in the spring of 1869 and served as

An 1874 U.S. Mint $10 gold pattern gave its value in everything from British pounds to German marks. It was produced by order of Mint Director Henry R. Linderman in response to a suggestion by Dana Bickford of New York.

The 1878 International Monetary Conference, also held in Paris, was called together by the United States as part of the provisions of the 1878 Bland-Allison Act. This conference did not generate the unity of the prior conference but it did lead to the production of some interesting U.S. patterns, including 1879 and 1880 metric gold $4 Stellas. The Stella (which came in flowing hair and coiled hair versions) would have been comparable in value to the Austrian eight florins, Dutch eight florins, the French 20 francs, the Italian 20 lire, and the Spanish 20 pesetas.

Mint director until early in 1873. Pollock was one of the first mint officials to suggest a reduced-weight silver dollar, and in his responses to Knox concerning the mint bill (submitted three days before those of Linderman), he expressed his support of Section 11, noting that "the reduction of the weight of the whole dollar is approved, and was recommended in my annual report of 1861."[11]

Similarly, in his Sept. 27, 1869, *Report of the Director of the Mint*, Pollock wrote of the need for the gold standard:

> Another function of the Mint, still more important in some respects, is to furnish a legal basis for the currency of the country. That legal basis, in its highest and most permanent sense, is *gold coin*; an unlimited legal tender, which does not promise to pay, but actually pays, is not a representative of property, but is property itself. It cannot satisfy hunger nor protect the human frame; but it will infallibly procure the means of doing so. It is not only a medium of exchange, but it has an intrinsic value, and is itself the standard of value; and, for the uses of money, it has and can have no rival or substitute. No country, not even the richest, need have a great deal of it. It is a scarce metal, and ought to be scarce; that is the very property which makes it fit for its purpose.[12]

Former Mint Director Robert Maskell Patterson (whose term of office ran from May 1835 to July 1851) believed, as did Linderman and Pollock, in the adoption of the gold standard. In his first reply to Knox, dated Feb. 10, 1870, Patterson queried Knox as to whether the revision of the mint laws was a simple recodification of existing statutes or if Knox was open to receiving suggestions and amendments. Knox must have replied favorably, for on March 5, 1870, Patterson again wrote to Knox and, at that time, he included his suggestions pertaining to the rough draft of the bill, along with his own amendment to Section 11 in which he advised dropping the silver dollar as had Linderman. Patterson's amendment to Section 11 of Knox's rough draft read:

> The silver dollar, half dime, and three-cent piece are dispensed with by this amendment. Gold becomes the standard money, of which the gold dollar is the unit. Silver is subsidiary, embracing coins from the dime to half dollar; coins less than the dime are of copper-nickel. The legal tender is limited to the necessities of the case; not more than a dollar for such silver, or fifteen cents for the nickels.[13]

The most influential mint official to object to any change in the weight or issuance of the silver dollar was James Ross Snowden, who had served as mint director from 1853 to 1861. Snowden, concerned with the possible confusion as to the standard of value, which he feared would be generated by the adoption of a lighter-weight silver dollar, conveyed his misgivings about the propriety of such a change in a March 10, 1870, response to Knox, stating:

> I see that it is proposed to demonetize the silver dollar. This I think unadvisable. Silver coins *below* the dollar are now not money in a proper sense, but only *tokens*. I do not like the idea of reducing the silver dollar to that level. It is quite true that the silver dollar, being more valuable than two half-dollars or four quarter-dollars, will not be used as a circulating medium, but only for [collector] cabinets, and perhaps to supply some occasional or local demand; yet I think there is no necessity for so considerable a piece as the dollar to be struck from metal which is only worth ninety-four cents. When we speak of dollars let it be known that we speak of dollars not demonetized and reduced below their intrinsic value, and thus avoid the introduction of contradictory and loose ideas of the standards of value.[14]

Andrew Mason, melter and refiner at the New York Assay Office, in a letter representing his own thoughts and those of officers at the assay office, expressed the same fears as had Snowden. Mason wrote, "the objections to changing the weight of the silver dollar are entitled to serious consideration."[15] In a subsequent letter, dated June 18, 1870, which was after the final draft of the mint bill had been submitted to Congress, Mason made it clear that he thought any change would hurt the standard of value, writing "The retention of the silver dollar, as at present issued, affords a standard of valuation for

Many believed that even if an international coinage was not adopted, U.S. coins should convert to the metric standard, as Knox had recommended in his report accompanying the mint bill. Shown are metric dollar and metric Goloid patterns. Goloid had been proposed by Dr. Wheeler H. Hubbell of Pennsylvania as a means of combining gold and silver in the same coin.

silver, and the demand for it at the regular coinage charge indicates its usefulness otherwise."[16]

The officers of the San Francisco Mint also objected to Knox's reduced-weight silver dollar because they thought it might interfere with previously existing contracts. In a letter to Knox dated Feb. 4, 1870, the officers questioned:

> Would not the proposed change in the weight of the silver dollar disturb the relative value of all our coinage, affect our commercial conventions, and possibly impair the validity of contracts running through a long period? Might not the dollar be retained as a measure of value, but the coinage of the piece for circulation be discontinued...[?][17]

Based on the suggestions of mint officers, particularly Linderman and Patterson, Knox decided to drop the subsidiary silver dollar from the final version of the mint bill. In his report accompanying the bill, under the subtitle "Silver Dollar-Its Discontinuance as a Standard," Knox wrote:

> The coinage of the silver dollar piece, the history of which is here given, is discontinued in the proposed bill. It is by law the dollar unit, and assuming the value of gold to be fifteen and one-half times that of silver, being about the mean ratio for the past six years, is worth in gold a premium of about three per cent., (its value being $1 03.12) and intrinsically more than seven per cent. premium in our other silver coins, its value thus being $1 07.42. The present laws consequently authorize both a gold dollar unit and a silver dollar unit, differing from each other in intrinsic value. The present gold dollar piece is made the dollar unit in the proposed bill, and the silver dollar piece is discontinued. If, however, such a coin is authorized, it should be issued only as a *commercial dollar*, not as a standard unit of account, and of the exact value of the Mexican dollar, which is the favorite for circulation in China and Japan and other Oriental countries.[18]

After incorporating his views and the opinions of the various coinage authorities, Knox sent the final draft of the new mint bill to Treasury Secretary Boutwell. On April 25, 1870, Boutwell in turn relayed the bill to the Senate Finance Committee Chairman John Sherman. Three days later, Sherman introduced the bill in the Senate, marking the beginning of a three-year journey through both houses of Congress, until it finally became law on Feb. 12, 1873.

From the writings of the coinage experts submitted to Congress along with the mint bill, it is clear that the removal of the silver dollar from the nation's coinage system was not concealed from members of Congress as free silver supporters and some red-faced congressmen would later contend. Instead, the proposals to change to a gold standard and end the coinage of the silver dollar were openly presented and, in fact, supported not only by the coinage authorities Knox consulted but by several influential members of Congress as well.

Despite three years of tedious movement through both houses of Congress (during which Knox's original measure was subjected to several modifications and spent much of its time under the scrutiny of the committees of both houses), the mint bill never once called for the continued coinage of the standard silver dollar. Attempt was made to include a subsidiary silver dollar of 384 grains and a 420-grain Trade dollar was eventually adopted, but at all times the averred purpose of the monetary standard provisions of the coinage measure remained securely linked to the adoption of gold as the sole unit of value. However, within this process, there was considerable manipulation by Pacific coast mining and bullion interests, led by William C. Ralston, who found an able assistant in former Philadelphia Mint Director Linderman. As will become clear in the following chapters, not all was aboveboard with the passage of this act and what meets the eye in official records concerning the mint bill only tells a slim portion of the story of the Crime of 1873.

Most of those responding to Knox's rough draft of the mint bill, including former Philadelphia Mint Director Robert M. Patterson, argued in favor of the adoption of a gold standard.

Chapter 9

THE PERFECT ALLY

Most writers who have examined the background of the Coinage Act of 1873 have concluded that Dr. Henry R. Linderman played only a minor role in this key piece of legislative history and then only as an above-reproach Treasury Department official. The truth is somewhat different. Surviving Linderman-to-Ralston letters from the Bank of California's archives reveal not only Linderman's close connection with William C. Ralston, who at that point controlled most of the Comstock, but also that he was well compensated monetarily by the prominent California banker during much of the time the mint bill was before Congress in return for tailoring several of the bill's key sections to favor the nation's mining interests. The true Crime of 1873 lies therefore not in the elimination of the silver dollar from the nation's coinage system, although this was likely a planned by-product of their manipulations, but in Linderman's using his influential role as an on-again-off-again Treasury representative to secure provisions in the nation's coinage laws that directly benefited private interests while lining his own pockets.

Henry R. Linderman was born on Dec. 26, 1825, to Dr. John and Rachel Linderman in Lehman Township, Pike County, Penn. At first, like Ralston, Linderman followed closely in his father's footsteps. Studying medicine at home, he eventually opened a practice in Pennsylvania, which he maintained for several years.[1] In 1853, he became a clerk at the Philadelphia Mint, rising to chief clerk in 1855, a position he held for the next 10 years, before resigning his post to go into private business. On March 4, 1867, President Andrew Johnson named Linderman director of the Philadelphia Mint, in which capacity he served until he was replaced by President Ulysses S. Grant in April 1869. In 1871, he was sent to Europe to study foreign currency systems. By 1872, he was back in the United States serving as a commissioner in charge of setting up a refinery in San Francisco, all of which culminated in his appointment to the newly created position as director of the Bureau of the Mint, in which office he served from April 1873 to December 1878.[2]

Just when Linderman first came under Ralston's influence is uncertain. However, by his August 1869 visit to San Francisco on Treasury business, shortly before he began consulting with John Jay Knox on the mint bill, Linderman had formed a close relationship with the California financier that would be reflected in his actions as a guardian of the bullion interests in Washington for much of the following decade.

For Ralston, it was a perfect alliance. In securing Linderman's services, he had found a good friend and a loyal ally with unmatchable Washington ties well beyond any of those possessed by his regular paid lobbyists, including direct access to the inner workings and decision-making at the U.S. Treasury, the White House, and within key Senate and House committee meetings. With Linderman's extensive background at the mint and his superior knowledge of complicated monetary theory—as well as a practical day-to-day knowledge of all matters relating to coinage, ranging from refining to metallurgy—Linderman was the ideal candidate to watch over Ralston's interests in Congress.

Perhaps most importantly, in Linderman, Ralston had found someone who, despite his lengthy record of government service, was willing to blur the line between the ethical and unethical to achieve his goals. For on the one hand, Linderman fervently believed in many of the provisions he helped guide through Congress for Ralston. On the other hand, he accepted payments in return for watching out for private interests, while continuing to take assignments from the Treasury Department. At least $8,500 in payments from Ralston (which exceeded the $5,000 annual salary he would later earn as director of the Bureau of the Mint) can be fairly well documented through the bank archive's letters as having been remitted to Linderman. Another $1,500 was requested by the Treasury official to cover additional expenses and was likely paid.[3]

Dr. Henry R. Linderman in a rarely seen photograph, taken on one of his visits to San Francisco. California Historical Society; Donated by Mrs. Scott Roundtree; April, 1969; Photographer Bradely and Rulofson; FN-21026.

In Linderman, Ralston also found someone who agreed with his economic philosophies, including the need for a gold standard (California had been nurtured on it and Linderman was a proponent of it), the importance of government support and encouragement of the growth of the domestic precious metals industry (believed to benefit the nation, which needed its product to return to specie payments), and the necessity of the removal of the government tax on the coinage of gold (which they both believed drove bullion out of the country and stood in the way of the expansion of U.S. business interests at home and abroad).

Since the days of the Civil War and the end of specie (coin) payments (which led to the release of the first greenbacks), California had shunned paper money in lieu of hard money in all manners of payments, passing legislation that stood up to state supreme court cases, requiring payment in gold when previously specified and prohibiting the use of paper money in the payment of taxes. But despite its great mineral wealth and unwavering passion for hard money, the Pacific coast often suffered chronic coin shortages. This left those whose primary trade was in money constantly looking for methods to keep the nation's gold at home. By the mid-1860s, merchants and bankers around California had become fairly united in their view that the one-half percent charge placed on the coinage of gold at the U.S. Mint since 1853 was an unfair tax and one of the primary reasons gold flowed away from this bullion-rich region, seeking markets (mainly London) where it would bring the highest price. In an 1866 letter, written at Knox's request and later brought before Congress, Ralston's associate, Louis A. Garnett, wrote that "If it be true that gold alone is the true measure of value, and the metallic worth of a country is the only safeguard to national and individual credit or solvency in periods of financial disturbance..." it would seem that all legislation should be directed toward its importation from abroad or its retention at home:

> Yet, strange as it may appear, all of our legislation upon this important subject has a direct opposite tendency. By imposing high mint charges upon the recoinage of foreign currency and exorbitant refining and revenue charges upon foreign and domestic bullion, it deters the one from seeking our markets and compels our own to seek the cheaper markets of other nations, or, rather where the smaller charges make its commercial value greater than its minting value at home.[4]

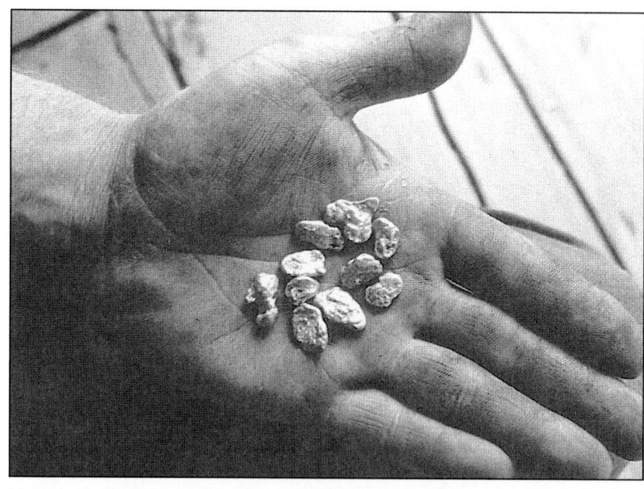

In the early days, following the California gold rush, Californians often relied on foreign coins and inconvenient gold dust and nuggets for currency.

Although free silver writers, including Nevada Sen. William Stewart (an active participant in the Jan. 9 and 10, 1871, Senate debate on the side of dropping the charge), would later claim that the lengthy battle in Congress over the coinage charge merely obfuscated the Coinage Act of 1873's real purpose (the secret adoption of a gold standard and the elimination of the silver dollar), the removal of the coinage charge was one of the key elements of the new bill, a change in the coinage laws the bullion interests had fought dearly to secure. The gold industry, which had drawn hundreds of thousands of emigrants to the West in the early 1850s, had, in recent years, seen its production wane. Relief from the coinage charge, many believed, would not only stimulate the mining industry but business in general as well. More gold in circulation in the form of coin would lessen problems with handling all manners of daily transactions. Plus, it was argued with some force, keeping gold bullion at home by dropping the charge, though costing the government approximately $200,000

A U.S. Assay Office was established in San Francisco in 1850 but at first only issued gold coins in $50 denominations.

in lost taxes, benefited the entire nation by turning the balance of trade in its favor and quickening a return to specie payments. Once such payments resumed, there would be no need for unbacked federal paper money which had depreciated against gold shortly after its release and plagued much of the country, causing confusion in business and domestic monetary transactions.

The May 21, 1869, issue of the *Virginia City Territorial Enterprise* gave some insight into the way in which the country was divided by varying currencies and the problems a traveler faced in this regard. Reporting on an article in the *San Francisco Times* favoring issuance of federal paper money redeemable in gold to facilitate trade between the Atlantic and Pacific states, the *Territorial Enterprise* wrote:

> At Corinne [Utah], the traveller going east strikes a greenback country; a country where the people look with astonishment and perplexity upon a gold coin, and scarcely know what to do with it. Prices, as far as the Promontory, are on a gold basis, east of that on a currency basis. Thus the traveller who starts from Sacramento pays $1 in gold for his meals, up to Promontory. Thence eastward he is agreeably surprised to find that the charge is only $1 in currency. On the other hand, the traveller bound west discovers, with a lengthening face, that the meal which only cost him $1 in currency at Corinne, requires $1 25 or more twenty miles west of that town.[5]

To make up for the lack of federal coinage on the Pacific coast, many private coiners began releasing gold coins. Shown are an 1850 Baldwin & Company $10 and an 1849 Mormon $20.

For Ralston there were other advantages to the removal of the coinage charge. Its elimination would not only draw more gold through his San Francisco Assaying and Refining Company on its way into U.S. coinage, but it would also offer the chance to make San Francisco a leading money center with the resources to expand its growing overseas trade, something he and the Bank of California would benefit greatly from.[6] There were everyday banking considerations as well. The Bank of California, like other banks, needed to have access to large amounts of gold, not just in bars but in coin form for the purposes of its wide-ranging (and in Ralston's case, often highly speculative) loans.

Ralston had already pumped millions into the Central Pacific Railroad, which tied up much of the bank's funds in slowly recouped loans, and similar amounts into his speculative ventures on the Comstock. He had survived the economic collapse and bank run of the 1850s, weathered rumored runs and acute coin shortages in the 1860s, and was ever aware of the bank's need to control as much of the region's money supply as it could to secure its survival against his overextended position and the coin shortages that were not uncommon in California's history.[7]

Even though California had large supplies of gold and silver, from the early days of the gold rush, its growth had been stilted by a lack of suitable and sufficient coinage. Circulation, at first, consisted of foreign coins and inconvenient gold dust and nuggets. What little official U.S. gold and silver coins that filtered to the West were needed to pay customs duties. The growth of the region's economy did not help, either, forcing bullion eastward in payment for a range of essential goods and supplies. To fill the void, a number of private enterprises began issuing gold coin. Some of these private issues were more reliable than others. Mormon gold coins, for instance, and the issues of Baldwin & Company were notorious for containing less gold than their inscribed dollar values.

A U.S. Assay Office was established in San Francisco in 1850, but did not begin issuing coins until 1851 and at first only in $50 denominations. A U.S. branch mint was finally authorized in 1852 and began taking deposits in 1854. It continued to operate out of an inadequate 60-foot square, three-story building located on San Francisco's Commercial Street until Congress appropriated funds and a new building was constructed on Fifth and Mission streets, which opened in 1874.

In design, many California territorial gold coins were similar to federal issues. Shown are an 1852 Moffat & Company $10 and an 1855 Kellogg & Company $20.

After the Civil War, the draw off of gold, spurred by a post-war boom in the East and the government's need to pay interest on the national debt, was of concern to Ralston and the entire Pacific coast.[8] The Bank of California, like other California banks, often found itself scrambling to obtain sufficient supplies of gold coin to meet the demands of its depositors. As David Lavender explained in *Nothing Seemed Impossible*, banks in San Francisco served as intermediaries in providing the necessary gold coin, by gathering unrefined bullion and taking it to the mint for refining. Some of this bullion would be placed in bank storage and others of it left with the mint for coinage. The amount that actually went into coinage, however, remained relatively small.[9]

Testifying before Congress' Select Committee on Retrenchment, on Sept. 4, 1869, that the nation's gold could be retained at home if the government allowed private refining of the bullion destined for coinage, San Francisco Assaying and Refining Company manager Garnett estimated that, out of the region's product of nearly $40 million in gold, not more than $6 million or $7 million went to the mint for coinage, and that most of this $6 million or $7 million in gold came from remote districts in the interior, where the difference between the commercial value of bullion and its coining value was not understood. Garnett told the committee that, because of coinage charges at the mint, the market value for unrefined gold bullion had been at one-half percent in favor of its export for the past two years, meaning most of it went abroad. He argued that the government duties on shipment of the bullion were $3 million more than the value of all of the gold that went to the U.S. Mint for coinage. Garnett told the committee:

> It is true I have sent in addition to that some nineteen or twenty millions of bullion to the mint, but I have done so knowing that we were sustaining a loss of three-eighths per cent. upon it. It is apparently a paradox to say that we would do so under such circumstances, but the directors of our institution, who are the principal bankers here, see that to stimulate enterprise, keep business and trade active, does them more good in the various ramifications of their business by keeping money easy than the three-eighths per cent. they would make on this amount of bullion by sending it to a foreign banker; and therefore they force it into the mint at a loss of three-eighths per cent. to them, hoping that this amount comes back to them again in stimulating the general business of the country.[10]

Jay Gould, who, along with James Fisk, attempted to corner the gold market in 1869.

The coinage supply problem became especially acute in mid-1869, just before Ralston and Linderman met in San Francisco, when Jay Gould and James Fisk attempted to corner the gold market in New York, forcing gold to a premium and draining off what supplies there were to the East. According to Ira B. Cross, in *Financing an Empire*, the Bank of California had always carried large supplies of gold bars, but these, of course, could not be used for over-the-counter transactions. "The United States Mint had shut down temporarily [due to a change in officers], thus making it impossible for the banks to have their gold bars minted into coins," Cross wrote. "Strangely enough there was at that time approximately $14,000,000 in gold coin locked up in the United States Sub-Treasury in San Francisco."[11]

This situation led to one of the more implausible tales often told of Ralston—one that originated with his friend, Asbury Harpending. The story, as related by Harpending, is that Ralston, hoping to avoid a run on the bank that would surely occur when it and other banks failed to produce enough coin to satisfy their depositors, asked Harpending to be at the bank at 1 a.m. and be ready for plenty of hard work. At the appointed time, Harpending and a friend met with Ralston and were soon heading to the nearby U.S. Sub-Treasury, where they removed sacks of gold coins to the bank, exchanging them at the Sub-Treasury for gold bars. When a threatening crowd gathered at the Bank of California's doors the next day, Ralston was able to avert a run by showing his anxious customers that the bank had ample supplies of gold coins. Once the danger had passed, Ralston switched the gold coins for the bullion, and no one was any the wiser. Considering the recent investigations and tight scrutiny under which the U.S. Sub-Treasury and branch mint were operating, it is unlikely this could have happened. However, whether the story is true or just a bit of folklore, it illustrates the desperate conditions Pacific coast bankers were placed in by suffering from an inadequate supply of coins. Relief in this instance occurred when the Treasury agreed to allow release of gold from the Sub-Treasury by coded telegram for deposits made in the East.

Shortly after this crisis, Knox began preparing the mint bill at Boutwell's request. Linderman was already convinced of the propriety of allowing a "free coinage" of gold, and most others Knox consulted, including, of course, the representatives from the Pacific coast, favored the removal of the charge. Therefore, in his report to Treasury Secretary George S. Boutwell, Knox featured the elimination of the coinage charge as one of the bill's primary provisions. Under the heading, "Repeal of the Coinage Charge," he wrote:

> The coinage charge at the French mint is about one-fifth of one per cent.; our present charge is one-half of one per cent. Our coinage charge it is now proposed to abolish, in order to conform to the practice of our own mint prior to the act of February 21, 1853, and for the reason that it should be the policy of the government to hinder rather than to encourage the export of bullion.[12]

To strengthen the point, Knox quoted Linderman from the latter's report about his 1869 visit to San Francisco. Linderman had written of the need to remove the coinage charge:

> My attention was attracted to the very small amount of refining and coinage executed at the branch mint at San Francisco, compared with the production of the country, and I was naturally led to inquire for an explanation. A due examination of the subject soon satisfied me as to the cause, which I found to be that, under our present system of mint laws, bullion has a higher commercial value for export than for coinage in the mint, which not only affects the local interests of that coast, but in view of the diminishing product of the precious metals, becomes a question of national importance. The reason for this is, that as gold and silver are chiefly valuable for the purpose of manufacturing money, the cost incidental to coinage necessarily determines the value of the bullion. I find, on comparison, and especially at San Francisco, that the expenses of coinage are much greater than abroad, and hence our metallic product commands a higher price in foreign countries than can be realized by its coinage at home. The principal charge tending to produce this result is that of half of one per cent. for coinage, which is above that of any other nation, and especially France and England, where most of our gold bullion is exported.
>
> The importance of this subject had presented itself in a measure to me while I was Director of the Mint [1867-1869], and in my annual report for 1868 I recommended its reduction from a half to a quarter of one per cent.; but my examination at San Francisco has led me to consider the subject more thoroughly, and I am convinced that it should be abrogated altogether, and that we should return to our uniform practice prior to 1853, which was to coin gold without charge, not only as an expedient for encouraging coinage, but as being more consistent with the theory of money as a universal standard of value.[13]

Linderman offered examples, using an unparted 42.24-ounce stamped bar (.892 fine gold, .98 fine silver, and .10 base metal) deposited at the San Francisco Mint, the Philadelphia Mint, New York Assay Office or the San Francisco Assaying and Refining Company, to illustrate the advantages of removing the coinage charge. In each case he demonstrated that, even with the variance in market values for gold from the East to West and the cost of refining, the bar would be worth from 99 cents to $2.63 cents more for deposit at the mint, once the coinage charge was dropped, than it would be to ship it abroad.[14]

Continuing his advocacy of dropping the charge, Knox reproduced a "recently published" article by "a very intelligent gentleman upon the Pacific Coast, who is thoroughly familiar with this question."[15] The gentleman, perhaps Garnett, wrote:

> While we are exporting our unrefined gold and silver to Europe, and our refined metals to China, we are importing gold from British Columbia, and silver from Mexico. While in the last ten years we have exported $612,000,000 of our native product, we have imported $157,000,000 of foreign treasure, and yet we receive no practical benefit from it as a means of increasing our metallic circulation; for it no sooner reaches our market than it commands a premium above its value in our mint for re-export, when it is in the form of bullion; and when in (foreign) coins it only entails a loss upon American commerce, as they are received abroad at a greater valuation than they will realize either in our market or at our mints; and we are, therefore, in every event, and under every condition of trade, the loser. That as the commercial value of gold as a commodity is greater than its value in our mints, our own production seeks other markets uncoined, and that of other nations avoids ours. While, however, there is a profit in the export of uncoined bullion, taken at its valuation in our mints, there is always a loss on the export of our coins taken at their current value. The result, therefore, of modifying our mint charges so as to conform to those of other nations would be to raise the coining value of gold at home above its commercial value, and thereby make it more valuable for coinage than for export. It would, therefore, all seek our mints for coinage; and when once coined would be the very last thing any one would want to ship, and never would be exported, except in cases of absolute necessity, and when no other medium of exchange could be procured.[16]

Of the coinage authorities Knox consulted in preparing the bill, only former Philadelphia Mint Director Robert Maskell Patterson (1835-1851) favored retention of the coinage charge, largely on the grounds that there had been a recent suggestion in England of reinstituting such a charge. Among those calling for its removal were former Philadelphia Mint Director James Ross Snowden (1853-1861), who noted that to do so would tend to increase the nation's gold coinage; William E. Chandler, former Assistant Secretary of the Treasury; and the officers of the San Francisco Mint.[17]

For their part, San Francisco Mint officers Gen. O.H. La Grange, superintendent; O.D. Munson, assayer; J.B. Harmstead, coiner; and J.P. Cochran, melter refiner, wrote:

> It will be observed that the officers of this branch are of the opinion that the seigniorage or coinage charge ought to be *entirely repealed* without reducing the weight of our coins; and further, that in the thirty-fourth section of the proposed law, (with the exception of the treasurer,) they venture with great deference to recommend (on the suggestion of the able and experienced assayer of this branch) that the entire charge for refining bullion deposited for coinage be abolished, or in other words that the government confer upon the mining interests of the country the benefit of a free mint. Some of the general reasons for this recommendation may be briefly stated as follows:
>
> 1. It is believed that the policy of our government should tend to the retention of American bullion at home rather than allow the difference between the mint charges of our own and foreign countries to operate as a premium to encourage its shipment abroad.
>
> 2. That such a modification of the law would to some extent stimulate mining enterprise, encourage an important but poorly paid branch of industry, and increase our annual product of precious metals.
>
> 3. That this charge, by raising the mint value of bullion above its market value for shipment, would increase our coinage, swell the volume of specie in circulation, stimulate the exporting of other commodities than gold and silver, to adjust balances of trade, and in some slight degree facilitate the resumption of specie payments.
>
> 4. The entire cost of refining the total bullion product of the country, say thirty-six millions, would not exceed $200,000, and we hazard the opinion that the advantages to be derived would many times exceed that sum.[18]

A couple of weeks later, Superintendent La Grange also pressed the point with Treasury Secretary Boutwell in a letter dated Feb. 7, 1870:

> SIR: Permit me in addition to the general suggestions made by the officers of this branch, to say that personally I am earnestly in favor of any measure that can be secured, having a tendency to bring the cost of refining and coining bullion in this country into such a relation with the cost of those operations in other countries as will abolish the premium now practically paid to exporters of our uncoined gold and silver.[19]

All was ready now for the mint bill to move to the floor of Congress. There the seemingly miniscule coinage charge gained top billing.

The San Francisco Mint began accepting deposits in 1854. The building soon proved to be too small. In 1874, the mint was moved to a much larger facility on Fifth and Mission streets.

Chapter 10

FREE GOLD

The mint bill, having emerged from the Senate Finance Committee, was introduced on the floor of the Senate on Jan. 9, 1871, where it instantly became the subject of a vigorous debate over the coinage charge question. During its stay in the finance committee, headed by Sen. John Sherman, the committee had approved an amendment calling for a three-tenths percent charge on coinage.

On Jan. 9, during the floor debate over the coinage measure (S859), a confused Sherman, in justification for the three-tenths percent charge, announced that a provision continuing the current one-half percent coinage charge had been in the bill when he presented it to Congress in the prior session and that most of the coinage experts John Jay Knox consulted had favored its retention, therefore, the reduction to three-tenths percent was of benefit to the mining interests.[1] Neither was true. The original bill did not contain the coinage charge, as Sherman suggested, nor did most of the experts Knox consulted want it retained. The amendment, therefore, raised a storm of protest from western senators eager to protect their constituents.

California Sen. Cornelius Cole was quick to object to Sherman's misstatement. "This charge I believe to be unjust and oppressive to those who are in possession of bullion and wish to convert it into coins," Cole complained. "With as much propriety, in my judgment, might any one who receives greenbacks or United States notes from the Treasury be charged a percentage for the printing of those notes. To convert bullion into coin is of no special advantage to the owner of that bullion. It is of advantage, however, to the country at large to have bullion converted into the coin of the United States."[2] Cole argued that the charge had the effect of driving bullion from the country, at the rate of between $10 million and $12 million annually. "This one half of one per cent. or three tenths of one per cent., as is proposed in this bill, is a sufficient inducement on the part of those who have bullion to let it go out of the country in the form of bullion in the payment of debts that they may owe abroad," he told the Senate.[3] Adding that the coinage charge had long been a subject of discussion on the Pacific coast, Cole said that the people there were "with wonderful unanimity" against the charge and "exceedingly anxious on this question."[4]

Great Britain allowed a free coinage of gold, which many on the Pacific coast believed drew gold out of the United States, to Europe, to be turned into British gold sovereigns.

Other senators, most hailing from the West, who fought against the charge during the two days of debate on this topic, voiced similar concerns, almost all pointing to the benefits England had enjoyed as a world money center after it adopted free coinage of gold, some 150 years earlier. Sen. Henry Winslow Corbett from Oregon, for example, said that, if gold could be retained at home, it would shift the balance of trade and cause an increase in exports of produce, such as wheat and cotton. It would also help speed a return to specie payments and make the country a center of the money trade, as in England. "We wish to make this country [the United States] the moneyed center of the world, and if we can reduce the coinage charge and retain the coin in our own country, rather than send it abroad, it will tend more than anything else to make us the moneyed center of the world," Corbett proclaimed.[5]

Sen. George H. Williams, also from Oregon, defended the elimination of the charge as a benefit not only to the Pacific coast but the nation as well. "It is not pretended that [gold] coin will not be exported if the charge provided for in this amendment should be abolished; but it will only be exported to meet the balance of trade that may exist against the United States," Williams said. "But now the exportation of bullion is a matter of commerce, for persons can go into the market in the city of San Francisco and elsewhere and buy up bullion, export it to England, and have it converted into coin free of charge, and make money in the operation; so that there is an inducement for exportation of bullion to Europe for purposes of speculation; and of course the more bullion there is exported to Europe the less will be converted into coin in this country, and to that extent the coin circulation of the United States will be reduced."[6]

By 1865, there were five British agency banks in San Francisco whose primary business was the purchase of bullion, some of it going toward London's trade with the Orient.[7] The existence and activities of such foreign banks on U.S. soil was not lost on the western senators, who were eager to point out that these agencies were large buyers of the region's gold produce, aided by the unfair coinage charge. Nevada Sen. William M. Stewart complained:

> It seems to me idle for us to quote as authority against free mintage and against the practice of England for the last one hundred and fifty years the opinion of one or two professors. What has been the result of her practice? It has enabled her agents to buy bullion all over the world. It has made England, which is not a bullion-producing country, the center of the bullion market of the world. It has given her merchants and her bankers the handling of the bullion of the world.[8]

Stewart also claimed the coinage charge fell upon every bullion producer, whether or not he had his bullion coined, explaining in a response to Sen. Sherman that the true market value of any bar of bullion was still its mint value, Stewart said of the problems facing a bullion producer:

> ...when he gets his bar in bullion in any place in this country the price of that bar of bullion is regulated where he sells it by the market value there, and the market value is always the mint value. Take it in San Francisco. You have a given number of ounces of bullion. You can get for it for shipment only the mint value, or perhaps a trifle more that somebody may give in order to get it. Bullion commonly sells at the mint value; that regulates its price. You charge one half of one per cent for coinage and that reduces the value of the bullion in that market one half of one per cent., and the man who sells his bar and does not have it coined has to pay that tax as much as the man who has his bullion coined.[9]

Sen. James W. Nye, also from Nevada, spoke of seeing cart loads of precious metals being spirited away in 1869, when gold flowed out of the West in response to Jay Gould's attempt to corner the market. Nye related:

> Mr. President, my mind is so constituted that I always doubt when I hear men theorize when I know to the contrary. I stood less than two years ago in the streets of San Francisco, in California, and in the dark day of a financial crisis there I saw cartloads of American bullion sacrificed to British buyers because they could pay one half of one per cent. more than we could, as their coinage was all free. The profits that day to the English bankers was double what the profits of this whole coinage is for twelve months to this nation. You give them one eighth of one per cent. advantage over the bullion buyers of our own country, and they can glean our own markets of the product.[10]

California Sen. Eugene Casserly, stressing the time and energy the Treasury had put into preparing the mint bill, chose to quote from Treasury Secretary George S. Boutwell's 1869 Treasurer's report as authority for dropping the coinage charge. "The coinage of the country is diminished in amount by the fact that in England and France the mint expenses are much less than with us," Boutwell had written. "It would no doubt have a tendency to prevent the export of the precious metals in the form of bullion, if the mint charges were to be reduced or altogether abolished."[11]

At one point during the debate, Casserly also asked that the testimony of William C. Ralston's associate Louis A. Garnett (given nearly a year prior to the Joint Committee on Retrenchment in San Francisco) be read into the record. Garnett had told the committee, "If we take off our coinage charge, with the low rate of refining that the private refiner [i.e., the San Francisco Assaying and Refining Company] refines at, the whole of our metallic product here at once becomes more valuable for coinage here than for export abroad."[12] When asked by the committee if gold would not still go abroad when the balance of trade was against the United States, Garnett responded:

> That is something we cannot avoid. We have to settle the balance of trade against us with gold in some sort; but now there is a constant incentive to send gold abroad when the balance of trade is not against us, but simply as a commodity which pays for its export abroad and a profit above the par of exchange. That is what is ruining us here.[13]

Besides, Garnett explained, even when the balance of trade was not in the United States' favor, the country was still importing bullion. "Take our own case," he said, "when we are exporting our fine silver to China and our unrefined metal to Europe, we are importing unrefined metal from British Columbia above us and the unrefined metal from Mexico below us; and yet the exchange in the aggregate, taking the entire country, is against us."[14] He added:

> In proof of this, we constantly find the fact in New York and the eastern markets and in ours, that when the market is well supplied with commercial bills in abundance, which the banker can cover his own exchanges with, he will not do it because the out-run on his bullion abroad will pay him a better profit than the discount of commercial bills, besides having a specie remittance, so that there is a constant tendency to export our bullion without reference to the balance of trade.[15]

However, when the bullion was in coin form, Garnett said, it would not be exported:

> ...because the ordinary wear and tear of our exact standard, which the imperfectness of manipulation and mechanics has never enabled us to obtain, is always a drawback on the export of coin. For instance, a twenty-dollar piece should weigh exactly five hundred and sixteen grains, but knowing it to be impossible to get exact weight the law allows a deviation of half a grain either way; it may weigh five hundred and sixteen and a half or five hundred and fifteen and a half grains. They generally try to keep it under that half a grain. Then there is the wear and tear of coin in use. Inasmuch as foreign coins when exported are treated as mere bullion, this is always a check against the export of our coins, and therefore our coins will never go abroad, if we can once convert our bullion into coin, unless as an absolute necessity....[16]

Garnett's argument, however, ignored years of experience that showed that coined gold and silver could and would be withdrawn from circulation any time either metal became more valuable as bullion than its nominal value as currency. Simply making certain that all U.S. bullion was converted into coin would not have kept it in the country, much less in circulation.

For his part, Sherman, one of only a few defenders of the charge to voice his opinion during the debate, claimed the coinage charge was "vital to the bill." The theory of the charge, Sherman told

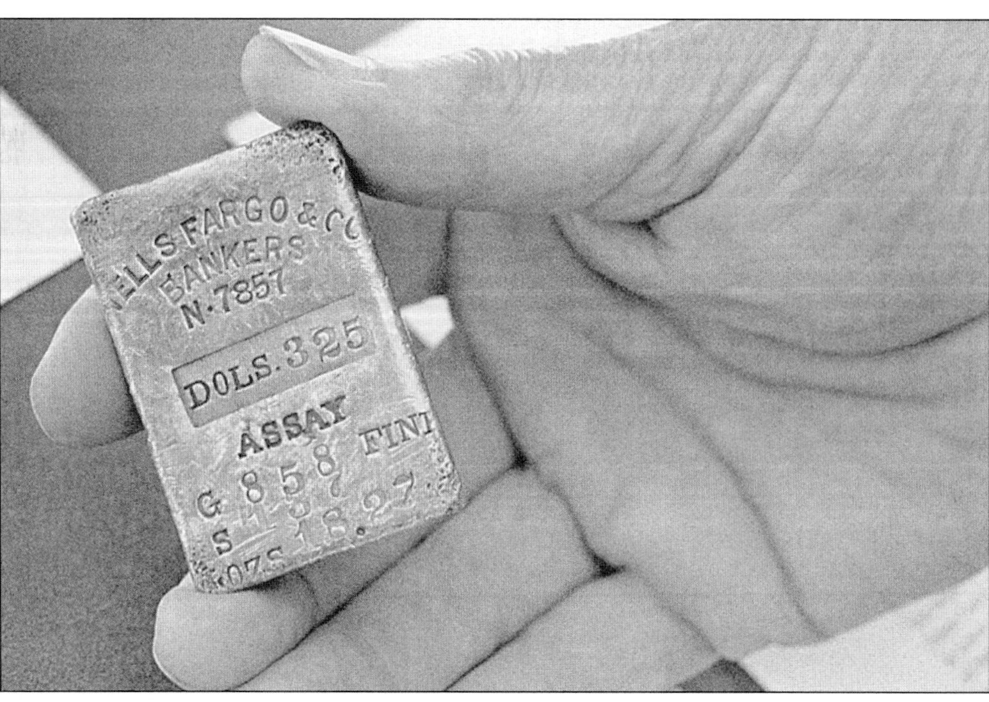

An 18.27-ounce Wells Fargo gold ingot stamped with its value in dollars and its gold and silver content.

the Senate, was that every process of government minting should be self-sustaining. Therefore, Sherman said, the Finance Committee, "after a careful consideration and examination of the question" decided to maintain the mintage charge, but at a reduced rate. The lower rate, he explained, had become possible because of increases in the quantity of gold being manufactured into coins and the cheapening of mint processes in the years since the coinage charge was adopted.[17] "I ascertained as nearly as possible the actual cost of converting standard bars into gold coin, and the concurrent testimony of nearly all is that it is about three tenths of one per cent.," Sherman told the Senate, and "At that rate we propose to leave the mintage charge."[18]

Also, in 1853, when the one-half percent charge was adopted, Sherman said the primary reason was to keep gold in the country:

> That was the main and leading object. It was argued, with a great deal of force, by eminent gentlemen then in this Chamber, that if a charge was put upon the coinage, as was done by all the nations of the world except England, the gold coin, which would then be more valuable as coin than as bullion, would not be exported until the balances of trade were settled by our commodities; that until bullion was exported, until wheat was exported, until cotton was exported, until all the other products of nature were exported, gold and silver coin would not be exported, because they were more valuable, made so by their greater cost.[19]

Citing the writings of European authorities, Sherman attempted to show that even in England, where a free coinage had been adhered to for more than a century, there had been a change of philosophy, and the reinstatement of the charge had only been postponed because of current discussions over an international coinage, which, if adopted, would require all nations to employ a common seigniorage. Sherman added that when you change bullion into coin, it makes it more convenient, not less, for use in export. Great Britain's sovereigns were regularly exported because of that nation's free coinage provision, according to the senator.

Sen. Justin S. Morrill of Vermont also spoke up in favor of the charge, arguing along the lines of Gresham's Law (i.e., bad money drives out the good) that as long as depreciated paper money continued to circulate, gold coin would not. Morrill told the Senate:

> The price of bullion is regulated by the markets of the world, not by the coinage stamp of the United States. Suppose, Mr. President, we were at the present moment to coin any amount of United States gold and silver, as long as we keep in circulation an irredeemable currency the coin will not come into circulation. It makes no difference how much we may coin the people will not see a dollar of it, not an eagle, not a dime more in consequence of its manufacture. That fact alone will not increase their ability to buy and hold it.[20]

The vote being taken, the amendments to the bill were passed by a narrow 25 to 22 margin, with 25 abstaining.

The following day, Cole asked for a separate vote on each amendment, after which he presented a letter "submitted to me by one of the most distinguished officers of this Government, received by him from probably the most skillful banker upon the Pacific coast."[21] The letter was from Ralston, hoping to add his weight to the argument. Ralston wrote:

> "The effect of this charge is to promote the exportation of the precious metals to other countries where no such charge exists. Gold bullion is actually worth one half per cent. more for export than for coinage. Hence the foreign bankers and importers, such as Rothschilds' agents, the managers of English banks or agencies, and a number of French and English firms, are constantly sending away all they can control, which is a large proportion of the entire product. The charge operates as a premium in their favor and against the enlargement of our coin base, which, at the present time especially, needs all the help we can give it, looking to the resumption of specie payments.
>
> "The coinage charge also operates indirectly to the prejudice of other exports, being an adverse element in the exchanges of the country, and thus affecting an immense volume of business. In proof of this I need only refer you to the well-known fact that while 'the true par of exchange results from the respective fine gold contents of the coins, the actual par depends upon the terms upon which gold bullion can be converted into such coins'...The charge of one half per cent. for converting our gold bullion into coin is that much against us in our exchanges with other nations, and inflicts a loss of millions of dollars upon the commerce of the country, while Government gains by it but the paltry sum of about one hundred and twenty-five thousand dollars per annum. Here is a point which our wise financial men at Washington appear to have overlooked entirely; a plain case of the policy which 'saves at the spigot and loses at the bung.'"[22]

Ralston's name would again be brought up on the floor of Congress by Sen. Sherman, who during the Jan. 10 debate complained that the effect of this act would be to force all of the gold produced in the United States into the mint in San Francisco. This declaration elicited a quick reply from California Sen. Cole, who told Sherman that there were other mints in the United States, "and we do not desire to have any more of it than properly belongs there."[23] Sherman retorted:

Louis A. Garnett, who managed the San Francisco Assaying and Refining Company, argued that once U.S. gold bullion was put into coin form, it would not be exported. Photos are not to actual size or proportion. The $10 coin at top measured 27mm in diameter. The $20 gold coin in the center was 34mm. The $5 coin was 21.6mm.

My friend knows very well that the gold will flow into the nearest mint, and there be melted and put in this form of gold coin; and this is to be done at the expense of the United States. Why should it not be left to be governed like any other matter of regulation and trade? This bullion is not the bullion of the United States. It is the property of private persons. Mr. Ralston, whose letter has been read here, handles more of this bullion than probably all the people of two of the greatest States of the Union [California and Nevada]—I believe he is cashier of the bank of California. And yet we are required, at the expense of the United States, to reduce all the gold product of this country into this convenient form for exportation, so that the mints of foreign countries may take our gold coin and melt it over without cost or loss or wastage…It seems to me that this will have a bad commercial operation. It may be of some benefit in a local way, by compelling a large manufacture in a local place, but in its effect upon the commerce of this country it must be injurious. It has been injurious in England. The opposite policy has been beneficial in France [France maintained a one-fifth percent coinage charge]. We have tried it for twenty years, and no complaint has been made except as to the rate.[24]

The question again being brought on the amendment, this time a voice vote of 36 to 14 overturned the proposed three-tenths percent coinage charge. Ralston had earned a temporary victory.

Chapter 11

MR. GUYESCUTES

After it passed the Senate, the mint bill was forwarded to the House of Representatives on Jan. 11, 1871, where it was immediately referred to the House Committee on Coinage, Weights and Measures for examination. On Jan. 13, the House ordered the Senate bill to be printed and recommitted. One day later, using the alias "Guyescutes," the bill's co-author, Dr. Henry R. Linderman, wrote to William C. Ralston, warning that if they could not get the coinage measure out of committee before the end of the 41st Congress, it would fail, leaving them "at sea again."[1] Misdated by Linderman as Jan. 14, 1870 (not 1871 as it should have been), the "Guyescutes" letter has laid completely undetected as to its author and its proper place in the sequence of surviving Linderman-to-Ralston correspondence since shortly after it was written.[2]

It begins a string of letters that reveal Linderman's continuing efforts on Ralston's behalf, which stretched beyond the passage of the Coinage Act of 1873 into his term as director of the Bureau of the Mint. Much of his activities for Ralston in relation to the coinage charge, maintaining Ralston's control over refining of government bullion, introduction of the Trade dollar amendment into the mint bill, and other matters were performed, for pay, during periods in which Linderman was also regularly being called upon by Treasury Secretary George S. Boutwell to attend to official duties for the U.S. Mint. It is likely one of the reasons Linderman signed code names to some of his letters to Ralston and marked most "Confidential."

Over the period between this first surviving letter, in January 1871, and the last one, in 1875, a few months prior to Ralston's death, Linderman employed at least two such aliases in letters to Ralston. "Guyescutes" appears only on the aforementioned letter, while "Old Man" was signed to some of the letters written in 1875, including one on Treasury Department, Office of the Director of the Mint, stationery!

The use of code names was also apparently one of Ralston's favorite pastimes. He assigned color-

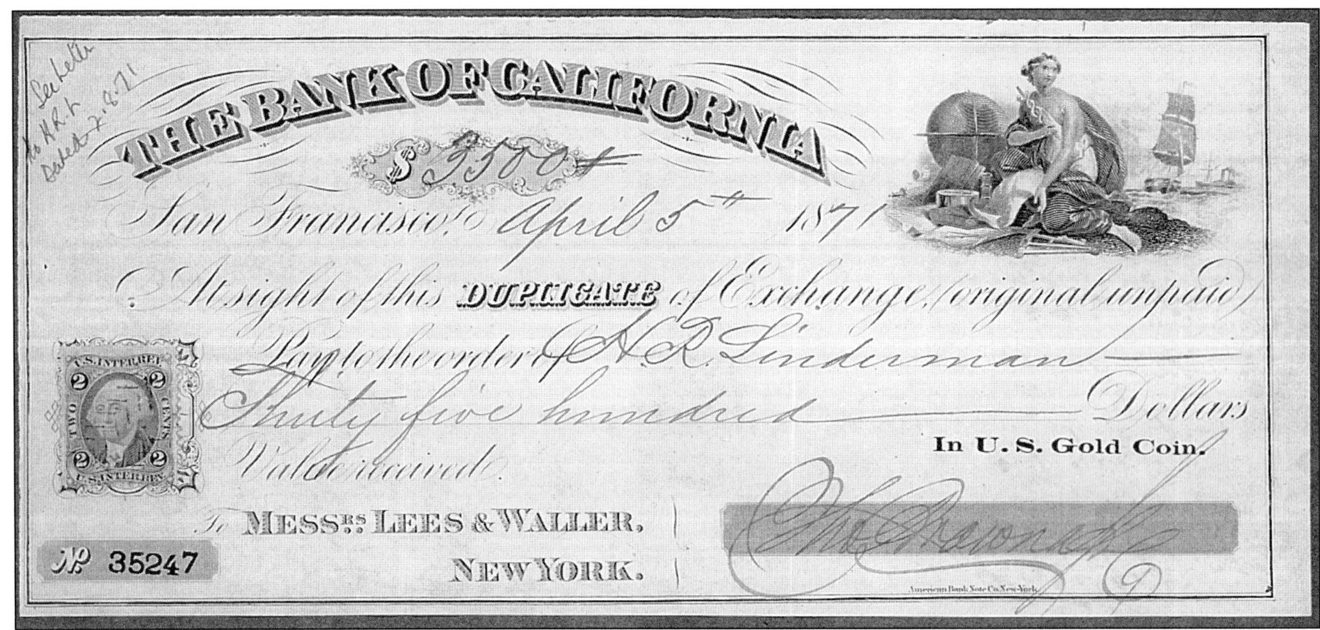
THE BANK OF CALIFORNIA
$3500
San Francisco, April 5th 1871
At sight of this DUPLICATE of Exchange (original unpaid)
Pay to the order of H. R. Linderman
Thirty five hundred Dollars
In U. S. Gold Coin.
Value received.
To Mess.rs Lees & Waller,
New York.
No 35247

Dated April 5, 1871, this Bank of California sight draft ordered payment of $3,500 to Henry R. Linderman through Lees & Waller in New York. In the same letter that William C. Ralston remitted this draft (reproduced elsewhere in this chapter), he also agreed to Linderman's request for an additional $5,000 for future services in pushing the mint bill through Congress. Courtesy of the Bancroft Library, University of California, Berkeley.

ful names to many of his associates, for use in letters and telegrams. For instance, Bank of California President D.O. Mills was "Monarch." Collis Huntington of the Central Pacific Railroad was "Hungry," and the Bank of California was "Bullion."[3] It can be assumed, therefore, that, in some cases, Linderman was just playing along. Though he no doubt would have preferred that none of his letters, coded or not, would ever come under public scrutiny.

In his Guyescutes letter, Linderman told Ralston he had been in regular contact with Louis A. Garnett, by letters and telegrams, keeping Garnett apprised of the bill's progress, and he had assured him there would be no difficulty in getting the bill out of the House committee and back on to the floor of Congress, in time to achieve its passage. Lately, however, Linderman had begun to worry.

"I had an interview with Judge [William D.] Kelley chairman of the coinage committee who intimated that the Bill might not be reported this session," Linderman wrote to Ralston.[4] Kelley, Linderman said, thought that Samuel Hooper, a member of the House Committee on Coinage, Weights and Measures (who would later take over the bill's leadership), might be "disposed to delay," plus "there appears to be some apathy in the House & a quiet opposition from Philad."[5] Linderman warned Ralston, "If it does not pass the House this session it fails on the day of adjournment and we will then be at sea again."[6] He also advised Ralston that, due to the risk to securing passage of the bill before the close of the 41st Congress, it would not be wise to bring up an amendment voiding two of the bill's provisions—one of which eliminated the office of Mint treasurer, and the other of which provided the Mint superintendent power to appoint employees without the nomination of operating officers. Both provisions likely dealt a blow to Ralston's long nurtured influence at the San Francisco Mint.

As a result of Linderman's "interview," Rep. Kelley agreed to call a meeting of the Committee on Coinage, Weights and Measures for the following Tuesday, with Linderman present "to explain any points that may be raised."[7] It would be one of several such committee meetings Linderman attended on Ralston's behalf.[8] Having made arrangements to remain in Washington until the end of the session, he urged Ralston to get California's congressional representatives worked up over the measure. Linderman wrote:

> [John J.] Knox appeared quite annoyed this morning—and asked, 'what do those California people mean writing and telegraphing [W.S.] Huntington [a Washington banker hired by Ralston as a lobbyist]. He knows nothing about the matter & comes to me & gets all information & &' I think it would be better to write to all your members in the House particularly [Aaron A.] Sargent and [Samuel B.] Axtell asking them to give special attention to the Mint Bill in the House. Sargent has a good deal in him and he should be impressed with the importance of the measure to the Pacific coast. What we want to do is to work up some enthusiasm and interests in the House in order to insure early action by the Committee on Coinage.[9]

With the mint bill passed, Linderman said, it would be an "easy matter to keep matters in good shape and it is not probable there would afterwards be any disposition to distrust its propositions."[10] The matters, Linderman referred to were, of course, the still-hoped-for elimination of the coinage charge and a provision allowing the exchange of refined bullion for unrefined, unparted bullion at U.S. branch mints, that, in reality, secured Ralston's monopoly over refining bullion deposited with the San Francisco Mint.

Although one 20th century historian claimed that Linderman was guilty of taking undue credit for just about everything associated with the Coinage Act of 1873, particularly in relation to the release of the Trade dollar, the Guyescutes letter shows the former Mint director's deep involvement with Ralston in matters relating to U.S. coinage, long before the passage of the bill.[11]

On Feb. 3, 1871, this time signing his own name, Linderman contacted Ralston to tell him that there had been some difficulty in getting action on the mint bill in the House, which he hoped would be resolved in the next couple of days. He would meet with President Ulysses S. Grant the following week to talk with him in reference to "the condition and prospects of our western mining interests."[12]

On Feb. 8, he again wrote to Ralston. By this time there had been some movement on the mint bill, but in the wrong direction. When the bill arrived at the House, it lacked a coinage charge, now the House committee was considering either reinstating the one-half percent charge in effect since 1853 or the three-tenths percent proffered unsuccessfully by the Senate and championed by Sens. John Sherman and Justin S. Morrill. Responding to a Jan. 28, 1871, letter from Ralston, Linderman wrote that there was "no doubt that both Sherman and Morrill got the Bill put quietly to sleep in the hands of the [House] Committee on Coinage," causing the delay, but that the pressure, "on which you [Ralston] materially aided," was beginning to show and there was hope for early action.[13] However, Linderman advised Ralston there was little likelihood of getting the coinage charge removed from the bill for some time to come. "We will probably have to submit, until another winter, to a coinage charge of 1/5 of one per cent.," a reduction to which he said he would put through the "Bullion Bill" (possibly code for "Bank of California Bill").[14] When the bill again appeared on the House floor in late February 1871, it indeed sported a one-fifth percent coinage charge.

"We ought to have a free coinage of gold," Linderman wrote, but there was strong opposition in both the Senate and the House. "Kelley was glad of the chance to let Hooper hold the Bill (on account of [his] Philad. interests). But we will march steadily forward until we bring the treatment of bullion and coinage, to a point that will place us on an equality with England & France."[15]

On Feb. 25, 1871, the mint bill finally emerged from committee. The House version of the bill was essentially the same as the one submitted by the Senate, except in respect to the coinage charge and the legal tender limit for subsidiary coinage, which was raised from $1 to $5 by the House substitute. However, the 41st Congress ended on March 3, 1871, without any further action, and the measure failed.

Six days later, Kelley reintroduced the bill (HR5) in the newly opened 42nd Congress, after which it was recommitted to await the appointment of a new Committee on Coinage, Weights and Measures. Realizing that the mint bill would not emerge from committee until the next session, Linderman, looking to cast a hopeful light on what had become a gloomy outlook, wrote in a March 26, 1871, letter to Ralston that if they could have succeeded in getting the bill out of the committee and onto the floor of Congress earlier, its passage would have been certain. Several things, however, had conspired against them, including chairman Kelley's procrastination (Kelley was a candidate for chairman of the

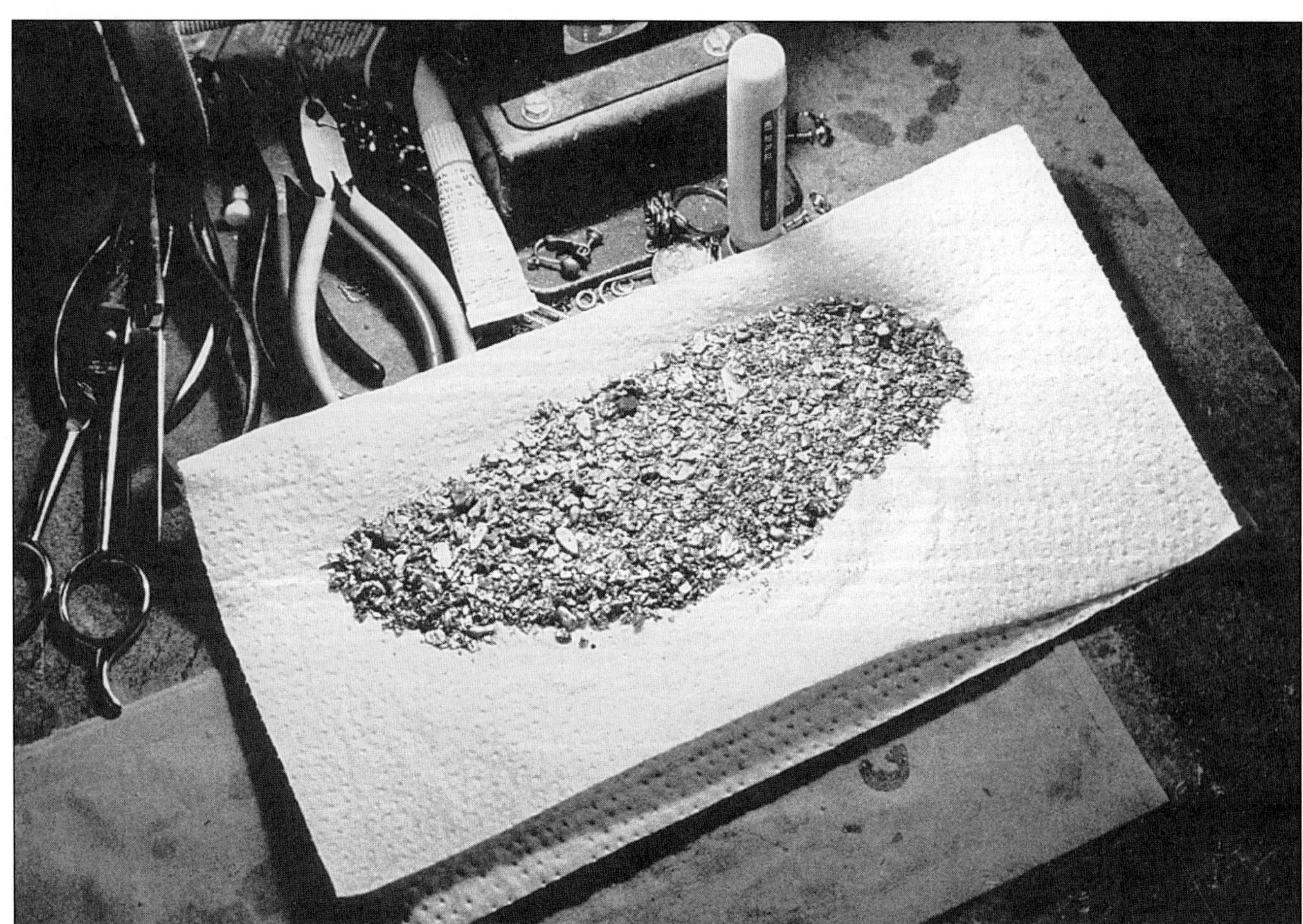

In the 1870s, to turn gold into coin, no matter what its original form, required the depositor to pay a one-half percent coinage charge. Linderman and Ralston hoped to remove the charge, which they both felt would help the mining industry and the nation.

House Ways and Means Committee, Linderman wrote, "and wanted no responsibility thrust upon him"); pressure from Philadelphia; the influence of Sens. Morrill and Sherman, "who undoubtedly wanted the Bill smothered to death;" and the complaint of someone, likely a congressman, who "grossly misrepresented matters" in claiming the attempts to repeal the coinage charge were based on saving the Bank of California $90,000 per year that would otherwise go to the U.S. Treasury.[16] "If the Sec[retary of the Treasury] & myself, had not pushed the Bill & circumstances occurred to strengthen our recommendations, it would never have been reported by the Committee," Linderman wrote. "Such is the temper & disorganization here, that the cowardly cry of 'Job' is fatal to any square measure of public interest, not backed by potential influences."[17] Linderman continued:

> There is no doubt that the true plan is, to push the Mint Bill through as a compact measure containing all necessary provisions (except the amendment of the House Committee for 1/5 of 1% coinage charge) desirable for the efficient conduct of the Mint business & the encouragement of refining by private enterprise. The Bill can be more easily passed than an isolated amendment for reducing or repealing the coinage charge & if the Bill is passed, it repeals the proviso in the present refining law limiting the provisions of the latter to the time of completion of the new Branch Mint. It is important to keep this in mind lest we may have to fight that matter over again.[18]

Having achieved much, all that was necessary to gain their goals, Linderman said, was:

> ...to continue our efforts in a quiet and prudent manner to insure success at the next session. Our contest will there be on the coinage charge & it is important that we put the Bill through the House with the coinage charge amendment struck out, & there is no doubt we can win. The Secretary, strongly favors a free coinage, and is well pleased with the results of the present refining system. I speak advisably on these points, Hooper is also for free coinage & Kelley too lately.
>
> A shrewd observer like yourself will not have failed to notice that we have a new order of things here. Things are much mixed in the House of Reps, and a clear majority for the Republicans on many questions cannot be depended on. This state of affairs will be clearly developed as time progresses. Again there is a strong disposition to remove all taxes that bear heavily on the industrial interests of the Country, and this must be taken advantage of to repeal the coinage charge.[19]

Assuring Ralston that he still had matters well in hand, Linderman added (in likely reference to Ralston's earlier battles not only to get the coinage charge dropped but also to secure a government refining contract for his San Francisco Assaying and Refining Company), "But you were correct when you said to me that it would take a year or two for things to settle down. Things make haste slowly here."[20] All that was really needed, Linderman told Ralston, was to continue to urge "officially" on the necessity of the service and the benefits to the country of cheap refining and free coinage to win passage of the provisions. (In a margin note, however, he added that, some time after June 20 a report showing the savings to the government, via private refining, should be prepared for inclusion in the Treasury secretary's annual report to Congress.)[21]

Serving, as he did, as a special agent for the Treasury, associated directly with the formulation of the mint bill at the request of the Treasury secretary, Linderman tried to walk a line between when he was performing "officially" for the government and when he was acting on Ralston's behalf. His letters show a constant self-absolution and pleading that, if he did not fully believe the causes he was working on for Ralston were also good for the nation, he would have never gotten involved. They also show an attempt, as much as possible, to structure the period of times in which he took payments from Ralston between times when he was "officially" in the Treasury's employ. However, the line is hardly straight and narrow. For instance, if, as he told Ralston, he helped the Treasury secretary save the bill from extinction in the House coinage committee, he did so during a period in which he was also in Ralston's employ. The same is true of when he suggested preparing material favorable to private refining for the Treasury secretary's report. There are other more egregious overlaps, as well, particularly those in late 1872, when he helped secure the Trade dollar for the Pacific coast bullion interests, while on dispatch from the Treasury.

Considering his close connections with the Treasury, and this bill in particular, Linderman was looked upon in the halls of Congress as a representative of the Treasury Department (as well as a likely candidate for head of the Bureau of the Mint being created by the mint bill).[22] For the Treasury Department, had Linderman's paid relationship with Ralston become known, the dangers were great. Charges of corruption and favoritism, which would certainly have spewed forth from Ralston's many competitors, leading to the "cry of 'Job'" Linderman so much feared, could have easily squashed the bill—placing Linderman and Grant's Treasury in a bad light. Years later, when Linderman was accused of taking Comstock mining stocks in payment from silver interests (a charge he vigorously denied), a congressional investigation was held and, at least one source says, caused him so much strain it resulted in his suffering a heart attack, leading to his death in early 1879. Therefore, considering Linderman's obvious need to conceal the true extent of his dealings with Ralston, urging things "officially" was not only smart politics but also his best way of continuing to appear above reproach.

A good example of Linderman's squirming to justify his actions, while still taking payments from Ralston, can be found in his March 26, 1871, letter. Writing to Ralston that Treasury Secretary Boutwell had recently commended him (Linderman) to various congressmen, including Kelley and Nevada Sen. James W. Nye, for rendering "invaluable services to the department and the Country, in mint and bullion matters," he told Ralston that they had suggested the importance of keeping him employed until the mint and coinage legislation was disposed, but he was not willing to enter into any such service as "it might interfere with my independence of action."[23] However, he would attend to any special matters that might arise (apparently meaning "for the Treasury"), "simply because it is better to keep these things 'in the family.'"[24] Linderman then asked Ralston for $3,500 for his services rendered up to that point and an additional $5,000 for his future efforts on the California banker's behalf:

> And now as to expenses and the future—for my services & expenses here, including anything that may be required in coming to Washington, off & on, or New York &c until 30th of June next, you will please send Thirty Five Hundred Dollars—on receipt hereof. I suppose you will desire to have me attend to these matters & the pushing of the Mint Bill next session say up to Sept 1, 1872—13 months, which will carry us to the expiration of your present refining contract [San Francisco Assaying and Refining Company] & by which time, I hope & firmly believe you will have all matters pertaining to refining and coinage in good shape. If so, I will make no engagement nor enter into any business which would interfere with the service indicated. I am willing to do so for the sum of Five Thousand Dollars, payable by January 1st, 1872. If I had not recommended both these measures, private refining & free coinage officially, before I undertook this business I would not do it at all. But I am strongly convinced of their propriety & necessity and it is a labor of love. Unfortunately I am not able to give my services without compensation.
>
> I would of course be perfectly willing to go on & attend to these matters as before, under the authority given in your letters & in conversation but I dislike to fix the compensation expenses &c after the work is done & it would be better for all concerned to have an understanding about the matter. Considering the expenses of laying around Washington travelling to & fro &c the amount left for services will be small.
>
> I leave the matter with you. If satisfactory to you I will as heretofore concentrate all my energies & influence to the passage of the Bill with the two essential features in it & the renewal of a satisfactory arrangement with the Refinery for renewing after the expiration of the present contract, and in any event believe me always
>
> Your Friend
> H.R. Linderman[25]

Although few of Ralston's responses survive, fortunately, in this case, a typewritten copy exists, as does the $3,500 sight draft. On April 5, 1871, Ralston replied:

> Yours March 26th to hand this morning, and enclosed please find draft for $3,500.00 in conformity with your wishes, and suffice it to say, we concur in all you suggest as to future compensation, and now allow me to repeat what I said to you verbally before your departure, viz. that we leave all our interests in your hands appertaining to the coinage charge question…and all other matters of this nature, and will depend on you solely to carry out and do the needfull in the premises, as in your good judgement may seem best and as I said then, we will take care of you, I like the way you put it, that the right things come right to business, and as I said we concur, so go ahead and do the needfull, as the circumstances may dictate requisite from time to time, and do not loose our trick trump every time…[26]

Setting aside the obvious conflict of interest and giving Linderman the benefit of the doubt that he squeezed all of his government services between his paid chores for Ralston would be nice but unrealistic. By late in the bill's history, his activities became so intermingled between his work with the Treasury and attempts by Ralston and Garnett to secure provision in the mint bill for a new trade coin that, in a March 1873 letter to Ralston, written after the mint bill had been signed into law, he even hinted that additional compensation might be in order![27]

In an Aug. 19, 1871, letter, written while Linderman was in London on Treasury business, he took time to aid Ralston and/or Louis A. Garnett in negotiating a deal with Grant & Company, "a powerful ring of speculators," for land in Sacramento, California, and kept both apprised of what was ahead for the mint bill.[28] After updating Ralston on the land sale, he wrote:

> I have kept Mr. Garnett advised of Mint bullion & coinage matters here & at home. My correspondent Mr. [William] DuBois Philad. Mint keeps me fully posted. I have examined the Brussels (Belgium) and Paris Mints.
>
> My purpose is to fight it out on this line until success or the latter part of fall comes, when I will return & proceed to Washington to give the Mint Bill an early start.[29]

The second session of the 42nd Congress would not open until Dec. 4, 1871, before which Linderman, as he told Ralston in an earlier letter, hoped to have a pamphlet offering a careful review of the mint bill prepared for distribution during the recess to new members of Congress. Saying that such a pamphlet would be extremely useful, he added, "You would be astonished at the general want of knowledge on this subject, not half a dozen men in Congress know anything about bullion manipulations."[30] It was a level of ignorance Linderman and Ralston could use to their mutual benefit.

Chapter 12

REFINED MONOPOLY

Congress may have lacked knowledge of bullion manipulations, as Dr. Henry R. Linderman suggested, but others keeping an eye on William C. Ralston and the Bank of California did not. This was especially true in relation to another lucrative provision of the mint bill—one that authorized the San Francisco Assaying and Refining Company's monopoly over refining bullion for the U.S. branch mint in San Francisco. It was a perk the Bank of California had fought long and hard to obtain and threatened to be lost with the completion of the new San Francisco Mint building. Ralston had been through too many battles since the mid-1860s, when the bank began its aggressive campaign for dominance over the Comstock, to let this happen.

It was during that period, it will be remembered, that the Bank of California came into possession of several of the ore-processing mills on the lode, translating their acquisitions into the Union Mill and Mining Company. While the bank crowd

Philadelphia Mint Director James Pollock at first objected to private refining of bullion deposited with the U.S. Mint. Ralston associate John Hewston Jr. found it necessary to obtain his support before the Treasury would authorize a contract with the San Francisco Assaying and Refining Company.

reigned over the lode, it also handled most of its raw ore processing. Once the ore was reduced at the mills and the precious metals extracted from most of the base materials, for many trade purposes, it still needed to be parted (separating the gold from the silver) and refined. It could then be formed into nearly pure bars or coins, at the discretion of the depositor. Under the San Francisco branch mint's control, this had proved to be a costly, wasteful, and time-consuming process that continually tied up the bank's money without interest. With the acquisition of the mills, the need for finding a cheaper, faster, more efficient means of bringing the metals to a level of refinement suitable to the whims of foreign trade—one that bypassed the strained capacities of the small branch mint—became more urgent. So, in 1866, along with former banking partners Eugene Kelly and Joseph A. Donohoe and others, Ralston and the Bank of California formed the San Francisco Assaying and Refining Company on Montgomery Street.[1]

Louis A. Garnett was appointed to head the new assay works' metallurgical operations and later became its general manager. Garnett, who was then in his early 40s, had nine years of experience in refining, including a stint as melter and refiner at the San Francisco Mint. A leading monetary theorist of his day, he would soon become Ralston's chief mentor on coinage matters and was in regular contact with Linderman and John Jay Knox in Washington, D.C., via telegraph. In his report accompanying the submission of the mint bill to Congress, Knox acknowledged Garnett along with the firm's assayer, John C. Hewston Jr., for their assistance in its preparation.

To assure the refinery's success and the bank's ability to obtain the federal coin necessary to transact business, Ralston had developed a close relationship with the U.S. Sub-Treasury and the mint in San Francisco—too close a relation for some tastes, as a congressional investigation was eventually ordered. Though it exonerated all involved, it alerted Ralston that there were those who would willingly block his path. Among these were Kelly and Donohoe, who had quickly dropped out of the arrangement with the Bank of California to become the assaying works' most vocal critics.[2]

Hoping to win an exclusive contract with the Treasury to refine all of the bullion deposited at the San Francisco Mint, Ralston dispatched Hewston to Washington to lobby for passage of a bill that would have secured the contract, and, by some contemporary accounts, spelled the end to the mint's antiquated refinery in San Francisco as well. Like Garnett, Hewston had extensive experience in such matters. After more than a decade of mint service in Philadelphia, as a melter and refiner, he was sent to San Francisco in the early 1850s, on orders from President Franklin Pierce, to oversee the set-up of the first San Francisco Mint. When the new mint opened, in April 1854, Hewston served as its coiner.[3]

In later years, he came into association with California Territorial gold coin producer John G. Kellogg. In 1860, Kellogg, Hewston & Co. was formed after the dissolution of Kellogg & Humbert (Augustus Humbert had served as the U.S. Assayer in San Francisco). This firm continued until 1866 when it sold out to the San Francisco Assaying and Refining Company, and Hewston became the new company's assayer.[4]

Arriving in Washington, Hewston went first to the Treasury Department, where, he later told Ralston, he was informed that the Treasury had no authority to issue the refinery a contract without congressional approval.[5] Apparently further clouding matters was the fact that California Sen. Cornelius Cole (perhaps at Donohoe, Kelly & Company's bidding) had already been to the Treasury, opposing private refining of mint bullion. Things were not any better in Washington, either. Kelly, from his New York Office, had raised a storm of protest in Congress that made it impossible for Ralston to win passage of his refining measure. Kelly and Donohoe, along with other assayers and bankers on the Pacific coast, feared that, besides giving the Bank of California a monopoly over refining, the contract would lead to the bank's direct control of the government mint.[6]

On June 25, 1868, Hewston, who had by this time wasted nearly a year in Washington, wrote to Ralston outlining the reasons for the delay and his recent successes. With the chances of obtaining congressional authorization at next to nil, he said, he had decided to go back to the Treasury, where he "tried quietly" again to secure a direct contract. This time, likely encouraged by learning that private refining of government bullion had been authorized by two prior coinage acts passed in 1853 and 1861, the Treasury was more agreeable. First, however, Hewston was told that he needed to obtain the endorsement of Philadelphia Mint Director James Pollock, who was on record as being opposed to private refining of mint bullion. In his June 25 letter, Hewston related to Ralston, "it was not easy but I returned yesterday from Phil. with such an endorsement."[7] A contract, he added, would be forthcoming. "As the case now stands the Secretary in a few days will give orders to [San Francisco Mint Superintendent Robert B.] Swain to contract with us or if not with us direct, with such party as are able to do all the work and that means us," he told Ralston. "[John Jay] Knox will write [a] private letter to Swain. Orders to [D.W.] Cheeseman [assistant Secretary of the Treasury at San Francisco] will be enclosed...to be delivered after the contract is completed."[8]

The contract apparently went through. Testifying before Congress' Joint Select Committee on Retrenchment, which met in San Francisco in 1869, former superintendent Swain (who had recently been replaced by the Grant administration) noted that, "Under instructions from Secretary McCulloch, last autumn I made a contract with the refinery here to refine all the bullion in the mint at eight cents an ounce; meantime we were charging the depositor eleven cents an ounce, which gave us a gain of three cents."[9]

Ralston's opponents got wind of the contract and rushed to stop it, introducing a resolution in the House and the Senate on July 13, 1868, looking to negate the current contract and repeal sections of the aforementioned 1853 and 1861 acts.[10] Three days after the bill's introduction in the Senate, Sen. John Sherman moved for the Senate to indefinitely postpone action on the measure, claiming that its provisions were already "disposed of by an amendment to one of the appropriations bills."[11] Approved on July 20, 1868, the amendment to the civil appropriations bill for the fiscal year ending June 30, 1869, to which Sherman referred, failed to repeal the earlier authority allowing outside refineries to perform services for the government but prohibited future contracts without Congress' approval. Attached to a provision granting additional funds for the completion of the Carson City Mint, the amendment read:

> *Provided*, That the Mint of the United States, and branches, shall continue to refine gold and silver bullion, and no contract to exchange crude or unparted bullion for refined bars shall be made until authorized by law.[12]

Ralston was not dissuaded. On Jan. 22, 1869, during the third session of the 40th Congress, new bills were entered in his favor in the House and Senate. Nevada Sen. William Stewart introduced S824, which authorized the exchange of refined gold and silver for unparted bars at the U.S. Mint and its branches. This bill was accompanied by a note from the Treasury secretary, giving his tacit approval.[13] On the same day, William D. Kelley brought a companion measure (HR1758 1/2) before the House. Donohoe and Kelly along with "other influential parties" (Pacific coast bankers and assayers) were quick to protest against the measure in a memorial to Congress. As the *Virginia City Territorial Enterprise* put it, it argued against "Mr. Stewart's bill excluding refining from the operations of the United States Mints."[14]

In their January 1869 submission to the House Committee on Coinage, Weights and Measures, signed by Donohoe, Kelly & Co., Milton S. Latham and several others, the bankers and assayers took issue with the way in which the assaying works had obtained its contract. Protesting against the measures pending in Congress, they wrote that they were surprised to see that the Treasury secretary and Philadelphia Mint director had recommended the pending bills. Despite any savings that might accrue from such a contract, the bankers and assayers wrote that, in a nation where annual production of precious metals stood at $80 million, there were dangers in placing the mint's refining into private hands. They added that they thought the matter had been settled the year prior, but had since learned otherwise:

> In June the [Treasury] Secretary issued an order to the superintendent of the San Francisco Mint to make a contract to refine bullion and receive in exchange fine bullion. Before the Secretary's order went into effect Congress passed a law prohibiting the Secty of the Treasury from making any contract to refine bullion and enacting that the Refinery shall be kept open. It was then supposed that the efforts of the San Francisco Assaying and Refining Company had been killed, but in this expectation the undersigned have been disappointed.
>
> In our protest of last spring we showed that the laws of 1853 and 1861 upon which the Secretary relied for his authority to issue his order of last June to the Superintendent at San Francisco, were passed by Congress without any knowledge of their purport, this the influence of designing parties for the special benefit of the latter.

> The San Francisco Assaying and Refining Company has had Mr. Hewston, their assayer, in Philadelphia and Washington nearly a year using all the influence of this wealthy company composed of six gentlemen to close the United States Refinery in San Francisco.
>
> The change in the law, as recommended by the Secretary will if adopted, have an effect quite contrary to its purport and would eventually result in a loss to the Government and in the establishment of a monopoly. Such a law will be for the special benefit of this San Francisco Assaying and Refining Company and against the wishes and interests of the public who have the largest stake in this subject and who understand it.
>
> The San Francisco [Assaying and] Refining Company charge less than the Government and do a large business; there is nothing to prevent the owners of bullion from having all their gold refined by this Company, they are not compelled to deposit in the U.S. Refinery. It may then be asked why does this company through the Government try to close the Refinery and thus compel all to carry grist to their mill?[15]

The protest went on to say that those signing the document remained on the most friendly terms with the men composing the San Francisco Assaying and Refining Company, "and beg not to be considered as saying that these gentlemen of large wealth and respectability would hereafter attempt to influence the appointment of officers and employees to the San Francisco Mint in order that such officers might subserve, their interest, to the injury of others, or of the Government."[16] But they might fail in business or sell off their company, and it was impossible to know afterward into whose hands it would fall:

> Therefore the undersigned for themselves, for the public and for the Government respectfully protest against being placed in the power of any company who could control both the bullion and the Mint on the Pacific Coast.
>
> With due respect to the Secretary of the Treasury, the undersigned beg leave to say that in his recommendation on this subject, as in most of his financial orders, his acts have met with the most unqualified disapproval.
>
> Believing, gentlemen of the Committee, that you will view the subject impartially and that you will decide that the interests of the public are paramount to the interests of this company, the undersigned have the honor to be, Respectfully,...[17]

The protest was apparently effective, as both of Ralston's measures failed. The next Congress, however, would be different. Ralston's representatives were able to attach an amendment to the annual civil appropriations bill that allowed the exchange of refined bars for unparted bars. On July 13, 1870, in response to the amendment passing the Senate the day prior, Kelly launched another broadside, relaying a copy of the bankers' and assayers' protest from the prior year to New York Rep. Samuel S. Cox in Washington, D.C. In the accompanying letter, signed "Eugene Kelly & Co," the bankers informed Cox:

> We have just received a telegram from Washington saying that 'A refining clause has passed the Senate.'
>
> This in all probability is the iniquity which designing parties have for so long a time and in so many different ways, been trying to force through Congress for the benefit of a few monopolists, and against which a large number of Bankers and others strongly protested in a communication addressed to the Committee on Coinage to H.R. in January 1869.
>
> We take the liberty to enclose a copy of that communication and protest bespeaking for it your attention. Time has but added strength to the statements and arguments herein made, let us hope that you will exert your influence to defeat the selfish scheme they refer to.[18]

Kelly was unable to avert passage of the amendment but likely had influence on the addition of a proviso, tacked on to it during the appropriations bill's stay in conference, ending private refining for the mint once the new San Francisco Mint was completed. (However, the mint bill, introduced in April 1870, if passed, would drop the time limit and assure that Ralston could continue to control much of the region's gold supply by diverting it through his refinery, despite Kelly's best efforts.)

As with the elimination of the coinage charge, the tactic employed by the bank crowd for securing passage, if not support, for the refinery measure was not only perseverance, aided by the passage of time ("Things make haste slowly here," Henry R. Linderman had told Ralston), but also to urge the benefits of such an arrangement to the nation as a whole. With the refining question, as with the coinage charge, Ralston had some legitimate points in this regard. For one, except for the New York Assay Office, the government's refineries were hampered by the necessity of continuing to use the outdated and wasteful nitric acid process for refining gold.[19] Private refineries in California employed a sulfuric acid process, which was cheaper, less wasteful, and would save the government money, provided it contracted out for its refining needs.

The Granite Lady

The first San Francisco Mint building having proved inadequate to handle the region's growing supplies of precious metals, Congress authorized construction of a new building. In 1867, 275 square feet of land at the northwest corner of Fifth and Mission Streets was purchased by government for the sum of $100,000. Two years later, the first foundations were laid.

In February 1873, Treasury Secretary George S. Boutwell appointed Gen. Samuel McCullough to oversee completion of the new mint, and work on readying the structure along the plans laid out by supervising architect A.B. Mullett proceeded briskly. By October 1874, the mint was nearly ready. "The Director of the Mint, Dr. H.R. Linderman, with the officers of the Mint in this city, and Mr. Arthur Orr, the coining-machinery expert [a member of the Philadelphia firm of Morgan & Orr], have been busily engaged in examining the machinery and apparatus at the New Mint; and, finding the same satisfactory, have agreed upon a plan for the transfer of coining operations from the old to the New Mint," explained the Oct. 29, 1874, issue of the *Alta California*.[1]

On Nov. 5, 1874, nearly 100 influential guests, including Linderman and several U.S. congressmen, braved a day-long downpour, to be on hand for the formal transfer of the new mint from McCullough to Gen. O.H. La Grange, who would serve as its first superintendent. In accepting the new mint, La Grange acknowledged that, in the past, there had been some problems with losses at the mint, but assured the new mint would continue to operate under the rule of "Strict accountability of officers and workmen; absolute security for the Government and the depositor." La Grange continued:

> We feel, sir, that in the near future, when San Francisco shall arbitrate the exchanges of more than half the world, our bankers and our merchants will find within these walls a constant, safe and perfect magazine to forge the peaceful weapons for the mighty conquests in which they will send the eagles on our coin farther than ever Roman eagles went, and win more prosperous and profitable victories than ever Roman legions won. And now, sir, that the cause of strife which has distracted our land for fifteen years, is passing rapidly away, we hope our statesmen will find time to attend to the financial question; and we are glad to have so fortunately placed at the commercial centre of the American gold coast so powerful an instrument as this Mint will prove for furnishing to all our people *honest money* [gold], which must always be the *guarantee of business safety and of national integrity.*[2]

The *Alta* praised Gen. McCullough for completing the new structure for $30,000 less than the initial $1.5 million appropriation. It then described the building in detail. Starting with the foundation, the *Alta* explained that its four-feet-thick basement walls were of Folsom granite and its exterior three-feet-thick walls "of free stone, steel colored, or what may be more properly designated a light gray," while its two main chimneys towered above the building 24 feet in height, and were richly ornamented in cast iron. The roof was made of iron but covered with copper and tinned on both sides.[3]

"The Fifth-street front is strikingly majestic, yet the huge columns, which cannot fail to command the attention and admiration of visitors, are finished with so much delicacy of workmanship as if they had been touched with the carpenter's plane," the *Alta* enthusiastically recorded. "The portico over the front entrance, which is about 64 feet in width by a depth of about 24 feet, is approached by a series of granite steps, nineteen in number, and is supported by six large stone columns…with heavy, ornamental bases and caps."[4] The *Alta* provided its readers with the dimensions for the melting, rolling, annealing, silver melting, and gold ingot rooms, heaping considerable praise on the layout of several of the first floor offices. Upon climbing 19 granite steps and swinging open the mint's massive front door, the *Alta* wrote, one followed a long corridor extending from one end of the building to the other, coming upon the offices of the cashier and receiving clerk, which it termed:

Known to collectors as the Granite Lady, the San Francisco Mint building at Fifth and Mission streets is shown here in 1976, following its restoration.

In this early 1970s photograph, Mint Director Mary Brooks points to impressions on a vault wall left by the stacking of bags of $20 gold coins.

THE MOST CONSPICUOUS APARTMENTS

In the building. Mahogany counters run the entire width of the rooms; they are handsomely carpeted and furnished with desks, and every appliance necessary, and present a lively, cheerful appearance. They run up the entire height of the building, are well ventilated and lighted, and in finish are said to be superior to like rooms in the Treasury Department at Washington. A handsome iron gallery runs around each office at the elevation of the second floor, the painting is bright and cheerful, and the fluted iron columns which stand out from the walls at regular intervals, are in part gilt and painted white. The magnificent yet delicate finish of these rooms, is alike creditable to Gen. McCullough and to the artists who have displayed their skill in ornamentation lavishly, and with undoubted taste. The eye is charmed with the beautiful blending of delicate tints with gold. The gallery is entered from the upper floor, the railings of which are painted in scarlet and gold. Thirty cream-colored pilasters, scattered in pairs around each room, create a beautiful effect. Eight windows in each apartment admit light from the court yard, and at night two large chandeliers in bronze and gold, each having twelve burners, will furnish these exquisite apartments with light. The floor in front of each counter is flagged with granite tiling two feet square.[5]

Known to collectors as the Granite Lady, the new mint building was not only a showpiece of modern design but served the nation, as an active minting facility, into the 1930s. In 1906, it earned considerable praise and service when a devastating earthquake destroyed much of San Francisco. Being one of the few public buildings still standing, it was pressed into use to aid in the emergency. Having been reopened in the 1970s as a museum and subsequently closed, efforts continue to preserve this landmark structure.

The San Francisco Mint was one of the few buildings to survive the earthquake and fires of 1906.

Rep. Samuel Hooper of Massachusetts gave some insight into the benefits depositors and the government derived from the provisions of the July 15, 1870, act, which allowed the continuation of private refining of bullion deposited with the mint. During debate over the mint bill, in April 1872, Hooper told Congress that the earlier act had served "to preserve to depositors the security of the Mint, assay and accountability, and at the same time have the refining done by the sulphuric acid process at the extensive and well-managed establishments of the Pacific coast."[20] Hooper estimated government savings at about three cents on every ounce of bullion refined and advised that there were other advantages, including, "the protection of the Government against the large losses of former years, amounting to over a quarter of a million dollars in the bullion fund, and which can only be accounted for upon the hypothesis (as claimed) that it 'went up the chimney.'"[21] He added:

> Private enterprise and ingenuity can refine bullion cheaper and better than the Government ever has done, or probably ever will do. As a matter of political economy this industry should therefore be fostered and encouraged; and as a matter of justice the committee believe that the Government, after having invited the investment of private capital in the business of refining, ought not to destroy that interest by useless and extravagant appropriations.[22]

According to Hooper, the nitric acid process then in general use at the mint yielded gold ranging from .990 to .993 fineness, while the relatively new sulfuric acid process provided a purer bar of gold. This was particularly important to Ralston and others in their overseas trade. However, the sulfuric acid process had its drawbacks. It required expensive buildings and machinery and emitted dangerous, highly noxious fumes. In the United States, only private firms in San Francisco (Ralston's among them) and the New York Assay office employed sulfuric acid as of that date. The Philadelphia, Carson City and San Francisco mints could not because of lack of room. Besides, Hooper told the House, "there are objections to its use in any building intended for coinage operations on account of its offensive fumes."[23]

If things make haste slowly in Congress, it may, also, have been because memories seldom faded. Hooper received immediate objection to the provision from those who suspected, rightly, that its true intent was to benefit influential Pacific coast constituents, namely Ralston and his cohorts. New York Reps. Clarkson N. Potter and Fernando Wood were among the most vocal. Potter argued that there were several sections of the mint bill that protected private interests and, in all, mitigated against its passage. After detailing past abuses (including the illegal bullion lending operation at the New York Assay Office), Wood told the House, "another flagrant case is the present scandalous job in connection with the private assaying company in San Francisco."[24] He went on to quote from a recent issue of the *New York Journal of Commerce* which charged:

> This job originated in a proviso adroitly interpolated two years ago in an appropriation bill for the San Francisco mint. It reads: '*And provided further*. That it shall be lawful, until after the completion and occupation of said branch mint building, to exchange at any mint or branch mint of the United States, unrefined or unparted bullion, whenever, in the opinion of the Secretary of the Treasury, it can be done with advantage to the Government.' A large private establishment in that city [Ralston's] under this arrangement secures an immense job of refining most of the gold thus treated on that coast at eight cents per ounce gross. The nominal charge at the mint there is eleven cents. During the last fiscal year $19,000,000 were deposited in San Francisco by the miners. The Government establishment should have received all [of] this from the owners, paid them for it at a charge, say, five cents per ounce gross, and then put it into fine bars of nine hundred and ninety-eight thousandths fine at a profit to the Treasury. Instead of that the mint there fixes the charge at eleven cents per ounce. This drives $13,000,000 direct to the private refinery, but $6,000,000 still reach the mint. Under this contract that, too, is handed over by official fingers to the private refinery. Eight cents per ounce is paid for having it turned into bars, mostly ranging from nine hundred and eighty-nine to nine hundred and ninety-three thousands fine, and then the mint takes it all (the $19,000,000) and gives coin for it. If the charge for coinage could be abolished, or reduced to less than its actual cost, as proposed in this bill [the mint bill], the [bank] 'ring' would have a still softer thing of the existing job. If the mint should part the gold as it ought, at a proper cost, the bars would be finer, and at least $10,000 be saved to the Treasury out of the silver mixed with the gold, which is now wasted or wholly unaccounted for.[25]

Rep. Wood then questioned how the provision could ever have appeared in the July 15, 1870, appropriations bill, complaining, in a grand showing, that he had searched the House and Senate proceedings as reported in the *Congressional Globe* to learn how it got there but was unable to do so.[26] He then called for a repeal of this proviso, "which can have no other tendency than to be productive of fraud," claiming that the entire business of smelting, refining, assaying, and coinage should be under exclusive control of the government. Wood charged that:

> Since soon after the discovery of gold in California these private refineries were warmed into existence in that State, and the first act, passed March 4, 1853, recognizing them, and inviting their cooperation for coinage purposes, was doubtless lobbied through Congress for improper purposes. A subsequent act of February 20, 1861, served to further encourage the establishment of private refineries. In San Francisco there are two of these establishments which have succeeded in assuming control of refining, and of excluding it almost entirely from the branch mint in that city. The result of this has been to entail considerable loss upon the United States, besides rendering insecure much of the bullion in the process of exchange. The present arrangement, so far as San Francisco is concerned, is open to grave suspicions of collusion. It is very evident that some one has influence enough to continue in existence an arrangement with these outside parties at the expense of the Government.[27]

The influence, of course, came from the Treasury, which had initiated the contract with the refinery, despite congressional objections, and supported private refining. It is uncertain whether or not Dr. Henry R. Linderman provided assistance on Ralston's behalf in the 1870 legislation. It is clear from his comments, in a report written shortly after his visit to California in late 1869, that, by that time, he was an advocate of private refining, or what he called the "true policy" the government should pursue in this regard.[28] Either way, by 1871, Linderman was definitely in the thick of the battle, fighting against officers of the New York Assay Office, who threatened to scuttle the provision in the pending mint bill, by contending that they could refine bullion cheaper than in San Francisco.

In his Feb. 3, 1871, letter to Ralston, written while the mint bill was still in the House Committee on Coinage, Weights and Measures, Linderman told Ralston of the battle, "The New York folks, through [Andrew] Mason, of the Assay office, are stirring up the question of cheap refining claiming to be able to do it at rates much below S.F.—<u>we have the matter well in hand.</u>"[29] Five days later, Linderman suggested to Ralston that he take a look at a letter to the editor, signed "C.H.S.," appearing in the Feb. 6, 1871, issue of the *New York Times,* on refining as conducted at the Philadelphia Mint and the New York Assay Office.[30]

The otherwise unidentified author wrote that the New York Assay Office, because of its use of sulfuric acid, could refine metal cheaper than the refinery at the Philadelphia Mint. But, because of government charges (which were based on the more costly nitric acid process), much of the bullion was still seeking foreign sulfuric acid-based refineries. "It would be a great saving to the nation to have their [Philadelphia's] expensive refining establishment abolished, its annual business being so small that it could conveniently be done in the New-York office in a single week," C.H.S. wrote.[31] He added that the spirit of the law concerning mint refining charges was to charge the depositor only the minimum necessary to cover expenses, which should allow the New York Assay Office, with its superior process, to reduce its rates. However, the New York Assay Office would not do so on account of recommendations from Philadelphia and the requirement that such charges be the same at all government institutions. "How long shall this last?" C.H.S. questioned. "How long shall Philadelphia rule New-York, and force its bullion, by extravagant and unlawful charges to seek European refineries, to the great expense and detriment of our merchants?"[32]

Of this letter, Linderman wrote to Ralston:

> The New York people could cut the knot if they had a man among them worth a snap, a little amendment to the appropriation bill would cut the Assay Off[ice] at once from the Mint <u>but this is not our funeral</u>.
>
> Those New York fellows have never felt easy in the stomach, since I smashed up their bar & coin loan business, & it will not return to them soon I think.[33]

More pressing, to Linderman, was quieting the debate being stirred up over who could refine metal cheaper—California or New York—which again boiled up on the floor of Congress in 1872. During the April 9, 1872, debate over the private refinery provision in the mint bill, Rep. Clarkson N. Potter of New York argued with Rep. Aaron A. Sargent of California over this topic. Potter claimed that it only cost the government 1.5 cents per ounce to refine gold at government assay offices as compared to 11 cents per ounce in California. Sargent countered that these figures did not take into account expenses for officers, workmen, buildings and equipment, and that in reality the charge at the New York Assay Office was 11 cents per ounce. Defending the provision allowing private refining, Rep. William L. Stoughton of Michigan added:

Heretofore eleven cents has always been the price charged by the Government for refining and parting gold. There were establishments upon the Pacific coast run by the sulphuric acid process that could part the metal cheaper than it could be done at the Mint. Consequently gold in the crude state was put in the Mint for the purpose of having the Mint responsibility, and turned over to these parties to be refined and parted, and they were paid eight cents for it, leaving a profit of three cents to the Government.

Now, it may be that it can be done a great deal cheaper in New York, because there we have provided an assay office, the buildings and the necessary workmen, and they are run by appropriations from Congress. When they have all that, of course they can refine the gold cheaper. But take that out of the account and they cannot refine gold any cheaper there than in San Francisco. I insist that it is cheaper for the Government to have the gold refined at private refiners in San Francisco, than to compel people to bring it all the way across the continent to New York to be refined. It is not the duty of the General Government to refine gold. The Constitution gives Congress power to make all law as relating to the coinage of money, not the refining of metals. That properly belongs to individual enterprise. It would be better to encourage the establishment of private institutions for that purpose, than for the Government to arrogate to itself a branch of business which is not guarantied [sic] to it by the Constitution, and which does not properly belong to it.[34]

In a May 19, 1872, letter to Ralston, while the bill was back in the House committee, Linderman wrote:

> As you have no doubt been informed I have had a fight since January, with the Assay Office, Eugene Kelly and the Chamber of Commerce (of N.Y.) in relation to the Mint Bill & particularly the refining section. I have kept them whipped all the while and don't mean to let them up until the Bill is finally disposed of.[35]

He added, "A rod is in the soak for them New York fellows & they will have it laid on unmercifully when the Bill again comes up..."[36] However, it was a slightly more costly rod than expected. Adding to the $5,000 he had already requested of Ralston for his services through September 1872, Linderman asked that an additional $1,500 be sent in the form of a draft or placed to his credit at the Bank of California's New York agency, Lees & Waller to cover "some extra expenses." "About a thousand of this amount I have already paid & the balance will be so required," he wrote to Ralston. "This will cover the matter."[37] Like the coinage charge, Linderman was now Ralston's champion of the refinery clause.

Chapter 13

GOLD STANDARD SECURED

By late 1871, inaction on the coinage measure, which had yet to emerge from committee in the House of Representatives, was causing concern at the Treasury. In his Dec. 4, 1871, *Report of the Secretary of the Treasury,* George S. Boutwell urged passage of the bill in the next Congress, stating:

> During the third session of the 41st Congress a bill was submitted for the organization of a Mint Bureau. The bill passed the Senate but failed in the House of Representatives; though not, as I am informed, from any objection to the principles on which it was framed. I urgently recommend the passage of a similar bill at the present session of Congress. All the Mints and Assay Offices are nominally in charge of the Treasury Department; but there is not, by authority of law, any person in the Department who, by virtue of his office, is supposed to be informed upon the subject; and no one on whom the Secretary of the Treasury can officially rely for information or advice in the management of this important branch of the public business.[1]

The bill finally came up for debate, after nearly a year of absence from the floor, on Jan. 9, 1872, at

During the April 1872 debate over the mint bill, several prominent congressmen openly favored making the U.S. gold dollar the standard of value and eliminating the 412 1/2-grain silver dollar. Coins shown inset are at actual size.

which time Rep. William D. Kelley strongly recommended its passage. Debate on that date centered on the salaries to be paid mint officials and the propriety of issuing subsidiary minor coinage. The following day, the bill was recommitted and reappeared in a substitute form (HR1427) on Feb. 9, 1872, under the leadership of Rep. Samuel Hooper. Hooper's substitute bill made a brief appearance on the floor of Congress on Feb. 13, 1872, but nearly two more months passed before it again came up for debate, by which time several important changes had been made to its contents.

The first of these revisions called for open bidding on nickel contracts, while the second new provision legalized the absurd method of issuing subsidiary coins in exchange for silver (a practice that John Jay Knox had adamantly opposed in his report accompanying the mint bill), and the third major revision provided for a 384-grain subsidiary silver dollar that, at one time, had been part of Knox's rough draft of the mint bill. The new subsidiary dollar was to have a legal tender value of up to $5 in any one payment, thus maintaining the gold dollar as the standard unit of value.

Free silver advocates would later contend that the demonetization of their beloved silver dollar had been accomplished surreptitiously, with little or no mention of the change in monetary standards during debates in both houses of Congress. This charge required them to ignore the rather extensive debate that occurred on April 9, 1872, during which four prominent congressmen repeatedly referred to the adoption of the gold standard.[2]

Hooper, who was now floor leader of the substitute bill in the House, made several references to the monetary standard change on that day. Others who commented directly on the change in standards included Reps. Stoughton, Potter, and Kelley. During his review of the various sections of the substitute bill, Hooper told Congress, in reference to Section 14 of the proposed bill:

> Thus far the section is a reenactment of existing laws. In addition, it declares the gold dollar of twenty-five and eight tenths grams of standard gold to be the unit of value, gold practically having been in this country for many years the standard or measure of value, as it is legally in Great Britain and most of the European countries. The silver dollar, which by law is now the legally declared unit of value, does not bear a correct relative proportion to the gold dollar. Being worth intrinsically about one dollar and three cents in gold, it cannot circulate concurrently with the gold coins.[3]

Hooper went on to explain the committee's endorsement of the single standard, by saying:

> As the value of the silver dollar depends on the market price of silver, which varies according to the demand and supply, it is now intrinsically worth as before stated, about three cents more than the gold dollar. By the act of January 18, 1837, the standard of the silver coins was increased to nine hundred thousandths fine, which reduced the weight of the dollar from four hundred and sixteen to four hundred and twelve and a half grains; the amount of pure silver, however, remained the same, namely, three hundred and seventy-one and one fourth grains. The committee, after careful consideration, concluded that twenty-five and eight tenths grains of standard gold constituting the gold dollar should be declared the money unit or metallic representative of the dollar of account.[4]

Hooper pronounced that, while the House Committee on Coinage, Weights and Measures could not take credit for the original preparation of the bill, the committee had given the bill careful consideration, "and have no hesitation in unanimously recommending its passage as necessary and expedient."[5]

Hooper also made several other references to the gold standard as he reviewed each section of the coinage bill. During his discussion of Section 15, calling for the redemption of abraded gold coins, he told Congress this provision was essential in order to keep the nation's gold coins, which were to become the unit of value, in good condition. In regard to the introduction of a subsidiary silver dollar, he explained:

> Section sixteen reenacts the provisions of existing laws defining the silver coins and their weights respectively, except in relation to the silver dollar, which is reduced in weight from four hundred and twelve and a half to three hundred and eighty-four grains; thus making it a subsidiary coin in harmony with the silver coins of less denomination, to secure its concurrent circulation with them. The silver dollar of four hundred and twelve and a half grains, by reason of its bullion or intrinsic value being greater than its nominal value, long since ceased to be a coin of circulation, and is melted by manufacturers of silverware. It does not circulate now in commercial transactions with any country, and the convenience of those manufacturers in this respect can better be met by supplying small stamped bars of the same standard, avoiding the useless expense of coining the dollar for that purpose.[6]

During the same debate, Rep. William L. Stoughton, a member of the Committee on Coinage, Weights and Measures, pointed to the necessity of making it perfectly clear by law that the gold standard was being adopted. He also listed the proposed gold coins including the gold dollar, which he observed would become the unit of value. Stoughton declared, by this bill, gold coins would be a legal tender, at their denominational values, for all sums, and:

> Aside from the three dollar gold piece, which is a deviation from our metrical ratio, and therefore objectionable, the only change in the present law is in more clearly specifying the gold dollar as the unit of value. This was probably the intention, and perhaps the effect of the act of March 3, 1849, but it ought not be left to inference or implication. The value of silver depends, in a great measure, upon the fluctuations of the market, and the supply and demand. Gold is practically the standard of value among all civilized nations, and the time has come in this country when the gold dollar should be distinctly declared to be the coin representative of the money unit.[7]

The next representative to address the House concerning the gold standard was Clarkson N. Potter of New York. Potter readily admitted that he supported the adoption of the gold standard but he objected to its installation until such time as specie payments resumed. Of his misgivings in regard to an early change in standards, Potter told Congress:

> Then, in the next place, this bill provides for making of changes in the legal-tender coin of the country, and for substituting as legal tender coin of only one metal instead as heretofore of two. I think myself this would be a wise provision, and that legal-tender coins, except subsidiary coin, should be of gold alone; but why should we legislate on this now when we are not using either of those metals as a circulating medium? The bill provides also for a change in respect of the weight and value of the silver dollar, which I think is a subject which, when we come to require legislation about it at all, will demand at our hands very serious consideration, and which, as we are not using such coins for circulation now, seems at this time to be an unnecessary subject about which to legislate.[8]

Rep. James Brooks, also from New York, expressed opposition, as had Potter, to the passage of any mint bill before the country resumed specie payments. Brooks found it incomprehensible that the House could be debating provisions for the coinage of gold and silver at a time when the country was being deluged with depreciated paper money. Just as Hooper began presenting the amendments to the bill, reading from the first section pertaining to the creation of the mint bureau, Brooks angrily objected to any discussion of the bill, charging:

> I move to strike out section one of the bill. I frankly avow that my object in doing so is to end this bill. It seems to me that this is the most farcical spectacle that Congress can present at this time, when Uncle Sam is covered all over with rags, from head to foot, and there is not a portion of his garments fit to wear in public, for all is so ragged; when no member of this House has seen a silver dollar or a golden eagle, except as a curiosity in a museum, for some four or five or six or seven years, and when there is no probability of seeing another golden eagle for some six or seven years to come. It seems to me to be the greatest of farces for this House to present such a spectacle as this, one fit for the pencil of Morgan or Nast in the caricatures of the day; this exhibition of two hundred and forty intelligent gentlemen deliberating upon the subject of coins and coinage; more especially when the Supreme Court of the United States has recently declared that gold and silver are no longer money, but that under the power in the constitution to coin money there is power to print in the Treasury building Treasury rags at the disposal and under the authority of Congress. What farce greater than this is ever enacted in any comic theater here or elsewhere? What is more calculated to excite ridicule in the country than so extraordinary a spectacle?[9]

California Sen. Aaron Sargent objected to Brooks' charge that there was no gold or silver in circulation, saying that Brooks "does not seem to under-

MR. 1873

No study of the Crime of 1873 would be complete, at least from a collector's point of view, without mention of the man who was known among numismatists as "Mr. 1873," Harry X Boosel. Boosel became famous for his collection of everything and anything related to the year 1873. He is credited with popularizing the 1873 "closed 3" and "open 3" varieties as well as his fascination with the Coinage Act of 1873.

Following the U.S. Mint's preparation and initial use of the coinage dies bearing the 1873 date, chief coiner A. Louden Snowden complained that the "3" in the date appeared more like an "8." To correct the problem, a new logotype showing an open "3" was introduced on all denominations except the half dollar, silver dollar and Trade dollar, and gold eagle. In the process, several rarities were created, including the proof 1873 $3 gold piece, which comes in "closed 3" and "open 3" varieties.

A change in the date punch led to the creation of the "open 3" and "closed 3" varieties of the 1873 coinage. The "closed 3" is at left.

stand that there are now some sections of the Union where gold circulates by the millions of dollars and that there are also some parts of the country where silver circulates by the millions of dollars." "Like cotton and sugar," chimed Brooks. "No, sir; but as coin," Sargent retorted. "Upon the Pacific gold and silver are the regular circulating medium, and there is nothing except a mere artificial barrier between that portion of the country and all the rest on account of the circulation throughout the Pacific coast of gold and silver."[10] The artificial barrier Sargent referred to was the pesky coinage charge, which, he had earlier explained, caused gold and silver to take wings and fly to other countries, robbing the United States of the benefit of the 70 million in gold and silver it produced per annum.

In response to Sargent, Rep. Potter declared that "No amount of legislation can make coin circulate for more than its intrinsic worth, except small coins for subsidiary purposes and within narrow limits; for if you stamp on the coin a false value, it will nevertheless circulate only at its true value."[11] Potter added:

> If, however, there are any excessive charges on account of coinage, I say reduce them. But if the gold and silver go away to other countries, it is because they are wanted as a circulating medium when they get to those countries, while we do not so use them here. I will go hand in hand with any man who wishes the country to get back to specie payments. But there is only one way in which that can be done. It is to make a dollar of legal tender paper redeemable and so equal in actual value to a real dollar. No contrivance of putting stamps upon these coins, or of recoining the coin and putting on another stamp instead of the present one, will make the coin worth one cent more than the real intrinsic value it possesses; and all measures to give a false and arbitrary value to the coin of the country will prove here, as they have proved everywhere, a delusion. And if that is one of the purposes of this bill then it is not a purpose which should commend it to our consideration.[12]

This led Rep. Kelley, who earlier in the day had been in an acrimonious battle with Potter over the proposal for uniform minor coinage, to query:

> I wish to ask the gentleman who has just spoken (Mr. Potter) if he knows of any Government in the world which makes its subsidiary coinage of full value? The silver coin of England is ten per cent. below the value of gold coin. And acting under the advice of the experts of this country, and of England and France, Japan has made her silver coinage within the last year twelve per cent. below the value of gold coin, and for this reason: it is impossible to retain the double standard. The values of gold and silver continually fluctuate. You cannot determine this year what will be the relative values of gold and silver next year. They were fifteen to one a short time ago; they are sixteen to one now.
>
> Hence all experience has shown that you must have one standard coin, which shall be a legal tender for all others, and then you may promote your domestic convenience by having a subsidiary coinage of silver, which shall circulate in all parts of your country as legal tender for a limited amount, and be redeemable at its face value by your Government.[13]

Kelley complained that Potter and Brooks were opposed to the bill simply because they wanted to maintain the full-weight silver dollar, so that their constituents (New York bullion dealers) could continue to profit from the exchange of their bullion for silver dollars at the New York Assay Office. This practice, according to Kelley, was costing the government enormous sums of money. He informed the Congress:

> Certain silver bullion dealers of New York are making from fifty thousand to one hundred and fifty thousand dollars a year out of your Government. One of them admitted to my colleague on the committee and myself, that his business averaged from one million eight hundred thousand to two million dollars a year, and that he put the silver into the Mint, and drew out for every two dollars, four half dollars and one ten-cent piece.[14]

Kelley, however, failed to note that, as the past practice of the mint, both in Philadelphia and at the New York Assay Office, had been to illegally exchange subsidiary coins for silver bullion (thereby splitting the government's seigniorage with the bullion dealers who would ship the new coins to more lucrative foreign markets where the coins could be traded at a premium), any issue of a subsidiary silver dollar would also profit bullion dealers in New York and elsewhere. This was especially true because the mint bill under discussion proposed to legalize exchanges of silver bullion for subsidiary coins for an additional two years.

Potter defended himself against Kelley's contention that he opposed the bill because he represented New York bullion dealers by reminding Kelley he was not the representative for the city of New York, but for an agricultural district that had no interest in the activities of New York bullion dealers. To this, Kelley responded, "We take you as Representative of the city of New York."[15] Kelley's attack on Potter may have been spurred by Potter's assault on Kelley during congressional debate over the mint bill on Jan. 9, 1872. At that time, Potter objected to passage of the mint bill on the grounds that the provisions relating to the contracting for the proposed

Besides dropping the silver dollar, the Coinage Act of 1873 also ended the minting of the two-cent piece, the silver three-cent piece, and the half dime. Photos are not to proportion or size. The three-cent piece measured just 14mm and the half dime 15.5mm. Both were smaller than the current dime. The two-cent piece measured 23mm.

nickel coinage would have given a monopoly to Pennsylvania nickel interests, so ably represented by Kelley. Just such a lucrative contract was something that Kelley had been hoping to obtain since the late 1860s, when a uniform minor coinage of copper-nickel was first proposed; therefore, Kelley was hardly in a position to condemn anyone for reacting in favor of a vested interest.

Subsequent to the conclusion of the April 9, 1872, House debate, the mint bill was recommitted, and on May 27, 1872, Hooper introduced another substitute bill (HR2934), which he assured Congress had met with universal approbation in the form in which it was offered. The major change, provided for by the substitute, was a slight increase in the weight of the subsidiary silver coins to the equivalent of 25 grams of silver per dollar of face value, in order to bring the nation's silver coins in line with Knox's international coinage suggestions accompanying the mint bill. Thus, the 384-grain dollar was adjusted upward to 385 grains.

During the May 27, 1872, deliberation, Hooper, hoping to avoid further delay, moved that the rules be suspended in order that the bill might be voted on without being read. This induced Rep. Brooks to counter with a motion for postponement until such time as his comrade, Potter, could be in attendance. Both attempts failed, as postponement was not allowed, and Hooper's move to suspend reading the bill was also defeated. The mint bill was brought up for a final vote and passed the House overwhelmingly by a vote of 110 to 13.

The bill having cleared the House, it was transmitted to the Senate on May 28, 1872, where, the following day, it was referred to the Senate Finance Committee. The bill was reported to the floor of the Senate on Dec. 16, 1872, recommitted, and reported back on Jan. 7, 1873. During its stay in the Senate Finance Committee, the House version of the mint bill was amended in relation to the nation's largest silver coin. The committee, probably at the Treasury's urging, dropped the subsidiary dollar and

During the Jan. 17, 1873, debate over the mint bill, California Sen. Eugene Casserly warned, "Nevada appears to be getting ready to deluge the world with silver." Less than two months later, the Consolidated Virginia began removing the first quantities of ore from what would come to be known as the Big Bonanza. Courtesy of the Nevada State Museum Photograph Collection.

substituted, in its stead, a heavier 420-grain Trade dollar that was to be used exclusively as a bullion piece for competition with the Mexican dollar in overseas trade with China, Japan, and other Asiatic countries.

The mint bill came up for final deliberation on Jan. 17, at which time, debate centered around concern expressed by Sen. Eugene Casserly of California over the redemption of abraded gold coins, a topic that the Pacific coast senator viewed as being of great importance, since his state's major form of currency was gold. The Senate's attention then turned to Casserly's rather ludicrous concern over retaining the eagle as the major reverse device on the nation's silver coinage. Treasury officials (namely Dr. Henry R. Linderman), as Sen. John Sherman explained, had requested amendment be made to allow the silver coinage to express the weight and fineness of the coins on each coin's reverse, as a means of aiding the promotion of an international coinage system. Casserly felt a sentimental attachment to the idea of retaining the eagle design feature then mandated for use on the reverse of the nation's silver coins. He lamented, "it will hardly be possible to think of a half dollar or a quarter dollar as being such a coin without the eagle upon it."[16] He asked Sherman if he was serious about the amendment, commenting that he wished to see the eagle preserved on the half dollar and quarter dollar, leading Sherman to gibe, "the eagle is preserved on all the gold coins in a size large enough to be caged," which brought about an outburst of laughter from his Senate colleagues.[17]

The laughter having subsided, Casserly, after further pleading, was able to rescue the lowly eagle, saving it from Senate extinction by a narrow vote of 26 to 24. The harrowing battle waged to retain the eagle caused Sherman to sarcastically respond, "as the Senate are so patriotic that they will not abolish the eagle, I hope they will be perfectly willing now

A substitute bill introduced by Rep. Samuel Hooper in May 1872 raised the weight of subsidiary silver dimes, quarters and half dollars to 385 grains. To denote the change, arrows were placed next to the date on coins minted in 1873 and 1874.

to hurry along with the bill."[18] Debate then turned to Casserly's amendment to remove the coinage charge on gold coins; his amendment, however, was defeated and, after all of the amendments were engrossed and the bill read, it passed the Senate.

The bill, as passed by the Senate, was sent to the House, which refused to agree to the Senate revisions, thereby requiring the appointment of a conference committee, comprised of members of both Houses, to resolve the differences. As a result of the conference committee's meeting—which was attended by Samuel Hooper (Massachusetts), Sherman O. Houghton (California), and Thompson W. McNeely (Illinois) of the House and John Sherman (Ohio), John Scott (Pennsylvania), and Thomas F. Bayard (Delaware) of the Senate—the Senate-authorized adoption of the Trade dollar won out over the House's subsidiary dollar. The crime was now a *fait accompli* as far as Linderman, William C. Ralston and others of the bank crowd were concerned. All that remained was President Ulysses S. Grant's signature.

With its increased weight, it was hoped that the new Trade dollar, authorized by the Coinage Act of 1873, would be accepted in the Far East.

Chapter 14

THE GOOD FIGHT

Feb. 12, 1873, was a dreary day, weatherwise, in the nation's capital. As preparations were in full swing for newly reelected President Ulysses S. Grant's reception, a major winter snowstorm was dumping six to eight inches of snow over much of the East, including Washington, D.C. Yet in the halls of Congress, especially among the Republicans, and at the White House, where finishing touches were being put in place for the evening's victory celebration, it was a day for rejoicing. This day would bring the counting of electoral votes in the House, packed "to suffocation almost," and the formal election of the president and vice president.[1]

Despite some grumblings in the daily press that he left too much of day-to-day government operations unchecked in the hands of his Cabinet, Grant remained a popular president. He won his second term handily over his opponent, *New York Tribune* editor Horace Greeley, in a popular vote count of 3,597,132 to 2,834,125. On the electoral vote side, it was even more lopsided. Greeley, who ran as the candidate for both the Democratic Party and the Independent Republican Party (the latter having been formed in 1872 to fight graft and dishonesty among public officials and urge civil service reform), took only six states, for a 286 to 66 tally.

Silver dollar coinage, which had been stopped in 1804, resumed on a small scale in the late 1830s with a design by Christian Gobrecht. The first Gobrecht dollars were struck at the old 416-grain standard. Later issues were at the 412 1/2-grain standard that would be employed with the introduction of the Seated Liberty dollar in 1840. Its coinage ended in 1873, when the Coinage Act of 1873 placed the nation on a gold standard.

On that same day, something more momentous happened. Vice President Schuyler Colfax signed off on the Coinage Act of 1873 in the Senate, sending the bill on to President Grant for his signature, thus ending the coinage of the silver dollar and, unbeknownst to anyone in the country at that time, sowing the seeds for the free silver debate that would consume America for much of the remainder of the century. True, there was some mention of the mint bill, and its provisions, in newspapers across the nation when it passed, but the bill was not big news. The Feb. 12 *Washington Star* devoted its front page to congressional hearings into the Crédit Mobilier scandal, a swindle of the Union Pacific Railroad by a construction company that tried to buy protection through stock payments to prominent Republican congressmen and a U.S. vice president. The following day, there was still no word of the bill's passage in the *Star*. The newspaper recorded that the snow had hampered attendance at the president's reception, and gave space to summarizing a speech in favor of a bill granting federal support to the Sutro Tunnel project in Nevada. The Comstock Lode, the *Star* quoted Rep. Nathaniel Banks of Massachusetts as saying, "was the richest and the largest [silver and gold strike] in the world, having yielded in the imperfect way its worked over a hundred and forty millions, and with the proposed tunnel it would yield from thirty to fifty millions annually." The Comstock's silver vein, Banks told Congress, was four or five times the length and width of Pennsylvania Avenue "from which some idea of its richness may be formed."[2]

The *Star* would not comment on the mint bill until several days later, and then only in the manner of reproducing its contents. This was, however, to be expected. The mint bill had been debated for years and was old news. Times were still good and the economy was robust, so there was little cause for concern. Although the first rumblings of the economic upheaval that would come to be known as the Panic of 1873 were felt in Vienna and Berlin early that year, it was not until security and brokerage firms in New York began bolting their doors late in 1873, followed by the collapse of one of the nation's leading banking houses, Jay Cooke & Company, that the devastating economic downturn began to exact its toll on the United States.

On the Pacific coast, where the Bank of California continued to reign over much of the Comstock, it was also a time for rejoicing for William C. Ralston, Louis A. Garnett and others who had spent years trying to secure passage of the mint bill. Ralston would take over as Bank of California president that same year and begin his active pursuit of making the Trade dollar scheme a success.

On the East Coast, likewise, Dr. Henry R. Linderman was also in a jubilant mood, as can be seen from a highly revealing and incriminating letter he wrote to Ralston on March 9, 1873, the day before he left from Washington, on an extended trip to Philadelphia, to make the "necessary arrangements [at the mint] for putting into effect on the 1st proximo the Coinage Act 1873."[3] Linderman gloated to his employer that, "With the exception of a very small coinage charge of 1/5 of one per cent I believe we have achieved all that we set out for" with the mint bill.[4] Among these achievements, Linderman related to Ralston, was a provision allowing mint depositors to exchange unparted, unrefined bullion for refined bullion at any U.S. mint (the battle had finally been won), a continuation of the provisions of refining acts passed in 1853 and 1861, which, Linderman said, "will keep the government from becoming a competitor with private enterprise" for the refining business ("I kept this point steadily in view throughout the entire contest," he added), and the issuance of a trade dollar ("Should this coin be favorably received in China it will prove the most important economic event for California that has yet happened," the new director raved).[5]

Linderman credited himself, Garnett and Ralston for helping to push this measure through—for without each of their aid "it had not the least chance." Linderman boasted:

> Never in the history of Legislation was a measure more carefully & persistently guarded than this Coinage Bill by me, and of course I could not have been there without some friends behind me.
>
> It cannot but prove beneficial to the Country, and the mining interest especially, and I trust that directly or indirectly you will share in it.[6]

During the years leading up to its passage, Linderman explained, he had subordinated everything else to achieving its passage, applying "the very best energies & services I was capable of rendering."[7] He then made a prediction which, if it had not been for the survival of the Linderman-to-Ralston letters, may have come true:

> It will never of course be known to the outside world what labor this measure has taken, nor will the mining interest ever likely know that they owe the reduction of the coinage charge primarily to you.—

For the steady support you have rendered I feel thankful.

But I cannot halt here. This measure must be put into intelligent and successful operation by its friends & the work naturally falls to me. I have not the least ambition or desire for the place (Director) but feel it incumbent on me to accept in deference to the general desire & my wish to see the measure put into operation.

I shall give immediate attention to the issue of the trade dollar and will try to get it out in acceptable form.[8]

In a guarded but highly revealing postscript, Linderman then left the door open for additional monetary compensation for his aid in pressing matters in Washington on Ralston's behalf, writing:

The last thing on this earth that you would have me do is to come to you in the shape either of a mendicant or official shyster but such is not my purpose. I simply desire to say then that my work is done. I leave the matter of any extra compensation entirely to you & whether you may do much, little or nothing at all, I shall be content, 'I have fought the good fight,' 'have kept the faith' and leave the rest up to you. In your own time & in your own way dispose of it. I should not now have mentioned the subject, but that I desire 'the deck cleared for action' and all matters off my mind before commencing my new work.

I shall put my oar in things here quietly but deeply & in the various contingencies that may arise in the next few years, will always remember & try to serve my friend R—always depend on that no matter what else may turn up.[9]

Best of all, from Ralston's viewpoint, whether or not he acquiesced to Linderman's request for additional compensation, he now had a close friend installed in the highest position within the U.S.

The Mexican eight reales had a long history of use and acceptance in China. Linderman and Rolston hoped that the new U.S. Trade dollar would take away some of its market.

Mint, something he would have occasion to rely on in the years to come. In the meantime, they could turn to the problems at hand, developing a way to win acceptance for the Trade dollar in the Orient and securing additional markets for the white metal. Through their close attention, the country had also been placed on a gold standard, the culmination of years of effort by those who believed ideologically that the true basis of money should be tied to only one metal—gold. In his first Mint director's report, written late in 1873, Linderman wrote openly of the switch in monetary standards under the heading, "GOLD THE STANDARD OR MEASURE OF VALUE; SILVER SUBSIDIARY." There he observed that, with the decline in silver associated with foreign nations adopting the gold standard, "...it is evident Congress acted wisely in establishing gold as the sole standard of value."[10]

Whether or not it acted wisely, there can be little doubt that the change in monetary standards was done openly, and not secreted from Congress by the Treasury or the bill's floor leaders, as some would later claim. Nor was there any need to hide the change. Unlike France and some other countries where battles raged over bimetallism, the great passion that existed in Europe for or against bimetallism did not yet burn in the United States and would not for a few years to come. Until silver fell significantly below paper, in 1876, bringing silver coins, which had been largely absent from pocket change since the days of the Civil War, back into circulation in great numbers, such arguments remained primarily on an intellectual basis.

Several in Congress and the Treasury, as we have seen, spoke openly and eloquently of the change in standards while the measure was before Congress, or wrote of their intentions in reports available to Congress and the public. Yet there was little objection. Those congressmen who years later complained that they had been duped into voting for the measure, including Rep. William D. Kelley, did so for political reasons, once the depression had turned the money question into a volatile topic for debate and silver's downfall had brought it to the attention of a new breed of monetary inflationists.

The fact that Nevada's senators and representatives voted in favor of an act that, in retrospect, appeared to be to their region's detriment has left historians to wonder why they would have done so and why it took three years for the silver interests to awaken to their mistake in allowing the bill to pass without the outlet for silver formerly provided by the now defunct silver dollar. In the process, most have concluded that congressional representatives of the bullion-producing states were not paying sufficient attention to the provisions of the mint bill—the high bullion value of the silver dollar having kept this coin out of circulation and out of the minds of those who should have guarded its future. But the real silver interests were paying attention. Throughout much of the time the bill spent in Congress, Ralston and his cohorts ruled the roost on the Comstock, and they made sure they got what they wanted—a coinage measure skewed with legislation prejudicial to the mining industry and the Bank of California. Only the coinage charge, now slightly reduced, remained to be taken care of, and this, too, would eventually come to pass, with Linderman's adept help. A meaty congressional bone was also tossed out to placate New York bullion dealers, who had in prior years made fortunes off the trade of subsidiary silver coins in Latin America and elsewhere. They won authorization for their previously illegal practice of exchanging silver bullion for subsidiary silver at the Philadelphia Mint and the New York Assay Office.

However, if the bullion interests were placated, what then of others in Congress? In assessing the reason why hundreds of other congressmen from non-silver-producing states did not protest the change in monetary standards, the traditional line among historians has been that the adoption of the gold standard by these legislators was more of a recognition of existing conditions than a planned switch to monometallism. Or, worse, that congressmen charged with putting this law on the books were bored by the recodification of the mint laws or failed to understand what they were doing in altering standards.[11] Although there may be an inkling of substance to all of these theories, it cannot be denied that the major framers of the measure clearly intended from the beginning to place the nation on a gold standard and drop the silver dollar. Nor can it be denied that many in Congress were well aware of the true intent of these provisions of the mint bill, whether or not they cared to admit it later.

Even by mid-1872, when Linderman and others became aware of the likely impact of the December 1871 German demonetization of silver, the intent of the framers of the coinage measure did not waver. They still fully supported the gold standard and believed the introduction of a new trade coin, and the replacement of the millions of fractional paper notes outstanding with subsidiary silver, would create a sufficient market for silver to prevent serious decline. At least in 1873 there was no reason to think otherwise. For much of 1873, the bullion value of a 412 1/2-grain silver dollar remained at or close to parity with the gold dollar. Two years later, in 1875, there still existed genuine hope that silver could be saved from depreciation. By that point, passage of the Specie Resumption Act had authorized replacement of worn fractional notes with subsidiary silver, the expected outpouring of silver from Germany was not as bad as previously projected, and the Trade dollar was showing some signs of acceptance.

The only thing that had changed by mid-1872 was that there was now tangible evidence of a coming decline in the value of silver that Linderman and Ralston could use to their advantage to raise urgency over passage of the long-stalled mint bill and its provisions for keeping gold at home. For, as Linderman would warn in a May letter to Ralston and again in his Nov. 19, 1872, report to Treasury Secretary George S. Boutwell, if silver fell in value because of the release of silver from Germany's monetary reorganization, those countries remaining on a double standard would serve as unwilling dumping grounds for the depreciated metal. In the United States, if depositors could still bring their silver to the mint under the old regulations (in effect as long as the mint bill languished in Congress) and turn it into standard dollars, redeemable by the government at face value, it would profit only the money speculators, and prove a serious threat to the economy and the nation's credit.

Linderman's clear understanding of the future for silver in the period prior to the passage of the mint bill, however, has led some 20th century historians, who noticed his November report to Boutwell, to again raise the specter of the Crime of 1873, linking the supposed collusion to the Treasury Department.[12] In essence, they charged that Linderman, acting on behalf of the Treasury, wrongly secreted his specialized knowledge of the impending decline in silver from Congress in order to obtain passage of the mint bill before monetary inflationists or silver standard supporters became aware of silver's future fate and made passage of the coinage measure much more difficult, if not impossible, to obtain. However, the contents of the aforementioned May 1872 letter from Linderman to Ralston and the fact that Linderman's Nov. 19, 1872, report to Boutwell (which received contemporary press coverage) served as the basis for the Treasury secretary's clear warnings to Congress of the future for silver prior to the bill's passage, cast serious doubts on the validity of such allegations.[13]

In his May 19, 1872, letter to Ralston (the same letter in which he requested an additional $1,500 for his services), Linderman told Ralston, "I have had translated for the use of the [House] committee the German coinage law (1871) together with Baron Northcomb's celebrated review of that law which he pronounces the greatest and most important economic measure of the present century."[14] At the time of Linderman's letter, the mint bill was in the House Committee on Coinage, Weights and Measures and would not emerge again until May 27, when Rep. Hooper brought it before the House and urged its approval. The economic review, Linderman continued, fully sustained the House committee "in two or three of the most important sections of our bill."[15] One of these was no doubt making gold the unit of value, as Linderman told Ralston:

> Germany having demonetized about $350.000.000 silver, the countries maintaining the double standard will be overrun with silver bullion. Unless we locate $50.000.000 in the U. States, in the next three years, unless this is done a serious decline in price is inevitable and this we must prevent by timely agitation & proper measures.[16]

Whether or not Linderman fully explained the likely impact of the German demonetization to the House committee or simply presented the translation and a review of the measure cannot be ascertained. However, it must be remembered, when dealing with the question of Linderman's intent and actions during this period, that Linderman was in Ralston's employ at the time.[17] Therefore, his primary motivation in anything he placed before Congress was to speed passage of the bill, convince the committee of the propriety of its provisions, and achieve the primary goals set forth by his employer. To do anything that might have jeopardized passage of the bill, which he, Ralston, Garnett and several California congressmen had devoted so much time to protecting and tailoring to their specifications, would have been unconscionable. If he did not believe that such information would have supported efforts to move the bill through Congress, he could have simply kept quiet—secreting it from Congress, along the lines suggested by the modern-day conspiracy theorists. Giving the information about the German coinage measure to Congress or placing it in a report to Boutwell, which then became part of Boutwell's December 1872 submission to Congress, would have otherwise been ludicrous.[18] This report, like Linderman's November submission to Boutwell, received contemporary press coverage. The Dec. 3, 1873, *New York Times*, for instance, carried Boutwell's report along with his warnings for silver. A synopsis of the report was also transmitted to Wall Street.

Certainly others besides Linderman, in Congress and the private sector, were capable of correctly judging the impact of a mass dumping of silver on the world's marketplace. Even Conrad Weigand, an assayer on the Comstock, as will be shown, was well aware of the German demonetization and its potential prior to the passage of the mint bill. Bankers and bullion dealers on both coasts were also likely in tune with the market implications of such a vast store of silver flowing out of Germany. It is more likely, therefore, that Linderman did inform the committee in May of what lay ahead for silver, in order to spur action on the mint bill.

Once the bill was passed, Linderman told Ralston in his May letter, the next step would be to replace the fractional notes in use since the Civil War with subsidiary silver coins, an action he viewed as part of the process of supporting the market value of silver. Meanwhile, in the fall of 1872, while Congress was in recess, Linderman again visited California on Treasury business, where he met with Louis A. Garnett, and likely Ralston, to discuss additional plans to avert the problems caused by the German demonetization—one of which was to introduce a special trade coin for use in the Orient, an idea that had been bandied about years before but had not come to fruition.[19] Once a decision was made to press for the coin, Linderman returned to Washington, where he entered his report to Boutwell on the problems facing silver, the need for quick action, and laid down the guidelines for the new coin.

For his part, Ralston set to work, shortly after Linderman's departure, contacting his business associates in the Orient (including representatives of the Yokohama, Japan, office of the Oriental Bank Corporation, the Bank of California's London agency) to see what they thought of the proposed new trade coin and whether or not it might win acceptance. On Nov. 7, 1872, nearly two weeks before Linderman's report to Boutwell, John Robertson, of the Oriental Bank Corporation, wrote to Ralston from Yokohama, saying he doubted the new dollars would find acceptance in Hong Kong or Japan, but the "Chinese may fancy them & this I think is your only hope. They are queer devils about dollars. The Chinese won't touch the Japanese silver dollars which are equal in weight & purity to Mexicans."[20]

In his Nov. 19, 1872, Treasury Department *Special Report of Examination of Branch Mints on the Pacific Coast*, penned along with Prof. John Torrey, Linderman was candid about his concerns for silver, parroting much of what he had told Ralston in May and outlining to Boutwell the results of his subsequent meeting with bullion interests on the Pacific coast. Linderman wrote that silver bullion annually pro-

Japan's .900 fine, 416-grain silver one yen was rejected by the Chinese.

Europe's Cast-Off

The first significant erosion of the price supports for silver came about as an indirect result of the Franco-Prussian War (1870-1871). The war, which lasted less than a year, was waged over a dispute between Prussia and France as to the rightful heir to the Spanish throne, and from a general eagerness on both sides to promote hostilities. It culminated in victory for Prussia, which laid siege to Paris late in 1870. The victory in turn opened the way for Otto von Bismarck to complete the unification of the various German petty states into the new German Empire, nominally under the control of William I (formerly the king of Prussia) who, after unification, took the title of German emperor. Prussia's victory also secured for the new empire an enormous indemnity of $965 million from France, a large portion of which was eventually remitted in the form of silver bullion.

Even with the surplus of silver bullion flooding into the German coffers, Bismark, the empire's first chancellor, opted to pattern the empire's new coinage system after that of Great Britain, by adopting a gold standard. In attempting to restructure the German coinage system, Bismarck found that it was necessary to eliminate the amalgamation of denominations that had come into general use in the various sovereignties before unification. The names and denominations of the circulating coins within Germany, before the formation of the empire, varied considerably. Prussia, for example, made use of the thaler and silber groschen, while Bavaria employed the thaler, gulden and kreuzers.

In December 1871, at Bismark's urging, the German Empire declared in favor of a gold standard, downgrading silver to use for exportation and in subsidiary coinage. In 1872, in order to implement the conversion to a gold standard, the empire began calling in all of the old silver coins still circulating in Germany. Germany's decision to shun silver and adopt gold as the privileged metal was at first felt primarily in the neighboring European countries, where the exiled German silver often clogged channels of trade, as it quickly depreciated in value. Between 1873 and 1879, Germany exported two-thirds of its silver supplies, ultimately resulting, when combined with increased production of precious metals worldwide, in a sharp decline in the value of silver bullion throughout the world.

Alarmed by the increased exportation of silver from Germany, which directly affected their economies, the member nations of the Latin Union (France, Italy, Belgium, Switzerland, and Greece), in 1874, moved to limit the product of full legal tender francs at the member mints, aiming toward the adoption of a gold standard. Other European nations also strove to control their burgeoning silver supplies: Between 1873 and 1875, Denmark, Norway, and Sweden entered into treaties, denouncing silver and adopting a gold standard; by 1875, Holland ceased coinage of silver and was followed the next year by Russia, which limited silver coinage to the amount needed for trade with China.

Along with its conversion to a gold standard, Germany adopted the mark.

duced at the mines in the United States had been increasing over the past three years to about $20 million per annum, "and a further increase in this product being quite certain, the future value of silver as compared with gold is a matter of national importance."[21] There were several causes at work now that could lead to silver's depreciation, Linderman told Boutwell, among these were the increased production along with demonetization by the German empire and other countries, and the change by some nations from its use in coinage to a preference for paper, all of which would bring large amounts of silver, that formerly went into coinage, on to the market.[22] Linderman estimated that at the time of Germany's enactment of its coinage law, in December 1871, there were some $350 million in silver in Germany, the equivalent of five years' total production of the globe. He wrote:

> Even if silver should be adopted by GERMANY, for subsidiary coinage, not more than $50,000,000 will be required for that purpose, which will leave $300,000,000, or about 9,000 tons, to be disposed of as bullion. A market for this immense supply of silver can only be found in such of the European States as maintain the single standard of silver, or the double standard of gold and silver, and in CHINA and the Indies.
>
> The facts above stated indicate the gradual but eventually certain adoption of the gold standard, and consequent demonetization of silver by all commercial countries. Not only is the tendency to adopt gold as the sole standard and measure of value, but to use paper money redeemable in gold, as the bulk of the circulating medium.
>
> The true policy of this country under these circumstances is to seek a market in CHINA for its silver bullion; and to do this it must be put in form to meet a favorable reception in that empire.[23]

Linderman related that the standard 412 1/2-grain silver dollar, which contained 371 1/4 grains of pure silver, had never been well received in China or in U.S. commerce ever since its introduction, because its bullion value was less than that of the old Spanish dollar and its successor the Mexican dollar, "both of which have played an important part in the commerce of the world."[24] When the U.S. silver dollar was introduced, the aim had been to set the new dollar at the same standard as the Spanish dollar, but the Act of 1792 had specified that the U.S. silver dollar contain 371 1/4 grains pure silver when it should have been within a fraction of 377 1/4 grains, Linderman wrote, adding:

> The mistake made in specifying 371 1/4 instead of 377 1/4 grains, was due to an error in determining the quality of pure silver in the Spanish dollar, the art of assaying being then imperfectly understood in this country. Dr. RITTENHOUSE, the first Director of the Mint, must have recognized the error, because the earlier issues of the mint correspond very closely to the Spanish dollar. His successor, however, caused the standard to be conformed to law, so that the dollar would contain 371 1/4 grains, which proportion of fine silver has never since been altered.
>
> Had the United States dollar been issued to correspond in content of fine silver to the old Spanish dollar, as was originally intended, it would no doubt long since have become an important agent of commerce.
>
> The silver dollar being a useless coin, both as respects circulation and commerce, should be abolished, and we should inquire whether some new medium may not be substituted, approximating in general character and value, which will meet certain commercial requirements becoming daily more pressing, without giving rise to any of those perplexing questions or complications resulting from the varying values of precious metals, under a double standard, and at the same time afford some relief to our mining industries, from the serious decline and further apparent depreciation in the value of silver.[25]

Leading up to his pitch for a heavier trade coin, Linderman told Boutwell that the establishment of a successful steamship line to China by the Pacific Mail Steam Ship Company and the connection with the oceanic cables, "which now nearly encompass the globe," were producing important changes in the way global exchanges were being transacted, thus giving San Francisco a bigger role in carrying out business for Europe with the Orient.[26] However, for a long time, much of the business of Europe and the United States with China and Japan has been done in Mexican dollars, which was a distinct disadvantage as, "...this coin has now practically become the money of account in those countries and of commerce with foreign nations, and so necessary has it become for this purpose that it readily commands about 8 per cent. premium both in London and San Francisco, *though intrinsically* worth only 1 6/10 per cent. more than our dollar of 412 1/2 grains."[27]

This, Linderman said, was a serious tax on the nation's commerce and its mining interests, as U.S. silver was being exported at a heavy discount. The Japanese being highly progressive and adaptive to the ways of other nations, Linderman explained, they had already adopted a gold stan-

The Hong Kong dollar, struck under British authority. A few years before the United States issued its Trade dollar for use in China, Great Britain sought to gain a greater share of the market by introducing its own coin as competition to the Mexican dollar. It enjoyed only a limited acceptance.

dard. The same, however, was not true of China, where their opposition to innovations was well known. Considering the magnitude of the nation's current commercial relations with the Chinese, along with the decreasing supply of Mexican dollars, Linderman said, the introduction of a new dollar that would be accepted by the Chinese could prove highly favorable. "After consulting with some of the leading business men of San Francisco, as well as with some of the most prominent and intelligent Chinese merchants as to its probable success," Linderman wrote. "I do not hesitate to recommend, in lieu of our old dollar, a new coin or disk, which shall be slightly more valuable than the Mexican dollar, to be made only upon the request of the owner of the bullion, and be paid for by him."[28] He added that it was not intended to make this new coin or disk legal tender in payment of debt:

> Its manufacture can therefore in nowise give rise to any complication with our monetary system, and neither in theory or principle differ in any respect from the manufacture of unparted or refined bars now authorized by law, except in being of *uniform* weight and fineness.
>
> If this new coin should be accepted at all as a medium in our trade with CHINA, it will doubtless very soon supersede the Mexican dollar, and there is no reason why it should not in a short time command a premium of 6 to 8 per cent.[29]

As the product of the nation's silver mines was presently being exported at an average discount of at least 2 percent, it would be an advantage not only to the nation's commerce but to its mining industry as well, Linderman reasoned. The trade of San Francisco with China direct, along with the exchange for account of the eastern cities and Europe would, he wrote, provide a safe outlet for silver and solve the perplexing proposition of its decline in the face of increasing production.

Linderman then suggested that the new coin might be named a "Silver Union" to differentiate it from the subsidiary silver coins and the gold dollar. By comparison, the new coin, which Linderman specified should be of 420 grains and contain 378 grains of pure silver, would weigh more than the Mexican dollar at 417 15/17 grains, the Japanese yen at 416 grains, and the current U.S. silver dollar at 412 1/2 grains.

After reviewing Linderman's report, Boutwell acted quickly, in his Dec. 2, 1872, *Report of the Secretary of the Treasury*, written less than two weeks later, he urged passage of the bill in the 42nd Congress, pointing to the German demonetization as a primary concern. Boutwell wrote that, in the past 10 years, the commercial value of silver had depreciated as compared to gold and that silver had come into disuse as currency in Germany and other countries. Therefore, he recommended no attempt be made to reintroduce it, noting:

> The intrinsic value of a metallic currency should correspond to its commercial value, or metal should be used only for the coinage of tokens [subsidiary coins] redeemable by the Government at their nominal value. As the depreciation of silver is likely to continue it is impossible to issue coin redeemable in gold without ultimate loss to the Government; for when the difference becomes considerable holders will present the silver for redemption, and leave it in the hands of the Government to be disposed of subsequently at a loss.[30]

Silver's use, Boutwell told Congress, should be restricted to commercial purposes and designed exclusively for commercial uses with other nations:

> Therefore, in renewing the recommendations heretofore made for the passage of the Mint bill, I suggest such alterations as will prohibit the coinage of silver for circulation in this country, but that authority be given for the coinage of a silver dollar that shall be as valuable as the Mexican dollar, and to be furnished at its actual cost. The Mexican dollar is used generally in trade with China and is now sold at a premium of about eight per cent. over the actual expense of coining. As the production of silver is rapidly increasing, such a coinage will at once furnish a market for the raw material and facilitate commerce between the United States and China.[31]

On Dec. 16, 1872, two weeks after Boutwell's report, the mint bill was reported to the floor of the Senate, recommitted, and reported back on Jan. 7, 1873. During its stay in the Senate Finance Committee, the 385-grain subsidiary silver dollar would be replaced with the new Trade dollar, a coin its promoters and most in California believed would be of great benefit to their financial well-being.

Chapter 15

RALSTON DOLLARS

Who, if anyone, should be credited with the placement of the Trade dollar into the mint bill is still a matter of debate. Some have argued that Louis A. Garnett was the primary force behind the amendment's origin. Others have said that William C. Ralston deserves the credit. There's also little doubt that, at least while things were going well, Mint Director Henry R. Linderman would have liked to have been known as its creator.

Of his father's claim, Porter Garnett wrote in a 1917 article for the *American Economic Review*:

> In the autumn of 1872, the late Louis A. Garnett of San Francisco, the present writer's father—then manager of the San Francisco Assaying and Refining Works—laid before Dr. H.R. Linderman, Superintendent of the Philadelphia Mint [sic], and subsequently the first Director of the Mint, under the act of 1873 establishing the Mint Bureau at Washington, the suggestion for the trade dollar. Mr. Garnett gave to Dr. Linderman a memorandum of all the essential facts and technical details as to weight and fineness, which he thought would justify the experiment and insure its success.[1]

Of the process by which the Trade dollar was then appended to the mint bill, Porter Garnett explained:

> During the last months of the period of two and a half years that the coinage act of 1873 had been pending in Congress, Mr. John J. Knox, then Deputy Comptroller of the Currency, undertook, at the direction of the Secretary of the Treasury, to formulate an amendment to the pending bill, authorizing the manufacture of the proposed disk. An attempt, however, had been made by some one in the department to alter the specifications and make it a 'metrical' coin, in the face of the ill-fated English experiment in Hong-Kong. It was only by an extended telegraphic correspondence that Mr. Garnett was able to avert this action, which would have been fatal to the success of the proposed coin.[2]

Porter Garnett's loyalty to his father aside, there is reason to believe that there was a wider range of influences for the coin's appearance in the mint bill than just Louis A. Garnett. Contemporary evidence of the involvement of the California silver interests in the Trade dollar amendment, for example, appeared in the *Virginia City Territorial Enterprise*, which on Feb. 4, 1873, less than two weeks before final passage of the mint bill, published a letter to the editor from Conrad Weigand, a former mint assayer, that not only linked Garnett with the Trade dollar amendment but Ralston and Milton S. Latham as well. Weigand, who was operating his own assaying firm, Weigand & Company, in Virginia City, claimed that the Trade dollar amendment had long been the work of Garnett, Ralston and Latham (a former California state senator who was manager of the London and San Francisco Bank). Weigand wrote to the *Territorial Enterprise* that:

> In December last though misled by the telegraph into the belief that Congress proposed issuing dollars of 440 troy grains in weight, you pointed out the fact that, instead of such inexplicable legislation, our great actual need is a market or demand for silver. At the same time you showed the chief causes of the alarmingly large discounts on silver bullion, and which threaten to become worse. Ignoring the minor influences, the great causes may be stated as
>
> First—The recent European abolition of silver as a legal tender for the payment of debts, except for very small amounts. This has thrown many tons of money-silver upon the manufacturing market. Of course that depressed the value per ounce of the metal in the great silver marts of the world. The wonder is that the depression has not been greater, especially in view of the second cause of depression, viz.: The unparalleled produce of silver in Nevada.[3]

Weigand declared that the only way to stop the discounts on silver was to find a market large enough to raise the value of silver in London, the great monetary exchange center of the world, and that:

> To create such a market has long been the study of William C. Ralston, Milton S. Latham, Louis A. Garnett and other philosophic financiers of San Francisco. With this object in view they have recommended to influential parties at Washington the addition to our silver money-dollar of a coined ingot or circular disk, to be known as a silver trade-dollar; its value to be about 2 per cent. greater than our money-dollar, and from three-quarters to 1 per cent. greater than the Mexican dollar. The Mexican dollar is both a current coin and hoard piece among the myriads of Asia. It is hoped that our trade-dollar by being made more

> valuable will in time supplant the Mexican dollar in Asia, and that the Asiatic demand, together with the anticipation of it, will both physically and speculatively relieve the London market, there raise the commercial value per ounce of silver, and in consequence enable buyers here to abolish present discounts and revert to former premiums upon our silver produce.[4]

As for Ralston, his early, as well as continual, involvement with the development of the U.S. Trade dollar can be verified by letters in the Ralston correspondence files.[5] From late in 1872 up until his death in 1875, Ralston was a driving force behind the introduction of the coin and what acceptance it ultimately gained in Far Eastern markets. So intent was Ralston at making the coin a staple in the Far East, that at least one of his correspondents in the Orient began referring to the coins as "Ralston dollars." A regular contact in this regard was John Robertson of the Oriental Bank Corporation in Yokohama, Japan. As has been mentioned, in late 1872, prior to the amendment's placement in the mint bill, Ralston called upon Robertson to test the waters for the new coin in the first of a series of correspondence that continued into 1875.

Of Ralston's connection to the introduction of the Trade dollar amendment, the *Territorial Enterprise*, of March 28, 1876, wrote:

> To the late Mr. William C. Ralston is due the origin of the present trade-dollar. As the silver accumulated from the mines his restless brain began to revolve around the problem of how to ship silver to China and Japan—the best markets in the world for silver—without losing the discount taxed on silver bars. He hit upon the thought that if a dollar could be made a trifle more valuable than the Mexican dollar perhaps the Chinese might be induced to accept it. He, with his usual energy, wrote his views to members of Congress, to the Secretary of the Treasury, and the Director of the Mint, and after a good while secured the legislation which authorized the coining of the trade-dollar.[6]

Beyond western advocates of the new trade coin, it must be added that Linderman was also a

1871 and 1872 patterns for the Commercial dollar. Like the Trade dollar, this coin was to be .900 fine and weighed 420 grains.

staunch supporter and did not mind taking credit for it. This likely led to a missive in the Nov. 21, 1874, issue of the *Alta California* written to mark Linderman's departure from that city by train, after overseeing the opening of the new San Francisco Mint. The *Alta* wrote:

> About two years ago Dr. Linderman made a visit to this coast in connection with Mint matters, and after his return to Washington submitted to Secretary Boutwell an elaborate and able report in relation to Mints and coinage, and especially to the production of silver bullion, and predicted the decline in the value of that metal which has since taken place, the causes for which he therein fully set forth. In the same report China was indicated as a market for United States silver, and the issue of the Trade Dollar recommended as the form in which the bullion would be most likely to meet with favor. The views of Dr. Linderman received the indorsement of the then Secretary of the Treasury and Congress, and the Trade Dollar was afterward authorized and issued, and has already become the commercial coin of the Orientals. In previous reports Dr. Linderman had called attention to the serious disadvantages to the country, arising from the high gold-coinage charge of the United States, and, under his steady lead, a reduction of the charge from the one-half to the one-fifth of one per cent. has been effected.
>
> The importance to the public of these two measures, has been partially manifested during the past year, but their real value could not be fully attained while the coinage capacity on this Coast was so limited as to be entirely inadequate to meet the demands for coinage, and especially of the Trade Dollar. This difficulty will disappear when the new Mint is in full operation.[7]

The *Alta* added that in connection with this, it was proper to say that "the United States Coinage Act of 1873 has been put in operation [the gold standard], without the disadvantages and embarrassments which appear to have attended similar reforms in other countries, and especially in Germany, and that fact naturally leads to the conclusion that our Mint officers and their coadjutors understand their business."[8]

Although the new refinery at the mint was not yet ready, the *Alta* reported that the mint was prepared to begin coinage:

> The new Mint will commence operations on or about the first of next month, on silver, coining Trade Dollars for a week or so, and then will coin up the gold that has accumulated. It is probable that during the month of December arrangements will be made for coining Trade Dollars so that a large amount will be kept constantly on hand at the Mint, and all parties wishing for them can be supplied at a moment's notice.[9]

Another piece to the puzzle can be found in Linderman's testimony before a congressional committee in 1876. Asked how the Trade dollar came into existence, Linderman told the committee:

> The silver dollar had been omitted in the coinage bill pending in Congress in 1872, and which had passed one House. I was on the Pacific Coast as a sort of special agent or commissioner for Mr. Boutwell in the fall of 1872. We were then looking for the commencement of the effect on silver of the German action, and, in discussion with some gentlemen there, it was suggested that we must look to China—some special market must be created or encouraged. Originally the Spanish dollar had been the principal commercial coin of the world; that dollar disappeared, and in time the Mexican dollar took its place, having within a fraction the same weight. The Mexican dollar contains 377 1/4 grains pure silver. We thought that we might work the trade-dollar into the place of the Mexican. This was the whole business. I recommended that in my report and it was acted upon in Congress, and it was merely intended for the Eastern trade.[10]

While it is clear that the Pacific coast silver interests played an important role in the creation of the Trade dollar, it is apparent from other documents and existing patterns that the idea for a U.S. trade coin, first termed a "Commercial dollar," dates back to 1870, if not earlier. John Jay Knox had mentioned it as a possibility in his report attached to the final version of the mint bill, submitted to Congress in April 1870. As part of his discussion of the reasons behind the planned elimination of the silver dollar, Knox had argued (much as Boutwell would two years later), that if it were deemed important to retain a silver dollar, then it should be preserved only in the form of a commercial dollar. Knox wrote:

> The present gold dollar piece is made the dollar unit in the proposed bill, and the silver dollar piece is discontinued. If, however, such a coin is authorized, it should be issued only as a *commercial dollar,* not as a standard unit of account, and of the exact value of the Mexican dollar, which is the favorite for circulation in China and Japan and other Oriental countries.[11]

Shortly after Knox's mint bill was submitted to the Senate, U.S. Revenue Commission Secretary Ezekial Elliott wrote to Knox on June 10, 1870, also advocating such a coin. After tracing the ill-fated history of the first U.S. silver dollar and the miscalculation that had been made in the attempt to base it on its Spanish model, Elliott suggested:

> It appears, therefore, that the existing silver dollar, although professedly based on the Spanish or Mexican silver dollar, does not fairly represent

> any coin ever issued from those mints; that it is merely a representative of the average of abraded Spanish-Mexican coins.
>
> The coins most in demand for oriental commerce were for many years the pillared Spanish-Mexican piasters; and such was their popularity that they continued to be preferred long after their intrinsic value had been considerably reduced by wear in use. The restoration, as a trade-coin, of a silver dollar, approximating to the old standard, to wit: one containing 25 grams of *pure* silver, is a subject which would seem to demand favorable consideration.[12]

Commercial dollar patterns were struck by the U.S. Mint as early as 1871. The first pieces, as with the later pieces proposed by Linderman's report, were to be 420 grains in total weight and .900 fine. Like the Trade dollar, as issued, the Commercial dollar patterns bore the weight and fineness inscribed on the coin's reverse. No other U.S. coin or pattern up to that date compares.[13] The mint continued to issue patterns bearing the Commercial dollar designation into 1872 and beyond, but in that year also began striking pieces bearing the legend "Trade Dollar."

Beyond the question of origin, however, the early existence of such patterns is also an indication of the intense interest 19th century America displayed for anything to do with the Orient. Contemporary newspapers on both coasts were crammed with tales of life in the Orient and the progress in overseas trade with China and Japan. By the 1860s, many doors to this mysterious world had swung open. Several delegations from Japan and China crossed the ocean to study western society or to negotiate treaties, offering real chances for trade expansion. This intensity heightened, in 1868, when Anson Burlingame, former U.S. minister to China, headed a delegation of Chinese diplomats visiting the United States, seeking diplomatic recognition for China, civil rights for Chinese citizens living abroad, and lowering of immigration restrictions. Ralston took time to entertain Burlingame and the delegation at his plush country home, Belmont.[14]

Despite such encouragements, Pacific coast merchants were keenly aware and considerably irked by the realization that, despite their prime geographic location in relation to China, they enjoyed only a small portion of this growing trade outlet. England, which controlled the supply of Mexican dollars, essential for trade with China, held a virtual stranglehold over commerce with the Far East. This disadvantage was especially disturbing to Pacific coast bankers, who regularly made a business not only in lending money to those engaged in importing tea, silk and other readily absorbed exotic products from the Far East, but also in trading bullion in that market. California bankers sent millions of dollars of gold and silver "treasure" via steamer each year either for sale to favorable markets or in payments of debts, and they wanted the playing field leveled.

It did not help matters that the British also held sway in California when it came to bullion purchases. Following the Civil War, California's economy was booming, a factor the British were quick to take advantage of. Ira Cross wrote that, during the decade of the 1860s, drawn by lucrative chances for investment made ripe by California's adherence to gold instead of depreciated paper, five agencies of British banking firms opened their doors in San Francisco. The first of these was the Commercial Bank of India, which set up a San Francisco office in 1863. Others included the British & California Banking Company Ltd., the Bank of British North America, the Bank of British Columbia (all three established in 1864), and the London & San Francisco Bank, operated by Latham, who established the San Francisco branch of this bank in 1865. "The five representatives of the British banking interests in San Francisco were not concerned with banking operations along lines similar to those which had been followed for the most part by the California bankers." Cross explained. "Instead, they devoted themselves primarily to the purchase and shipment of bullion, to making advances on securities, merchandise and on shipments of gold and silver, and to the issuance of letters of credit."[15]

An example of the scope of these bullion shipments can be seen in the Aug. 5, 1869, issue of the *Alta California*, which reported that, on that day, $663,377.23 in silver bars, Mexican dollars, gold bars, gold coin and gold dust had been shipped to China and Japan, via steamer. The greatest amount came from the Bank of British North America, which dispatched $265,203.93 in silver bars to Japan, while the Bank of California shipped $16,000 in Mexican dollars to Japan, and $30,488.04 in silver bars and $28,000 in Mexican dollars to China. With silver and gold supplies relatively tight, the newspaper reported, these figures were down from the prior year, when $777,888.19 in treasure was hoisted onto the same steamer.[16]

Six days later, the *Virginia City Territorial Enterprise*, under the heading "Trade with China," recorded that Chinese trade from its 14 custom houses, as tracked by the chief of the Revenue Bureau in Peking, had risen from an export/import

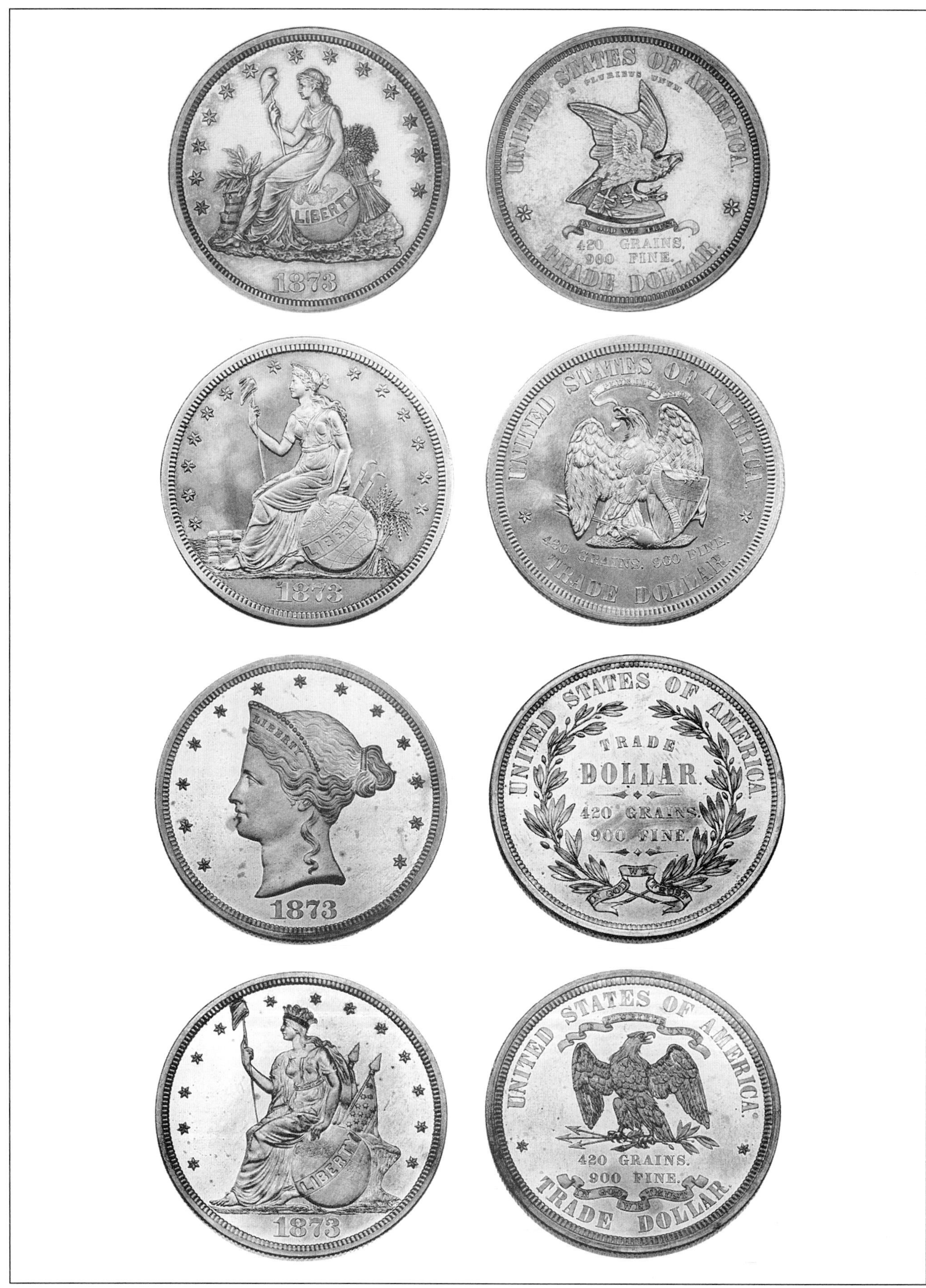

A selection of Trade dollar patterns. The first pieces with the Trade dollar designation were struck in 1872.

total in 1864 of 105,300,087 taels (a tael being worth roughly $1.50 at the time) to 140,235,946 by 1868. In most years, imports led exports. In dollars, the 1868 export/import total was more than $210 million, with the amount of revenue collected on this commerce at nearly $14 million. When broken down between the nations of the world, however, the *Territorial Enterprise* found that Great Britain and its dependencies realized 123,062,454 taels ($184.6 million) and the United States just 7,416,069 taels ($11.1 million), while all other countries accounted for 9,757,428 taels ($14.6 million).

"A portion of this trade may subsequently fall to our credit," the *Territorial Enterprise* wrote. "Nevertheless it will be seen that our trade with China is comparatively trifling, compared with that of Great Britain. Nor is it increasing any in proportion to the increase of that of the latter power."[17]

The fact that not only was there a need to find a means of eliminating this lopsided trade deficit but also that such an expanded outlet might someday be required simply to bolster silver prices was also understood. There had been all kinds of predictions as to the future wealth of the Comstock in the years leading up to the discovery of the Big Bonanza—some from government geologists and others from leading miners—but no one could be certain what the future would hold. The Comstock had experienced long periods of barren rock in the years prior and might soon tap out. On the other hand, it could flood the market with silver. This made many wary of any movements in world markets for the metals and brought some to predict the worst.

Taking good-natured jabs at one such doom and gloom forecast in the *San Francisco Bulletin*, the May 14, 1869, *Territorial Enterprise* wrote that the *Bulletin* had warned readers that circumstances might be in the works that could cause a great change in the relative value of gold to silver. The *Bulletin* observed that in 1844 the ratio of gold to silver had been 12 1/8 to 1 but, by 1863, silver had been devalued somewhat, as the ratio stood at 15 to 1. This decrease in the value of silver, it said, would have been worse had it not been for the Asiatic market. The *Bulletin* contended that when silver was not wanted to carry on world commerce, "this vastly increased production, aided by the fact that it is only a legal tender in small sums, would make it almost a drug in the market but for the fact that China and Central Asia buy from $50,000,000 to $75,000,000 of foreign silver coin and bullion every year and quietly melt this down, and, for all known commercial purposes, withdraw it from the circulation of the world."[18] The great silver market of the world was China, the *Bulletin* added, and "so long as this and other Asiatic countries have more to sell than to buy, the exchange will go on in the old way—silver for tea, silk and rice."[19] If this market changed in the other direction, as a prominent Chinese statesman had told the *Bulletin* it might, all of the silver hoarded in China during the past 300 and 400 years would come out of hiding and flood into the United States and Europe. If that happened, the *Bulletin* glumly predicted of silver's future:

> It will probably cease to be used as a circulating medium, and be employed principally in the manufacture of coal-scuttles and other domestic utensils. The silver mines of Nevada will be abandoned, for the same reason that copper mining has been suspended in California—not because of their exhaustion, but because the metal they produce will be comparatively valueless. It will be sold by the ton, like pig-iron, and will pay for working only when found in deposits too rich, like the ores of the Eberhardt, to be reduced by ordinary processes.[20]

The *Enterprise* joked that with the completion of the transcontinental railroad (which had been linked four days prior at Promontory Point, Utah), the Chinese silver might soon be on its way, and, if this were so, it could be the reason behind the recent refusal of banks in the area to accept silver in payments over $5. "We are not getting alarmed; yet, that a panic may not be inaugurated here," the *Territorial Enterprise* smirked, "we will continue to receive silver in payment of subscriptions to the ENTERPRISE, and will instruct our carriers to collect in the same depreciating currency."[21]

However, by 1872, it was not the threat of Chinese dumping silver that was of concern, it was the change to a gold standard by Germany. The urgency for adoption of the long debated mint bill was ratcheted up a notch, as was the need to win a greater share of the Oriental market for silver from Great Britain. If more of Europe would soon be resisting silver, as it appeared it would, the markets for this metal would be considerably narrowed.

A Feb. 5, 1873, letter to the State Department from David A. Bailey, U.S. Council at Hong Kong, to Assistant Secretary of State Charles Hale, forwarded to Treasury Secretary George S. Boutwell (who brought the matter before the House of Representatives on Feb. 10, 1873, two days before the Coinage Act of 1873 was signed into law), raised the Trade dollar concept from a level of regional significance to one of national importance.[22] In his letter, Bailey called for increased American banking facilities in the Far East, and for the issuance of a trade coin equal in weight to the Mexican dollar in order to eliminate the surcharge levied on American commerce engendered by being forced to negotiate through London banks. Bailey explained that the balance of trade between America and Europe was generally against the former, stating:

> This deficit is made up by both North America and South America sending bullion and specie to Europe. The United States imports [goods] from China, Japan, the Philippine Islands, and East India, annually, to the extent of about (approximately) $50,000,000 (Mexican money). By far the greatest portion of this import is paid for by America in London. Thus the United States annually adds to the debts already existing against her in Europe the amounts of her imports from the East.[23]

Bailey noted that London bankers, for the advantage of serving as middlemen, charged a 2 percent commission, and all told, this method of financing trade with the Far East taxed U.S. commerce between 3 and 4 percent on each transaction. He recommended, with the completion of the transcontinental railroad and the opening of a direct steamship route to the Far East, that American bankers consider establishing branches in China and Japan and thereby take control of the American-Asiatic trade. If they did so, Bailey said, "There is no saying that the time may not come when the stream of bullion and dollars, now leaving Mexico, Peru, and other South American countries, will flow into one great reservoir, one of the great commercial centers of the United States, whether it be New York or San Francisco, and that there the balances of the whole world will be adjusted."[24]

As a corollary to this, Bailey also advocated the minting of a trade coin to meet the requirements of Asiatic trade and, more specifically, China. He wrote:

> Permit me to express the opinion that—
>
> 1. A dollar with the same intrinsic value as the Mexican, to serve for currency in China, should be coined by the United States.
>
> 2. A sufficient quantity of these dollars should be shipped on trial, and, if possible, a declaration obtained from the Peking Government declaring them a legal tender in all trade transactions and for payment of Custom-house dues, and forbidding their being chopped.
>
> 3. The dollars to be, once for all, of a uniform coinage, and as closely resembling the Mexican dollar as may be expedient.[25]

If the plan was successful, Bailey said, gold coin would soon flow into the United States, "and instead of America shipping her gold and silver in bars to Europe, she will find a vast market for her coins in the East, and get, thereby, an enormous hold on this great trade."[26]

Bailey's second point, shipping quantities of the new coins to the Orient on trial and urging their legal recognition, was basically the course Ralston took in promoting the Trade dollar. Shortly after the first Trade dollars were struck, Ralston shipped samples to Robertson in Yokohama. In a Sept. 8, 1873, letter, Robertson told Ralston he had passed the new coins on to Hong Kong, as there would be no use for them in Japan. Japan had by this point gone through the first years of its currency conversion under the Meiji Restoration government and had dropped silver in favor of a gold standard. Robertson was, however, able to receive a favor-

The Trade dollar as issued in 1873.

able editorial about the coin in an issue of the *Japan Herald*, he told Ralston, by plying the editor with a "brandy and soda" and five of the new coins for his watch chain.[27]

What was really needed, Roberston wrote, was an official proclamation making the coins acceptable in the payment of customs duties. In an Oct. 8, 1873, letter, Robertson again pointed to the necessity of obtaining a proclamation to convince the Chinese to use the coin and warned that Ralston's earlier suggestion, "to sink John Bull" in winning acceptance of the Trade dollar, would not be wise, as the English still controlled Hong Kong and would be necessary in securing the proclamation.[28]

At a couple of points during their trans-Pacific communications, the discussion turned to whether or not a bit of tipping of Chinese mandarin (local officials) might not speed the process, but this was deemed unwise. It would, however, be prudent, Robertson told Ralston in his Sept. 8, 1873, letter, to keep the French "sweet," as they controlled Saigon—and "a few dollars officially spent might get an official proclamation there."[29]

Despite the Oriental Bank Corporation's efforts on Ralston's behalf, the Chinese people were slow to warm to the new coin. In a Sept. 29, 1874, letter, Robertson seemed resigned to the impossibility of securing the sought-after proclamation, writing to Ralston that, "Trades are not yet a <u>legal tender</u> anywhere in this part of the world; but they seem to <u>beep</u> in Hong Kong pretty well, and as long as holders could buy to what they wanted with these it is not so much matter about their being a 'legal tender' a good <u>commercial</u> tender is just as good as a <u>legal</u> one."[30]

On Dec. 21, 1874, after returning from a trip to China, he again wrote to Ralston, this time telling him, "I am now 'cracking your whip' about the <u>Trade Dollar</u> and by next mail I hope to tell you more."[31] Things were all right in the south of China with the Trade dollar, Robertson told Ralston, but the north was still uncertain. In Hong Kong, there was still opposition as well, especially from the Hong Kong and Shanghai Bank and the London and San Francisco Bank, which favored the Hong Kong dollar, struck under British authority. He hoped, however, to have the Trade dollar accepted as a legal tender between banks locally.

In February of that year, Ralston turned to Linderman for help, writing to the Mint director inquiring as to the cost of placing the coins in certain Chinese and Japanese ports for the use of the Navy Department to further enhance their acceptance.[32] Linderman replied with the figures and likely shipped the coins, as well.

Ralston kept up the pressure until his death in August 1875, not willing to give up on the coin or the lucrative measures provided by the Coinage Act of 1873. Sen. John Sherman thus correctly informed the Senate on Jan. 17, 1873, during debate over the mint bill, that "the 'trade dollar' has been adopted mainly for the benefit of the people of California, and others engaged in trade with China."[33] It might also justly be said that its adoption was as the result of pressure applied by the existing silver interests as well.

The lack of protest by silver bullion producers to the removal of the standard silver dollar from the mint bill, therefore, becomes understandable, when one weighs the benefits these interests derived from the bill's provisions against any perceived losses. Ralston, Latham, Garnett, and other San Francisco financiers looked upon the reduction in the minting charge and the anticipated market created by the new Trade dollar and were evidently content in the belief that these provisions would benefit themselves and the country through increases in their trading position relative to other foreign powers and, in particular, London. They also likely viewed the adoption of a gold standard, which had maintained California through the toughest times, as prudent for the rest of the nation as well. As Linderman told Ralston in his May 19, 1872, letter, the true course must be to force gold on the East, not paper on the West.[34] The mint bill would do just that.

Chapter 16

WORTHY REASONS

On Oct. 14, 1896, in a speech before Boston's Twentieth Century Club, former Treasury Secretary George S. Boutwell told his audience of the likely reason why Nevada Sens. William M. Stewart and John Percival Jones voted in favor of the Coinage Act of 1873:

> There is historical evidence tending to show that they had sufficient and worthy reasons as representatives of the silver mining interest for assenting to the suspension of the coinage of the silver dollar. In 1872 silver was at a slight premium as compared with gold. Therefore the privilege of coinage of the dollar was of no advantage to the owners of bullion.
>
> The Mint Bill had a new and attractive feature. It provided for the coinage of a dollar that was to contain 420 grains of standard silver, and was to be known as the trade dollar. The Mexican dollar, which contained about 416 grains, was then sold at a premium, and it was used extensively in the China and India trade.
>
> It was the expectation of all concerned that the trade dollar, from its added value, would take the place of the Mexican dollar in the immense trade of the East. My own confidence was great. Indeed, the thought of failure never occurred to me. Unfortunately, the stolidity of the Chinese and the force of habit among that people were not considered by us. From long use they had become accustomed to the Mexican dollar. They refused our trade dollar, notwithstanding its greater weight.
>
> We coined and put into circulation, at home and abroad, about 36,000,000 pieces, many of which were afterward recoined as legal-tender dollars under a special act of Congress.

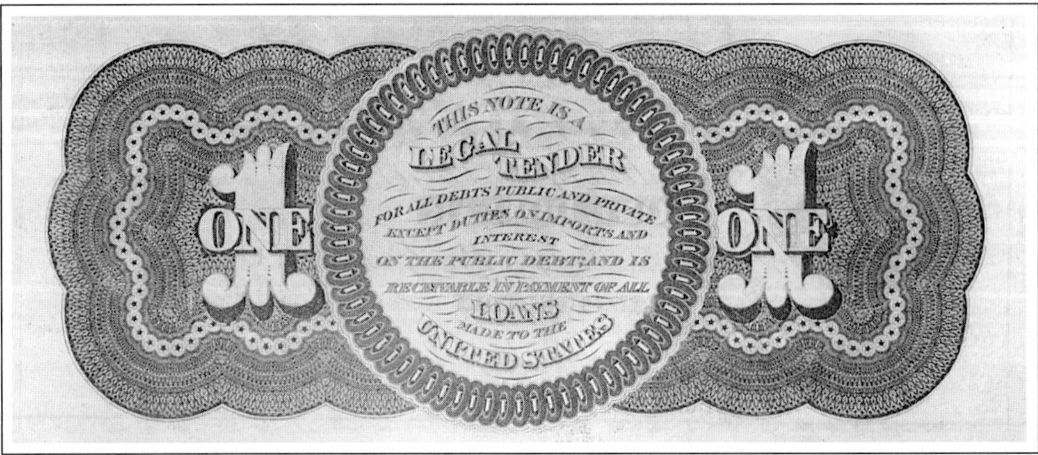

California, Nevada, and Oregon maintained an allegiance to gold while much of the rest of the nation used United States notes. Many on the Pacific coast, therefore, favored the gold standard.

> With the failure of that undertaking came the crusade against the act of 1873. Whether the two events sustained to each other the relation of cause and effect, I cannot say.[1]

There is reason to believe that Boutwell's contention is correct, at least in terms of the primary capitalists and financiers of the bullion industry in California and Nevada and, in particular, William C. Ralston, who, besides seeking an outlet for the stepped-up production of silver emanating from Nevada mines and attempting to seize from London greater control over financial transactions with the Orient, were not concerned about the survival of the silver dollar. This is not to say that everyone on the Pacific coast favored its elimination, simply that those with the greatest amount of power to wield their influence in Washington likely did. Certainly, in Ralston's case, if he or Louis A. Garnett had any qualms about the silver dollar's disappearance, they would have had little difficulty in getting Dr. Henry R. Linderman's attention at any time during the bill's lengthy stay in Congress or, in particular, in late 1872, when they held discussions with Linderman over how to address the eventual impact of the silver dumped on the world market by Germany. It is more likely, then, that Ralston and Garnett favored the adoption of the gold standard, as did many of the leading money philosophers on the Pacific Coast. The dropping of the silver dollar or its reduction in weight was a necessary part of this process.

One contemporary in the region who was concerned about the elimination of the standard silver dollar was assayer Conrad Weigand, who wrote of his misgivings to the *Territorial Enterprise*, less than two weeks before the mint bill's final passage. Weigand was afraid that any alteration to the weight of the standard silver dollar would lead to confusion in resolving existing contracts, which had presumably always been based on a silver dollar of exactly 412 1/2 grains. But Weigand's comments show his own confusion as to the monetary standard provisions of the bill, and his objections appear to be based more on a concern for industry standards of valuation of contracts and stamped bars than any predilection to bimetallism as such.

In his Feb. 4, 1873, letter to the *Virginia City Territorial Enterprise* Weigand mistakenly warned readers that, unless assayers in the vicinity protested proposed changes in the mint bill, the Trade dollar of 420 grains would become the new nominal standard of valuation, causing a necessary downward adjustment of 1 8/10 percent of the assayer's value stamp (which denoted how many coined dollars could be struck from a given bar containing silver). He complained:

> Mssr. Ralston, Latham and Garnett, well knowing that many contracts are based on the silver dollar of 412 1/2 grains (the weight not being specified), and that the whole American bullion trade is based upon the same valuation, did not propose to Congress to make any change in the weight of the silver money-dollar. They did recommend, *besides* the unaltered money-dollar, that a new trade-dollar should be authorized and issued. But, through Senatorial stupidity, the amendments passed in the Senate have *substituted* the trade-dollar for the money-dollar.[2]

Weigand was apparently unaware that at no point during the bill's three-year stay before Congress was the standard silver dollar provided for in its provisions. His qualms over a change in the valuation of the number of grains of silver that legally constituted a dollar in silver are similar to the concerns expressed exactly three years earlier by the officers of the San Francisco Mint. In their Feb. 4, 1870, response to John Jay Knox on his rough draft of the mint bill, which called for a subsidiary dollar of 384 grains, they had queried:

> Would not the proposed change in the weight of the silver dollar disturb the relative value of all our coinage, affect our commercial conventions, and possibly impair the validity of contracts running through a long period? Might not the dollar be retained as a measure of value, but the coinage of the piece for circulation be discontinued...[?][3]

This confusion is one of the reasons given for not assenting to a subsidiary silver dollar, as first proposed by Knox and later appeared in a House version of the bill. Though such a coin may have helped absorb silver, Linderman and others were worried about the mixed message it sent by presenting a coin with a dollar face value but no longer the gold equivalent. In arguing against the 384-grain dollar in his March 10, 1870, letter to Knox, former Mint Director James Ross Snowden expressed these concerns, saying he did not like the idea of reducing the dollar to the same "token" level as the other subsidiary coins, declaring, "When we speak of dollars let it be known that we speak of dollars not demonetized and reduced below their intrinsic value, and thus avoid the introduction of contradictory and loose ideas of the standards of value."[4]

In voicing his consternation over the elimination of the "money-dollar," Weigand also claimed that Ralston, Latham, and Garnett, who

Former Philadelphia Mint Director James Ross Snowden had objected to the release of a 384-grain subsidiary silver dollar, believing it would cause confusion.

he said were largely responsible for the Trade dollar amendment, opposed the elimination of the standard silver dollar. There is, however, substantial reason to believe that Weigand erred in his judgment of the motives and monetary standard philosophies of the aforementioned California bullion interests. Mary Ellen Glass, who presented a portion of Weigand's letter in her *Silver and Politics in Nevada: 1892-1902,* found, similarly, that, "There is some evidence, indeed, that the capitalists and major mine owners of the Comstock supported the demonetization to their own profit."[5]

This conclusion is not farfetched, especially when one reviews the advantages provided to the bullion interests in this coinage measure and when one takes into account that California and Nevada had long advocated and maintained contracts in gold, regularly shunned and criticized the use of seemingly unbacked federal paper money, and would likely, as a majority, have preferred that the rest of the nation did so, as well. Also, before the complexion of the so-called silver interests changed—due to the discovery of the Big Bonanza—the prevailing silver interests, Ralston and company, had little interest in the future of the standard silver dollar. As Linderman explained in his November 1872 report to Boutwell, it was a useless coin for their purposes, which revolved largely around trade with the Orient. This point is dramatically confirmed by the extremely low mintages of standard silver dollars at the western branch mints, as compared to production of the same coins at the Philadelphia Mint, during the years 1870-1873.[6]

Mint records show that, while Philadelphia churned out record numbers of the standard silver dollars in 1871 and 1872, with a combined total mintage of 2,890,210 silver dollars for years that the mint bill was before Congress, the western mints—at San Francisco and Carson City—struck a meager 293,000 silver cartwheels over the same period. Obviously there was no great demand for the coin, either for trade with the Orient or in domestic circulation in the West. Being lighter in weight than its Mexican rival, the standard silver dollar was often viewed as a hindrance to increasing trade with the Orient rather than a benefit.[7]

It is also likely that Ralston, Latham and Garnett agreed with the Treasury Department's position relative to the need for adopting the gold standard to insure proper backing for the dollar in trade relations with foreign nations, who were themselves all moving toward monometallism. Sticking with gold had seen California, Nevada and Oregon through earlier panics and tough times of the Civil War, while the rest of the nation was blanketed with depreciated greenbacks, fractional notes, postage stamps (used for a time as change) and private tokens to make up for the lack of federally coined money.

Even into 1874, by which time paper money had made some inroads in the West and a national party had been formed in Indianapolis calling for its increased printing, Californians still readily voiced their allegiance to gold, crediting it with keeping them out of the ravages of the depression that had, by this point, engulfed the rest of the nation. In an editorial under the heading "Real Money," the Dec. 25, 1874, issue of the *Alta California* wrote:

> The advocates of an irredeemable paper currency made a constant howl a few years since about the disloyalty and impolicy of California's adherence to gold; but they seem to have discovered the error of their ways of late, for they preserve a most discreet silence. If ever facts exposed the folly of a theory conclusively, it has been done in this case. Two years ago both great political parties of the country declared, in their national platforms, that measures should be taken for the resumption of specie payments; and though the promise thus made has not been fulfilled, it is still obligatory; and the leading financiers and commercial centres continue to call on Congressmen to remember the conditions under which they were chosen. Every year some new event occurs to demonstrate the folly of using money that has no fixed value. Contracts made in it are in the nature of gambling ventures, and the risk increases with the time before payment is to be made, and with the possibilities of fluctuation.[8]

The *Alta* then quoted from the Dec. 18 issue of the *Chicago Tribune*, which praised California's stubborn allegiance to gold, writing:

> A year ago, when the panic passed over the United States as a destructive blast, destroying wealth, sweeping away the accumulations of years, and leaving in its trail an unprecedented annihilation of credit, industry and production, the Pacific States were untouched. They had not dabbled in the unclean things. They had not erected a paper standard as variable as the wind. The panic found them buying and selling and keeping accounts in dollars, and not with fluctuating and uncertain and irredeemable paper. They did business in money, and not with protested promises. They dealt with property at its value in money, and not fictitious values founded upon bets as to the value of greenbacks at a future day. They had no margins invested in the chances of the rise and fall of paper; they dealt exclusively with real values in real money. There

Hoarding of coins during the Civil War also led to the introduction of money substitutes, including copper Civil War tokens, which served in the place of one-cent coins.

> was no collapse there, because there was no speculation or gambling in the money invested. There was no shrinkage of values because of the shrinkage of money. The money of California remained unchanged, and the property representing like money knew no shrinkage. While the banks of the rest of the country closed their doors, and even the savings banks refused, for want even of depreciated paper, to pay their depositors, the banks of California were undisturbed, paying all demands in coin.[9]

From the discovery of gold in California in 1848, the production of that state's mines placed California in the unusual position of conducting the majority of its payments in gold, while, at the same time, the federal greenback currency won only limited acceptance and use. This point was made abundantly clear during the Jan. 17, 1873, Senate debate over government redemption of abraded gold coins. At that time, Sen.

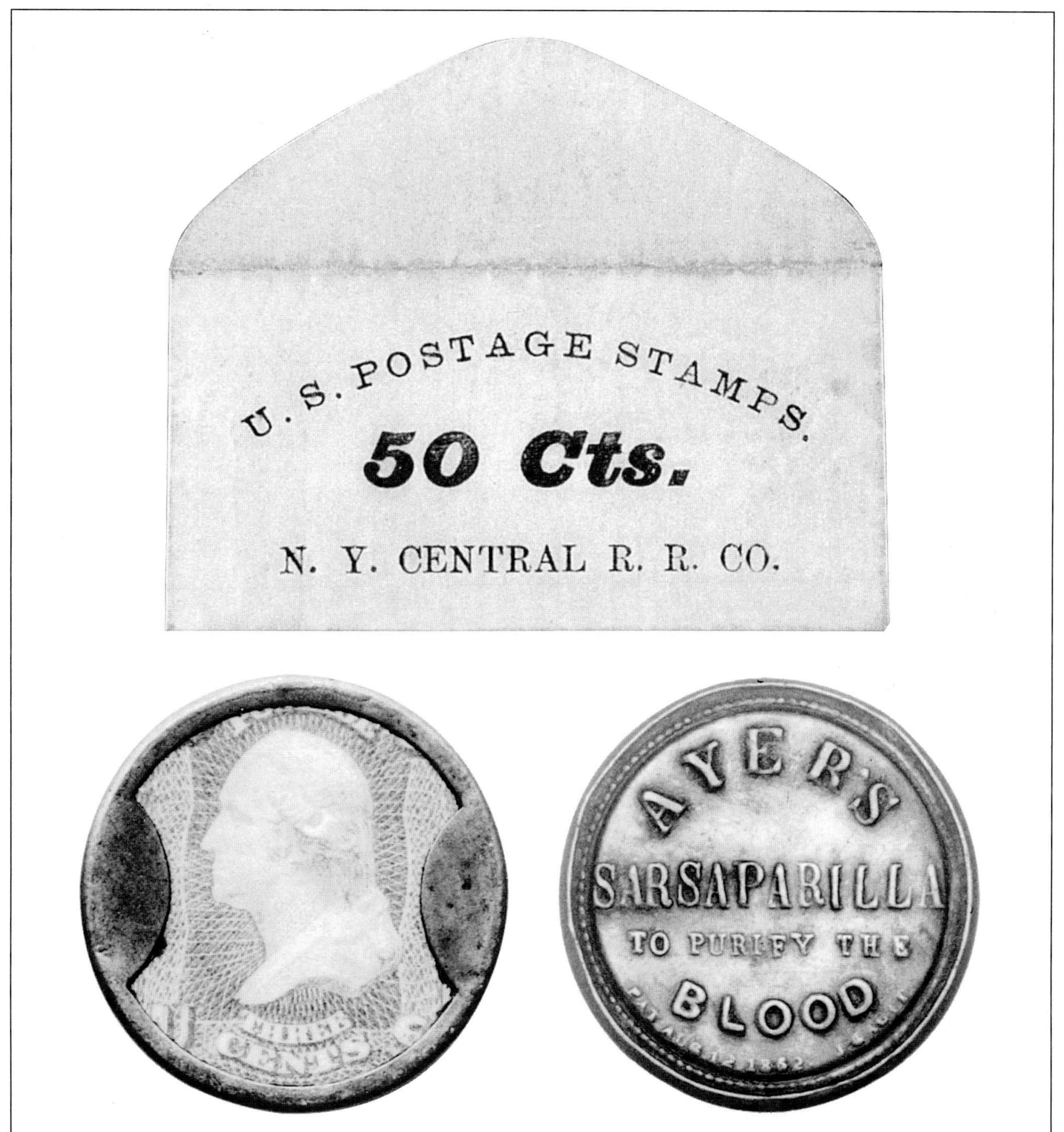

Postage stamps were also used as money during the Civil War. The stamps were often housed in envelopes or metal encasements for ease of handling and protection from damage.

The small coinage of silver dollars at the Carson City and San Francisco mints during the years just prior to the passage of the Coinage Act of 1873 serve as a good indication that the standard silver dollar was not wanted for trade with the Orient.

John Sherman contended that Californians had insisted on circulating gold in lieu of the government's fiduciary paper currency and were now attempting to force redemption of worn and mutilated gold coins on the rest of the country. To this charge, California Sen. Eugene Casserly responded that paper money had always been accepted in San Francisco and at a premium to that of Sherman's home state of Ohio. However, due to the large production of gold, "our whole system of values was based upon gold coin," not necessarily by choice but through economic necessity.[10] He lamented:

> Yet we are constantly met when we seek to do anything to relieve the people of California in reference to the condition of the coinage there by the reproach that we insisted on keeping in California the gold coin of the country. Why, Mr. President, was it wrong for a State when she had the right to choose between two kinds of lawful money—greenbacks or gold—to choose that kind which formed her currency, and more than that, which formed her entire standard and basis of value?[11]

David Lavender, who relied on Ralston's correspondence in preparation of his biography of the Bank of California's leader, supported the contention that California bullion interests advocated the gold standard for the nation. Lavender wrote that Linderman, Knox, Ralston and Garnett all wanted to make gold the only standard when the government resumed specie payments. In California, the real reason was that gold had long been symbolic of a sound economy and "Only the stability of gold, Californians were convinced, would maintain the price of domestic bonds, real estate and foreign exchange."[12] Linderman, Lavender said, had other reasons for preferring gold in that, like other conservative economists, he was sure that the price of silver was going to drop. If it did while bimetallism was still in force, silver owners would then melt their bullion and have it transformed into silver dollars for payments of debts, causing price structures to collapse, while trade with Europe (which needed to be handled with gold) would suffer and the government supplies of gold would be drained.[13] "To prevent this, the Linderman-Knox-Garnett school of economists decided that the new mint bill they were preparing should drop the silver dollar from the list of coins that the government would mint," Lavender wrote.[14]

There is no reason not to believe Ralston and Garnett, at least, were aware of the Treasury Department's stand on the adoption of a gold standard and the need to eliminate the standard silver dollar. This position, as previously mentioned, was published in several congressional documents, including John Jay Knox's report, which was part of the original bill submitted to Congress, and was freely espoused by Linderman, who spent a considerable portion of his time on the Pacific coast, holding frequent discussions with the bullion interests, including Ralston and Garnett.

They were also attuned to the problems created by too much silver in circulation and too little gold. Since the first years of the Comstock, silver had been somewhat of a drug on the Pacific coast. In 1869, the Bank of California and Wells Fargo reacted by restricting the amount they would take in payment of debts. While the rest of the country anxiously awaited the resumption of specie payments and the removal of fractional notes, the West was often buried in the white metal and left looking for ways to get rid of it. The Trade dollar seemed to offer a real solution.

In late 1874, Linderman was again back in California, this time in preparation for the opening of the new San Francisco Mint at Fifth and Mission streets. Of its formal transfer from the construction crew to Mint Superintendent O.H. La Grange (planned for Nov. 6), the Oct. 29, 1874, *Alta California* reported, "The Director [Linderman] expresses his determination to so arrange Mint matters on this coast as to insure the coinage of trade dollars in such quantities as will meet the increasing demand of the same."[15] All were hopeful in the West that the Trade dollar would soon be keeping the new mint's presses running non-stop, as the heavier silver coin won respect in overseas markets and solved the problems of an overabundant silver supply.

Chapter 17

FAILED EXPERIMENT

In late 1872, the promoters of the Trade dollar were only able to make an educated guess as to the hidden potential of yet untapped ore pockets that lay below the Comstock, and they justly believed that the introduction of the Trade dollar would go a long way toward shoring up the value of silver. But by 1876, further demonetizations and restrictions placed on silver's use by the Latin Monetary Union, made it apparent this was unlikely to happen. The economic depression had worsened, demonetized foreign silver glutted and clogged world marketplaces, vast increases in the domestic production of silver threatened to still further erode silver's already unstable value, and the ill-fated Trade dollar was beginning to enter domestic circulation in the United States. It was a recipe for disaster in which the Trade dollar was a key ingredient.[1]

The Trade dollar's failure to gain acceptance and use over its competitor, the Mexican dollar, would not have been as devastating had it remained a mere bullion coin with no legal tender quality. However, the Coinage Act of 1873 had allowed the bullion piece the same $5 legal tender limit given the nation's subsidiary silver coins; therefore, even before the Chinese fully rejected the Trade dollar, it was placed into circulation in the United States as a legal tender coin, something its originators professed to have hoped to avoid. Upon entering circulation, the Trade dollar fell immediately to discount, in the face of weak silver prices and its lack of acceptance in payment of government obligations.

Bullion brokers were quick to grasp that they could make huge profits by unloading millions of the depreciated Trade dollars on the unsuspecting public at the coin's stated face value. Trade dollars, which could be purchased at 80 to 90 cents (depending on the silver market and the trade locality), were especially popular with unscrupulous employers who realized a decided advantage by paying their employees' wages in the cheapened silver coins. The unwanted Trade dollars at first became a nuisance to bankers and merchants in the West, who, in order to avoid loss, either had to totally refuse to accept the coins or take them only at a large discount.[2] Not long after, the problem spread eastward.

Still, even with these problems, many on the Pacific coast remained hopeful that the Trade dollar

In the early years of its coinage, many of the Trade dollars were shipped to China. The Carson City Mint struck 124,500 of the coins in 1873. Today gem specimens are scarce.

and silver could recover. The April 14, 1876, issue of the *San Francisco Post* reported:

> The shipment by the steamship Lotus yesterday was one of the largest made in some time. Nearly $700,000 in silver, over one-third of which was in trade-dollars, was exported to Hongkong on speculation by the Chinese merchants of this city, and it is estimated that a sum nearly as large will go out by the next steamer. It was stated yesterday that the Bank of California, London and San Francisco Bank, Nevada Bank and other heavy banking institutions were refusing to sell silver coin, and were hoarding it for the purpose of meeting the demands of business, as silver coin was scarce. Inquiry at those institutions shows that the banks are not hoarding, but at nearly every one of them the same reply is given, to the effect that silver is much scarcer than the public imagine.[3]

The *Post* suggested that, although a great deal of stress had been placed on the enormous amount of silver being extracted from the Bonanza mines, world silver production had been falling off as compared to gold. It wrote:

> Take the six years closing with 1875 and the annual average yield of gold was $104,000,000, while that of silver was only $63,500,000, [it] looks as if the plethora in silver in the market just now was owing to artificial causes and could not last, because the yield of silver is not sufficient to keep it permanently at that point. There is not the slightest danger of its depreciation, but every reason to expect the appreciation from the moment of its monetization on a large scale in this country.[4]

Three months later, in July 1876, silver fell off drastically, the bullion value of a 412 1/2-grain silver dollar bottoming at 79 cents. In an ill-conceived attempt to fix the problems with the Trade dollar without ending its coinage, Congress passed the Act of July 22, 1876, revoking the coin's legal tender status and restricting its coinage to the amount needed to meet export demand. This move, however, did not stop its entry into domestic circulation, nor did it provide relief for the holders of millions of the depreciated, and now totally demonetized, trade coins. This would not occur until several years after the Treasury ended regular Trade dollar coinage.

But if others in the country were becoming alarmed, Mint Director Henry R. Linderman was not. He maintained that the coin was continuing to win acceptance in its intended market. Throughout his term as Mint director, Linderman was positive, to the point of exuberance, in each of his annual reports, when it came to discussing the Trade dollar. A good example is his 1877 report, submitted a little more than a year after the coin's legal tender status had been revoked. "The trade-dollar," Linderman wrote, "continues to grow in favor in China, and the demand at San Francisco for the past fiscal year for export to that empire averaged over $687,000 per month, and in some months more than twice that amount was exported."[5] Linderman suggested that the coin would likely someday supplant the Mexican dollar. To demonstrate that there were already signs of this happening, Linderman related that, in October of that year, when a banker in San Francisco telegraphed London asking at what price Mexican dollars could be sold in that city, he learned that there was little demand for that coin for export. Instead, it was being used for melting purposes. Linderman also noted that Chinese residents in San Francisco were paying a 2 percent premium above the price of Mexican dollars for U.S. Trade dollars in London, which confirmed that there was a decided preference for the U.S. Trade dollar.

"The testimony of intelligent bankers, thoroughly familiar with the Chinese exchanges, (recently given before the United States Treasury commission in San Francisco) shows conclusively that the coinage of trade-dollars has been attended with decided advantages both as respects our commercial and mining interests, and there can be no doubt but that it should be continued on a scale equal to the requirements for export to China," Linderman wrote.[6]

In this same report, Linderman, who was by this time arranging large-scale purchases of silver from the bonanza firm for use in U.S. subsidiary coins, quoted from the U.S. Treasury commission investigation, in which he took part, to show that the Trade dollar was making headway in the Orient. In some very leading questions, Linderman and others on the commission tried to tailor the responses from the Pacific coast bankers and bullion interests they interviewed to prove that the Trade dollar was of a great benefit to the country as well as the Pacific coast.

Some of the most convincing testimony in this regard came from M.M. Tomkins, an agent for the Hong Kong and Shanghai Bank, who had formerly worked as a bullion exchange clerk for the Bank of California. Tomkins told the commission that the great demand in the last three years for silver had been in the China trade and that it had become more advantageous to buy that silver in San Francisco than in London—a demand that did not exist before the Trade dollar. The questioning from the commission chairman continued:

Chopmarks, placed on the coins by merchants in the Orient, attest to the use of these coins as they were originally intended.

Q. You are now [the] agent of a banking corporation with its headquarters in Hong-Kong?—A. Yes, sir.

Q. Its principal place of business is in Hong-Kong?—A. Yes, sir, its head place is there.

Q. Does it have an office in London?—A. Yes, sir; and also in Shanghai, Yokohama, and all through Eastern India.

Q. So far as your knowledge extends, is it or not a fact that the larger portion of bullion for the requirements of your bank in China and Japan is shipped directly from here?—A. Fully one-half; not more. This year there has been a little more shipped from London, as the rate has been more than enough higher here to cover the rate of exchange, interest and all, over there. Last year we shipped more from this port.

Q. What effect on the bullion-market here has the coinage of trade-dollars had, in your judgment?—A. It has been of great benefit to the silver-producers, in bringing silver up in this market.

Q. It has been the means of converting a large amount of silver into a convenient form for shipping?—A. Yes, sir.

Q. They have to a great measure, taken the place of the silver circulating in that country?—A. Yes, sir; they have not thoroughly supplied it, but they are crowding it out of the market, and taking the place of it to some extent.

Q. Trade-dollars are now practically current in Hong-Kong, Canton, Foo-Chow, Ah Mow, and Ong Chow?—A. Yes, sir.

Q. And are working their way as far south as Singapore?—A. Yes, sir; the largest shipments are made to See Kung for the purchase of rice.

Q. How much do you think the silver market here has appreciated? How much benefit are the producers of silver deriving to-day from the mere fact that the government is coining trade-dollars?—A. I should fancy fully the cost of transportation between here and London, 2 per cent.[7]

In questioning by Linderman, the Mint director tried to affirm the need for continued coinage of the Trade dollar:

> Q. Suppose the government [were] to afford facilities for the coinage of as many trade-dollars as the trade required here, converting all of the silver itno [sic; "into"] trade-dollars, what would be the ultimate effect on Mexican silver by diverting it this way instead of to London?—A. If the demand for China was great enough to work them all off, it would necessitate the bringing of Mexican dollars here, or they would bring the crude silver here. That demand for it increases every year.
>
> Q. Then, as a business man, familiar with this entire subject, and viewing it in all of its points, do you think it to the advantage of the United States and the Pacific coast to keep up a liberal coinage of these trade-dollars?—A. Decidedly.[8]

In response to further questioning, Tomkins estimated that every $1 million in silver shipped from San Francisco to the Orient "leaves about $30,000 in San Francisco in refining charges and commissions, rates, &c."[9]

Ironically, while Linderman worked to portray the Trade dollar's future as a rosy one, Treasury Secretary John Sherman, to whom Linderman submitted his report, was calling for an end to its coinage. In his aforementioned Dec. 3, 1877, Treasurer's report, Sherman wrote of problems with the coin:

> By the coinage act of 1873 any person may deposit silver bullion at the mint to be coined into trade-dollars of the weight of 420 grains troy, upon the payment of the cost of coinage. This provision was made at a time when such a dollar was worth in the market $1 02 13/100 in gold, and was designed for the use of trade of China, where silver was the only standard. By the joint resolution of July 22, 1876, passed when the trade-dollar in market value had fallen greatly below one dollar in gold, it was provided that it should not be thereafter a legal tender, and the Secretary of the Treasury was authorized 'to limit the coinage thereof to such an amount as he may deem sufficient to meet the export demand for the same.' Under these laws the amount of trade-dollars issued, mainly for exportation, was $30,710,400. In October last it became apparent that there was no further export demand for trade-dollars, but deposits of silver bullion were made, and such dollars were demanded of the mint for circulation in the United States, that the owner might secure the difference between the value of such bullion in the market and United States notes. At the time, the mints were fully occupied by the issue of fractional and other coins on account of the Government. Therefore, under the authority of the law referred to, the Secretary directed that no further issues of trade-dollars should be made until necessary again to meet an export demand. In case another silver dollar is authorized, the Secretary recommends that the trade-dollar be discontinued.[10]

Linderman had acknowledged, in his report, that there was some problem with the coins entering domestic circulation and that there had been an order from the Treasury secretary to suspend coinage in October. But while the Treasury secretary claimed it was because of a lack of export demand and called for termination of the Trade dollar, Linderman apparently viewed the suspension as temporary. "There are weighty reasons why the trade-dollar should not be coined for domestic circulation," Linderman wrote, "but it is hardly worth while to state them, since the law provides very clearly that they shall be coined only to meet the export demand, and leaves no discretion as to their coinage for any other purpose."[11]

In the following year's report, while Treasury Secretary Sherman was announcing that as many as 4 million Trade dollars had been placed in circulation in the states east of the Rocky Mountains and more were likely to return from China, Linderman maintained a positive front, continuing to promote the coin's overseas successes. In a joint letter from the Oriental Bank Corporation and the Hong Kong and Shanghai Banking Corporation, published with his Mint director's report, a representative of one of the banks was so effusive over the success of the Trade dollar that it leaves more of the taste of a piece commissioned by Linderman and supporters of the coin than a legitimate report. The representative exclaimed:

> Late advices from San Francisco report that so great is the demand for trade-dollars for shipment to China, that the California mint is unequal to the task of turning out the coin fast enough to satisfy requirements. This is, in our estimation, evidence powerful enough to convince the most skeptical as to whether the United States trade-dollar has been a success or not. It is the best dollar we have ever seen here, and as there can be no doubt as to the standard and purity being maintained, it will become more popular day by day, and, we doubt not, ultimately find its way into the north of China, where the people are prejudice against innovation. Trade-dollars are current by count at Singapore, Penang, Bangkok, and Saigon; they are current by weight at Swatow, Amoy, Foochow, and Canton. In Hong-Kong they are not a legal tender, and the banks will only take them from each other by special arrangement; but the Chinese take them freely in Hong-Kong when they want coin of any description, which is very seldom, as they prefer bank-notes, and only take coin from the banks when they require to export it from the colony. In the South of China, the Straits and Cochin China, the trade-dollar is well known and passes without comment along with the clean [not chopmarked] Mexican dollars, but in Shanghai and the northern ports it is unknown, and is not likely to be current for a length of time.
>
> My opinion is that ultimately it will be current all over China; it is the best coin that ever has been

China produced very little gold and silver coinage during this period. Large copper cash coins and shoe-shaped silver ingots, known as sycee silver, served as currency in many parts of the country.

> imported, and, being produced at the fountain-head of silver, can be laid down more cheaply than any other dollar. The reliable character of the coin (for weight or purity) is a further consideration which might be favorably entertained.
>
> China requires many millions of dollars annually, and while the clean Mexican dollar will be imported for the North of China, the trade-dollar will be imported for the South. I would roughly estimate that the San Francisco steamers will bring from four to six lacs (four to six thousand) of trade-dollars each fortnightly trip, all the year round. I base this estimate upon the experience of last season's requirements.[12]

Linderman said this and other testimony he reproduced elsewhere in his report, "establish satisfactorily the fact that the trade-dollar has proved beneficial to the Chinese, the American merchant, and the producer of silver."[13] However, the reports Linderman referred to are a bit less enthusiastic and generally recorded a lack of circulation, except in southern ports.

In response to requests for information on the use of the Trade dollar made by U.S. Minister to China George F. Seward, writing on July 1, 1878, from Peking, Chester Holcombe replied, "From these you will see that the coin in question has obtained no circulation in China, except at Amoy, Canton, Foo-Chow, Swatow, and the Formosa ports" where it was preferred to the Mexican dollar.[14] From Amoy on May 2, 1878, consul J.A. Henderson observed, "The American trade-dollar is and has been for more than two years past in use at the ports in this consular district, though not so extensively as the Mexican."[15] From Chinkiang on March 12,

1878, consul J.C.S. Colby wrote, "In response to the inquiry made in your No. 27, in regard to trade-dollars, I beg to say that there are none in circulation at this port, and, from the best information I can gather on the subject, any effort to introduce them commercially would be attended with a considerable loss to the introducer, as they would not be received except at a discount of at least five per cent. as compared with the Mexican dollar, now in universal use here."[16] Council Isaac F. Shepard responded on March 8, 1878, from Hankow, "...I have to report, from inquiries of merchants and the bank, I cannot learn that an American trade-dollar was ever seen in Hankow."[17] Frederick Baudinel, U.S. vice-consul from Newchwang, replied, on Feb. 27, 1878, "...I have the honor to state, the trade-dollar has come into circulation at this port, but only to a very limited extent; it is sold at a premium as a curiosity to dealers from the interior, but can only be passed at a discount in general business."[18] The vice chairman of the Shanghai Chamber of Commerce, F.B. Forbes, wrote, on March 30, 1878, "The dollar has been imported in small quantities and has failed to make its way, having always been refused at its full value, while application to the Taoutai for assistance in introducing it has led to no result beyond a declaration of the inability of the officials to move in the matter, as the currency of this port for trade purposes in sycee silver."[19] Similarly, U.S. consul O.N. Denny responded from Tientsin on Feb. 14, 1878:

> In reply to your dispatch of the 5th instant, I have the honor to say that the American trade-dollar is not known as a circulating medium at this port. As you are aware, nothing will be received in payment of obligations in the interior but sycee silver or copper cash, and the same rule is also observed at this port in most all transactions.[20]

As he had in his prior year's report, Linderman again acknowledged there had been a problem with Trade dollars entering domestic circulation. This began, he said, in late 1877, when "the larger portion" of a mintage of Trade dollars at San Francisco (estimated, by Sherman, at 4 million coins) that were supposed to have been shipped to China were instead sent by bullion depositors to the Mississippi Valley and eastern states. Still, Linderman urged the continued coinage of the Trade dollar, restricted for export, as the coin had "attained such a favorable position in China, it would not appear to be advisable to repeal the law authorizing its coinage."[21]

By the time regular production of the Trade dollar finally ended, in 1878, the unwanted coins had gravitated eastward, congregating in sections of the country where the majority of citizens were either illiterate or unaware of the coin's true value. Five years after regular coinage ended, the Trade dollar was still such a burden that the *New York Times* lamented, on June 6, 1883:

> It is a curious illustration of how firmly a vicious form of currency can get itself rooted in this country that at a meeting of the produce trade yesterday, there was a decided difference of opinion as to the proposition to refuse trade dollars at par. These nondescript and bastard coins, which are no more legal tender than are the Japanese yen, which, moreover, are worth less than their nominal value, still circulate in considerable quantities. The Post

The 1878-CC is a Trade dollar series key. Almost half of its 97,000 mintage is believed to have been melted prior to the coin's release.

> Office, of course, does not take them; they are refused on railways running out of town, on the elevated roads, and on some of the horse car roads, but they still maintain their hold in the retail trade. As they were coined purely on private account, everyone of them now in circulation has yielded a fraudulent profit to some swindler. One controlling influence in maintaining them is that of the fact that the Government of the United States every month swindles the people in a like manner, through the 'standard dollar' out of $400,000, or the snug sum of $5,000,000 a year.[22]

The beginning of the bimetallic agitation, which, by 1878, provided a partial victory to the forces of free silver, through the passage of the Bland-Allison Act, requiring the government to purchase at market value between $2 million to $4 million worth of silver per month (to be used for the production of full legal tender standard 412 1/2-grain silver dollars), led to a rather ironic and financially ridiculous episode in American monetary history. As the lighter silver dollars were readily received as full legal tender, their heavier, and intrinsically more valuable, counterparts, the Trade dollars, were shunned and excluded. Many of the unwanted coins, after being purchased at a discount, found their way back to the melting pots, where they were magically transformed into the beloved, but lighter-weight Morgan silver dollars.

All told, John M. Willem Jr. determined that, "as of July 1, 1881, the United States had minted 35,963,558 Trade Dollars, including 8,758 proof pieces for collectors. Of these, 27,700,754 had been exported, 2,074,812 of these had come back, leaving a total in the United States of 10,337,616 pieces."[23] Beginning in 1878, Willem said, Congress began receiving petitions urging government redemption of the unwanted Trade dollars.

A memorial that graphically illustrates the problem caused by their circulation and the irony of the situation was submitted to Congress by the New York Mercantile Exchange. On Feb. 3, 1883, its members complained:

> We are put to great inconvenience and pecuniary loss by a coin known as the trade dollar, which is not a legal tender in payment of debts, and which, not withstanding, is so largely received and recognized as a dollar by the community that we cannot without loss of trade individually refuse to accept it in payment, and which, being not taken on deposit by the banks, and not accepted in payment of dues to the Government, we are compelled to sell at a discount.
>
> Some persons employing operatives make a practice of buying at a discount these coins and paying them at par value to their operatives, who again pay them to retailers of goods, and these, again pay them to us, and we, not being able to deposit them or pay them in large amounts to our creditors, are compelled to sell them to brokers at a discount for legal money. It results that there is a continual loss falling upon us, and a corresponding profit reaped by such unscrupulous persons.
>
> The United States Government coined and put into circulation said trade dollars, made them a limited legal tender, and subsequently repudiated them by taking away their legal-tender function and refusing to receive them for its own duties.
>
> The present status of this coin causes it to be a nuisance to us and disgrace to the nation. It seems to us absurd that a coin containing 420 grains of coin silver should be refused the legal-tender function as a dollar, and be forced thereby to a discount, while a coin containing 7 1/2 grains less of coin silver should be given that function, and thereby kept at par.

After 1878, Trade dollar coinage consisted of proofs for collectors.

> We respectfully urge upon Congress that it restore to the trade dollar its legal tender function, and that it receive it and issue silver certificates for the standard silver dollar.[24]

The severity of the Trade dollar problem was such that President Chester A. Arthur called for their redemption in his 1884 message to Congress, saying:

> While trade-dollars have ceased, for the present at least, to be an element of active disturbance in our currency system, some provision should be made for their surrender to the Government. In view of the circumstances under which they were coined and of the fact that they have never had a legal-tender quality [sic], there should be offered for them only a slight advance over their bullion value.[25]

In his 1884 Treasurer's report, Treasury Secretary Hugh McCulloch wrote:

> The Secretary suggests that the existence of the anomalous trade-dollars should be no longer tolerated. Originally coined for purposes of foreign trade, and given a limited legal-tender quality in this country, they have not only been deprived of that quality by law, but have also ceased to perform the function for which they were created.
>
> Some million of them, variously estimated at from six to ten, are held in various parts of the country, awaiting the action of Congress. Although intrinsically more valuable than the standard dollar, their bullion value is only about 86 cents. If it be considered unfair or impracticable to accomplish their surrender at their bullion value merely, a small advance on that value might be offered for them. The offer should not remain open longer than one year.[26]

The 1884 and 1885 proof Trade dollars are legendary rarities. Just 10 of the 1884 coins are known and five of the 1885s. An 1885 Trade dollar sold at auction in 1997 for $907,000.

After almost 10 years of waiting, holders of the unwanted Trade dollars—coins Linderman had once declared to Ralston could prove to be "the most important economic event for California that has yet happened"—were rewarded for their patience on March 3, 1887, when Congress agreed to a six-month redemption period in which Trade dollars could be exchanged at the mint for standard silver dollars, or subsidiary silver coins, at face value. By this method, Willem estimated, one-fifth of the original mintage was eventually redeemed.

Collecting Trade Dollars

If you are interested in collecting a coin with an exotic history, few U.S. coins can top the Trade dollar. Despite its poor 19th century reputation, many collectors are drawn to this series by Mint engraver William Barber's attractive design and the pure romance of a coin that was used in the Orient. Struck for commercial use only from 1873-1878, the series features a number of relatively low-mintage dates that are quite scarce, even in circulated grades. Unlike the Morgan dollar series, where certain dates and mints can be collected in circulated grades for under $20, all of the Trade dollars retail at above $100, even in the lowest collectible grades. In Mint State-65, there are several noted rarities, including all of the Carson City dates.

As millions of these coins went overseas, many were mutilated with chopmarks, applied by Chinese merchants, and thousands of others either never returned or were transformed into Morgan dollars. Therefore, mintage figures can be deceptive. The 1878-CC, considered a series key, shows an official mintage of 97,000, however, it is believed that nearly half of the mintage was melted prior to release. Mintages provided here are for regular-issue coins, not proofs.

After 1878, only proof issues for collectors were struck. The series ended in 1885. The 1884 and 1885 proofs are legendary rarities. Only 10 of the 1884 coins are known and just five of the 1885s. An example of the 1885, graded Proof-65, brought $907,500 in a 1997 auction.

Pieces bearing chopmarks—sometimes obliterating the design—generally bring lower values. However, from a purely historical sense, the "chops" identify that the coin at least saw service in the Far East, as was its original intent, and, therefore, are fascinating in their own right.

Prices given here represent current retail prices at the time of publication as compiled for *Coin Prices* magazine. All prices are approximates of what you can expect to pay a dealer to obtain one of the coins (they are not offers to buy or sell) and may vary with subsequent upward or downward movements in a particular series or the coin market as a whole. Prices can and do vary from dealer to dealer, as well.

As with other U.S. coin series, slight differences in grade can mean hundreds, or thousands, of dollars in value. Learning to grade is crucial to any successful venture into the coin market. Check the section on Morgan dollar collecting for listings of some helpful references to grading and counterfeit detection, along with additional collecting tips.

While there are a number of reference books that focus on the Morgan and Peace dollar series, there are very few that look at the Trade dollar. A classic in the field is John M. Willem Jr.'s *The United States Trade Dollar: America's Only Unwanted, Unhonored Coin,* published by the author in 1959 but now available in reprint. A recent work, the two-volume *Silver Dollars & Trade Dollars of the United States: A Complete Encyclopedia* by Q. David Bowers, provides in-depth analysis of each date and mint, including the various varieties.

TRADE DOLLAR PROFILE

1873

Mints: Philadelphia (397,500), Carson City (124,500), San Francisco (703,000). **Timeline**: President Ulysses S. Grant begins his second term in office. Coinage Act of 1873 signed into law on Feb. 12. Congress censors congressmen Oakes Ames and James Brooks for their involvement in the Crédit Mobilier scandal. Congress passes the "Salary Grab" Act, raising congressmen's salaries retroactive to the beginning of the term. The act is later repealed. In September, Panic of 1873 begins a six-year economic depression. New York brokerage firms begin closing their doors late in the year with the failure of the prominent banking firm of Jay Cooke & Company. William Marcy "Boss" Tweed is convicted on 102 counts of fraud. Jules Verne's *20,000 Leagues Under the Sea* is published. Memorial Day is recognized as a legal holiday in New York. Survivor wins the first Preakness Stakes. **Average commercial ratio of silver to gold:** 15.93 to 1**. Average value of silver in standard 412 1/2-grain dollar:** 1.03.

Date	G-4	VG-8	F-12	VF-20	XF-40	AU-50	MS-60	MS-63	MS-65	Prf-60	Prf-65
1873	100.	110.	125.	165.	250.	325.	1000.	3500.	12,000.	1750.	12,000.
1873CC	150.	175.	225.	450.	700.	1200.	2100.	25,000.	80,000.	-	-
1873S	130.	145.	160.	180.	260.	375.	1200.	6000.	25,000.	-	-

1874

Mints: Philadelphia (987,800), Carson City (1,373,200), San Francisco (2,549,000). **Timeline**: Mark Twain and Charles Warner characterize the post-Civil War era as The Gilded Age, one of political corruption and economic speculation. Grange agitation leads to passage in Wisconsin of the Potter law, regulating intrastate freight rates. Passage of a currency act restricts the number of greenbacks in circulation to $382 million. Barbed wire is invented by Joseph F. Glidden, forever changing the open range. Thomas Nast uses an elephant in one of his *Harper's Weekly* cartoons to symbolize the Republican Party. The Greenback Party is organized in Indianapolis. Philadelphia opens the first public zoo in the United States. Gold discovery in Black Hills confirmed. **Average commercial ratio of silver to gold:** 16.16 to 1**. Average value of silver in standard 412 1/2-grain dollar:** 99 cents.

Date	G-4	VG-8	F-12	VF-20	XF-40	AU-50	MS-60	MS-63	MS-65	Prf-60	Prf-65
1874	120.	130.	150.	185.	240.	340.	700.	3500.	15,000.	1000.	12,000.
1874CC	80.00	90.00	105.	165.	240.	350.	1000.	5500.	40,000.	-	-
1874S	70.00	80.00	95.00	120.	165.	250.	675.	3000.	30,000.	-	-

1875

Mints: Philadelphia (218,900), Carson City (1,573,700), San Francisco (4,487,000). **Timeline**: Congress passes the Specie Resumption Act, which reduces the number of greenbacks in circulation from $382 million to $300 million. Specie payments are to resume by Jan. 1, 1879. Coinage of the 20-cent piece is authorized by Congress. The "Whiskey Ring" is revealed, a conspiracy between distillery owners and U.S. Internal Revenue Service officers to defraud the government through nonpayment of Federal liquor taxes. More than 200 indictments are handed down. William "Boss" Tweed escapes from prison and flees to Cuba. The first Kentucky Derby is held at Churchill Downs, Ky. Aristides wins. **Average commercial ratio of silver to gold:** 16.64 to 1**. Average value of silver in standard 412 1/2-grain dollar:** 96 cents.

Date	G-4	VG-8	F-12	VF-20	XF-40	AU-50	MS-60	MS-63	MS-65	Prf-60	Prf-65
1875	260.	350.	425.	525.	675.	800.	1850.	4000.	13,000.	1050.	6500.
1875CC	80.00	90.00	105.	130.	200.	375.	900.	3000.	40,000.	-	-
1875S	60.00	70.00	85.00	100.	120.	210.	500.	1250.	7000.	-	-
1875S/CC	275.	325.	400.	525.	695.	1100.	1900.	-	-	-	-

1876 **Mints**: Philadelphia (456,150), Carson City (509,000), San Francisco (5,227,000). **Timeline**: Congress strips legal-tender status from Trade dollar, as millions of the coins begin to circulate in the United States. Greenback Party holds its first national convention in Indianapolis, Ind. It nominates Peter Cooper of New York for president and Samuel Carey of Ohio for vice president. Republican Rutherford B. Hayes faces off against Democratic Samuel J. Tilden in a disputed election. William "Boss" Tweed is captured in Spain and returned to the United States to serve out the remainder of his sentence. Alexander Graham Bell receives patent for the telephone. Centennial celebrations are held with an exposition in Philadelphia. Gen. George Armstrong Custer loses his life and all of his command in the Battle of the Little Bighorn. Richard P. Bland introduces a measure calling for restoration of the free and unlimited coinage of silver. Colorado becomes the 38th state in Union. **Average commercial ratio of silver to gold:** 17.75 to 1. **Average value of silver in standard 412 1/2-grain dollar:** 90 cents.

Date	G-4	VG-8	F-12	VF-20	XF-40	AU-50	MS-60	MS-63	MS-65	Prf-60	Prf-65
1876	70.00	80.00	100.	125.	165.	400.	675.	1250.	7500.	1050.	6500.
1876CC	125.	145.	180.	220.	325.	450.	2100.	20,000.	75,000.	-	-
1876S	60.00	70.00	85.00	100.	120.	210.	475.	1250.	10,000.	-	-

1877 **Mints**: Philadelphia (3,039,710), Carson City (534,000), San Francisco (9,519,000). **Timeline**: President Rutherford B. Hayes is officially named president by the newly created Electoral Commission and is inaugurated as the nation's 19th President. Federal troops are withdrawn from the South as "carpetbag" rule ends. Chief Joseph of the Nez Percé Indians surrenders after a four-month retreat in an attempt to reach Canada. He is only a few miles short of his goal when forced to surrender to save the tribe's women and children. B&O railroad workers strike in Martinsburg, W.Va., protesting against a cut in wages and an increase in rail cars. Gov. Henry M. Mathews calls out the militia, but workers stop the train carrying the troops from leaving the station, setting the station on fire. Twelve people are killed. Flag Day is observed for the first time this year. **Average commercial ratio of silver to gold:** 17.20 to 1. **Average value of silver in standard 412 1/2-grain dollar:** 93 cents.

Date	G-4	VG-8	F-12	VF-20	XF-40	AU-50	MS-60	MS-63	MS-65	Prf-60	Prf-65
1877	60.00	70.00	85.00	105.	130.	210.	525.	1750.	16,000.	2000.	19,000.
1877CC	130.	150.	190.	260.	370.	600.	1275.	12,000.	70,000.	-	-
1877S	60.00	70.00	85.00	100.	120.	210.	475.	1250.	8000.	-	-

1878 **Mints**: Philadelphia (900, all proofs), Carson City (97,000), San Francisco (4,162,000). **Notes:** 1878-CC—44,148 Trade dollars were melted at Carson City in 1878, possibly 1878-CCs. **Timeline**: John Sherman, head of the Senate Finance Committee during the Coinage Act of 1873's stay in Congress, is selected by President Rutherford B. Hayes to fill the post of Treasury secretary. Reacting to the strikes of the prior year, the Knights of Labor is formed in an attempt to organize all workers into a single union. California Sen. Aaron Sargent introduces an amendment to Constitution that would have allowed women the right to vote. It finally wins approval in 1919. Thomas Edison receives a patent for the phonograph and organizes the first electric light company. The first commercial telephone exchange is opened in New Haven, Conn. The Greenback Labor Party, a coalition of the Greenback and National parties, forms in Toledo, Ohio, and calls for the free coinage of silver. The Bland-Allison Act is passed. Coinage of the Morgan silver dollar begins shortly thereafter. **Average commercial ratio of silver to gold:** 17.92 to 1. **Average value of silver in standard 412 1/2-grain dollar:** 89 cents.

Date	G-4	VG-8	F-12	VF-20	XF-40	AU-50	MS-60	MS-63	MS-65	Prf-60	Prf-65
1878	-	Proof only	-	1100.	1250.	1500.	-	-	-	3200.	22,000.
1878CC	425.	525.	675.	850.	1750.	2100.	5500.	13,500.	67,500.		-
1878S	60.00	70.00	85.00	100.	120.	210.	475.	1250.	7000.	-	-

Date	G-4	VG-8	F-12	VF-20	XF-40	AU-50	MS-60	MS-63	MS-65	Prf-60	Prf-65
1879	-	Proof only	-	900.	950.	1100.	-	-	-	2450.	22,000.
1880	-	Proof only	-	900.	950.	1100.	-	-	-	2450.	19,500.
1881	-	Proof only	-	950.	1000.	1250.	-	-	-	3000.	20,000.
1882	-	Proof only	-	950.	1000.	1250.	-	-	-	3100.	20,000.
1883	-	Proof only	-	1100.	1200.	1400.	-	-	-	3200.	20,000.
1884	-	Proof only						Eliasberg, Apr. 1997, Prf-66, $396,000.			--
1885	-	Proof only						Eliasberg, Apr. 1997, Prf-65, $907,500.			--

Chapter 18

SAVING SILVER

Following the Civil War, most monetary conservatives favored a resumption of specie payments but were in disagreement on how to achieve this goal. Hugh McCulloch, who rose to the post of Treasury secretary in 1865, hoped for a quick resumption (believing that the federal paper issues were merely war-time expedients) but ran into trouble with his contraction policy, which brought the number of outstanding United States notes down from approximately $400 million (the war-time high had been $449 million in mid-1864) to $352 million. The rapid tightening of the money supply was too much and was halted by Congress in 1868.[1]

Among the problems Congress faced with legislating a return to specie payments was the enormous war debt. In 1860, before war broke out, the national debt stood at just shy of $65 million but by 1865 it had ballooned to nearly $2.7 billion.[2] Most of this was interest-bearing debt, based on war-time bond sales, and finding a method to either pay off the debt, or (as ended up being the case) spreading its dismissal out over a number of years through additional bond sales, would slow any return to specie payments until the Treasury's gold reserves could grow and the debt be safely reduced.

To prevent any moves by those who advocated paying off the debt in paper money, and calm public fears, Congress passed the Public Credit Act in 1869, asserting that the government "solemnly pledges its faith to make provision at the earliest practicable period for the redemption of United States notes in coin."[3] Under Treasury Secretary George S. Boutwell's leadership, the administration made no further advances toward a rapid retirement of greenbacks, the Treasury secretary apparently preferring to allow time for the economy to improve and public credit to strengthen in the hope that both would eventually return federal paper to parity with gold and allow their redemption without draining the Treasury's gold reserves.[4] By the time Dr. Henry R. Linderman was appointed Mint director, in 1873, Boutwell had, however, left the Treasury and Assistant Treasury Secretary William A. Richardson had taken over.

Though the economy remained strong, silver, as Linderman predicted, had begun to slip; the bullion value of a silver dollar dropping to a low of 98 cents in 1873, while averaging just above $1. The new Mint director, however, had already formulated a plan to support silver prices and, at the same time, inch the nation closer to specie resumption. Besides promoting export of the metal in the form of the newly authorized Trade dollars, he would set the nation's mints to work producing an increased number of subsidiary silver coins, while making plans, as he had told William C. Ralston in 1872, to place the coins in circulation in lieu of the millions of fractional notes still outstanding.

There were some good reasons for doing so—speculative and practical. First, Linderman believed that the issuance of $50 million in subsidiary silver coins (in place of the like ceiling on fractionals) would help bolster the price of silver and, thereby, aid the nation's mining industry. Second, the life expectancy of the fractional notes, issued in three-, five-, 10-, 15-, 25- and 50-cent denominations, was only nine months as compared with coins, which, it was judged, could withstand 50 years of circulation, cutting replacement costs. Third, if specie resumption were to some day be ordered, as most in the Treasury hoped, a ready supply of silver coins, issuable on demand, would be needed.

Despite the intentionally limiting aspects of Section 28 of the Coinage Act of 1873, Linderman wasted no time instituting his own liberal interpretation of when the subsidiary coinage exchange provisions of that portion of the coinage law should take effect and how they could best be reconfigured to benefit the nation. Under John Jay Knox's final draft of what became Section 28 of the mint bill, subsidiary silver coins were to be issued only in exchange for gold coins and in sums of not less than $100. This limitation was placed

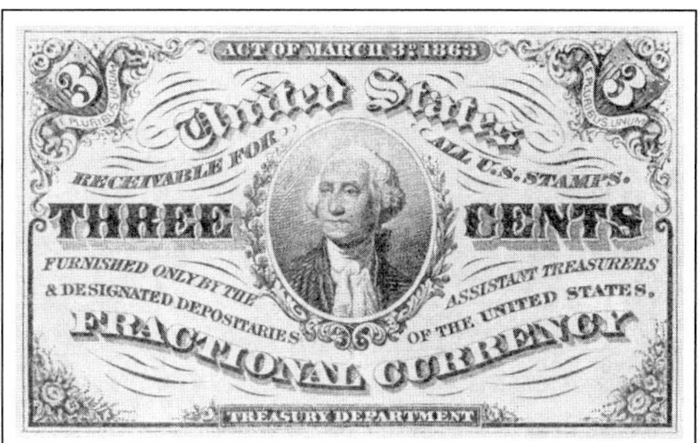

Fractional paper notes had been issued since the days of the Civil War. They came in a variety of denominations.

there with special emphasis by Knox because the prior illegal, but generally followed, practice of allowing the exchange of silver bullion for subsidiary coins had, at times, placed too many of the coins in circulation. The Act of 1853 had reduced the weight of the silver half dimes, dimes, quarters and half dollars to a 384-grain subsidiary level and given the coins a restricted legal tender status in an attempt to keep the coins in domestic circulation. It also established a bullion fund by which any silver needed for coinage could be purchased by the mint at market value and in exchange for gold—the intent being to limit the number of coins to what was actually required for circulation.

The first of several directors to subvert this provision was Mint Director George N. Eckert, who, in the early 1850s, began buying silver above market value and in exchange for the new subsidiary silver coins. The country was soon flooded with subsidiary silver coins that, due to their legal tender

Arrows and Rays

With the discovery of gold in California, and in Australia, Congress' attempts to find a suitable mint ratio for precious metals were dashed, as the intrinsic value of the dollar rose to $1.03. Since the minor silver coinage contained the fractional equivalent of silver in the dollar-sized coin, the minor coins also became subject to melting and exportation. The country was thus quickly denuded of silver.

In California, one contemporary observed that, in the early 1850s, silver was in such irregular supply that "the shrewdest operators" imported silver coins from France, Spain and Mexico, to be used as change. The coins were judged by size, so a French five-franc, Mexican dollar, and any coin of a similar size passed as a dollar, while half dollars and their equivalents were scarce, being in heavy demand by gamblers. "This forced such a premium that eighteen dollars in silver would commonly bring twenty dollars in gold," according to this observer.[1]

In an attempt to alleviate the problem and return silver coins to circulation, in 1853 Congress authorized a reduction in the weight of the minor silver coins to 384 grains, while retaining the dollar at full weight. To denote the change, arrows were added at the date on the Seated Liberty half dimes, dimes, quarters and halves. The quarter and half dollar also featured a glory of rays surrounding the eagle for the 1853 coinage. The arrows were retained on all of these coins through 1855. Rare examples exist, struck in 1853, at the former weight and without the arrows or rays. The 1853-O half dollar without arrows, of which only three specimens are known to exist, is a celebrated rarity in this regard.

In 1853 all of the nation's silver coins, except the dollar, were reduced in weight to a 384-grain subsidiary level.

George N. Eckert, Philadelphia Mint director from 1851-1853, was the first to allow the illegal exchange of silver bullion for subsidiary silver coins.

status of just $5 in any one payment and nonacceptance for government obligations, immediately fell in value.

The overabundance of subsidiary silver coin was, however, to be short-lived. In 1858, Canada adopted a decimal system of coinage, based on the dollar, but lacked the quantity of coins necessary for its implementation. U.S. subsidiary coins filled the void. Additional markets in Latin America and the West Indies had also developed and drew off more of the coins.

With the outbreak of the Civil War, hoarding of all precious-metal coins began, leading to the suspension of specie payments in late 1861, leaving as the basic circulating currency various forms of paper money, including private and state bank notes, and government-issued Demand notes and United States notes. The Demand notes, authorized by Acts of July 17 and Aug. 5, 1861, with more than 7.25 million issued, were not backed by gold but were acceptable in payment of government duties and by a Treasury circular issued just prior to the suspension of specie payments were made payable in coin. The United States notes, which were also known as Legal Tender notes, because of the wording of the payment obligation, were first issued on March 10, 1862. By the end of the war, $432 million were outstanding. (All of these federal paper issues were generally referred to as greenbacks, although the term originated with the Demand notes, which had a green-colored back.)

As the war dragged on, greenbacks depreciated in value against gold, falling at one point to 30 cents on the dollar. As they depreciated, the nation's fractional coins became worth more as bullion than as currency and quickly disappeared from circulation. By mid-1862, subsidiary silver coins were absent from circulation everywhere except on the Pacific coast where there was an overabundance.

As he was drafting the new mint bill, Knox kept in mind the problems caused by the illegal subsidiary coin issues, writing in his report accompanying the bill:

> The act of February 21, 1853, provides that the silver coins of smaller denomination than one dollar 'shall be paid out at the mint in exchange for gold coins at par in sums not less than one hundred dollars.' It was evidently intended that these subsidiary or token coins should be issued only in exchange at par for gold coin. But the practice at the mint for many years has been to purchase all silver bullion offered at about $1 22 1/2 per ounce, which is above the market price, paying therefore in silver coin. The ounce of silver purchased is worth $1 25 in the silver coin issued, weight for weight, so that the government really reserves a seigniorage of two and one-half cents per ounce. The effect of the mint practice has been to put in circulation silver coins without regard to the amount required for the purposes of 'change,' creating a discount upon silver coin, and bringing loss upon holders of any considerable amount. These coins are a legal tender for five dollars, but they are not received at the custom house in payment of duties except for fractional portions of a dollar. The coins thus issued have accumulated, and are now at a large discount in Canada and California, and will again become burdensome at home when brought into circulation. The correct method of issuing silver coin is as was originally contemplated: to purchase with gold such an amount of silver bullion at market rates as is needed for coinage into fractional parts of a dollar; to issue the silver coins only in exchange for gold at par, and to require the manufacture of such coinage to cease whenever there is evidence of a redundancy. In the proposed bill the language is clear and explicit on this point, and these silver coins are made a legal tender for sums less than one dollar.[5]

Rep. Samuel Hooper, who brought the mint bill before the House in April 1872, said similarly:

> Prior to the suspension of specie payments in 1861, silver coins appear to have been issued in excess of the requirements of the public, and were at times sold at a small discount from their nominal value, probably for the reason that they could be obtained at the Mint at less than their nominal value. The principle or system of issuing silver coins at their nominal value, in exchange for gold only, is undoubtedly the correct one, as it gives the Government the benefit of the seigniorage, and restrains their issue to the wants of the public for these subsidiary coins.[6]

However, by the time Hooper was outlining to Congress the proper method for issuing subsidiary silver coins, the measure had already been amended from Knox's original version to allow for a continuation of the exchange of silver for subsidiary coins for another two years. This proviso, or continuation of the "present practice," as Hooper termed it, was necessary, Hooper told Congress, "to meet the special requirement for the subsidiary silver coins in commercial transactions with some of the South American States."[7]

In order to keep additional subsidiary coins from being produced in the West, where the coins had become a nuisance, the proviso limited issuance to the Philadelphia Mint and the New York Assay Office. New York bullion dealers were, of course, pleased with the extension. They had been enjoying a lucrative business taking their silver bullion to the New York Assay Office, which was paying

The over supply of small silver coins created by the illegal exchanges of silver bullion for subsidiary silver coins did not last. With the start of the Civil War, it became hard to get change in most parts of the country. **Frank Leslie's Illustrated Newspaper,** ***April 4, 1863.***

Shown are a Demand note (top) and a United States note.

above market for silver, and exchanging it for subsidiary silver coins that would be immediately exported either to Canada, Latin America or the West Indies. One of these dealers had testified in the prior Congress that he had made $75,000 to $100,000 a year off of the practice.[8]

During the April 9, 1872, debate over the section of the mint bill calling for a uniform copper-nickel minor coinage, Rep. William D. Kelley charged that, since the 1850s, New York bullion dealers had been "growing fat and greedy upon the defects in our Mint laws..."[9] Kelley observed that a change in the coinage system would afford a loss to New York bullion dealers—the only people Kelley believed were likely to object to the proposed changes to the minor coinage or favor retention of the full weight silver dollar. In reference to the defects, Kelley said:

> All other Governments pay the expense of minting by the difference between the intrinsic value of subsidiary coins and the value at which they circulate and at which the Government redeems them. And such was the law of this country until by a ruling of Mr. [James] Guthrie, when he was Secretary of the Treasury [1853-1857], the Mint was ordered to receive silver from private individuals and coin it. Now, it so happens that a constituent of the gentleman from New York [Rep. Clarkson N. Potter] has been taking advantage of that ruling and deposited silver to be made into half dollars and other silver coins; and for every two dollars' worth of silver deposited by him he gets four half dollars and one ten-cent piece, or the equivalent thereof. He has, as he stated to my colleague (Mr. HOOPER, of Massachusetts) and myself, been doing a business of from eighteen hundred thousand to two million dollars per annum, giving him as profit an annual income equal to the salary of the President for the presidential term.[10]

Despite any benefit the proviso gave New York bullion dealers, there was another, unforeseen problem with the extension. It opened the door for Mint Director Linderman to generously adapt the bill's provisions to his own special agenda—namely creating a domestic market for silver by pushing through silver payouts at government offices in place of greenbacks.

The Panic of 1873, which began in September, led to a widespread spate of calls for specie resumption, and Linderman and the Treasury lurched at the opportunity by beginning payments of subsidiary silver, in late October, at government offices. By the time of new Treasury Secretary William A. Richardson's Dec. 1, 1873, report to Congress, the Treasury was in the second month of its campaign to

Preparing the new Demand notes at the U.S. Treasury.* Harper's Weekly, *Oct. 19, 1861.

restore silver to circulation. "The recent fall in the price of gold, together with the depreciation in the market value of silver, as compared with gold, which has been going on for some time, has enabled the Director to coin silver, to be paid out instead of United States notes to advantage," Richardson wrote of their action. "Availing himself of this opportunity, the Director caused to be purchased as much silver bullion as could be conveniently used in giving employment to the mints, when not engaged in the more important business of coining gold, and the same was so coined and paid out."[11]

Outlining his scheme in his Nov. 1, 1873, *Report of the Director of the Mint*, written a few days after the payments began, Linderman was careful to quote only the proviso to Section 28 and not the section's primary restriction concerning issuance.[12] Although he admitted that the proper mode of releasing subsidiary silver coins was in exchange for gold, he suggested that compliance to this be delayed until specie payments resumed. Linderman wrote:

> In the mean time it is quite certain that the depreciation of silver and appreciation of United States currency will, before long, enable the Government to purchase silver bullion with gold, coin it on its own account, and pay out the resulting silver coins at their nominal value. At the present rate for silver and premium on gold, the operation would net the Treasury about 10 per cent. This plan could not, it is believed, do injury to any interest, but would be productive of much benefit to the precious metal mining interests and business of the country at large, and should be adhered to until specie payments shall have been resumed on a substantial basis; after which these coins should be issued only in exchange at par for gold coins, and thus restrict the issue to the actual requirements of the public for the purposes for which such coins are intended.[13]

Thus, as Linderman explained, the government would, from time to time, buy silver bullion at the market value in gold for the manufacture of subsidiary silver coins, which could be paid out in exchange for gold at par in sums of not less than $100 (as provided for in Section 28); the government would also continue to purchase silver bullion to be paid out in subsidiary silver coins for the use of bullion dealers in their shipments to Latin America and elsewhere until Feb. 12, 1875 (as authorized by the proviso to Section 28); and the government would purchase silver bullion at gold value and manufacture it on government account into subsidiary silver coins, which were to be paid out "at the discretion of the Treasury Department and according to its convenience."[14] He explained that the last method was necessary for the government to realize full seigniorage on the issue of subsidiary silver coins by taking advantage of the strong value of paper in relation to silver. What he did not mention, but must have known, was that, although "at the present rate" this plan afforded a profit to the government and a chance that coins could enter and remain in circulation, if silver's value rose above paper, either through an appreciation of silver in relation to gold or a drop in the greenback's value to gold, it would drive the coins out of circulation.

At least for the moment, though, the fall in the value of gold and silver played into Linderman's hands. By October 1873, silver coins began to show up in circulation around the country, startling many in the East who were not familiar with the coins. The Oct. 29, 1873, issue of the *New York Times* reported of silver's sudden reappearance:

> The low price of silver has brought a large amount of it into circulation. Silver dimes, half-dimes, quarters, half-dollars, and even dollars, are given out as change for currency over bar and restaurant counters with the utmost nonchalance by the attendants. People go about chinking the silver coin in their pockets, feeling that they are possessed of money the solid value of which is unmistakable, and it is paid out again more reluctantly than the paper currency in vogue so long. The coin is generally fresh from the Mint, and it is examined critically and with curiosity by many who have never seen American coin before. It is bought by the restaurant-keepers for circulation among their customers, and serves as a good advertisement of the places issuing it.[15]

Around this same time, news emerged from the Treasury that, with the recent fall-off in the value of gold, it was considering release of silver coin over-the-counter at government offices. The Oct. 26, 1873, *New York Times* reported (in a dispatch from Washington datelined Oct. 25) that the Treasury had intended to begin releasing silver the week prior, but preparations were not completed. "The Secretary does not expect that there will be a great demand for the silver," the *Times* related.[16]

The *Times* explained how the payout of silver might commence:

> The Secretary of the Treasury has received many inquiries relative to the contemplated issue by the Treasury Department of silver coin to take the place of currency in making payments by the departments. The Secretary does not know exactly how much will be paid out. He expects that it will be convenient for him, next week, to issue about $200,000, in the regular course of business, but this will depend somewhat upon circumstances. If gold

> should go up, silver would not be paid out, nor would it be sold again to bankers for speculative purposes. It is not to be expected that the Treasury will begin now to pay out silver coin for every purpose, and thus exhaust immediately the entire amount held by the Government. One illustration of the manner of making such payments was presented by the Secretary to-day, who said that if a person should present a check for $225 40, the chances were that he would receive $5 40 of the amount in silver. The determination of the department is to issue silver to whatever extent it can be conveniently done; and as there is bullion sufficient to coin about $200,000, within a week this will be used as a beginning.[17]

In an interesting article in the September 1939 issue of the *Pacific Coast Review*, George L. Anderson cited reports in several contemporary newspapers to show that the Treasury actually intended not only to release silver but to do so in exchange for greenbacks—a step which many apparently viewed as a precursor to a full resumption. "There was a general disposition [at the time] to regard the exchange of silver for greenbacks as the forerunner of gold resumption and the beginnings of a movement to place the business of the country on a hard-money foundation," Anderson wrote. "One writer [in the Nov. 6, 1873, *Augusta Republican*] concluded an expression of this sentiment with the following statement: 'The Goddess of Liberty will once more sport her cap in our pockets, and the soiled photographs of defunct statesmen and financiers return to the vaults of the treasury; and but a little distance behind the white gleam of silver we see the red and yellow glow of returning gold.'"[18]

According to Anderson, the commotion raised by the announcement of the Treasury's scheme led to the department being flooded with requests, from throughout the country, to swap greenbacks for silver. Before such exchanges began, the Treasury, however, backed down. Anderson theorized that it did so because someone at the Treasury realized that any such issue would be illegal. He wrote that Treasury officials discovered the:

> …fact that certain specific provisions of the coinage act of February 12, 1873, prohibited the payment of silver coin except for certain purposes and exchange for paper currency was not included in the list. Under the provision that the subsidiary silver coins were legal tender for amounts not exceeding five dollars they could be paid out to that extend on account of government obligations and a revision of the plan of that nature was ordered in a Treasury circular issued October 27, 1873. It was addressed to the Treasurer of the United States and contained the following order:

> You will please, after the receipt of this letter, and until otherwise ordered, pay public creditors, should they desire it on account of currency obligations, but not in exchange for currency, a sum not to exceed five dollars in any one payment, in silver.[19]

As the Treasury, or least the plan's architect, Linderman, was fully aware of the illegality of the exchange of silver for paper, it is more likely that the *New York Times*' Oct. 29 assessment of why the Treasury changed course is nearer the mark. In a dispatch datelined the day prior, the Oct. 29 *Times* recorded:

> The payment of silver in sums of $5 and under, to the Government creditors, was to-day begun at the Treasury Department. There was, however, no exchange of silver for currency. It was found by the extend of demands that came when the announcement of the intention of the Treasury in this respect was published, that the unlimited payment of silver with the amount of coin on hand, and the limited capacity of the mints in turning out silver coin, was entirely impracticable. As was stated in these dispatches last week, the mints are now employed in coining gold to their fullest capacity, and can do but little with silver till the gold demand is less. It is still hoped that when the coining of silver can be resumed, the exchange of it for currency may safely begin.[20]

The payments were immediately popular. The Oct. 30, 1873, *Times* observed:

> At the Sub-Treasury it was learned that nearly all of the applicants for payment had taken $5 of their dues in silver, as permitted by the late order of Secretary Richardson. A considerable amount of silver was disbursed during the day.
>
> Mr. Floyd, at the Assay Office, had received instructions from Washington to make its bullion fund available as far as practicable in carrying out the project of the Treasury Department for silver resumption. This bullion fund includes about $1,000,000 in silver. The Government can at any time obtain possession of 500,000 ounces of fine silver, which will make $692,000 in coin. The officers of the Philadelphia Mint have been instructed to use two-thirds of its entire capacity in the coinage of silver, and it is expected that from $1,000,000 to $1,500,000 can be turned out every month.
>
> Many large orders had been received for silver, as soon as it is a par with greenbacks, by bankers in New-York, and not only from Texas and the South, but also from large manufacturers throughout the West, who want it in payment of their workmen, and also from the proprietors of New-York hotels, who want it for a similar object.[21]

The Treasury's plan for a silver resumption would be short lived. Not long after Richardson's glowing report to Congress, a fall in the value of paper led silver coins to disappear from circulation, causing the Treasury secretary to suspend further releases.[22]

The failure of the coins to remain in circulation did not go unnoticed. Contemporary newspapers regularly referred sarcastically to the Treasury's failed actions at a specie resumption. For example, the *Alta California* termed it "Richardson's absurdity," and the *San Francisco Chronicle*, called it "Judge Richardson's scheme to resume specie payments without letting the country know it."[23] This, however, did not dissuade Linderman. He pressed ahead with plans to produce and issue subsidiary coins in preparation for the day when full specie resumption would be ordered.

During the period between Linderman's late 1873 report and his following year's submission, the nation slumped deeper into depression, while Congress became mired in debate over the economy. In the wake of this, support for currency inflation mushroomed in Congress, turning a bill introduced by Sen. John Sherman (S617) that would have ordered specie resumption by Jan. 1, 1876, into what came to be known as the "Inflation Bill," restoring the number of greenbacks to pre-McCulloch contraction levels, and eliminating the resumption clause. Grant's subsequent veto and the failure of soft money men to muster the votes to override spelled the end for this hotly debated measure.

With the opening of the second session of the 43rd Congress on Dec. 7, 1874, there would be a renewed push by sound money forces for specie resumption. Linderman, who, through his close ties with key legislators in Congress, was likely aware of plans to push for specie resumption legislation in the upcoming session, wrote in his Oct. 13, 1874, Mint director's report that unless there were a material advance in the price of silver or a depreciation in the gold value of the paper dollar, the mint could continue to avail itself of the method of purchasing and producing subsidiary silver coins he adopted the prior year. Taking advantage of an unusual shortage of subsidiary silver on the Pacific coast, Linderman again broached the idea of a silver resumption, observing that, barring a significant advance in the price of silver or a weakening of paper against gold, the low price of silver assured that the government could, at any time, purchase enough silver at an advantage over issuing paper to begin wide-scale payouts of subsidiary coins. Linderman wrote:

> The first effect of any considerable issue of subsidiary silver coin would be the disappearance in the New York market of the difference between the bullion and market value of these coins. They would next be sent to the Pacific coast and Texas in such amounts as to compel merchants and others to avail themselves of the provision of law limiting the legal tender of such coins to $5. After a time they would begin to enter more or less into general circulation in other sections of the Union, and, as the paper money approached parity with gold, gradually expel the fractional notes.[24]

Noting that the proviso in Section 28, granting a two-year extension to the legalized exchange of silver bullion for silver coins at the Philadelphia Mint and the New York Assay Office would soon expire (Feb. 12, 1875), Linderman advised that it not be renewed because, "the issue of subsidiary and token coins should be entirely under the control of the Government, and kept within such limits as will protect the public from the inconvenience and loss which would attend a redundant issue."[25] The most vitally important factors in preventing this, he said, were a restriction on the amount to which the coins would be accepted as legal tender and limiting the number of coins in circulation to the requirements of the public need for small change.

Admitting once again that such issues should properly only be made in exchange for gold, he reasserted the Treasury's right to coin as many subsidiary silver coins as needed, putting off compliance with the mint bill's issuance provisions until the yet-to-be-determined date of specie resumption, when gold would form the basis of the currency. Until then, he wrote, "...the Government may manufacture on its own account, and under favorable circumstances pay out, silver coins, at its pleasure and convenience, to the extent required to meet any legitimate demands for the same."[26]

In Linderman's mind, the amount manufactured was limited only to what he deemed necessary to supply enough coinage to replace the fractional currency and bolster the silver market, even if these coins went immediately into storage and remained there indefinitely. Linderman added that it was not within the province of his report to consider the question of the substitution of subsidiary silver for fractional notes, which had yet to be authorized. "The determination of the proper time to commence the preparation in that way for a specie basis, as well as the policy and expediency of the measure, will no doubt receive due consideration by the proper authority," he wrote, while assuring that "...the mints are, or soon will be, in condition to meet in a reasonable time all the requirements of the country for coin, and which of course would be augmented when it shall be determined to withdraw the fractional currency."[27]

Two months later, Congress would be locked in a battle over the measure that would come to be known as the Specie Resumption Act. Passed by Congress on Jan. 8, 1875, and signed into law six days later by President Ulysses S. Grant, the act called for a reduction of the number of United States notes in circulation from $382 million to $300 million and allowed the resumption of specie payments after Jan. 1, 1879. Also among its provisions was the authorization for the redemption of the fractional currency with subsidiary silver coins Linderman had wanted and the elimination of the seigniorage on gold and silver coinage he and Ralston had fallen short of achieving with the Coinage Act of 1873. As to the replacement of the fractional notes, the bill provided:

> That the Secretary of the Treasury is hereby authorized and required, as rapidly as practicable, to cause to be coined, at the Mints of the United States, silver coins of the denominations of ten, twenty-five and fifty cents, of standard value, and to issue them in redemption of an equal number of fractional currency of similar denomination, or, at his discretion, he may issue such silver coins through the Mints, the sub-Treasuries, public depositories and Post Offices of the United States; and, upon such issue, he is hereby authorized and required to redeem an equal amount of such fractional currency, until the whole amount of such fractional currency outstanding shall be redeemed.[28]

Whether or not Linderman was involved in framing this measure—which most historians have credited to Sen. Sherman for its introduction and contents—is unclear. The idea to exchange the subsidiary silver for the fractional notes, a small portion of the entire resumption process, was not Linderman's alone. In 1869, for example, the U.S. Mint began producing a series of "Standard Silver" 10-, 25-, and 50-cent patterns for a new coinage that would replace the fractional notes, in preparation for specie resumption. Championed by then Mint Director James Pollock, the new coins were to have been of the same .900 fineness as the silver subsidiary coins then in use but would have been smaller in size and lighter in weight to further discourage hoarding and export. Except for a few patterns, struck in variety of metals and denominations, nothing came of Pollock's proposal. However, by late 1874, when Linderman wrote his annual report, the story was different. The Treasury not only supported the general idea of replacing the fractional notes with coins, but Linderman, with his clout as director of all of the nation's mints, began formulating plans for the changeover, apparently confident that the "due consideration" by Congress would be short in coming.[29]

Some clear evidence of his involvement with the Specie Resumption Act, while it was before Congress, can be found in one of Linderman's "Old Man" letters to Ralston. Penned on Jan. 7, 1875, one day after what was then being termed the Senate Finance Bill passed the House, this letter reveals his behind-the-scenes efforts in relation to an apparent move by Ralston's regular nemesis (Eugene Kelly) on the refining business, his keen interest in the measure's subsidiary silver provision, and his intention to see this "silver resumption business safely launched" before giving up his position as Mint director (as his salary—$5,000—he said, was too low).[30] Linderman wrote:

> The Senate Finance Bill passed the House to-day and only awaits the executive approval to become a law & which it will no doubt receive. This bill among other things removes the gold coinage charge and thus after a four years contest victory perches on our banners. It has indeed been a long and weary struggle but we had finally reversed the policy of the country and to its great benefit beyond doubt.[31]

The battle was not an easy one, Linderman explained, and ran right into Kelly, who continued to oppose Ralston's monopoly over private refining of government bullion in California. "Things got pretty hot and the result doubtful," Linderman related. "I was compelled to take a hand in the fight to save the day."[32] Kelly's man, Edelman, it seems, had presented a paper, titled "Comments on the Finance Bill," attacking Ralston's control of the refining business with the intention of having it read before the House during expected discussion of the Senate Finance Bill. The paper, via a circuitous route from Rep. Horace Maynard, chairman of the House Committee on Banking and Currency, to Samuel Hooper, had been forwarded to Linderman's attention. "The 'Old Man's' hand was about however and got it in shape for a severe shot which I will give it sure," Linderman boasted to Ralston.[33]

Of the finance bill's provision allowing the exchange of subsidiary silver for fractional notes, Linderman complained to Ralston that an editorial in a recent issue of the *Alta California* was unwise. The editorial, which appeared in the Dec. 26, 1874, *Alta*, just prior to the bill's passage, argued that any subsidiary coins would likely disappear as soon as they were released because of a premium on the coins for export, and that the provision was, in reality, a renewal of "Mr. Richardson's absurdity of two years since."[34] The absurdity the *Alta* was referring to was the release of subsidiary sil-

An 1869 Standard Silver 10-cent pattern.

ver coins Linderman had directed but which failed when federal paper money fell in value.

"The mining section of the country should be the last to complain of the measure as anything which will tend to make a home market for silver and prevent serious depreciation should commend itself to it," Linderman scolded Ralston, adding, "Now all this is d—d [damned] provoking especially when our own friends needlessly & recklessly put in their hammer."[35]

A letter writer to the Jan. 7, 1875, issue of the *National Republican* (whom the *Alta* probably correctly surmised had connections with the Treasury) would challenge the *Alta's* editorial, claiming that the newspaper's calculations were wrong. The eight percent premium on subsidiary silver the *Alta* had argued would help draw the coins out of circulation, the letter writer explained, only existed because of the demand in Latin America for the coins. Once that demand was met by full production of the mints, the premium would disappear, and the excess coins would enter circulation in the United States.

"Suppose the Government had $15,000,000 of subsidiary silver coin ready for issue, and the Mints coining such pieces at the rate of $1,500,000 per month, is it at all probable that the demand from two or three of the least important of the South American States would not soon be met?" he wrote. "If so, the coins would circulate in the United States until they could be exported at a profit as bullion, and such a condition of affairs would not arise unless there should be a material advance in the price of silver bullion or depreciation of the greenback dollar."[36]

At the present rates, this could not happen, the writer boldly proclaimed:

> Silver coins to the amount of $500,000 could not be sold at this time in New York city for anything above their bullion value, and for the reason that the sum mentioned would more than meet any demand for such coins as money.
>
> It will not matter much if two or three millions of the subsidiary coins go to Central or South America annually, as it would have no perceptible effect on the value here, provided redemption be commenced with a sufficient stock of coin on hand and the Mints are operated to their full capacity.[37]

However, just as this letter was being written, the value of the greenback fell below silver in relation to gold, which indeed caused the subsidiary silver coins to be withdrawn from circulation. Linderman explained in his Nov. 20, 1875, Mint director's report, however, that this unfavorable market for the release of the coins was likely to be temporary. According to Linderman, "A very gradual contraction of the legal-tender notes and a moderate revival of business will, it is probable, by the time the necessary stock of silver coin to commence the redemption can be prepared, reduce the gold-premium to such a point as will insure the success of the measure."[38]

Linderman offered a similar assessment in the June 16, 1875, issue of the *San Francisco Chronicle*, under the heading "Silver for Coinage, Dr. Linderman's Views of the New Coinage Law," datelined June 1 from the *New York Times*. The *Times* correspondent having interviewed Linderman about the silver coinage provisions of the Specie Resumption Act, recorded in a report dictated by Linderman, that the "proper authorities" had, as early as 1872, correctly judged the effect of Germany's change to the gold standard "and in the Coinage Act of 1873 gold was in effect declared to be the standard of value and the legal-tender silver dollar abolished."[39] In the same act, the Trade dollar was adopted specifically for the China market and:

> Subsequently another measure, and one which is calculated to have an important bearing on the value of silver, was adopted. We refer to the law providing for the substitution of silver coin in the place of the fractional currency. The decline in the value of silver will not, it is hoped, have to go much further to meet the appreciation of the United States legal-tender notes, which should follow their gradual withdrawal and cancellation, and a moderate revival of business in this country. All doubts as to the practicability of maintaining the circulation of silver will in that contingency disappear, and it is quite probable that, soon after the substitution is well under way, and full provision made for meeting the demands of China for the trade dollar, the depreciation of silver will be arrested...[40]

With this in mind, under Linderman's direction, the nation's mints began setting production records for subsidiary silver coins that would not be matched for decades to come. While in 1874, the total mintage of dimes by the San Francisco, Carson

Implementation of the provisions of the 1875 Specie Resumption Act led to greatly increased coinages of dimes, quarters and half dollars in 1875 and 1876.

City and Philadelphia Mints reached 3,190,817, the 1875 coinage, under the provisions of the Specie Resumption Act, was eight times as much, 24,065,700. The breakdown of the individual mints for that year is equally as startling and explains why these coins remain in great supply for collectors at moderate prices. The Philadelphia coinage total jumped from 2,940,000 to 10,350,700 in 1875, and the San Francisco Mint, with its new minting facility in operation, saw its meager 240,000 mintage from the prior year soar to 9,070,000. Totals for the half dollar coinage were also highly inflated, rising from 2,813,300 in 1874 to 10,235,500 in 1875.

Mintage figures for the dimes, quarters and half dollars grew again in 1876. This was most dramatic in quarters, which had witnessed only a moderate increase in 1875. In 1876 the Philadelphia Mint alone struck 17,817,150 quarters. Totals for all mints rose from 863,900 in 1874 to 5,113,500 in 1875 to 31,357,150 in 1876.

The massive government purchases of silver for such coinage led some to suspect that those behind the subsidiary silver coinage provisions of the Specie Resumption Act did not really care if the coins were released into circulation. During the March 16, 1876, debate over the act that ultimately authorized the exchange of the fractionals for silver, Rep. Abram S. Hewitt of New York told Congress:

> But there is such a thing as luck, even in legislation, and the republican party have always had their share of it, and it was never more manifest than in this silver business, as I shall endeavor to show. At the date of the passage of the resumption act, and for some months thereafter, the price of fine silver in London averaged 56.99 pence, practically 57 pence per ounce. But meanwhile the Big Bonanza began to pour into the markets of the world its marvelous product of silver. I have no doubt that the promoters of the resumption act knew perfectly well what was going to happen, and thought it would not be a bad thing if they could get a cash market for $40,000,000 of their product, and especially for a goodly pile of it before the general market was affected by the enormous yield of silver. Mark how carefully the act is to instruct the Secretary to proceed to coin the silver as rapidly as possible, and yet how indifferent it is as to the paying out of the coins. In fact it would suit the bonanza party better that they should not be paid out at all. The very best thing that could happen to them would be to transfer the bullion from their mines to the United States mints and let it lie there. This would be a sale of the mine better than the Emma operation, without any 'curses coming home to roost.' Well, it appears by the report of the Director of the Mint [Linderman's 1875 submission] that these bonanza gentlemen were pretty successful in getting rid of their silver before it fell in value. He purchased $12,658, 054.68 up to the 1st of October last at an average of 111.4 cents per ounce, which is the equivalent, as near as may be, of 56 1/2 pence per ounce in London. The price last week in London is 52 5/8 pence per ounce, a fall of nearly 4 pence per ounce, which, on the quantity purchased to October 1, makes a difference of nearly $1,000,000, and including that since purchased, of over $1,000,000 out of the Treasury into the pockets of the 'big bonanza' party. No wonder that the Secretary was directed to hurry up with the coinage, while no one was found to hurry up the issue of the coins.[41]

The overabundance of subsidiary coins as a result of the Specie Resumption Act led to low mintages of subsidiary coins in later years. In 1886, for instance, only 5,886 quarters were minted.

Hewitt complained that this was not the only benefit the silver interests had obtained through the passage of the Specie Resumption Act, noting correctly that the same act removed the gold coinage charge. "No doubt the financial wiseacres of the republican party believed that the stamp of the United States Mint would keep these double eagles at home, and were willing to pay 1/5 of 1 per cent. for this benefit, which no one will deny would have been cheap at the price; but, as the Secretary was not prepared to hoard gold as well as silver and there was no use for gold in this country, it went abroad under laws more powerful than the clauses of the bonanza act, and will continue to go until a practical scheme of legislation is devised looking to the certain resumption of specie payments," Hewitt said.[42]

The "luck, even in legislation" he had referred to at the beginning of his diatribe, Hewitt explained, was that silver had fallen so much in the past four months that it would be possible to put the coins into circulation without their leaving the country or being melted. One month later, on April 17, 1876, with silver still trading below paper, Congress was able to safely order the Treasury to begin the exchange of fractional currency without a loss. By the Act of July 22, 1876 (the same legislation that stripped the Trade dollar of its legal tender status), Congress also officially allowed the exchange of subsidiary silver for United States notes. Treasury Secretary Lot M. Morrill, writing in his Dec. 4, 1876, report to Congress, recorded that, immediately upon passage of the act on April 17, 1876, the Treasury began issuing silver subsidiary silver coin in redemption for the fractional notes and, with the authority granted on July 22, 1876, began exchanging silver coin for legal tender notes "as rapidly as the coinage at the mints would permit."[43]

However, there was an unforeseen danger to the quick release of these coins. While the Treasury doled out dimes, quarters and half dollars in record numbers, the value of silver drifted low enough in world bullion markets to draw millions of previously issued silver coins back from Canada, Latin America and the West Indies. Coins thought to have been melted began flooding into the United States in great numbers. Banks soon refused to accept the coins on deposit or in large payments, while businesses that handled large amounts suffered losses.[44]

In December 1878, Treasury Secretary John Sherman was forced to order the suspension of subsidiary coinage; and the Act of June 9, 1879, provided some relief by allowing the redemption "in sums of twenty dollars, or any multiples thereof" of the depreciated coins.[45] Even by 1885, with annual mintages of dimes, quarters and half dollars down to more normal levels, the Treasury still had $31,694,365 in subsidiary silver in its vaults waiting to be paid out.[46]

Linderman's plan had not saved silver as he hoped. On the other hand, it did provide an additional mar-

Shortchanged

One of the shortest-lived series of U.S. coins, the 20-cent piece, was ostensibly the brainchild of Nevada Sen. John Percival Jones (a hero of the 1869 Gold Hill fire). The haulting of half-dime coinage by order of the Coinage Act of 1873 and a general shortage of minor coinage in the West, led Jones to enter a bill in Congress in February 1874 calling for a 20-cent coin. The new denomination was expected to alleviate problems with daily transactions. As merchants often priced items at 10 cents, customers paying with a quarter dollar were being forced to take a dime in change and forfeit five cents. As Dan De Quille explained of the situation in Virginia City:

> The money in circulation is wholly gold and silver coin, and the smallest coin in use is the bit, or ten-cent piece—sometimes spoken of as a 'short bit,' as not being twelve and one half cents, the 'long bit.' There being no smaller change in use than the dime, the bit passes for the half of twenty-five cents. Thus whenever a customer throws down a quarter of a dollar in payment for a drink or a cigar, he gets back a dime, and so has paid fifteen cents for his 'nip' or smoke. The new twenty-cent pieces, of which Senator Jones of Nevada is the father, will, however, cure this little ill.[1]

The coin's placement at five grams in weight, it was also believed, would make it convenient as an international coin, fitting in with the other silver coins, which had been adjusted upward in weight to a metric standard in 1873. The size and resemblance of the 20-cent piece to the Seated Liberty quarter, however, led to confusion and brought about its elimination as a coinage denomination in 1878.

The first year of mintage was the largest, with 1,155,000 struck at the San Francisco Mint, an additional 133,290 minted in Carson City, and a low 39,700 coined at the parent mint in Philadelphia. After that, mintages of the 20-cent piece dropped sharply to 15,900 in 1876 in Philadelphia and 10,000 at Carson City. The latter is a great rarity, as most were melted at the mint. Less than two dozen specimens are believed to have escaped the melting pot. Only proofs for collectors were issued in 1877 and 1878.

Unlike the dimes, quarters, half dollars and silver dollars of the period, the edge of the 20-cent piece was plain (not reeded) and the word "Liberty" was raised on the surface rather than recessed.

The 20-cent piece was only issued for four years. Its similarity in size to the quarter dollar apparently led to its rejection by the public.

ket for the metal during the heyday of the Comstock Lode. It is likely that, back in May 1872, when Linderman told Ralston of his scheme to replace the fractional notes, he earnestly believed such an action and the success of the Trade dollar would achieve his goals and be good for the government at the same time. If nothing else, he was certain it would be good for his friends on the Pacific coast.

In a March 14, 1875, letter, written less than two weeks after the close of final regular session of the 43rd Congress (which had passed the Specie Resumption Act), he wrote to Ralston, again under the alias "Old Man," telling his former employer, "Your community certainly have reason to be thankful for some of the legislation of the last Congress, the government's bullion operations come as a benefit to your section in a time of severe depression caused by an unusual drain of coin."[47] He then suggested that the Pacific coast newspapers had overlooked the services of California Sen. Aaron Sargent in the adoption of the sections of the act in relation to the elimination of the coinage charge and redemption of fractional notes with silver coins. "The importance of the latter, as lending strongly to arrest the downward tendency of the value of silver cannot well be overestimated," Linderman wrote. "Although the ground had been pretty well prepared[,] the services of Sargent were put in at the right moment and with his usual good sense of adroitness, and effectiveness. It appears to me that a proper commendation of his services in these matters should be given in your newspapers... Having lead the fight in the matter of free coinage, since 1867, and as respects silver coinage for ten years, I can appreciate the valuable and timely services of Mr. Sargent."[48]

A few days later, Linderman again wrote to Ralston, announcing that once he got the mints up and running producing subsidiary silver coins, he would make plans to travel to the West and look over the situation. Linderman would indeed make the trip to the West in 1875, where he toured the Comstock mines. It would be the last time he would see his old friend, Ralston, alive.

Chapter 19

A FATEFUL DAY

The year 1875 started out on a high note for Mint Director Henry R. Linderman. With the passage of the Specie Resumption Act, he could now officially begin the work of putting the nation's growing supply of silver into coinage. "I intimated clearly to [Louis A.] Garnett some time ago that we would have to ship doré silver from the West to supply the refineries of the Assay Office at N.Y. & Mint Philad.," Linderman wrote to William C. Ralston in his March 16, 1875, "Old Man" letter. "We must drop all theories and deal with facts and circumstances as they exist.

"By keeping the price down and all our operations strictly within the law we can market all our silver bullion at home & meet the Government demand for coinage. We certainly do not want any silver bullion from abroad."[1]

Once all of the mints were engaged in producing the small silver coins, he told Ralston, he would be compelled to travel to the West to "look over the ground carefully and come to [a] conclusion as to a general plan of operations."[2]

While Linderman was optimistic, on the Pacific coast some dark clouds were looming on the horizon for his old friend Ralston. Although the generally unflappable Ralston continued plodding along from one grandiose scheme to another (including the completion of the magnificent multi-story, multi-million dollar Palace Hotel he was building with Comstock partner William Sharon in the heart of San Francisco and an attempt to take over the Spring Valley Water Company, which controlled water distribution to San Francisco), his mounting debt and constant need to invent new sources for cash to back his ever-expanding list of ventures had placed him in serious financial trouble. Cracks, that cut to the very foundation of the once mighty Bank of California and would soon widen enough to admit a glaring light on the poor management decisions being made by its popular and powerful leader, were beginning to show.

During most of the 1860s, Ralston had been the undisputed master of the Comstock, controlling the majority its mines, its bullion, its primary mills, its railroad, its lumber supply, its water, and its banking through a menagerie of companies all under the bank crowd's handpicked leadership. Likewise, within California, there was hardly an enterprise that he or the bank did not have a direct hand in or had not backed financially. By the early 1870s, however, this was no longer true—at least not on the Comstock. A series of lapses and ill-timed investments hastened the erosion of the bank crowd's monopoly. One of the major breaks occurred in 1872, while Sharon's attention was focused elsewhere. It was then that former Bank of California director Alvinza Hayward and mine superintendent John P. Jones, aware that the Crown Point was about to hit bonanza, were able to wrest control of the mine away from the bank crowd's Union Mill and Mining Company and reap a fortune in the process. Worse was yet to come, however, from four Irishmen, who shortly after the mint bill passed gained an important foothold on the Comstock. In the late 1860s, John W. Mackay, an experienced miner, who first made a name and fortune at the Comstock's Kentuck Mine; James G. Fair, who had also knocked around the mines for years, including a stint as superintendent of the Ophir; and two experienced, and likewise wealthy, San Francisco stockbrokers, James C. Flood and William S. O'Brien, made their first foray into mastering the lode by edging out Ralston and Sharon at the Hale & Norcross.

It was a bitter blow to the bank crowd. Sharon had won control of the mine for the crowd's newly formed Union Mill and Mining Company in 1868, after a lengthy and costly stock battle that saw Hale & Norcross shares climb from $300 to more than $7,000 in just one month.[3] Unfortunately, shortly after the Union Mill and Mining Company took over, the mine went into borrasca, and stock prices tumbled. Convinced that the mine still held plenty of ore that could be profitably worked, if properly managed, Mackay, Fair, Flood and O'Brien (who operated in Virginia City as Fair & Mackay and in San Francisco as Flood & O'Brien) began quietly buying up stock. Not long after they took over, the Hale & Norcross hit a profitable

By the mid-1870s, despite its sterling reputation, the Bank of California was in trouble. In late 1875, shortly after Ralston took over as president, it would collapse under a day-long siege. Bank staff photo courtesy of the California History Room, California State Library, Sacramento, California. Bottom photo courtesy of the Bancroft Library, University of California, Berkeley.

vein. From 1869-1870, under the bonanza firm's management, the mine paid out $728,000 in dividends, providing additional capital for exploration and a widening of the bonanza firm's wedge into the Comstock.[4]

The firm soon began buying up other claims, including the Bullion and the Savage, neither of which produced paying ore, and taking up ground on the north end of the lode, between the Ophir and the Best & Belcher, on a combination of previously unproductive claims known collectively as the Consolidated Virginia. In 1873, their speculative purchases paid off when miners on the Consolidated Virginia struck a vein of low-grade ore. Judging the likely direction of the vein, the bonanza firm quietly secured the adjacent property, organizing it under the banner of the California Mining Company. On March 1, 1873, the Consolidated Virginia began hoisting the first major quantities of ore up from the 1,200-foot level through the Gould & Curry shaft, sending stock prices on all Comstock properties upward.[5] In October 1874, when work began on the 1,500-foot level, Consolidated Virginia miners encountered the main ore body, a stope so wide and so rich that even the best of Comstock mining men had a hard time suppressing their excitement. Dan De Quille, the *Virginia City Territorial Enterprise's* veteran reporter, boasted of a tour he took of the Consolidated Virginia that the mine's workings were like a subterranean town, with some 800 to 1,000 men toiling below "on a solid mass of ore of the richest description."[6]

"Even here, well toward its south end—as far as explored—the ore body is by no means small, being over nine and one half rods in width!" De Quille

The Consolidated Virginia encountered the main body of the Big Bonanza around the 1,500-foot level. The discovery sent stock prices soaring. This view of the mine's hoisting works is believed to date from around 1900. Courtesy of the Nevada State Museum Photograph Collection.

exclaimed. "This is not a mixture of ore and worthless rock, but is a solid mass of rich silver ore, which is sent to the mills just as it is dug or blasted down—ore that will pay from $100 to $300 per ton. As thirteen cubic feet make a ton of ore, we have here for every block of ore three feet square from $200 to $600 in pure silver and gold."[7]

De Quille was not the only one swept up in the silver fever. Eliot Lord wrote that most who judged the bonanza, which ran into the California, placed the figure at $500 million to $600 million, while Philipp Deidesheimer, developer of the square-set timbering system used throughout the lode, proclaimed its value at around $15 million.[8] Robert E. Rogers, a chemistry professor at the University of Pennsylvania, who had lately been employed by the U.S. Treasury overseeing installation of the refinery at the new San Francisco Mint, was a bit more conservative than some, but was still wide of the mark. After touring the Consolidated Virginia on July 16 and 17, 1875 (the first of those days in the company of Mint Director Linderman), he wrote, "On an inspection of the official surveys exhibiting the galleries and cross-cuts, it would seem fair to conclude that with proper allowances, the ore-body equals an amount which, taken at the actual assays, would give as the ultimate yield of the two mines, $300,000,000; but to guard against the chance of overestimating, I take the assays at one-half that ascertained, which will place the production at not less than $150,000,000."[9]

Historian Grant Smith put the average per ton value from 1873-1882 at $105 on the Consolidated Virginia. The total tonnage removed was 809,275, with a market value of $61,125,757. The adjacent

California mine, which averaged $98 per ton, extracted 588,586 tons for a total of $44,031,733 during the same time frame.[10]

Upon his arrival on the lode, sometime in July, Mint Director Linderman was like a kid in a candy store, unable to contain his excitement. He was now able to see, firsthand, the mineral wealth over which he was the government's lord and seized the opportunity for publicity for his subsidiary silver coinage plans by touring the Consolidated Virginia in mid-July, accompanied by San Francisco Mint Superintendent O.H. La Grange and a correspondent for the *New York Tribune*. The impressionable reporter gushed in his July 31 feature for the *Tribune,* that the Mint director had remarked, upon emerging from the mine, that "he had never seen so much money in his whole life, and never expected to see so much again," adding, "Dr. Linderman thinks the Nevada mines will have a great deal to do with the return to specie payments. He sees no reason why silver should not be in general circulation now instead of small notes and fractional currency, as the low price of silver in the London market makes a greenback dollar by quotation worth the more by one or two cents."[11]

The excitement over the Big Bonanza sent stock prices soaring for all lode properties during the latter months of 1874. In a desperate attempt to regain their former position on the Comstock, Sharon and Ralston began sinking millions into acquiring stock in the often water-soaked Ophir, hoping that it would share in the neighboring Consolidated Virginia's success at the lower levels. After another fierce and costly battle, they gained control of the Ophir by paying Elias Jackson "Lucky" Baldwin $2.7 million for his 20,000 shares.[12] Baldwin was the lucky one, Ralston was not. In early January 1875, just as the Senate was passing the Specie Resumption Act, the overheated market broke. Stock prices plummeted across the board.

The Consolidated Virginia, which had been driven up to $790 before the market peaked, was worth a paltry $40 by the end of the February. The story was as glum for the Ophir. Ralston lost, by one estimate, $8 million.[13] Sharon, however, survived. According to an oft-repeated story, he had disposed of his shares short, just prior to the market tumble. Some said he even leaked the rumor that triggered the collapse, announcing that there was no bonanza at the Ophir, thereby heartlessly taking his friends, including Ralston, down in the market free-fall. Once the market settled, he was then able to quietly buy shares at greatly reduced prices from those he had helped to ruin. Whether this treachery-laced story is true is uncertain. In Ralston's case, it did not matter. His losses on the Comstock, though substantial, were only part of an increasingly grim story. [14]

Although Ralston had been seriously overextended in the past, he had always been able to find a way to escape the darkest situations. In 1873, for example, when bank officials, being harried by the bank's creditors, discovered that $3.5 million in unsecured loans were due from the Kimball Manufacturing Company, the New Montgomery Street Real Estate Company and the Mission Woolen Mills, companies owned by Ralston, he was able to turn to his father-in-law, John D. Fry (who became rich with Ralston's help on the Comstock) to come to his and the bank's aid by assuming $3.4 million in debt, in exchange for all collateral and securities held by the bank.[15]

The money had, for a time, rescued the overly ambitious and, at times, less-than-prudent Ralston, but by the summer of 1875, he was again in too deep. Money was again tight, and his old methods of securing enough gold to keep the bank and his ancillary business ventures afloat were not good enough.

In 1869, when gold coin was in short supply, Ralston had found inventive ways to survive, convincing the Treasury to allow gold transfers by coded telegraph messages to the San Francisco Sub-Treasury and, the story goes, secretly transferring gold coins from the Sub-Treasury to the bank, in order to avoid a run. In 1875, however, the situation had changed. There was a similar shortage of gold coin, but his debts were higher and his methods of escape more questionable and less effective. With the depression raging, gold had gone to a premium in the East and would remain there for quite some time, siphoning off large amounts of California's yellow lifeblood.[16] Between Jan.1, 1875, and Aug. 26, 1875, a fateful day for the Bank of California, the high price of gold on the East Coast drew off more than $30 million in gold, an increase of $15 million over the prior year.[17] With the price of wheat being high, another $5 million had been lost moving that year's product to market, forcing depositors to withdraw funds just at a time of scarcity of coin.[18]

The Aug. 26, 1875, *San Francisco Chronicle*, under the heading "A Tight Money Market," reported that much of the region's cash was in the countryside, for the purposes of "moving the crop," but:

The Ophir mine in the early 1900s. Ralston and Sharon had hoped it would share in the same kind of good fortune at the lower levels as enjoyed by the bonanza crowd's Consolidated Virginia and the California. Courtesy of the Nevada State Museum Photograph Collection.

> Besides this the drain of gold to the East has been heavy for several months past, and only diminished quite recently, the shipments last week having scarcely exceeded $125,000. About $15,000,000 is supposed to be necessary to make the local market easy. When four or five millions are withdrawn, its absence is seriously felt.[19]

The *Chronicle* found another cause for the tightness closer to home, in the opening of the Nevada Bank of San Francisco by the bonanza firm, which had absorbed some $10 million. The *Chronicle* wrote:

John Mackay, one of the four Bonanza Kings. Courtesy of Nevada State Museum Photograph Collection.

> The establishment of their new bank with an immense capital, and a large amount of ready money for the use of borrowers, afforded Flood & O'Brien the opportunity which they desired of withdrawing money from circulation. They first began to loan with less freedom. Then they commenced to supply the public, hungering for stocks and expecting a big deal in the Fall, with all the shares they could stagger under, thus absorbing private hoards drawn from savings banks and old stockings. Everybody who wanted California and Best & Belcher was allowed to have it to satiety. The sales of California have been immense, 150,000 shares having been thrown on the market within a month by brokers in the confidence of the bonanza kings. Last week they drew from the Bank of California $1,800,000 which they had there, refusing certification and demanding the coin. This they placed as a special deposit with Donohoe, Kelly & Co. The expectation was that the bank ring, presumed to have great liabilities, and to be keeping in their vaults an immense amount of certificates of favorite stocks, which they could not use as ready money in case of need, would be compelled to throw them all, and especially the coveted Ophir, on the market. The expectations were realized. Money became scarcer day by day. The Bank of California began to contract and shorten it loans, and ask its stock-operating customers for money....[20]

To escape his problems, Ralston had also turned to illegal methods of freeing up money, including ordering all of the gold bullion (some $2 million worth) at the San Francisco Assaying and Refining Company to be converted at the San Francisco

The Consolidated Virginia and California joint shaft, known as the "C & C," which was sunk to the east of the Consolidated Virginia shaft. Courtesy of the Nevada State Museum Photograph Collection.

C.&C.SHAFT

Mint into coin. He then charged the bullion, most of which was owned by others, to his own account, going in debt to the refinery for $2 million. He also began over-issuing stock in the Bank of California, 13,180 shares in all, which raised more than $1.3 million in the process, while borrowing another $300,000 on Southern Pacific railroad bonds that had been left in his trust.[21]

None of it worked. On Aug. 26, 1875, the Bank of California closed its doors amid a daylong siege by anxious depositors, clamoring to remove their money. The Aug. 27, 1875, *Alta California* covered the bank's fateful last hours under Ralston's leadership in great detail. Shortly after the bank opened for business on Thursday, Aug. 26, "it was noticed that something like a run...was in progress," the *Alta* recorded.[22] A leading firm of financiers withdrew $45,000, and nervous stockbrokers, many of whom had large amounts of money in Bank of California checks, pulled their deposits out of the bank.

By early afternoon, the run had become such that the normally large afternoon crowd mingling outside of the bank on California Street began to take notice, excited further by a false rumor that Milton S. Latham's London & San Francisco Bank had refused to receive checks on the Bank of California. "After two, the rush became still greater, and the crowd of anxious men, nervously handing in their checks and eagerly clutching the proffered coin in return, steadily increased, until the counters were invaded by a throng several lines deep," the *Alta* wrote.[23] So troubling was the crowd that bank officials partially closed the doors and stationed guards to keep order, and members of the companies of the Second Brigade, fearing a riot, assembled at their respective armories. "The force of paying tellers were kept very busy receiving checks and counting out the coin; as each happy recipient of a lot of twenty-dollar gold pieces left the counter, an anxious depositor took his place, and so the run went on," the *Alta* related.[24]

At 2:35, nearly a half hour before scheduled closing time, the bank was forced to shut its doors. "All who exhibited checks, however, were admitted through the wicket by the police officer on guard," according to the *Alta*. "The tellers continued to pay the checks of those who were fortunate enough to reach the desk ahead of their struggling neighbors, up to sixteen minutes of three, when a messenger from Davidson's Bank arrived, pushed up to the desk, and presented a check for $5485. Mr. Ralston said, 'We will not cash any more checks to-day.' This finally closed

Shift change at the C & C joint shaft. Courtesy of the Nevada State Museum Photograph Collection.

business for the day, and the disappointed holders of checks withdrew."[25]

Ralston would later tell a *San Francisco Chronicle* reporter that he first noticed the run at about 1 p.m., when depositors began lining up at the counter six to eight deep. "By 2 o'clock the bank was full and they began to crowd on the sidewalk in front of the bank," Ralston told the *Chronicle*. "We kept paying out money as fast as possible, but it was like pouring water into a knot-hole. I saw that it was no use to hold out, that we could not weather the storm, and, knowing that we must face the music, at about 25 minutes to 3 I had the doors closed."[26] Ralston estimated the amount withdrawn in coin alone at $1.4 million.

The doors of the Bank of California having closed, in desperation the mob turned its attention to the National Gold Bank and Trust Company located across the street. One anxious depositor lunged forward, clutching a $10 bill. Presenting it to the teller, he cried, "'For heaven's sake, give me coin for this—it's the last dollar I've got in the world.'"[27]

At the Bank of California, a woman "ghastly with paint and rouge," finding the bank closed, tried in vain to gain entry into the bank through a closed window, "declaring she would have her money, every cent of it, and if her John wasn't out to sister Abigail's in Amador, he'd see that her hard-earned savings wasn't stolen, you bet your life he would."[28] Elsewhere, wild rumors spread. One claimed that Ralston had hanged himself in the rear anteroom of the bank, and that his corpse, surrounded by his grieving family, was being guarded by a squad of police. Others said several distraught depositors had blown their brains out, "and that one stock broker, having failed, had gone stark mad, and was dancing a maniacal hornpipe among baskets of stock certificates in his back office."[29]

Gen. Thompson, the National Gold Bank and Trust Company's cashier, assured a reporter for the *Alta* that the suspension at the Bank of California was likely temporary, and it would no doubt reopen the following morning. But it would not. Shortly after 3 p.m. the officers of the Bank of California began to meet behind closed doors. The meeting ran until about 5:30. Representatives of the press were then led into an anteroom of the president's office to await the close of the directors' meeting. Soon Ralston emerged, looking to the *Alta* reporter as if he was hoping to repress any sign of agitation, and led reporters into his office.

"I will make a few preliminary remarks, gentlemen, which I do not care especially to have taken down," Ralston began. "Of course, in the confusion that has taken place to-day and during this afternoon, it will be impossible for us to do anything or say anything, for a few days, by which time we will make up a statement to present to the public. A resolution has been adopted by the Board, and is being copied here, which we will give you for publication in the morning papers, which tells all that we have to say on the subject. I will add, on my own behalf, however, as an officer of the Bank, that there is no question whatever as to the ability of the Bank to meet all its obligations, and leave considerable surplus aside."[30] The resolution read:

> The Trustees are under the painful necessity of stating to the creditors of the Bank of California, and to the public, that the Bank has been compelled to suspend business. At this moment of excitement, and without reports from the Agencies, they are not prepared to make a statement as to the situation of the Bank, but they are now examining into it critically, and will at the earliest possible moment make a definite report.[31]

Although Ralston was in no mood for questions, the reporters pressed, and the *Alta* recorded:

> Q.—Will you resume business to-morrow, at the usual hour? A.—No, sir; we will not resume.
>
> Q.—How soon do you propose to resume business? A (After some hesitation).—We don't expect to resume.
>
> Q.—Not at all? A.—No, sir.[32]

The same Ralston said was true of the Bank of California's agencies in New York, Gold Hill and Virginia City, which were quickly told to shut their doors. The questioning continued:

> Q.—What occasioned the suspension? A. (With a slight smile)—Scarcity of coin.
>
> Q.—Is there a scarcity of coin in the city? A.—Scarcity of coin in circulation—scarcity of coin obtainable.[33]

Ralston said $4 million had been withdrawn from the region for the wheat crop, adding that the gold shortage was not expected to let up until October. "You see we are here with a metallic currency, and this is one disadvantage—when you get to the bottom of the tub you can't lift yourself up," he told the *Alta*.[34] But he was just covering for more serious troubles, the source of which few could no longer doubt.

Not long before this interview, in a desperate attempt to gain money, Ralston had begun selling off his assets at bargain prices, disposing of his

William C. Ralston appears with the officers and staff of the Bank of California in this 1874 photograph. Ralston is seated at center, below the painting of D.O. Mills. Courtesy of the California History Room, California State Library, Sacramento, Calif.

half interest in the Palace Hotel to William Sharon, in May, for $1.75 million in cash and his stock in the Virginia and Truckee Railroad to former bank president D.O. Mills for $900,000.[35] On Aug. 22, he asked Sharon and Mills for help to save him from ruin. Mills came through with $75,000, but it was too late.[36] Word of Ralston's sell-off had apparently leaked out, making stockbrokers jittery. Joseph King, who was running a brokerage at the time of the bank's collapse, wrote in his history of the San Francisco Stock and Exchange Board that when his partner, B.F. Sherwood (one of Sharon's brokers), returned from a trip to the East, he expressed his concerns to Sherwood about the stability of the Bank of California, "I told him the brokers were talking quietly, among themselves, about the large transfers of real estate by the officers of the bank, and as we had a large balance to our credit it would be wise to protect ourselves."[37]

On Aug. 25, prices on the San Francisco stock market skittered sharply downward. The Ophir quickly dropped 17 points, and the Consolidated Virginia lost 45 in the wake of a large sell-off by the bank crowd.[38] *The San Francisco Chronicle* reported that while there was no panic, there was something akin to it, as "Small operators who have been dealing largely in margins gathered on the sidewalks and in the corridors of stock rooms, and whispered with white lips: 'The crash, it comes! It comes!"[39]

The following day, Sharon placed a large sell order on most of his mining stock, including the Ophir, sending the market into a free-fall, leading stocks dropping 20 points.[40] King, who claimed to have learned the morning of Aug. 26 that the bank would not open the following day, dispatched his brokerage's clerks, loaded down with canvas bags, scurrying around the city to cash all of his company's checks, whether or not they were drawn on

In 1869, Ralston had been able to escape a coin shortage when the Treasury agreed to allow the release of gold coins from the San Francisco Sub-Treasury for deposits made in the East. By 1875, however, he was in too deep. Many still chose to believe that a shortage of gold coin, rather than poor management decisions, caused the bank's collapse.

the Bank of California.[41] Other brokers did the same. The large firm of Edward F. Hall was one of the first, withdrawing $250,000. Parker & Fry cashed all of its checks and had $150,000 in its safe by nightfall.[42]

"Maurice Schmitt presented $14,000 in checks to Nicolson, the paying teller, at the Bank of California, at 11 o'clock in the morning," King wrote, and "Was eventually referred to Mr. Ralston, told to wait a short time and re-present them, and then told his own banker of the matter, who begged of him not to mention the incident, as the Bank of California was as solid as any bank in the city. He obtained the money a short time afterwards."[43]

As the afternoon crowd swelled on California Street, the situation grew desperate. The Bank of California was short of bullion, and it was Ralston's fault. He had left the bank's normal reserves fall to dangerously low levels in the months prior, disguising the fact by various means, including writing checks to the bank from his own account and placing "cash tags" on the checks, which allowed the checks to be counted as part of the bullion reserve even without coin on deposit.[44] When the Bank of California's directors met at Sharon's house on the evening of Aug. 25, it was revealed that there was only really $500,000 in reserve, not the $2 million the books called for, the rest was in the form of tags signed by Ralston.[45] The directors asked for help from Flood & O'Brien, who were in the process of opening the Nevada Bank of San Francisco, but were turned down. So the bank opened the following day, only to witness a collapse that sent shock waves across the United States.

The *New York Tribune* covered the collapse in detail, its correspondent blaming the bank's failure on the "special weakness" its principals, Ralston and Sharon, had for a "miscellaneous" of ventures, as it ran down a laundry list of Ralston's enterprises including the Palace Hotel, being built by Sharon and Ralston at an estimated cost of $7 million, the Mission Woolen Mills, Cornell Watch Company, Kimball Manufacturing Company, West Coast Furniture Company, Artificial Ice Company and many others to show how widely the bank's money had been diffused. "I suspect the Californians are the most inveterate gamblers in the world, and if ever the United States should be 'cornered' to the money market it would be by a Californian," the *Tribune* correspondent wrote.[46] Also condemned were Ralston's and Sharon's extravagant lifestyles, the *Tribune* correspondent labeling Ralston, "an exaggerated type of the prevalent San Francisco millionaire," indulging in a fine country mansion, fine houses, fine dinners, and fine company. "He 'entertained' and did not stint."[47]

In California, however, most focused not on Ralston. Few were yet ready to believe he was in trouble. It was more likely that the tight money supply was the real culprit. This was the tact the *Alta California* took in a report penned on the evening of the bank run:

> The suspension of the Bank of California was received by the public as the news of a calamity hardly second to any that the city has heretofore experienced. The event was caused by that growing scarcity of coin to which we have frequently called attention. It is in no respect a failure since there is no possibility of loss. The assets of the bank are of the best description. The stockholders of the bank are the wealthiest men in the town, who are all individually responsible. The means of payment are, therefore, ample, but the present scarcity of coin makes a slight delay necessary. We have frequently called attention to the long continued drain of coin from the city.[48]

The *Alta* estimated that for the year up to Aug. 1, 1875, some $36.89 million in gold had been sent east, with additional shortages caused by the draw off of the wool and wheat markets.

Wild rumors also surfaced as to reasons for the region's shortage of gold coin. Some charged, as had the *San Francisco Chronicle*, that Flood & O'Brien could have averted the problems but were hoarding coin. Word on the street was that, the day before the collapse, the San Francisco Mint had begun work on striking $2 million in gold coins and had turned out some $300,000 in $20 gold pieces for Flood & O'Brien. "They say that their [Flood & O'Brien] money is loaned out, but it is asserted, on the other hand, that the loan is simply to their associates, Mackey [sic] and Fair, and that the loan is locked up in the vaults of Donohoe, Kelly & Co. Of course, rumors are easily spread and not very reliable," the Aug. 28 issue of the *Alta* reported.[49]

Others, noticing the large transactions being conducted by the Treasury with the bonanza firm for the purchase of silver for subsidiary coinage, came to believe that the draw off had been acerbated by the government. Queried by an *Alta* reporter if the large sum of gold, said to have been sent East, had gone through the San Francisco Sub-Treasury, Sub-Treasury head William Sherman replied that this was all in the form of subsidiary silver coins:

The run on the Bank of California (shown at far right) began to be noticeable in the early afternoon of Aug. 26, as the crowd outside of the bank began to swell. Courtesy of the Bancroft Library, University of California, Berkeley.

> The gold did not go East. The silver was coined here. Millions of dollars have been coined here and sent East as silver coin. By the law of Congress for the redemption of fractional currency, the Secretary of the Treasury is authorized to buy bullion and coin it into subsidiary coin. They have been doing that. They have bought millions in this market. They have bought mostly of Flood & O'Brien, I think.[50]

Pressed further, Sherman insisted the gold obtained from the bonanza firm did not go east. "The money was paid out of this office on the requisition of the Secretary of the Treasury into the Superintendent of the Mint, the bullion fund," Sherman said. "He used it for the purchase of silver, and has been so using it for months. The silver has been coined and sent East in large quantities, though some of it is now on hand in the Mint."[51]

Some also blamed the erratic stock market for siphoning off the gold. Stockbroker Sherwood denied this, telling the *Alta* that merchants and traders had helped strain the reserves of area banks by taking out loans to take advantage of the high rate of gold in the East. Sherwood explained:

> The two primary causes have been what I have told you[:] the large remittances to the East to get the high rate of gold, and the remittances to the interior to harvest the grain crop. I think that the condition of our Coast, financially, is upon a sound basis; but it is these extraordinary causes that has brought this thing about. Money for stock don't go out of the country, but merely changes from one hand to the other. It does not make a scarcity of money. But the trouble is, there was not money enough to afford a circulating medium and there was a want of confidence; and of course the failure of the Bank of California created a further want of confidence and that has made a drain of coin which would take it out of its usual channels.[52]

Fortunately, the bank run was largely confined to the Bank of California and the National Gold Bank and Trust Company. The latter, along with the Merchants' Exchange Bank, closed its doors the following day but would soon reopen. On Friday morning, Aug. 27, crowds again formed and turned their attention to Latham's London and San Francisco Bank, only to find it had plenty of reserves to meet the demand. By the time the *Alta California's* reporter gained entrance to Latham's office, at around 3 p.m., the bank had paid out $900,000. Latham told the reporter that the bank's New York correspondents had forwarded nearly a half million to the bank and were offering an additional million should it be needed. The panic, as far as Latham was concerned, was over.[53]

The U.S. Treasury was also quick to act to relieve the pressure. Linderman, who was in Carson City on the day of the collapse, traveled to California where he negotiated the purchase of large quantities of Comstock silver in return for gold.[54] The Aug. 30, 1875, issue of the *Alta* reported:

> We are authorized to state that negotiations between the Mint authorities and Messrs. Flood & O'Brien, for the purchase of the entire outrun of Con. Virginia mine of the next thirty days, are in progress, and the Director of the Mint, who is now here, is in telegraphic communication with the Secretary of the Treasury on the subject. It is expected that the purchase will be completed today, and will insure to our distressed market a large supply of gold coin from the Treasury.[55]

The *Alta* also reported that production at the mines would be increased, and that coinage at the San Francisco Mint had been stepped up as well. "There are over $3,000,000 in gold coin in the Sub-Treasury of this city," the *Alta* related. "If a large portion of this money be applied to the purchase of bullion for the Mint, it is apparent that the money market must be relieved, supposing, as we do, that the coin so obtained will not be 'locked up.'"[56]

In an article datelined Aug. 30 from San Francisco, the Aug. 31, 1875, *New York Tribune* reported that, at the request of the Comptroller of the Currency (John Jay Knox), Linderman had made a thorough examination of the books and assets of the National Gold Bank and Trust Company and found everything to be is satisfactory condition. "He will report on the same to the Comptroller," the *Tribune* wrote. "The bank will be left free by the Government to manage its own affairs."[57] Ralston and the Bank of California would not be that lucky. The day the bank closed had proved fateful. The following day would be much worse.

Chapter 20

RALSTON'S DEMISE

After executing a deed conveying all of his property (including his beloved country home, Belmont) to William Sharon, and submitting his resignation as bank president, at the request of the bank's board of trustees, William C. Ralston left the Bank of California in the mid-afternoon of Friday, Aug. 27, broken and penniless. By the *Alta California's* account, he departed by the bank's Sansome Street entrance, walked quickly up Sansome to Clay Street, then to Stockton Street, on his way to the Neptune Bath House at North Beach. Wet with perspiration from the mid-day's unforgiving sun, he paused for a while, sitting on one of the stringers. There he was observed, by three boys, pulling papers from his pocket, ripping them to shreds and scattering the pieces in the water below. Ralston asked one of the boys if he thought it was too cold for a swim. Having received assurance that it was not, he walked back to the beach staying close to the shoreline as he continued toward the bathhouse, retrieving more papers and bank deposit books from his pockets, tearing them likewise to pieces as he plod slowly along. The first of two pieces later recovered read "—wrote—the last letter—going to send—Phil som—" on its front and on its back, "—write this—." The second piece read, "—Dear sister—No. 7—"[1]

Arriving at the bathhouse a little after 3 p.m., Ralston threw down a half dollar and asked for some towels. Clarence C. Richards, the bathhouse keeper and son-in-law of its owner, Joseph Dunkerly, complied. In the meantime, Ralston talked cheerfully with some children playing near the bathhouse door. Noticing he was perspiring heavily, Richards became concerned for Ralston's health. "I said, 'Mr. Ralston, you are sweating a great deal,' and he answered, saying, 'Oh, I'll rub myself well and take a shower-bath before I go in."[2]

Handing Richards his coat, vest and pants, Ralston admonished, "I want you to put these away for me and be very careful with them. They contain valuables."[3] Among the contents of his pockets were much of what he still owned, a pocket watch and chain, gold studs, keys, a small sum of money, two pocketknives, two ivory tablets and a number of papers.

Having changed into his swimming drawers, Ralston left the bathhouse. Walking out to the end of a small wharf, he dove in, swimming out toward Alcatraz Island, playfully diving and floating on his back at times. He was out about 600 yards before two other bathhouse patrons on shore noticed something was wrong. "What is the matter with that gentleman who just went into the water?" said one of them. "See, he is floating on the water and making no signs of movement."[4] Richards yelled to his father-in-law, Dunkerly, that Ralston was drowning, after which he jumped into a boat and began rowing out in Ralston's direction. Dunkerly headed for the coroner's office to report the death.

The motionless Ralston was now being carried along with the tide toward Selby's Lead Smelting Works. Before Richards could reach him, M.J. Clarke, engineer of the lead works' small steamer, the *Bullion*, anchored about 400 yards away, had arrived in a small boat and, with great difficulty, lifted Ralston in to it. Clarke would later testify that he had observed Ralston swimming but thought nothing of it, until he saw men from shore pointing to where Ralston was, "...I saw that there was something the matter with him, and I looked again, and he was making unusual squirming in the water, as though he was in a fit, or something of that sort; I saw that he was swimming as though he had a fit, or something of that kind, in the water, and he would roll over and dive down and come up again, and, it was unnatural, the way that he was working; it was not as swimmers usually do; he would roll over and go down and come up; I think I noticed it three different times."[5]

Clarke believed at first that Ralston, who was head down in the water, was dead, so he decided to secure a rope to his arm and body and haul him to shore, "but when I came to tie the rope around his other hand I saw he was alive, at least I imagined he was; I could feel him moving in my arms; I felt his flesh quiver...."[6] Instead,

The scene of William C. Ralston's death. The Neptune Bath House is in the foreground. Above is Selby's Lead Smelting Works. The steamer Bullion is anchored just offshore. Courtesy of the Bancroft Library, University of California, Berkeley.

Clarke pulled Ralston out of the water and into the boat and then rowed for shore, depositing Ralston on the beach on Bay Street, between Leavenworth and Hyde.

Once on the beach, Clarke and others sprawled Ralston's limp body over a barrel, rolling him back and forth, attempting to drain the water from his lungs. Among those who rushed to Ralston's aid were Theodore Bee, assayer at Selby's Lead Smelting Works, and three swimmers, Oscar Meysel, F. Giamboni and C. Balzarini. "'I rubbed his feet and tried to warm him up," Meysel told the *Alta* of the rescue efforts. "On the arrival of the doctor, we tried to restore him by artificial breathing. I blew in his mouth for about three-quarters of an hour, while the doctor pressed on his stomach."[7] They continued to labor over Ralston in this manner, but it was to no avail. "The first half hour he seemed to warm up, but gradually after that I felt that his lips were getting colder. I did all I could to try to bring him to life again," Meysel said.[8] The crowd around Ralston continued to swell.

Dunkerly arrived at the coroner's office at around 3:30 p.m., where the deputy coroner and an *Alta* reporter, making his daily rounds, had a hard time accepting that the drowned man was Ralston. Nevertheless, somebody had drowned, and a dead wagon was dispatched. Rumors spread throughout the city that it was Ralston, but still were not widely believed.

The *Alta's* representative, who rode aboard the dead wagon, along with the deputy coroner and Dunkerly, reported that:

> The long black box on wheels, driving rapidly down the avenue, attracted all eyes and certainly deepened the general sensation. Along the rough and unpaved thoroughfare we drove along until reaching a rise in full sight of the smelting works. We saw several figures tearing wildly up the high bluff and over the sandy stretch to the beach beyond, which was hidden from sight. Lashing up the horse, the end of the road was soon reached. Jumping out, and taking a fence at a run, the three were quickly struggling through the deep sand down to the beach below. The first sight that met the eye was a few coarse bags stretched upon the

> sand, on which was lying a stout man, destitute of all clothing except a pair of bathing drawers. A small crowd of boys, sailors, longshoremen and bare-headed women were grouped around, while five men were energetically manipulating the body with the purpose of winning back the almost flown spark of vital fire. The lower limbs were rubbed by coarse though kindly hands, with salt, the arms flexed, the chest pressed upon and released at regular intervals, while holding the head in his lap was a young German who had glued his lips to those of the almost inanimate man, and was forcing his own life giving breath into the speechless mouth.[9]

The tragic news having spread, others arrived on the scene, including San Francisco Mayor Otis and Ralston's father-in-law, J.D. Fry. It was indeed Ralston, and he would soon be pronounced dead. "The smoke from the lead works had covered all the standing objects, the sands and the bluff, with a melancholy gray tone which, together with the slow, measured swash of the incoming tide on the beach, made this strange and sad scene more solemn and affecting," the *Alta* wrote. "Every one seemed overcome by the presence of death, the talk of all being little and in a low tone, while the many bare-headed women gathered around the body of the late millionaire looked deeply compassionate, while tears were in the eyes of many."[10]

Ralston's body having been placed in the dead wagon, he was first taken to his San Francisco residence at Leavenworth and Pine streets. Later the body was moved, by procession, to Fry's home, where Ralston's wife and two daughters had been staying since the bank's collapse.

Once the city's stunned residents came to accept that Ralston was dead, the question became: How had it happened? Rumors sprang up that Ralston, who had been ruined and further humiliated by being asked earlier that same day to turn in his resignation, had committed suicide. These rumors were especially popular among San Francisco newspapers opposed to the bank crowd but were also picked up nationally. The Aug. 28, 1875, *New York Tribune* reported that Ralston was seen sitting on a clay bank near the smelting works, tearing up several pieces of paper and throwing them into the water. A "search was made for the pieces, but none could be found," the *Tribune* wrote. "It is also reported that he [Ralston] was seen to drink from a phial before going into the water. The general impression is that he took poison before entering the water."[11]

Dr. Valentine Newmark, who had tended to Ralston on the beach, fixed the cause of death as apoplexy, saying, "although I had been told it was a case of a drowned person, from examining him I did not think that there was any case of drowning at all; he had the appearance of a man who had died from apoplexy; his face was flushed and livid, perfectly blue, a glassy stare in his eyes and the pupils dilated; his face had not the look of a drowned man."[12] Newmark explained that, "If a person much over-heated and fatigued suddenly plunges in the water, the blood would be driven from the surface of the body to the internal organs, and the heart or brain are more particularly liable to suffer from such a shock; such a shock might cause apoplexy; the longer a man remained in the water, under such circumstances, the greater the liability to a chill; remaining in the water might have, as it were, a cumulative effect."[13]

Strangely, Ralston, who had been in a regular habit of taking such swims, had been warned just prior to his death by his friend, Mint Director Henry R. Linderman, that such a practice could prove fatal. The Aug. 28 issue of the *Alta* recorded:

> Dr. Lindermann [sic], Director of the United States Mint, and a personal friend of Mr. Ralston, not longer than ten days ago, talking to him of his habit of going in bathing after having concluded the business of the day, strongly advised him against continuing the practice. He warned him that he would some day be seized with cramps while out of his depth and drown. The peculiar, tired and nervous condition produced by a hard day's work, would tend most strongly to produce this disastrous result. Mr. Ralston, on this advice, gave up his bathing for a considerable time, but eventually returned to it, and for the past two weeks has been bathing constantly.
>
> A physician who saw Mr. Ralston's remains at his residence late yesterday afternoon states that the expression of the face, the color and general appearance of the body, gave him the conviction, in the strongest manner, that the deceased had met his death from a spasm or apoplectic attack, which could have been caused by suddenly entering the cold waters of the bay with overheated blood and in a state of great mental and nervous excitement.[14]

Others, however, continued to cling to the suicide theory. In its Aug. 29 issue, the *Alta* wrote, "There are journals even in this city [the *San Francisco Call* and the *San Francisco Bulletin*] which are so rash as to give currency, without foundation, to the painful rumor that the death of Mr. W.C. Ralston was suicidal."[15] Apparently unaware of the circumstances behind Ralston's forced resignation as Bank of California president, it added:

> The unexpected blow struck by the Board of Trustees of the Bank of California, in requesting his resignation, completely stunned the man who stood at their mercy, reduced by his own act [assigning his

property to the bank] to poverty to save the bank and preserve his honor. Why the Trustees acted as they did seems unaccountable, under the circumstances in which they were placed; but this is not proper for us to discuss. The resignation of Mr. Ralston was promptly handed in, and this last act was the straw that broke a strong back. He left the bank bewildered in mind. He was homeless, abandoned and out of business. He walked fast—anywhere, reaching the North Beach probably before he thought what he was doing.[16]

The *Alta* said his demeanor, while walking to the beach and during his regular swim, showed that "he was not only sane, but also not desirous of taking his own life." Claiming his death was likely the result of the day's mental excitement and his overheated blood, it scolded the *Call* and the *Bulletin*:

> In justice to his memory, the press should correct any inadvertent errors which they have made in noticing his death. The result of the autopsy has not yet been made known; but the investigation before the Coroner affords only proof that our statement is correct.[17]

The funeral was planned for Sunday, Aug. 29, but had to be postponed until Monday, when Ralston's brother, A.J. Ralston, could be in attendance. Ralston's body was packed in a rosewood ice box, with a plate-glass top for viewing. "On Saturday evening and during all of yesterday Col. Fry's house was besieged by visitors anxious to obtain a view," the *Alta* wrote.[18] All around the box were placed rare and exotic flowers by the attending mourners who represented all classes of San Franciscans. "Crosses, crowns, wreaths, anchors, massive bouquets, and garlands of the rarest and most exquisite flowers filled the air with their perfume and expressed the symathies [sic] and respect of hundreds."[19]

In the meantime, most buildings were draped in black, including the Bank of California, the San Francisco Stock Exchange, the Kimball Manufacturing Company, the West Coast Furniture Company, and Windel's Carpet Cleaning Works. Other

Many of William C. Ralston's enterprises are depicted in this memorial printing. At upper left is the Palace Hotel. At middle left is Gold Hill. At bottom left is the Kimball Manufacturing Company. At top right is the California Theatre. At middle right is the Pacific Rolling Mills. At bottom right are the Cornell Watch Company and the West Coast Furniture Company. Flanking Ralston's portrait are, at left, the California Silk Factory and, at right, the Mission Woolen Mills. Shown below Ralston is the Bank of California. Courtesy of the Bancroft Library, University of California, Berkeley.

stores along San Francisco's Montgomery Street placed life-size drawings and paintings of Ralston on exhibit, wrapped in black crepe.[20] Flags throughout the city were flown at half-staff.

Among the pallbearers would be many of San Francisco leading citizens and Ralston's close associates, including former Bank of California president D.O. Mills, William Sharon, Sen. Cornelius Cole and Louis A. Garnett. Long before 9 a.m. on Aug. 30, the streets around Calvary Church, where the services were to be held, were lined with people. "The people swarmed into Union Square, and soon it presented a solid square of humanity."[21] The funeral cortege from Col. Fry's house was evident by the approach of a platoon of police—the crowd parting as the hearse made its way to the church.

"At 11:25 A.M. the casket, preceded by the Rev. Dr. Hemphill, and borne by a detachment of Co. C. First Infantry, and followed by Mr. Ralston's colored body servant, the pall-bearers, the employés of the Bank, mourning relatives, bankers, Boards of Brokers, the Odd Fellows, Regents of the University, members of the Chamber of Commerce, entered the church and was placed in front of the pulpit."[22] The procession into the church was accompanied by the playing of Beethoven's funeral march. At the pulpit, Rev. Hemphill lamented:

> That William C. Ralston, *our* William C. Ralston, is gone. We are sad. We are sick at heart. A word can start the tear in every eye. He had been with use these twenty years—his name and fame and fortune woven into the history of our city and our State—the top and crown of this vast commercial fabric, which he, more than a dozen men that you could name, helped to build, and yet not lifted above the people because of pride of place or a pride of intellect; but walking on our levels still, familiar, friendly, neighborly always and everywhere—a stranger to the pride of riches—the same in mien and spirit when controlling millions as when a salaried official on a Mississippi steamer—kind, considerate, tender, truehearted, helpful to all who were drifted across his path, ready to spend himself and be spent for others who were weak and struggling, to work for them, to help them to
>
> UPBUILD THEIR SHATTERED FORTUNES.
> San Francisco does well to put on the symbols of sorrow. There is no one like him left that I know of. His death is an immense loss to the city and the State. Such was he: the rich man's peer—the poor man's friend. His very presence was a power; we were confident so long as he was not afraid. There was something in his look of buoyancy and triumph, in his manly bearing, in his sympathy, in his capacity for work, in his genuine, irrepressible interest, in his smile—something so reassuring in his way of saying that he had struggled through it all himself—that you were convinced that though you might be over-freighted with heavy and great cares, you would yet be able to shake them off.... [23]

Following the services, the cortege escorting Ralston to his burial included several regiments of the National Guard; clerks and employees of the Bank of California; regents, faculty and students of the University of California; members of the Chamber of Commerce; members of the San Francisco Stock Exchange and the Pacific Stock Exchange; the officers and employees of the Mission Woolen Mills; employees of the Kimball Carriage Manufacturing Company, the West Coast Furniture Company, the Cornell Watch Company and workmen of the Palace Hotel, numbering around 1,800, all wearing crepe on their arms.[24]

"The cortege moved from Powell and Geary streets to Post, to Stockton, to O'Farrell, to Taylor, to Geary, to Van Ness avenue," the *Alta* recorded. "The streets and house-windows were packed with people along the entire route, and the cross streets were lined with vehicles of every description. It appeared as though the entire population had decided to testify their respect to the dead by following his remains from his house to his final place of rest."[25]

Ralston's widespread influence in the business world, along with his generous support of charitable organizations, assured that beyond his critics, many would come to praise him. A.A. Cohen, the bank's longest running depositor, having maintained an account with Ralston for 21 years, remembered Ralston by saying he never knew a man who understood the principles of exchanges better:

> He knew just where the best place was for him to remit, and the way he could do an exchange business to the best advantage; for he kept run of the transactions of the general monetary system of the country. For instance, sometimes it is better to remit to New York; sometimes it is better to remit to China; and he made exchanges in that way, so as to give the bank the greatest possible profit on the transactions made.[26]

Cohen claimed, in his early years in banking, Ralston was considered, among the business community, a very cautious and prudent man in his banking transactions. He added, "I have no doubt, if the same characteristics which marked the first years of his business life had been continued until the present, the bank would not be in the situation it now is."[27] Cohen credited Ralston for sticking with the Comstock through its tough times, saying, in answer to a question from the *Alta* about Ralston's enterprises:

> A.—To him probably more than any other man on this Coast is due the credit of the great discoveries that have even recently been made on the Comstock lode. Very soon after the first discovery of silver ore there, when everybody held aloof to see what was coming, and afraid to venture anything, Ralston started an agency of the Bank at Virginia City, under the management of Mr. Sharon; and with the capital that they were enabled to furnish there, they assisted very materially the earlier developments that were made on that lode. After the failure of ore that was first found in the Ophir, the Gould & Curry and Mexican, and some of the Gold Hill mines had given out, and the price of the stock had dwindled down to almost nothing, a great many people here urged him to withdraw the capital of the Bank from Nevada; but he always refused believing much greater developments would be made in the future than had been made at that time. And if he had listened to others, and not exercised his own vigorous judgment the State of Nevada would have been a mere fraction of what it now is, or what it would have been a few years ago; perhaps not to-day. But a great many developments that have been made in different parts of Nevada probably would not have been made, if that course recommended him by his friends had been taken.[28]

Ralston's close friend, Henry F. Williams, termed him, "the most unselfish man I ever met," explaining that he readily aided those who were just getting started.[29] When a Mr. Soule, who for years had been employed at San Quentin in the manufacture of mechanical implements, came to Ralston with the idea of starting a similar enterprise in San Francisco, only employing wayward youth, Ralston provided $10,000 to launch the now successful enterprise. Likewise, when another mechanic came to Ralston with the idea for a business manufacturing edge tools, Ralston gave him $2,500, despite the fact that the man had no security to offer. "He has always been the first man to come forward and contribute to aid our industrial exhibitions and all our public enterprises," Williams said of Ralston. "He was the most reliable person they had. They could call upon him with a certainty of aid."[30]

Gen. George S. Dodge, vice president and acting president of the Pacific Stock Board, similarly lauded Ralston, telling the *Alta* his death was great loss to the Pacific coast, "He was foremost in all the enterprises that tend to develop a new country, and would listen always to everything of importance that came before him." Dodge related of his last talk with Ralston, on Friday morning, the day Ralston died: "Mr. Ralston said to me that he had commenced and was going to give his undivided attention to the settlement of the affairs of the Bank of California; that he had reduced his expenses by closing his house, and that he was going to commence at the bed-rock again and build up for himself, and to save every depositor and every one that had interests in the bank; he had that morning closed his house in pursuance of this design, and removed his family to Colonel Fry's."[31]

Ralston would be praised throughout the city. The various exchanges, including the stock boards, produce exchange, merchants exchange and many others, issued proclamations. Civic societies and associations all favored him as well. Pastors at churches, throughout San Francisco, preached of the great man and took the opportunity to school their congregations on the uncertainty of riches. One preacher proclaiming, "Will it not be possible for God to emphasize more impressively these words of the Holy Writ: 'Let not the rich man glory in his riches.'"[32] At Plymouth Church, Rev. T.K. Noble said of Ralston:

> For years he had spent his money with a liberal hand: he lived like a prince; he entertained like a king; but, on Friday last, he was sitting by his golden throne, with bowed head—dethroned, but kingly still. 'I am not given to boasting,' he said, 'but let me retain this throne, and I pledge you my word that not a dollar shall be lost by a single creditor.' His request was refused—wisely, or unwisely, I am not competent to decide; and what then? Did he give utterance to bitterness, or animosity? On the contrary, he calmly resigned his trust, and then made over his entire possessions for the benefit of these creditors—his railroad interests, his manufacturing interests, his palatial home in Belmont, his houses in the city, and even his horses and carriages were surrendered, and surrendered without a murmur; and gathering up a few souvenirs of the past, he went out of his home penniless to begin life anew. To my thinking, this was grandest act of his singularly successful life.[33]

On Sept. 8, 1875, Ralston's friends gathered for a special meeting, conducted by George W. Smiley, a leading broker. Nearly 90 vice presidents of the new organization formed out of the assembly were elected. The *Alta* estimated that some 20,000 packed in Union Hall or milled around outside for presentations, raising Ralston's stature to mythic proportions.

Many took umbrage to the attacks of the *San Francisco Bulletin* and *Call* of the local press, who, they believed sought to bring a great man down. Thomas Fitch proclaimed, "I say, my fellow-citizens, that WILLIAM C. RALSTON was stung to death by the blood-sucking vermin of the press."[34] Of the charges made by the local press, Col. W.H.L. Barnes added:

> Now, they say, he sought to rob the city. When it is asserted that, from his earliest coming here, he was

> engaged in plundering the city, our answer is—the public's answer to the world, will be—His record is in the monuments of public industry and private enterprise that sparkle and blaze all over your city, which, but for him, so far as human knowledge goes, as far as human eyes can see, would never have had a solitary moment's life. (Applause.) He never sought anything from the city or State; the stream of public beneficence never flowed in towards him. He was a man without selfish ambition—a man of the people, who, though he spent his vast wealth for your sakes; who, though he entertained like a Prince with a boundless magnificence, like the stream that rises in the mountain, flowing ever on, deepening and widening; yet not one drop of that generous stream which he shed upon all of us, ever came back to him. He was a giver. He was a bounteous giver, prodigal if you please, wasteful if you please, but he gave. He was no hoarder of money; he was no miser; he was no public or private usurer. He gave. From the first hour that he came, and until the last hour of his life, he was giving. (Applause)[35]

In the end, a resolution was adopted by those in attendance, among the provisions of which were, "to record, in unmistakable language, their utter condemnation and abhorrence of the savage brutality and cruelty of certain of the daily newspapers of this city" and call for merchants to stop advertising in the San Francisco *Bulletin* and the *Call*.[36] Speeches and resolutions were also offered in the street with similar results.

The Bank of California would be reorganized, under Sharon's direction, reopening on Oct. 2, 1875, to again become one of the nation's major banks. Sharon would take over Ralston's home, Belmont, and withstand a suit by Ralston's wife, Elizabeth.

Linderman, who was in San Francisco on the day of the funeral and likely paid his respects to his departed friend and his widow, would continue to purchase Nevada silver, most of this coming from the bonanza firm, and push for acceptance of the Trade dollar he and Ralston had worked so hard to obtain. With the growth of the Free Silver Movement, there would be a new silver dollar to contend with and charges of corruption that would erupt just before his death in 1879. Times were changing. Life on Comstock, and throughout the nation, would never be the same.

Chapter 21

SILVER'S REBIRTH

The birth of the Free Silver Movement, which would result in the reinstatement of the standard silver dollar, can be traced to 1876, three years after the passage of the Coinage Act of 1873. Spurring the rise of the movement and the new allegiance to silver were a combination of factors stemming from the Panic of 1873 and the collapse of silver prices. The panic led to the closing of more than 10,000 businesses during the ensuing six years of depression. Hardest hit were the nation's laboring classes and its agrarians, who struggled under mounting debts (and in the case of the farmers, falling produce prices), further invigorating the rise of various associations of malcontents who, as the depression worsened, looked to identify the cause of the nation's economic woes and, increasingly, came to blame it on a shortage of money. Over the next several decades, debates raged on the floor of Congress and in the nation's press over the propriety of growing the supply of money, either through increased printing of paper or restoration of an unlimited coinage of the silver dollar.

Although advocates of monetary inflation were in evidence well prior to the Panic of 1873 (including the Greenback Party's forerunner, the National Labor Reform Party, which, in its 1872 platform, called for "a purely national circulating medium based on the faith and resources of the nation"), they increased dramatically in number and influence after the panic began, leading to congressional

The Panic of 1873 led to the formation of the Greenback Party, which sought an increased printing of federal paper money.

support for raising ceilings on the number of greenbacks and national bank notes in circulation. On Nov. 25, 1874, agitation over currency inflation coalesced in the formation of the Greenback Party in Indianapolis, Ind. The *Alta California*, which regularly lampooned attempts to grow the supply of inconvertible paper money, jested of its founding:

> The new currency party, just organized at Indianapolis, proposes to go it on the general idea of an old German of whom General Robert Toombs told the President last Spring. During the hard times of '37, when money was scarce and the State Bank was at its wits' end, this astute financier of the rural districts came to Milledgeville and sought his representative in the Legislature. 'Mr. Toombs,' says he, 'we must have more money. We're obleeged to have more money.' 'Well,' says Toombs, in his brusque way, 'how are you going to get it?' 'Out of the State Bank,' says the financier. 'But,' says Toombs, struck by the earnestness of his constituent, 'how is the State Bank to get it?' 'Stamp it,' says the financier. '*Stamp* it,' roared Toombs; 'and how is it going to redeem the money it stamps?' 'Why,' Mr. Toombs, says he, 'that's just what I' a-comin' to. You see, Mr. Toombs, *I'm agin' redemption!*'[1]

In May 1876, the Greenback Party held its first national convention, in Indianapolis, where Peter Cooper, a millionaire philanthropist from New York, was nominated as its candidate for president. Samuel Carey, of Ohio, was tabbed for vice president. In its 1876 platform, the party called for a repudiation of the 1875 Specie Resumption Act, which threatened to limit the currency supply.

Linking with discontented laborers to form a coalition between the Labor Reform and Greenback parties in 1878 on a joint platform, the greenbackers were able to elect a number of congressmen. However, they lost considerable influence when the provisions of the Specie Resumption Act went into effect on Jan. 1, 1879, reducing the amount of United States notes in circulation and making the remaining notes redeemable in gold. The party again nominated candidates for president and vice president in 1880 and 1884, but after that faded from stature.

Taking paper money's place, as the preferred inflationary vehicle for the remainder of the century, would be silver, which, as silver prices weakened and greater supplies entered circulation, took on an appeal that far outstripped any engendered in the greenbacks. This was particularly true among the nation's hard-pressed agrarians, many of whom had remained suspicious of paper but would come to embrace the free silver dogma that the demonetization of silver had been engineered by the wealthy to increase the value of gold and further burden the working masses in debt.

Still, despite its more wide-ranging appeal, the abandonment of easily printed paper for silver, by those who favored monetary inflation, was not immediate or all encompassing. It was not until 1876, well after the depression began, that silver began to be looked on as a viable inflationary tool, and even then, there was considerable resistance from hard-line soft money supporters. Some thought that the supply was still too small to serve their purposes. Others continued to view silver as another form of hard money, to be held in disdain with gold. J.S. Moore wrote contemporarily of this phenomenon in the March 1877 issue of the *North American Review.* Chastising William D. Kelley, who backed the gold standard during debate over the mint bill but now favored currency inflation, Moore wrote:

> On February 9, 1872, a bill to demonetize silver was introduced in the House of Representatives, and out of this bill eventually grew the demonetizing Act of 1873. It is a remarkable fact that the chief inflationists, like Mr. Kelly [sic] and others, were anxious and voted for this measure. The inflationists up to within a recent period when silver became depreciated looked upon that metal with the same aversion as they looked upon gold. The philanthropic inflationists maintain that gold and silver as money are the enemies of labor, of enterprise, and of the people.[2]

Irwin Unger expressed a similar view in *The Greenback Era: A Social and Political History of American Finance, 1865-1869*. Of the lack of objection of the soft money interests to the proposed elimination of the standard silver dollar during debate over the mint bill and their silence on the subject for years after the bill's passage, Unger asserted that, while silver was overvalued in relation to gold, it held no attraction to soft money men. This fact being demonstrated by the vote in House, where the bill passed 110 to 13, meaning that almost every soft money man supported it. "In fact, until well into 1876 and even 1877 silver was regarded as just another variety of specie, of hard money," Unger wrote.[3] However, once they got by their initial prejudice against coin:

> ...the paper money men almost universally embraced the new panacea. The greenback ideologues saw it as a renewed opportunity to put off the evil day of resumption and at the same time scale down the federal debt without hurdling the barrier of the 1869 Public Credit Act. The more pragmatic greenbackers hoped for relief to private debtors from the new form of 'cheap money.' Among the soft money men of the prairies, silver seemed to be the answer to problem of rural taxes and rural debts.[4]

There are additional market- and circulation-related reasons for the three-year gap between the silver dollar's removal from the nation's coinage system and the first outcries against the Coinage Act of 1873. While it is true that silver fell below par with gold in 1873, confirming Mint Director Henry R. Linderman's suspicions, it was not a total collapse. From 1873-1875 silver maintained a high enough price in relation to paper that even the reduced-weight subsidiary silver coins could not be released into circulation without disappearing. By 1876, however, several factors served to strengthen public perception of the need for an expandable money supply and to spark awareness that silver could serve that purpose. As the depression grew worse and credit tightened, Unger explained, the lack of available currency was further exacerbated by the Specie Resumption Act of 1875 and Treasury Secretary Benjamin Bristow's liberal interpretation of its greenback redemption provision, which greatly reduced the amount of currency in circulation. The tightening of credit also coincided with peak production of silver on the Comstock Lode; the unexpected rejection of the Trade dollar by the Chinese, with the massive entry of the depreciated silver dollars into domestic circulation; record production of silver dimes, quarters and half dollars, which began to be released into circulation that year; and the continuing effects of silver's new role as a monetary outcast abroad. After years of being held at a premium or near par with gold, silver fell drastically—the silver value of a standard silver dollar dropping to below 80 cents by mid-year. With the depression raging, the stage was set for the standard silver dollar—once legal tender in payments of all debts, public and private—to become the oppressed darling of a new inflationary movement, which sought an immediate return to bimetallism.

Charges of corruption in the passage of the Coinage Act of 1873 were quickly forthcoming, stirred by the writings of George Weston, a former abolitionist newspaper editor and a Boston merchant, who, through a series of letters to the editors of many of the nation's leading newspapers, launched debate over the silver question.[5] In his first letter, published in the March 2, 1876, issue of the *Boston Globe*, Weston argued that the Constitution of the United States legally provided for the maintenance of the double standard, allowing that nothing but gold or silver coins could be considered as a tender for payments of debts, "and no political ingenuity or corruption can get rid of it so long as the Federal Constitution remains unaltered."[6]

Weston claimed that throughout history, the bimetallic standard had been nearly the universal practice of mankind and was so installed in the United States up until the surreptitious passage of the Coinage Act of 1873. Weston explained:

> The practice in this country conformed to the plain letter of the United States Constitution during more than two generations, and down to February 12, 1873, when, without discussion in or out of Congress, and without notice or warning of any kind, there were surreptitiously inserted in a long act relating to the Mint, two sections, providing for the coinage of the trade dollar and of fractions of the dollar, not to be a legal tender for sums exceeding five dollars, and forbidding any silver coinage except of such trade dollars and fractional parts of the dollar.[7]

According to Weston's analysis, the coinage legislation "was as selfish in its origin as it was surreptitious in the manner of its introduction," intended to augment the public and private debt for the benefit of foreign and domestic bankers.[8] He insisted that, until 1873, gold and silver had been on an equal footing and that:

> The demonetization of silver dates only with the acts of February 12, 1873, and June 22, 1874, which are unconstitutional as respects private debts, and scandalously corrupt as respects the national debt, the burden of which they increase by a heavy percentage. The people who are to pay this debt, and who received nothing for it but depreciated paper, are entitled to the benefit resulting from the richness and abundance of newly discovered silver mines, and if they are wise and firm they will insist upon it and obtain it.[9]

Weston having leveled the first blow in what was to become a lengthy campaign waged to reinstate the free coinage of the silver dollar, other influential newspapers expanded on his theory that the removal of the silver dollar was a result of an overt conspiracy. Slightly more than two months after Weston's first letter appeared in the *Boston Globe*, the *New York Graphic*, on May 9, 1876, pondered, "it would be interesting to know exactly who proposed and engineered through Congress the bill which demonetized silver in this country."[10]

Pleading, as had Weston, that the silver dollar had been made a unit of value from the settlement of the country and that the switch to a monometallic standard caused gold to appreciate in value, while prices in general declined, the *Graphic* told its readers that, through the demonetization of the silver dollar, "silver bullion became a drug on the market. Resumption was pushed indefinitely ahead, and business of all kinds was paralyzed."[11]

The *Graphic* contended that the coinage legislation of 1873 aided rich capitalists; therefore, it was obvious who engineered the bill's passage through Congress, and that without a doubt, "if the matter were investigated it would be found that a few leading financiers and their Congressional attorneys, backed by the great moneyed institutions, smuggled the measure through Congress."[12]

On July 8, 1876, the *Cincinnati Commercial* parroted the *Graphic's* concern over a bondholder's conspiracy, noting:

> During the disappearance of the precious metals from circulation in this country, the old double standard was abolished by indirection. Of course this was not done accidentally, but systematically and in the interest of the holders of securities, with the purpose of increasing the weight of debts, public and private.[13]

Ten days later, on July 18, 1876, the *Cincinnati Commercial* expanded on its conspiracy charges, claiming that there had been British involvement in the bondholder's plot and asserting, "the only persons who seem to have known anything about it were two or three Congressmen, and the agents of European bankers, who were lively with information. There is the strongest suggestion of the use of 'British gold' in this legislation that we have ever seen."[14]

The free silver crusade having been launched, newspaper editors throughout the country joined in the battle, expressing their views on the silver question. The restoration of the double standard became the primary objective of the free silver camp, and along these lines, the *Cincinnati Commercial* became one of the most influential editorial leaders of the crusade. On July 23, 1876, the pro-silver newspaper expanded its attack on those who, it claimed, were responsible for the downfall of the silver dollar, angrily charging that:

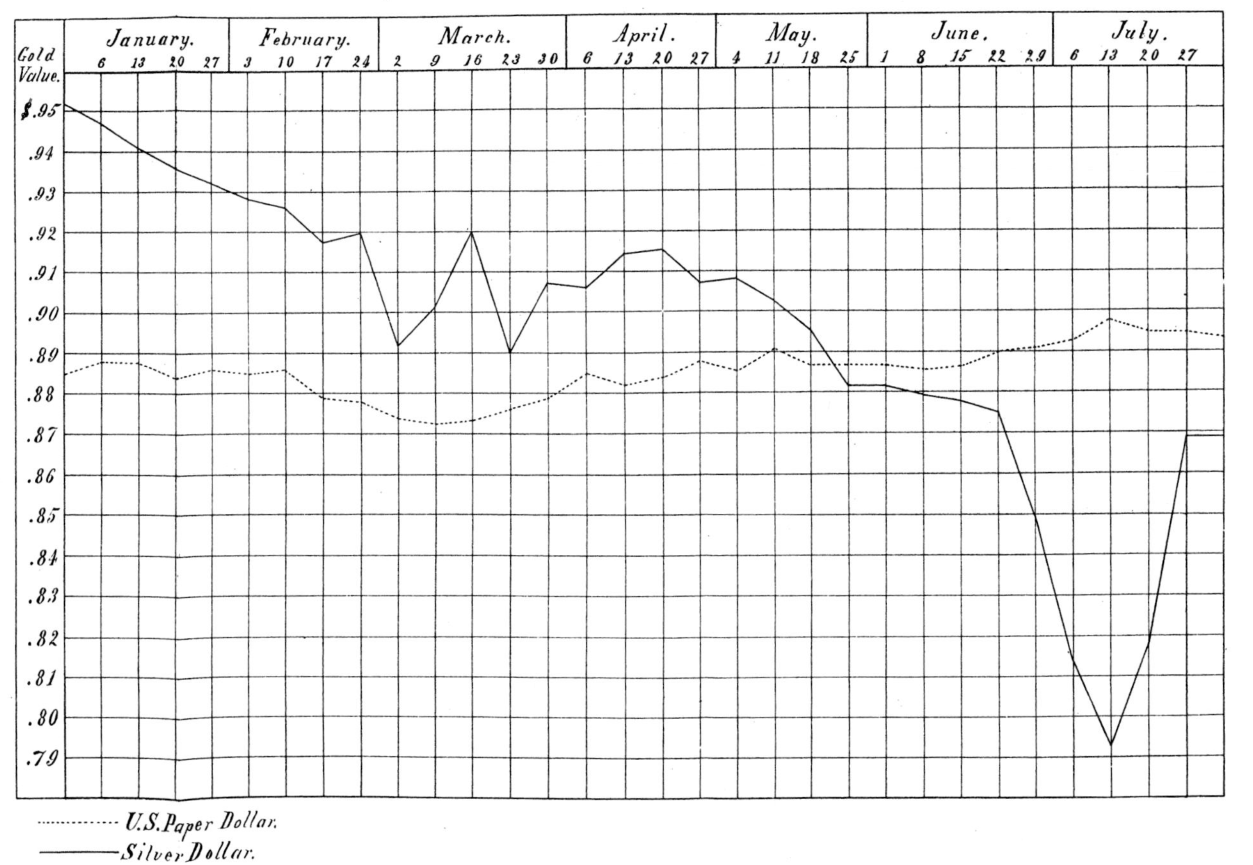

This diagram, from the 1876 Report of the Director of the Mint, shows the decline in the value of the silver dollar, as compared to the paper dollar, during the first six months of 1876.

> The people of the United States have had the standard changed on them in the dark, and now those guilty of this tremendous wrong would brazenly take advantage of it. Their object was to increase the purchasing power of gold, and then say: 'Behold we have boosted gold twenty per cent. We took away the silver dollar, which was worth 104, and by placing the standard, contrary to the policy of ALEXANDER HAMILTON, in one metal, gold—we have brought down the price of silver to eighty cents—making a difference of twenty-four cents on the dollar.' This, then, is the measure of the success of their conspiracy—and they presume to charge those who would restore the people's rights in silver with being inflationists and repudiationists—and above all in impudence, with proposing to disturb the standard, if the standard is such a sacred thing?[15]

By September 1876, when Weston's 13th letter, expressing his views on the silver question, appeared in the *Chicago Tribune*, his ideas were receiving widespread acceptance and, along with the writings of other influential free silver newspapers, helped to raise the silver issue to one of national importance. In his letter concerning "The Secret and Fraudulent Character of the Silver Demonetization of 1873-4," printed in the Sept. 9, 1876, issue of the *Chicago Tribune*, Weston, for the first time, reviewed the congressional debate over the Coinage Act of 1873 and the passage of the Revised Statutes of 1874, which he claimed surreptitiously eliminated the silver dollar without informing the public of the true intent of the measures. According to Weston, the people of the United States know when a subject is debated or when it is not debated, and they know that the silver question was not discussed or written about until 1876, "two years after the mischief of demonetizing silver was consummated...."[16]

While he was willing to admit that the passage of the mint bill was covered by the press, Weston surmised that it would have taken a skilled eye to determine that, even though the Coinage Act of 1873 halted the coinage of the silver dollar, the actual demonetization was accomplished one year later, when the Revised Statutes of 1874 took away the coin's full legal tender status. In answer to those who defended the coinage act by asserting that, because it appeared before three or four sessions of Congress, had been printed on numerous occasions and, therefore, should not have gone unnoticed, Weston charged that the elimination of the double standard did escape attention, as shown by the lack of discussion on the matter, in and out of Congress, "and it is idle to controvert that by the circuitous and inferential argument that it might have attracted attention, or even ought to have attracted attention. It did not, as a matter of fact, and that is the end of it."[17]

Not only was the act ignored by Congress and the public, according to Weston, but "the time selected [for its passage] was skillfully chosen to escape attention...," because in 1873 and 1874, the entire currency circulation in the United States was comprised of paper money, thus nothing could have been more boring to Congress or the people than coinage legislation, "and, providing such an act was long enough—and this contained seventy-four tedious sections—what opportunity more admirable could be conceived of for slipping in almost anything, with the connivance of the few men having the matter in charge?"[18]

In summarizing the Senate debate over the mint bill, Weston found that, for the most part, deliberations centered around a contest between the western senators and the chairman of the Senate Finance Committee, John Sherman, over the coinage charge, and that "not one word about demonetizing silver, or abrogating the double standard was uttered by any Senator."[19] Of the progress of the bill through the House of Representatives, Weston wrote that the House bill, as introduced by Samuel Hooper, provided for a silver dollar, but the House did not move to demonetize the silver dollar. He stated that, "there was no demonetizing of the old silver dollar in Mr. Hooper's bill and no assertion in any form, direct or implied, of any authority in Congress to demonetize any gold or silver coin of full weight and standard."[20]

When the bill returned to the Senate late in 1872, Weston noted that the Senate substituted the Trade dollar for the House's 385-grain subsidiary dollar without discussion, and:

> This was undoubtedly an assertion of a power in Congress to demonetize silver of full weight, but that was added at the end of the legislative proceedings in relation to the matter. It formed no part of the bill, the printing of which eleven times, and the consideration of which during successive sessions, are now so ostentatiously paraded. It was one of those things so often slipped into laws at the very last moment, and essentially changing their character. The Senate adopted it without observation, and the House never acted upon it at all, except to reject it *pro forma* and send the bill to a conference committee.[21]

The final blow to the silver dollar, by Weston's account, came about as the result of a clause fraudulently inserted into the Revised Statutes of 1874 that reduced the legal tender status of all silver coins to five dollars, of which he asserted, "that this was inserted improperly and without the knowledge of Congress is not attempted to be denied. That it was contrived and fraudulent in the

Free silver supporters argued that there was no legitimate reason for ending the coinage of the standard silver dollar in 1873. Its removal from the nation's coinage system, they claimed, was aimed solely at increasing the value of gold.

interest of those who profited by it, is an inference not difficult to be drawn."[22]

The ranting and raving of Weston and others, who strove to reinstate the free and unlimited coinage of the silver dollar, led Congress, by mid-1876, to compose a special commission to look into the silver question and to report its findings, along with recommendations, to Congress. The commission, comprised of members of both Houses, as well as other technical experts, at first held their sessions in New York, but moved to Washington, D.C. in December 1876, when Congress reconvened. Members of the commission included John P. Jones, Lewis V. Bogy, and George S. Boutwell from the Senate; Randall L. Gibson, George Willard, and Richard P. Bland from the House; along with William S. Groesbeck, Prof. Francis Bowen, and the man whose letters had focused public attention on the issue, George M. Weston, who served as the commission's secretary.

After completing its study, the commission submitted its two-volume report to the Senate on March 2, 1877. Most of the commission's members favored the majority report, advocating a return to bimetallism, while only two objected and issued minority reports. They were Sen. Boutwell, who as Treasury secretary had been intimately involved in the legislation, and Prof. Bowen.

The majority report concluded that demonetization had been affected solely to aid the creditor classes, stating:

> Germany and the United States demonetized silver in 1873. At that time it was neither depreciated nor unsteady in value, nor had any change occurred in the relative production, consumption, or distribution of the precious metals to indicate its depreciation in the future, nor was any actual or probable depreciation assigned as a reason for its demonetization. The average flow of silver to India was undisturbed, and the Big Bonanza in the Comstock Lode was undiscovered. Manifestly, the real reason for the demonetization of silver was the apprehension of the creditor classes that the combined production of the two metals would raise prices and cheapen money unless one of them was shorn of the money function. In Europe this reason was distinctly avowed.[23]

The commission also complained that "the act when passed was not read except by title, and it is notorious that this transcendent change in the money systems of the country, affecting the most vital interests, was carried through without the knowledge or observation of the country."[24] Expanding on their charge that the country was largely unaware of the change in monetary standards affected by the bill, the commission concluded:

> If it had been generally known that any such vital question as the demonetization of silver was lurking in the bill, it would have aroused the most wide-spreading discussion throughout the country, as is shown by the present debate upon remonetizing it, which is only the same question in reverse, and which, it is apparent, will dominate all other public questions until it is settled.[25]

The commission was correct in assuming that the silver question would dominate public discussion, which it did for the next two decades. The inherent popularity of the silver movement, which was then still in its formative stages, sent politicians scurrying to cover their tracks as charges that they had voted for the notorious coinage act began to hamper their political ambitions. It became politically expedient for those congressmen who had voted in the affirmative and found themselves required to explain their actions, to claim that they were entirely ignorant of the true intent of the bill, at the time of passage, having been hoodwinked by an elaborate cover-up into voting for a measure that they would normally have opposed.

One such chameleon, who eagerly jumped on the silver bandwagon, denying any foreknowledge of the change in monetary standards, was William D. Kelley, who had on numerous occasions blatantly defended and encouraged adoption of the gold standard on the floor of Congress. Kelley developed a sudden case of amnesia, claiming during House debate on March 9, 1878, that he was totally unaware that the mint bill planned to drop the silver dollar, and that:

> In connection with the charge that I advocated the bill which demonetized the standard silver dollar, I say that, though chairman of the Committee on Coinage, I was ignorant of the fact that it would demonetize the silver dollar or of its dropping the silver dollar from our system of coins as were those distinguished Senators, Messrs. BLAINE and VOORHEES, who were then members of the House, and each of whom a few days since interrogated the other: 'Did you know it was dropped when the bill was passed? 'No,' said Mr. BLAINE; 'did you?' 'No' said Mr. VOORHEES. I do not think that there were three members in the House that knew it. I doubt whether Mr. HOOPER, who, in my absence from the Committee of Coinage and attendance on the Committee of Ways and Means, managed the bill knew it.[26]

Kelley, again testifying before Congress on May 10, 1879, concerning his role in the passage of the Coinage Act of 1873, bombastically claimed:

> All I can say is that the Committee on Coinage, Weights and Measures, who reported the original bill, were faithful and able, and scanned its provisions closely; that as their organ I reported it; that it contained provision for the both the standard silver dollar and the trade-dollar. Never having heard until a long time after its enactment into law of the substitution in the Senate of the section which dropped the standard dollar, I profess to know nothing of its history; but I am prepared to say that in all the legislation of this country there is no mystery equal to the demonetization of the standard silver dollar of the United States. I have never found a man who could tell just how it came about, or why.[27]

Of course, Kelley needed only to question himself in order to determine how and why the silver dollar was demonetized, for he had been a leading advocate of the monometallic standard and, as his statements during debate over the mint bill clearly show, he knew very well that the standard silver dollar had been expunged from the House version of the coinage bill in favor of a subsidiary silver dollar.

The early writings of the Free Silver Movement, based on a reasonably intellectual appeal, such as those of Weston and the United States Monetary Commission, did not, however, become the mainstay of free silver rhetoric. Instead, the popularity of the free silver cause was to be spread, by the movement's most influential and prolific writers, through the promotion of elaborately played out scenarios of international intrigue based, as we shall see, on emotional appeals, common to righteous causes and deliberately fabricated evidence offered as the true history of the Crime of 1873.

Chapter 22

BLOODY FOOTPRINTS

Less than one month after George Melville Weston's first letter opposed to the demonetization of silver appeared in the *Boston Globe*, Horace White, a former editor of the *Chicago Tribune*, answered Weston's charges in a letter to the New York financial weekly, *The Public*, published on March 23, 1876. In his letter to *The Public*, White explained that, recently "My attention has been drawn to an article, somewhat extensively circulated in the press, attributed to the pen of Mr. George M. Weston on the subject of silver as a legal-tender."[1] White complained of Weston's theories on the money question, stating:

> He has studied his subject just far enough to get wrong, and to mislead others; and since the subject of silver legal-tender is becoming an important one, by reason of the late decline in the value of that metal, as compared with gold, it is important that a false start should be checked as soon as possible.[2]

Weston had argued that the demonetization of silver had been purposely calculated to increase the public debt in the interest of bondholders, and he predicted that, once the public became aware of the real reasons behind the demonetization of silver, the Coinage Act of 1873 would be repealed. Also, Weston theorized, that, as most of the public debt had been entered into during a period in which the silver dollar of 412 1/2 grains and the gold dollar of 25 8/10 grains were by law equal legal tender, the government would be justified in repaying creditors in silver rather than in gold. White, however, contended that at the time when most of public debt was incurred the silver dollar was a forgotten coin, and that the general understanding among creditors was that payment of their bonds was to be made in gold. Any alteration of the true spirit and intent of such contracts, White said, would result in a loss of dollars and cents. As to Weston's revelation of what he claimed were the real reasons behind the demonetization of silver and his disclosure of a means by which the public debt could be expunged, White retorted, "there is no cash value in Mr. Weston's discovery—not a dime!"[3]

White and other gold advocates, while they sometimes differed as to whether the Act of 1834 (which changed the legal ratio of gold to silver) or the Act of 1853 (which placed the minor silver coins at a subsidiary level) was responsible for silver's loss of status, agreed that silver had, in reality, been demonetized long before the passage of the Coinage Act of 1873. Pro-gold authors also claimed that the enactment of the law of 1873 marked the legal recognition of a natural economic movement to a gold standard. As a pro-gold writer, in the July 24, 1876, issue of the *New York Tribune*, put it, "I have said that silver was actually demonetized by the act of 1834 rather than by the act of 1873, and that the latter simply recognized a state of affairs already existing."[4]

Another author, who adopted a similar viewpoint, was Henry Varnum Poor. Poor, in a July-August 1878 article in the *North American Review*, determined that the demonetization of silver had been effected by the Act of 1853:

> The effect of the act of 1853, consequently, was to place the country effectually upon a mono-metallic basis—as much so as if the silver dollar itself had been reduced to the position of a subsidiary coin—the only currency from our own Mint left in circulation being gold, and the subsidiary silver coins of denominations of less than one dollar.[5]

After explaining that the silver dollar was absent from circulation prior to the passage of the Coinage Act of 1873, Poor justified the Act of 1873 by asserting that it:

> ...produced no change in the monetary condition of the country, and no change whatever, except to remove an obsolete provision from the statute-book. That this act was not devised by the rich as a cunning and cruel method of oppressing the poor, by increasing the amounts to be paid by them, is sufficiently shown by the fact that it substituted the lower standard [gold] in place of the higher. The measure, consequently, if that had any design of the kind, was conceived wholly in the interest of the poor against the rich. It had no other design than to adapt the currency to the convenience and wants of the country; the dropping out of the silver dollar being one of the least important of the measures to be accomplished.[6]

William Stewart, who made his fame on the Comstock before becoming a U.S. Senator from Nevada. Stewart was a leading free silver advocate.

Pending coinage legislation, which eventually resulted in a partial victory for free silver advocates, through the Feb. 28, 1878, passage of the Bland-Allison Act, reinstating a limited coinage of the standard silver dollar, led an association of eastern bankers to submit a memorial to Congress, in January 1878, expressing their misgivings about the planned reintroduction of the silver dollar. In their memorial, representatives of the banks of New York, Boston, Philadelphia, and Baltimore charged that the standard 412 1/2-grain silver dollar, which throughout its history had been subjected to exportation, had never really earned a place in the country's coinage system. They reminded Congress that:

> ...from 1834 the silver dollar bore a large premium in gold, and was taken for export as fast as issued. It was from that date to be found in this country only in the cabinets of numismatists and collectors of rare and curious objects, so that practically the 'dollar of the fathers' never had a place as an active member or portion of the currency.[7]

The bankers also believed that the Coinage Act of 1873 came about as a natural progression in the monetary evolution of the United States. They claimed:

> Whatever may, at this stage of the discussion be thought of the Act of 1873, it is certain that it effected no change whatever in the ideas and habits of our people, or in the trading or monetary operations of the country. It merely gave the form of legal enactment to usage or customary law. It only declared that gold should continue to fill the place that it had filled, and perform the functions that it had performed from the foundation of our government. It was an act in the strictest harmony with the policy and course of all commercial nations.[8]

For the most part, while free silver authors tantalized their readers with thrilling accounts of international intrigue, pro-gold authors, in their defense of the 1873 coinage legislation, mundanely tabulated the number of columns of debate over the coinage bill found in the *Congressional Globe*, theorized about the culmination of a natural evolution of the country's monetary system, and counted and recounted the number of silver dollars struck by the mint since its foundation, to show that very few people ever held one of the coins. Their analyses of the history and economic impact of the Coinage Act of 1873 were undoubtedly more factually based than those offered by the free silver camp but certainly made for less stimulating reading. Pro-gold authors preferred to overcome the menace of free silver through the use of fact-based rational arguments. This, however, proved to be a formidable task, for every time sound money authors exposed a fallacy in the free silver rhetoric, diligent defenders of the silver dollar scrambled to plug up the gaps in their tale of conspiracy. Free silver authors did not seem to mind when one of their several cherished affidavits proved to be false; they simply explained to their supporters that the evidence, believable or not, had been received from a reliable source that was above reproach. Besides which, in the final analysis, free silver authors argued, it was not essential to prove who committed the crime, what was important to understand was that a crime had been committed and needed to be rectified, by reinstating the full and unlimited coinage of the silver dollar, which, in their opinion, would bring the country back to prosperity.

Free silver stories, which grew in complexity as the movement gained momentum, vary as to exact origin of the conspiracy that led to the Crime of 1873 but, most often, they eagerly linked Great Britain, under the dominance of the wealthy Jewish financiers, the Rothschilds, to the scheme to demonetize silver and increase the value of gold. This myth gained such a wide circulation, that it even received an airing in 1890 on the floor of the Senate. On May 22, 1890, Sen. John W. Daniel of Virginia blasted Great Britain for attempting to take over the United States by bringing about the demonetization of silver. In his verbal assault on the motherland, Sen. Daniel caustically charged:

> Far-reaching in her provision of events, Great Britain sought by the wiles of commerce to accomplish what she had failed to do here by force of arms and had but partially done abroad, and to-day, as the wheat of her myriad of Indian ryots takes the place of our American product in the Liverpool market, she beholds the triumph of a policy which has narcotized American brains, corrupted American morals, and impoverished American farmers. While some of our economists amuse ignorant readers by copying English phrases about 'the best money,' 'the fixed and invariable value of gold,' and talk scholastically about 'intrinsic value,' England gathers her golden harvests, piles up her 'cent per cent.,' and laughs in her sleeve at our ignorance and our folly.[9]

Other free silver mythographers told of an elaborate renumbering scheme, by which the removal of the silver dollar was overlooked in the Senate during final debate over the mint bill in December 1872. This, they said, was engineered by Sen. John Sherman of Ohio, upon whom they also looked askance for his activities in relation to the 1867 Paris International Monetary Conference and its call for a universal coinage based on gold.

While free silver authors thrilled their readers with tales of international intrigue in relation to the so-called Crime of 1873, pro-gold authors fell back on the lack of silver dollars struck since the founding of the U.S. Mint to show that the coin had never held a substantial place as part of the nation's currency supply.

Among Sherman's chief detractors was Sen. William M. Stewart of Nevada, Adolph Sutro's early ally on the Comstock, who became a powerful proponent of the free coinage of silver. He, along with other free silver writers, argued that Sherman had purposely prolonged the January 1871 debate over the amendment to place a small coinage charge on the minting of gold, in order to mask the true intent of the coinage bill—which he said was to bring about the secret demonetization of silver. In a Sept. 5, 1893, speech, Stewart queried:

> If the Senate had been advised, as Mr. SHERMAN says that he was, that no silver could, under that bill, be deposited at the mint for coinage, is it probable that it would have spent two days in hot debate over the question of taxing bullion which could not be deposited, and therefore never could be taxed?[10]

In questioning Sherman's motives for advocating a coinage charge, Stewart found that, "I can draw no other inference from his course at that time than a purpose to conceal the fact that the silver dollar had been omitted."[11]

Of course, by this point, Stewart had conveniently forgotten that he had participated in the debate on the side of the removal of the coinage charge, as promoted by the Pacific coast bullion interests, who believed it helped drive gold out of the country. The debate over the inclusion of the coinage charge led to the defeat of Sherman's seigniorage amendment, causing Sherman to vote against the entire bill. Stewart, however, postulated that the defeat of the minting charges was not the real reason behind Sherman's negative vote, saying of Sherman:

> He knew very well that his vote would not defeat the bill nor endanger it in the slightest degree; but by voting against it he made the Senate believe that he attached more importance to a charge of three-tenths of 1 per cent on the coinage of gold (and of silver bullion, the coinage of which on private account had been abolished) than to the systematizing of the various confused mint laws of the country, by a measure which had been the labor of experts so eminent as those he describes.[12]

Stewart also claimed that Sherman was aware of the long-range impact of the coinage bill that demonetized silver; therefore, "is it not barely possible that knowing that fact, he desired to avoid the odium of voting for it which would attach after its far-reaching consequences should have been realized?"[13]

To free silver advocates, the thought that Sherman, a U.S. congressman, could be coerced into a subterfuge that would eventually benefit European bankers and bondholders was not farfetched. After all, they explained, the Grant administration had reeked of corruption, the Crédit Mobilier scandal being a prime example. This, they claimed, had been an era in which normally honest men set aside their ethical values and gave in to the lure of wealth; therefore, it was not inconceivable that Sherman could have succumbed to greed.

To promote their view that the congressmen who were involved the passage of the Coinage Act of 1873 had been spirited down a path of monetary greed by European bankers, free silver theorists found that it was necessary to procure direct evidence of European involvement in the construction and passage of the coinage act. By searching the *Congressional Globe*, they stumbled across their second scapegoat, the English bullion authority, Ernest Seyd.

According to the standard free silver theory of European bribery and intrigue, cultivated and nourished throughout the history of the Free Silver Movement, Seyd had not only offered advice on the text of the coinage bill, as mentioned by Rep. Samuel Hooper during House deliberation of the mint bill on April 19, 1872, but he was in the United States during the debate over the coinage bill, in order to deliver the bribe money for the Rothschild syndicate. Seyd, according to this popular theory, had been empowered by the syndicate with a fund of 100,000 British pounds ($500,000), with which to bribe the American Congress and insure the demonetization of silver.

Sarah E.V. Emery, a fanatical analyst of American economic history, who boldly discovered seven separate instances of corruption in the history of the United States, presented one of the most detailed and widely quoted of the Ernest Seyd myths.[14] Emery's theory gained such popularity that beyond being quoted by other free silver authors, it was offered by Rep. Thomas C. McRae of Arkansas, in a June 6, 1890, speech before Congress, as undeniable evidence of Seyd's involvement in the demonetization of silver.

Emery laid out the Seyd myth in her 1887 book, *Seven Financial Conspiracies which have Enslaved the American People*, in which she detailed Seyd's involvement, saying:

> But it was not the American capitalist alone who entered into this murderous scheme for demonetizing silver. In the *Banker's Magazine* of August, 1873, we find the following on this subject:
>
> In 1872, silver being demonetized in France, England and Holland, a capital of $500,000 was raised, and Ernest Seyd of London was sent to

this country with this fund, as agent of the foreign bond holders and capitalists, to effect the same object (demonetization of silver), which was accomplished.

There you have it, a paid agent of English capitalists sent to this country with $500,000 to buy the American Congress and rob the American people. In corroboration of this testimony we read from the *Congressional* Globe of April 9, 1872, page 2304, these words:

Ernest Seyd of London, a distinguished writer and bullionist, who is now here, has given great attention to the subject of mint and coinage. After having examined the first draft of this bill (for the demonetization of silver) he made various sensible suggestions, which the committee adopted and embodied in the bill.[15]

Other such supposed evidence of Seyd's involvement was offered by Gordon Clark in his 1896 *Handbook of Money*, in which Clark presented the eyewitness account of 62-year-old Frederick A. Luckenbach of New York, the inventor of Luckenbach's pneumatic pulverizer, who in his affidavit sworn to in Denver on May 9, 1892, claimed to have visited with Seyd in London early in the year 1874. At that time, according to Luckenbach, Seyd related his role in the demonetization conspiracy. Luckenbach testified that Seyd told him that, "he could relate the facts about the corruption of the American Congress that would place it far ahead of the English Parliament in that line."[16] After promising not to reveal anything that was said during Seyd's lifetime, Luckenbach quotes Seyd as telling him:

'I went to America in the winter of 1872-73, authorized to secure, if I could, the passage of a bill demonetizing silver. It was to the interest of those I represented—the governors of the Bank of England—to have it done. I took with me £100,000 sterling, with instructions if that was not sufficient to accomplish the object to draw for another £100,000 or as much more as was necessary.'[17]

To further support the validity of the Luckenbach affidavit, which Clark says first appeared in the *Rocky Mountain News*, Clark avowed that it must be genuine, because it appeared in "a very able and influential journal,"[18] published by the Honorable T.H. Patterson of Denver County, "a lawyer and orator as well as editor, and one of the best-known men of the West."[19] Patterson, in turn, explained, in his introduction to the Luckenbach affidavit, how the information was obtained for publication. Patterson stated that the affidavit was the result of the efforts of Mr. M.H. Slater, the chairman of the executive committee of the Colorado State Silver League, who having learned that Luckenbach had the information, "waited upon him and induced him to put the whole story in explicit form and give it to the public."[20]

Clark, offering further support as to the validity of the Luckenbach affidavit, proudly relayed to his readers the news that Luckenbach was an exemplary citizen, saying:

Frederick A. Luckenback [sic], in short, is a citizen of the Denver, a native American, a man of character, means, and large business connection, both in his own country and in Europe. His long and friendly acquaintance with Ernest Seyd is undisputed, and has been publicly admitted by Mr. Seyd's family.[21]

As a final glowing proof, not only of the genuineness of the document, but also of the subversive efforts practice by the American press to suppress the truth on the money question, Clark stated that Slater had submitted the Luckenbach affidavit to the Associated Press and they refused to handle it, then:

What better evidence is required, that [sic] this simple item, to prove that the American Press, so far as concerns its great combination of 'metropolitan journals,' is thoroughly 'subsidized' by the bank and bullion trust of Europe and America? On the money question no truth can be got into that press, and no truth can be got out of it.[22]

This well-developed tale of international intrigue, revolving around Seyd's supposedly corrupt activities, began to lose some of its glitter when pro-gold authors revealed that Seyd was not an advocate of the gold standard at all, but was, in fact, one of Europe's most ardent supporters of bimetallism, having written several influential tracts favoring European retention of the double standard. As Rep. James Thompson McCleary, in his article "The Crime of 1873," in the June 1, 1896, issue *of Sound Currency*, explained:

The fact is that Seyd, Wolowski and Cernushi were the three great champions of silver in Europe. They fought for it as knights of old fought for their lady loves. And it is the basest ingratitude for the friends of silver in this country to blacken the fair name of the greatest champion of their cause.[23]

Forced to admit that Seyd was in reality a champion of their own views, free silver authors adjusted their stories, but they continued to maintain that he was directly responsible for the demonetization of silver in the United States. The National Silver Executive Committee, in its 1890 report, *Silver in the Fifty-First Congress*, simply explained that Seyd became an advocate of bimetallism after the mint bill had been passed. Meanwhile, Clark, who freely admitted that a Feb. 17, 1872, letter from Seyd to Rep. Hooper showed that Seyd had objected to the demonetization of the silver dollar, was still unwilling to totally absolve Seyd of wrongdoing.

Clark graciously acknowledged that, under ordinary circumstances, Seyd would have been true to his convictions, but Seyd:

> ...as 'adviser of the Bank of England,' was forced to postpone his theories, when that huge octopus came to see its fat prey in the United States. He was in a difficult position. For the time, he was serving his country, his friends and his blood, as against a country that England, at heart, still regards as a rebel to her throne and policy.... Though untrue to his deepest convictions, he is to be blamed somewhat as Americans blame the unfortunate Major Andre, whom Washington hanged with heart-felt sorrow. Andre was a true Englishman; and so, by position, was Seyd.[24]

Baseless accusations made against Seyd, like the preceding example, angered Rep. McCleary, who complained:

> There is a certain class of people to whom any story that lowers an honored name is always welcome. For them no proof was needed in support of this story. There are others who are slow to believe as true that which ought not to be true, but who have heard this story so frequently and so positively stated that some of them may regretfully half admit to themselves that there must be a modicum of truth in it somewhere. They will be glad to be assured, as I now assure them, after very careful study of the subject, that the whole story is an unmitigated falsehood, without even the shadow of foundation.[25]

Free silver advocates became so wrapped up in their belief that an increase in the nation's money supply through the free and unlimited coinage of the silver dollar would alleviate the problems of the debt-ridden middle and lower classes, while thwarting the efforts of the moneyed classes of the world to control the nation's growth through a stranglehold of gold, that they frequently resorted to altered and spurious documents to support their cause. For example, Emery, in *Seven Financial Conspiracies which have Enslaved the American People*, mentioned earlier, either as a result of her own ingenuity or by quoting from a previously altered free silver source, had grossly misquoted Rep. Hooper's congressional statement in regard to Seyd. Emery's transcription of Hooper's April 9, 1872, statement, regarding Seyd's contribution, mysteriously contained, among other inaccuracies, the three additional words "is now here" in order to convince her readers that Seyd was in the United States during the passage of the mint bill.

Emery's charges, which were frequently offered in Congress as proof of a conspiracy, were challenged by Sen. George F. Hoar of Massachusetts. On Aug. 22, 1893, he presented the Senate with the actual letter from Seyd to Hooper, proving beyond question that Seyd had advised Hooper to retain the silver dollar. Shortly thereafter, Hoar informed the Senate that Seyd's brother and his son had co-authored a letter to the *New York Evening Post*, denying the charges made against their relative and avowing that Seyd had (as actually was the case) not been in the United States since 1856. A little more than a month later, on Sept. 28, 1893, Hoar, continuing his attack on the misconceptions of the Free Silver Movement, read to his Senate colleagues the real text of the *Congressional Globe* for April 9, 1872, in order to illustrate the free silver authors' deceptions.

As for Emery's quotation from the August 1873 issue of *Bankers' Magazine*, Rep. McCleary discovered that "this proves to be another forgery, as no such paragraph appears in the Bankers' Magazine for August, 1873, or in any other number of that periodical, so far as a careful search by the editor can disclose."[26] The fact that Emery's quotation did not appear in the *Bankers' Magazine* did not, however, dissuade Clark from attesting to the validity of the quotation. Clark claimed that the quotation in question had been originally brought to light by Gen. A.J. Warner, and defended Mrs. Emery, stating:

> ...General A.J. Warner, in the first edition of his 'Appreciation of Money' (Henry Carey Baird & Co., publishers, 1877), said: "The '*Bankers' Magazine* for August, 1873, contains this important item: 'In 1872, silver being demonetized in France, Germany, England, and Holland, a capital of one hundred thousand pounds ($500,000) was raised, and Ernest Seyd, of London, was sent to this country with this fund, as the agent of the foreign bondholders and capitalists, to effect the same object, which was successful.'" The New York *Bankers' Magazine* now contains no such item. On personal inquiry of General Warner it has been ascertained that within a year or so after the 'Mint Act' became a law he certainly cut the extract from one of the current financial publications of the day—either from some one of the various bankers' magazines or from some similar source which *referred* it to the *Bankers' Magazine*. Later the quotation was used by Mrs. S.E.V. Emery in her 'Seven Financial Conspiracies,' and she has been roundly abused (even in Congress) for misquotation, but with no real ground, as the facts here evince.[27]

Even though an investigation, conducted by Alfred T. Storey, an English correspondent to the New York publication *The Voice*, established that Seyd had signed the record books of his firm on several occasions between October 1872 and March 1873, the period in which free silver writers alleged that Seyd was in the United States, Clark was not convinced and suggested that the records may have been forged:

Now the statement of the correspondent of *The Voice*, in regard to Ernest Seyd's letter books, has been confirmed by the unquestioned authority of Moreton Frewen, and is no doubt perfectly true. *But it proves absolutely nothing that is claimed for it.* For Ernest Seyd was perhaps the ablest man living in 1873 both as writer on metallic money and in forecasting the future. If such a man had desired to make a record of his presence in London during a brief absence, how easy it would have been to do so by such simple aids as a little good copying-ink and a few sheets of letter-paper, with signatures prepared in advance of their use.[28]

If the preceding argument was not convincing, Clark explained that it did not really matter, as:

One Thing is Certain

Some one bearing the name, and claiming to be, Ernest Seyd, was in New York and Washington in 1873. In Washington, he moved prominently, with a generous display of wealth, but quietly. His name was naturally kept out of hotel registers and the local papers, though he ran some risk of putting it on file. For instance, the Washington *National Republican* of January 18, 1873, contained this item:

The Coinage and Mint Bill passed by the House at the last session, was up in the Senate yesterday, and, after the adoption of several amendments, passed. An eminent foreign banker gives it as his opinion that the bill as it came from the House was the most effective step that had been yet taken toward the resumption of specie payments.

In January, 1873, what 'eminent foreign banker' but Ernest Seyd had been consulted regarding the 'Mint Bill,' or knew anything about it? He was the one 'foreign banker' to whom it had been specially sent, through the Bank of England. But in respect to the 'House bill' and 'the resumption of specie payments,' the bill simply *prevented* silver from being of any use for that purpose, by robbing it of its legal-tender value, and confining its debt-paying power to five dollars—of course against which 'the eminent foreign banker,' Ernest Seyd, had vigorously protested when he first knew of it from Samuel Hooper. In regard to the 'resumption,' the House bill and the Senate bill were *exactly alike*. But, when Mr. Seyd visited Washington in 1873, 'the eminent foreign banker' was recommending the 'Coinage and Mint Bill' for just what he knew it would *not do*. In short, he was not dealing in the truth, but was busy with the work of misdirection and attorneyship. Still, his better nature ultimately prevailed, and he was prompted to his talk with Mr. Luckenbach. He probably desired that the world should know the facts after his death. Ernest Seyd was in no sense a *little* man.

Such are now the conclusions of Americans having the largest knowledge of all the facts.[29]

Populist author Ignatius Donnelly, an avid propagandist of free silver mythology, was unwilling to entertain any evidence of Seyd's innocence. In his book, *The American People's Money*, published in 1895, Donnelly employed several fictitious characters, through whom he expressed his views on the money question and Seyd's involvement in the alleged conspiracy.[30]

The main characters in Donnelly's free silver novel include James Hutchison, president of the Trader's and Mechanic's Bank of Chicago and Hugh Sanders, a farmer from Shelbyville, Ill., both of whom, along with several other passengers, are depicted en route via train from Chicago to the Pacific coast. During their cross-country journey, Sanders, the farmer, lectures the Chicago banker, Hutchison, on the virtues of free silver and the evils of the gold standard.

In regard to Seyd, Donnelly, through his agrarian character, Hugh Sanders, defends the Luckenbach affidavit stating:

But it will be observed that while, there is a denial of the fact that Ernest Seyd was in the United States in 1872, there is no denial that the Seyd family was well acquainted with Mr. Luckenbach, or that he dined with them in London in 1865; or that Ernest Seyd and he held such a conversation at the dinner table. If Mr. Luckenbach had invented the whole story, if he did not know Ernest Seyd, if he was a fraud, they would have said so most emphatically, for he had assailed the good name of their father and brother before the whole world.[31]

When banker Hutchison confronted Sanders with the Seyd family denial that Ernest Seyd had been in the United States during the deliberation over the coinage bill, the farmer questioned:

'Where is the proof of that?' asked Mr. Sanders. 'And observe that Hooper says it was 'submitted to nearly all the mint experts in the country.' That is, in the United States. If Mr. Seyd was not in America, why was he the only expert in England to whom the bill was submitted? Why was he PICKED OUT? And is it not strange that the only English expert selected was the same man Luckenbach dined with in London, in February, 1874—and this fact is not denied by Seyd's relatives,—and to whom Seyd stated that he had been the instrument used by Bank of England to bribe Congress. The links of the connection are all there. Ernest Seyd tells Luckenbach that with $500,000, furnished by the governors of the Bank of England, he had bought the demonetization bill through Congress.[32]

Donnelly's interpretation of Rep. Hooper's congressional statement was by far too literal, and his indictment of Seyd required an unyielding belief in a highly questionable document released to the free silver press in 1892, more than a decade after Seyd became the popular scapegoat of free silver writers. To Donnelly and, for that matter, to most free silver writers, it did not matter that Seyd's relatives denied that Ernest Seyd had anything to do with the demonetization of silver, because such evidence was merely human testimony, and as Donnelly's character Sanders explained, "if you were to accept the denials of guilt of the convicted criminals, or their friends...the prison houses would all be empty."[33]

The simplistic forms of evading the truth, practiced by Donnelly and other free silver writers, were masterfully refined by the free silver movement's leading storyteller, William H. "Coin" Harvey, who, like Donnelly, was able to find fault in any "human testimony" that denied English involvement in the Crime of 1873. In a July 1895 debate with Roswell G. Horr in Chicago, Harvey provided listeners with a glimpse of the inductive reasoning by which he was able to justify ignoring evidence to the contrary and condemn England for the demonetization of silver. Harvey retorted:

> Mr. Horr says that I have no proof that the scheme was concocted in London to demonetize silver in the United States. When I was a boy I went into a courthouse one day to hear a criminal trial, and I heard a lawyer say 'When a crime is committed and you want to detect the criminal, look for the man that is benefited by the crime.' (Applause.) Reasoning by induction will more invariably locate the criminal than any uncertain human testimony.[34]

At least one free silver author, E.J. Farmer (pseud.), in his book, *The Conspiracy Against Silver or a Plea for Bimetallism in the United States*, published in 1886, saw any attempt to defame the righteous cause of the Free Silver Movement as direct evidence of a joint conspiracy between the enemies of silver in the United States and in England. Farmer raged:

> The parties who concocted that law understood its purpose, however, and no doubt received their reward, whether it was in 30 pieces of gold, or more. They as completely sold out the nation, as Judas sold out Christ, and yet we have apologists for that transaction all over the country to-day. When the people became aware of how their interests had been sacrificed to the 'golden calf,' they demanded the re-instatement of silver and with great difficulty procured it, in an emasculated form, in the Bland Bill passed February 28, 1878. There it was that the enemies of silver began to pour out the vials of their wrath, and to predict the direst evils that ever befel a nation. These conspirators have kept up their Cataline assemblages ever since, and, backed by England, have their daggers ever ready to strike down the silver dollar. No statement is too false for them to make; no scheme to dastardly too attempt—the exaltation of their golden idol is their one song, and as priests to this golden Juggernaut, they smile to see the wreck and ruin its gilded wheels have wrought; while around this car may be seen the bloody footprints of the British lion.(35)

Chapter 23

PARTIAL VICTORY

By the latter part of 1876, with the Free Silver Movement still in its infancy and the first complaints of George Weston and other free silver writers being heard, bills began popping up in the House calling for restoration of the free and unlimited coinage of the 412 1/2-grain silver dollar at the old 16 to 1 ratio. One of the first of these measures was introduced by former gold-standard friend Rep. William D. Kelley. The measure that would succeed, however, the Bland bill, was brought before the House by Rep. Richard P. Bland, an early free silver backer from Missouri, who as a youth had worked in the Nevada silver mines, and in the 1890s, came to be viewed as serious contender for the presidential nomination.[1] On Feb. 28, 1878, with modifications made in the Senate by sound money advocate William B. Allison, the bill passed over President Rutherford B. Hayes' veto. Today known as the Bland-Allison Act, it required the Treasury secretary to purchase, at market price, "not less than two million dollars worth per month, nor more than four million dollars worth per month [of silver]" and cause the same to be coined monthly "as fast as so purchased" into silver dollars.[2] Additional provisions called for silver's use as backing for paper silver certificates, which could be obtained by bullion owners in exchange for a minimum of $10 in silver, and for the president to invite all nations of the Latin Union and other European nations deemed advisable to join in a conference "for the purpose of establishing, internationally, the use of bimetallic money, and securing fixity of relative value between those metals..."[3]

In calling for the new coin, free silverites argued that, since most earlier contracts and government bonds had specified only "coin" in payment, not specifically gold or silver, the latter, which was readily available and could be used to expand the money supply, bolster the price of silver, and return a nation still stinging from depression back to prosperity, be accepted for payment of all debts, public or private. The July 14, 1870, act authorizing the refunding of the national debt, for instance, had called for the sale of 5, 4 1/2, and 4 percent bonds that would be redeemable in "coin of the present standard value," which free silver advocates could argue was any legal-tender dollar coin produced by the U.S. Mint, whether it be gold or silver.

However, by tradition, monetary conservatives observed, such bonds were sold for gold, and using depreciated silver would have damaged credibility. In his 1877 *Money and Legal Tender in*

A pattern for the new standard silver dollar authorized by the 1878 Bland-Allison Act.

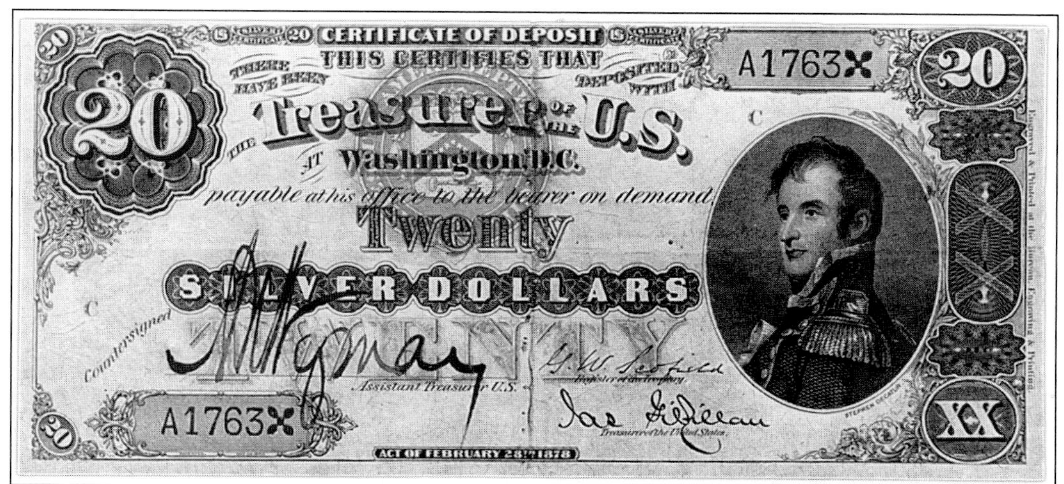

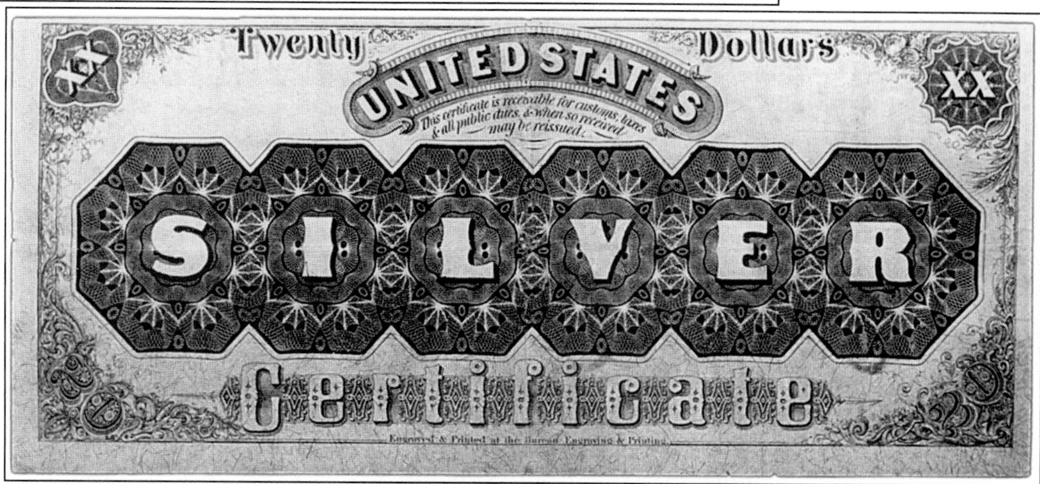

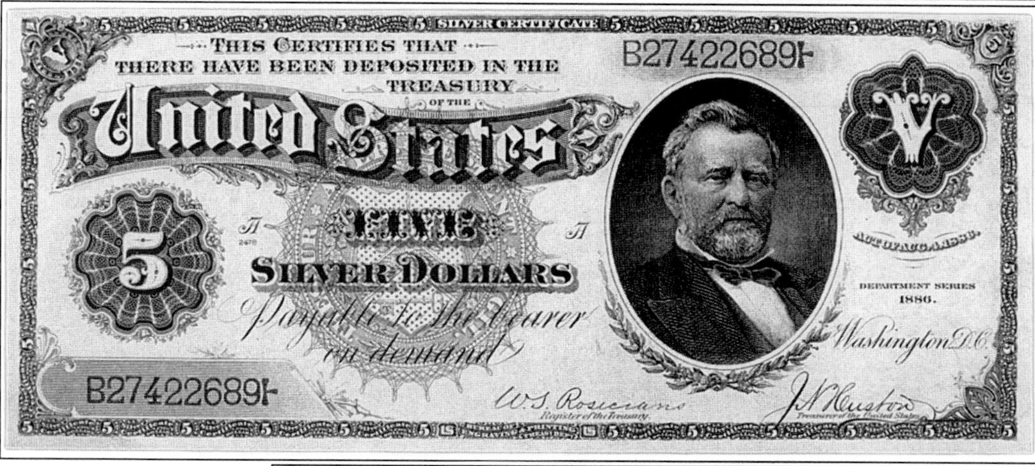

The Bland-Alllison Act also authorized the release of silver certificates, which were backed by silver.

the United States, written while the Bland bill and similar measures were still pending in Congress, Mint Director Henry R. Linderman wrote that, "It is a well known fact that settlement for all bonds, issued under the provisions of this Act, has without exception been made on the basis of 25 8/10 grains of standard, or 23 22/100 grains of fine gold to the coined dollar, and the purchasers and holders of such bonds very naturally expect to receive payment in 'gold coins of standard value' equal to the coins in which their subscriptions were made and paid."[4] Thus, Linderman warned, "Not withstanding the option as to payment in gold coin or silver dollars given the Government by the law, the fact that the bonds have been taken and settled for on the gold basis, and that silver, in the mean time, comparing its commercial value with that fixed by law in the silver dollar, has materially depreciated, renders it very doubtful, to say the least, whether the United States could with justice pay either the principal or interest of its bonds in silver dollars."[5]

It was the fear of the effects of just such a repudiation of former debt that served as the substance of President Hayes' veto of the Bland-Allison Act. Hayes contended that the provisions of the act, which would allow for the new silver dollars "to be a legal tender at their nominal value in all debts and dues, public and private, except where otherwise expressly stipulated in the contract," would have an injurious effect on any bonded debt incurred since the passage of the Coinage Act of 1873, when the silver dollar was still trading at around $1.03.[6] "It is well known that the market value of that number of grains of standard silver [412 1/2] during the past year has been from 90 to 92 cents as compared with the standard gold dollar," Hayes wrote. "Thus the silver dollar authorized by this bill is worth 8 to 10 per cent less than it purports to be worth, and is made legal tender for debts contracted when the law did not recognize such coins as lawful money."[7]

Hayes sympathized with those who believed that the return of the silver dollar to circulation would bring the coin's value to parity with gold, but added, "The capital defect of the bill is that it contains no provision protecting...preexisting debts in case the coinage which it creates shall continue to be of less value than that which was the sole legal tender [when] they were contracted."[8] Hayes concluded:

> It is my firm conviction that if the country is to be benefited by a silver coinage it can be done only by the issue of silver dollars of full value, which will defraud no man. A currency worth less than it purports to be worth will in the end defraud not only creditors, but all who are engaged in legitimate business, and none more surely than those who are dependent on their daily labor for their daily bread.[9]

Within hours of his veto, Congress had overturned it. Patterns for the new dollar coin having been produced as early as 1876, coinage began on March 11, 1878, with the first specimens, struck in proof, presented to President Hayes, Treasury Secretary John Sherman, and Mint Director Linderman. Linderman was appointed by Sherman to oversee a committee arranging for purchases of silver for the new dollar coin and began by aggressively pursuing his contacts on the Pacific coast, who at first proved reluctant to sell at the price the government was offering.[10] In his Nov. 1, 1878, *Report of the Director of the Mint*, Linderman wrote, "Soon after the passage of the act authorizing the coinage of the standard silver dollar, and an attempt being made to procure the requisite bullion for its coinage at the mints on the Pacific coast, it was found that the producers and dealers would not sell silver to the government at the equivalent of the London rate, but demanded in addition thereto an amount equal to the cost of bringing it from London and laying it down in San Francisco."[11] So Linderman worked to bring the Philadelphia Mint up to full production capacity to meet the $2 million to $4 million per month coinage demand for dollars and, for a time, turned to purchasing foreign silver to make up for the shortfall.[12] In July, 1878, according to Linderman, the "principal holders of bullion on the Pacific coast," no doubt the bonanza firm, "receded from their position and accepted the equivalent of the London rate, at which price sufficient bullion was purchased to employ the mints at San Francisco and Carson on the coinage of the dollar."[13] First-year mintages of the new dollars were high, including 10,509,550 coins from Philadelphia, 2,212,000 from Carson City, and 9,744,000 from San Francisco. These totals far exceeded the entire standard silver dollar coinage by the U.S. Mint since it began striking dollar coins in 1794.

By this point, however, Linderman had bigger problems than price resistance from the bonanza firm or the reinstatement of the silver dollar he had helped remove from the nation's coinage system. In June 1878, a congressional investigation was launched by Rep. John Montgomery Glover of Missouri into Linderman's past activities as Mint director. Among the chief charges were that Linderman had accepted payments, in the form of stocks, from Pacific coast bullion interests, and rigged his government reports to help bolster the value of Comstock mining stocks.

In its June 17, 1878, issue, the *New York Tribune* began relating what little is known about the investigation:

> Washington June 16—Mr. Glover's committee has been investigating the conduct of the Mint Bureau, and has submitted its report to the President and the secretary of the Treasury. The latter, after examining it, has concluded to take no action in the premises until an inquiry is made which shall be fair to Dr. Linderman, the director, and shall give him full opportunity to defend himself. The accusation which Mr. Glover's committee makes against Dr. Linderman, but upon which no judgement should be formed until he has had opportunity to reply to it is in substance that he caused stock jobbing reports of the natural resources of the Comstock Lode to be published; that he purchased silver at greater than the market rates; that he employed a man in San Francisco who was not needed; and that a member of his family received payments from persons having duties with the bureau.[14]

Linderman, it is clear, had considerable ties with the Pacific coast bullion interests and was not above raving about the Comstock Lode in his official reports—though this was likely more the result of over enthusiasm than a matter of writing reports aimed at "stock jobbing." Interestingly, though, the committee was not alone in such an observation. During the March 16, 1876, House debate over the release of the subsidiary silver coins, former Linderman ally William D. Kelley, joked that Linderman's annual reports were poorly veiled advertisements for the Comstock. Exaggerating some, Kelley gibed:

> The report of the Director of the Mint is little more than an advertisement of old Townsend's genuine sarsaparilla. (Laughter.) It is a pamphlet molded upon the advertising pamphlets of that physician, whose sands of life are nearly run. Pages of it are covered with evidence of the increasing value of the stock of the mines on the Comstock lode, and its bulk is swollen so that it is inconvenient for carriage by the insertion of maps of mines and their machinery, intended to demonstrate the truth of his advice to the people that if they want to buy stock in the Comstock mines they had better do it at once. (Laughter.)[15]

In its June 18, 1878, issue, the *New York Tribune* continued its coverage into the congressional investigation. Under the headline, "Dr. Linderman Not Frightened," the report, received by telegraph, explained:

> Washington, June 17—Republican members of Mr. Glover's committee report that no consultation has he held with them in regard to the accusations against Dr. Linderman. The Republican member of the sub-committee which was appointed to inquire into this matter has not even been informed in regard to it. The whole evidence submitted by Dr. Linderman in defence was taken at 5 o'clock in the afternoon, and he had not even been examined by the committee when the so-called report was given out. A Republican member of the committee, who has heard all of the testimony, says there is not a particle in it which reflects upon him that is not wholly hearsay.
>
> Dr. Linderman says that Mr. Glover has treated him with conspicuous unfairness. The director says that no report has been made by the Glover committee, and that, so far as he knows, the investigation has not been finished. He says that the credible

Coinage of the new dollar began in 1878. First-year mintages exceeded the total of all silver dollar coinage up to that date.

The Linderman Collection

Although much of Henry R. Linderman's more questionable activities, in relation to the Coinage Act of 1873, have remained unknown until now, collectors have long been aware of his considerable use of his position as Mint director to assemble a premiere personal collection of coins, patterns and restrikes, highlighted by a specimen of the "King of American Coins," the 1804 silver dollar. Noted numismatic author Q. David Bowers, in his *The Rare Silver Dollars Dated 1804*, wrote recently in this regard:

> Henry Richard Linderman, M.D., was a brilliant man. There is no doubt of this.... However, Linderman, while in charge of the Philadelphia Mint, took ample advantage of the prerogatives offered—official and unofficial—and his private collection of rare coin was thus augmented by many newly created rarities, the equals of which could not be obtained by numismatists in the private sector.[1]

The full extent of Linderman's activities, as the nation's leading behind-the-scenes coin collector, did not become apparent until several years after his death in 1879. In 1887, his collection was placed up for auction by Lyman H. Low & Co., with the sale planned for June 28, 1887. The catalog was a feast of off-metal rarities, restrikes and other stellar U.S. coins. Low explained in the sale's opening paragraph:

> Although the collection offered on the following pages embraces but 188 lots, we are confident that an inspection of the Catalogue will show that the sale which it announces challenges all previous American Sales in the point of average quality and high value,—by whatever standard it may be measured. The pieces described cannot fail to elicit a lively interest among American collectors, for, aside from the extreme rarity of many of the patterns, trial pieces, etc., the entire collection has a character so marked, and so peculiarly its own, that it may fairly be regarded as without a compeer in its special line.[2]

Chief among these pieces was a Class III specimen of the 1804 silver dollar. Coinage of the silver dollar having been halted in 1804, U.S. Mint records showed that 19,570 silver dollars were struck that year. Until the early 1960s, the mystery of what happened to all but a few remaining specimens in collectors hands was largely unsolved. Some theorized, in differing stories, that almost the entire mintage was lost at sea. Others claimed the coins had been melted.

In their 1962 book, *The Fantastic 1804 Silver Dollar*, Eric P. Newman and Kenneth E. Bressett cleared up much of the mystery by showing that the first pieces bearing this date were not struck in 1804. Rather, the first 1804 silver dollars were minted in the early 1830s for inclusion in presentation sets to be given to foreign dignitaries. The mintage total was, therefore, for 1803-dated dollars.

In subsequent years, additional 1804 dollars, with slight variations, were surreptitiously produced by Mint employees. Linderman's specimen is of this later origin, despite the fact that his wife, Emily, appeared before Justice of the Peace Charles W. Hobrook in July 1887, shortly after the sale was to have taken place, claiming her husband had informed her that his specimen was an original and had been obtained by installment payments, Linderman not feeling able to pay for the coin all at one time.[3] This interesting document is reproduced in the Newman/Bressett book. Today the coin is on display at the American Numismatic Association's Money Museum in Colorado Springs, Colo. The Low auction described the lot as such:

Henry R. Linderman's Class III specimen of the rare 1804 silver dollar. Courtesy of the American Numismatic Association.

Continued On Page 201

and legal testimony before the committee does not and cannot convict him of any improper official conduct, nor show anything against his integrity as a man. The testimony to his prejudice is simply hearsay, and would not be received by any court of law in the land. Dr. Linderman also asserts that the whole case against him has been made up by discharged employés, and that it is nothing less than a conspiracy. He says that he does not propose to fight the case in the newspapers nor does he intend to take any steps until the report and the testimony are before the public. Dr. Linderman does not deny specific facts, and will not say whether he employed his son [Henry], whether he dealt in Bonanza stocks, whether his family received $1,000 from the San Francisco Mint, nor whether he employed persons of improper character contrary to law. He is very defiant, however.

Dr. Linderman says Glover's vindictiveness has been known to him for months. As far back as April Mr. Glover wrote a letter to a gentleman threatening Dr. Linderman and indicating an intention to destroy him. This letter is now in the director's possession, and shows that Mr. Glover the day it was written, went to President and asked for Linderman's removal. The whole force of the Mint Bureau is being employed on the books, and it is the impression that Mr. Glover will let nothing except garbled reports of the testimony go out, but

Continued From Page 200

40 **Dollar, 1804.** A **beautiful sharp proof;** evenly centered, edge lettered. The finest known specimen of this valuable coin. This piece has the advantage over the few existing specimens, in being the property of the late Director of the Mint, Dr. Linderman, which alone is a guarantee of its being struck in the U.S. Mint; it is from the same dies as that in the Mint Cabinet...At previous sales, inferior specimens have sold for $1,000 and $1,200. The perfection of the one now offered should command a large advance on all preceding prices.[4]

Another highlight of the collection was Lot 55, a 16-piece set of the 1868 regular-issue coins struck in aluminum, "mounted in perforated frame between glass, and bound, book-form, in fine morocco case with clasps."[5] The cataloger added that the set was believed to be unique. Linderman obtained the set while serving as Philadelphia Mint director from 1867-1869. The U.S. Mint had been experimenting during this period with determining the practicality of using aluminum as a coinage metal.

Andrew W. Pollock III, in *United States Patterns and Related Issues*, reports the existence of at least two sets like Linderman's and possibly a third, all in proof. According to Pollock's research, the sets were prepared at Linderman's request as presentation gifts, with four sets ultimately ordered.[6] In 1979, one of the sets was sold as part of Bowers and Ruddy Galleries' sale of the Garrett Collection. Offered as Lot 396, the catalog description noted, "The importance of this set, preserved today in its original state, cannot be overemphasized. Certainly it ranks as one of the most rare and significant Philadelphia Mint products of the 1860s."[7] It sold for $40,000.

Other rarities in the Linderman sale included two examples of the famous 1827 quarter dollar, the first described as "Proof, struck from rusted die..." and the second, "Proof; equally perfect and desirable."[7] Restrikes are known, having been made using rusted dies with a flat base to the "2" in the denomination. Linderman's were likely of this origin. Less than 10 originals are accounted for, along with a dozen or so restrikes. The scarcity of all such pieces is shown in that, at the time, the cataloger of Linderman's collection stated that a specimen "in the Foster Ely sale (Nov. '86) brought $210."[8]

Also featured in the Linderman collection was a large selection of desirable patterns, including, of relevance to this study, sets of 1873 Trade dollar patterns in copper, silver and white metal; 1874 Dana Bickford $10 international coinage patterns; and 1878 pattern dollars by George T. Morgan and William Barber.

The sale, however, never took place. The government stopped the auction. Linderman's collection, minus the off-metal pieces, was finally sold on Feb. 28, 1888, by Scott Stamp & Coin Company, Ltd. The note at the beginning of the Scott offering observed of the missing lots:

> After mature consideration of all the questions of law and equity involved in the sale of trial and experimental pieces formerly classed as 'pattern' pieces, made at the United States mint, the government has allowed us to sell the celebrated Linderman collection. The decision of the government can be summed up as follows:
>
> 'The sale of Experimental pieces made in 1888 or thereafter, and of pieces struck from dies of accepted designs, unless in the metal in which the coins were issued for circulation is prohibited.' The latter portion of the decision is retroactive and covers the period prior to 1888, as well as that subsequent to it.[9]

Thus, Linderman's 1868 aluminum set was withdrawn. More than a dozen other lots from the original sale catalog, were either removed entirely or, in the case of multiple-item lots, reduced as to content. Despite the removals, several rare coins successfully sold, including Linderman's 1804 silver dollar, which brought $470; the 1827 quarter dollars at $81 and $88; the 1874 Dana Bickford international coinage pattern for $90; and a six-piece silver Trade dollar pattern set which went for $22.

Linderman's beard has grayed and his hairline receded in this painting made during his term as director of the Bureau of the Mint.

Former President Ulysses S. Grant (fourth from the right) on an 1879 tour of the Comstock. At far left is John Mackay and at far right is James G. Fair. Courtesy of Special Collections Department, University of Reno Library.

> will keep everything in its one-sided shape until Dr. Linderman's term of office is about to expire in December next, and then use it to defeat his reappointment.[16]

In his *Bonanza Mines of Nevada: Gross Frauds in the Management Exposed*, Squire P. Dewey, an original incorporator of the Ophir (who by 1878 had become a seriously disgruntled stockholder of now well-depreciated Consolidated Virginia shares), charged not only that in 1875 the bonanza firm had paid Philipp Deidesheimer to make his robust estimates of the value of the Big Bonanza to drive share prices up but also that "the most ingenious device to divest the public of doubt and distrust and especially of suspicion that the expert opinions had been improperly influenced..." was to get Mint Director Linderman to visit the Consolidated Virginia on two official tours in the summer of 1875, where Bonanza King James Fair led him around, convincing him of its overinflated wealth.[17] Linderman then returned to Washington and wrote enthusiastically of the Big Bonanza, quoting extensively from the overblown findings of Prof. R.E. Rogers, in his 1875 *Report of the Director of the Mint*, Dewey said. "This report," Dewey claimed, "was the bait that captured Eastern capital. Even the officials highest in authority, including the President of the United States, members of the Cabinet, and heads and subordinates of departments, were lured into confidence and became contributors to the exchequer of the bonanza firm."[18]

After reviewing the contents of Linderman's report, Dewey, who had been aware of the June 1878 congressional committee investigation of Linderman, wrote, "Recent investigations at Washington of official transactions of Linderman have disclosed the fact that the wife of that gentleman became the owner of a large number of bonanza shares at or about the time of the disinterested report by her husband, as above quoted."[19] Whether or not this is true is uncertain. Dewey, a San Francisco real estate investor and "self-important man," who lost heavily in the Comstock, is pretty much decried by Comstock historian Grant Smith as a quack, who had brought suit against the bonanza firm in 1878 to recover some of his losses and made scurrilous charges in the *San Francisco Chronicle* and his 78-page 1878 *Bonanza Mines* pamphlet.[20] The latter, Smith characterized as "a clever piece of evasion and misrepresentation...so convincing to the uniformed that it has been quoted as authoritative by some writers, especially by the authors of two recent books of no value."[21] By the time of Dewey's pamphlet, Comstock stocks had depreciated to a slim fraction of their former value, ruining many in the process. According to Dewey, in January 1875, shares in Consolidated Virginia were trading at $140, but by Dec. 1, 1878, they had fallen to $8 per share. Dewey calculated (adjusting for lost interest and subtracting dividends and dividend interest) that on the 540,000 shares the capital stock had been divided into, each shareholder had suffered a loss of $110.54 per share as of Dec. 1, 1878.

Of Dewey's claims against Linderman, Smith wrote:

> Squire P. Dewey, in his vicious pamphlet entitled 'The Bonanza Mines,' printed in 1878, charges that the Director of the Mint, Dan DeQuille and Deidesheimer were bribed with stock to make their extravagant reports. It meant nothing to Dewey that Dan DeQuille was above suspicion and always broke, and that Dedesheimer went through bankruptcy a few months after the crash with liabilities $534,000. The reader will be shocked at the suggestion that the Director and, necessarily, Professor Rogers, were bribed.[22]

The *Dictionary of American Biography* recorded of the 1878 investigation into Linderman's activities:

> The anxiety caused by these investigations, after the strenuous work of the year before, proved too much for his [Linderman's] health; he was not on duty after November, and his death followed in January. No conclusive report on the investigations exists, but there is no question as to Linderman's personal integrity. He was an exceptionally able director of the mint at a period when efficient conduct of the office was particularly difficult.[23]

Considering Linderman's dealings with William C. Ralston, it is fairer to say that, although Dewey was likely a crank and Linderman was an able Mint director, the book on Linderman's innocence in this question should remain open.

In his Nov. 1, 1878, *Annual Report of the Director of the Mint*, one of his last official duties before his death on Jan. 27, 1879, Linderman wrote that

The Savage mansion in the 1870s. It served as the Virginia City office of the Savage mine and home to its superintendent. The building still stands. A plaque on its front relates that former President Grant spoke from its second floor balcony on Oct. 27, 1879, following a parade in his honor.

purchases of bullion for the new silver dollar began in March 1878 and up to Sept. 30 17,925,701.99 fine ounces had been procured at an average price of 117.47 cents per ounce fine.[24] During 1878 alone the U.S. Mint struck 22.49 million silver dollars between the Philadelphia, San Francisco and Carson City facilities. In 1885, the same year President Grover Cleveland called for a repeal of the Bland-Allison Act, the Philadelphia Mint produced 17,787,930 Morgan dollars on its own. The total of all mints for that year was a healthy 28.69 million. The following year, mintages would top 30 million. Most of this coinage was dispatched immediately into Treasury vaults and saw only limited use in circulation. It was, however, popular among speculators, who found the exchange of the continually depreciating silver dollars for gold to their decided benefit.

A Pauper

Despite any stock payments he may or may not have taken from the Bonanza Kings (or his celebrated coin collection, which his wife would later put up for auction), Henry R. Linderman's estate records suggest that, at the time of his death, he had little more than the clothes on his back. Estate records filed in the Supreme Court of the District of Columbia, Jan. 16, 1880, on behalf of his widow, Emily, and his son, Henry, read:

> In Re Estate of Henry R. Linderman. The petition of Emily Linderman and Henry Linderman respectfully represents that they are citizens of the United States and residents of the City of Washington; that said Emily is the widow and said Henry the only child of Henry R. Linderman late of said City deceased and are both of full age; that the said Henry R. Linderman died at the said City of Washington, the place of his last domicile, on the 27th day of January 1879, intestate; that he left no personal property except his clothing wearing apparel and a clause against the United States of from $300.00 to $400.00 on account of his salary.
>
> The petitioners therefore pray that letters of administration upon the estate of the said Henry R. Linderman may be granted to the said Emily Linderman and that they may have such other and further relief as the nature of the case may require.[1]

The document was signed an attested to by Emily Linderman and Henry Linderman. On that same day, Justice Charles P. Janus agreed to make Emily administrator of the estate, "upon her filing of a proper fund in the final amount of eight hundred dollars with securities satisfactory to the Court."[2]

In his Dec. 8, 1885, State of the Union message, President Cleveland announced that, since 1878, 215,759,431 silver dollars had been coined, yet "up to the present time only 50,000,000 of the silver dollars so coined have actually found their way into circulation, leaving more than 165,000,000 in the possession of the Government, the custody of which has entailed a considerable expense for the construction of vaults for its deposit."[25] In addition, he said, there was some $93 million outstanding in silver certificates obtained through the deposit of silver with the government. "If continued long enough," Cleveland warned, "this operation will result in the substitution of silver for all the gold the Government owns applicable to its general purposes."[26] Increasingly, he said, customs payments were being made in silver or silver certificates (which by the passage of the Bland-Allison Act were made legal tender for all debts, public and private), making replenishing the gold reserves impossible. Further, Cleveland warned, it might lead the government to be in the position of being required to pay silver for its obligations, increasing the hoarding of gold, which had already begun. Cleveland scolded:

> When the time comes that gold has been withdrawn from circulation, then will be apparent the difference between the real value of the silver dollar and the dollar in gold, and the two coins will part company. Gold, still the standard of value, and necessary in our dealings with other countries, will be at a premium over silver; banks which have substituted gold for the deposits of their customers may pay them with silver bought with such gold, thus making a handsome profit; rich speculators will sell their hoarded gold to their neighbors who need it to liquidate their foreign debts, at a ruinous premium over silver, and the laboring men and women of the land, most defenseless of all, will find that the dollar received for the wage of their toil has sadly shrunk in its purchasing power.[27]

Silver dollar mintages would remain high over the next several years. However, the continued high coinages only added to the bloated backlog of bags of silver dollars stacked in Treasury vaults and did nothing to restore the continually sagging price of silver bullion.

Free silver forces would win another victory with the July 14, 1890, passage of the Sherman Silver Purchase Act, which required the Treasury to purchase $4.5 million in silver each month, "or so much thereof as may be offered in each month," to be paid for in Treasury notes redeemable in either gold or silver coin and usable in all payments of public and private debts.[28] Further, it required that, of this $4.5 million, $2 million of it would be turned into standard silver dollars each month until July 1891, after which "as much as may be necessary to provide for the redemption of the Treasury notes herein provide for..." would be minted.[29]

Again, against the predictions of free silver advocates, silver failed to return to parity with gold. After rebounding slightly in wake of the act's passage, it drifted lower. By 1893, when Cleveland called for the repeal of this act, in the hope of breaking the nation out of another major depression, the silver in the standard silver dollar was worth less than 52 cents.[30] Worse yet, the drain on the nation's gold reserves had brought the government stores below the $100 million level set by the government for the redemption of other notes in circulation. "Between the 1st day of July, 1890, and the 15th day of July, 1893, the gold coin and bullion in our Treasury decreased more than $132,000,000, while during the same period the silver coin and bullion in the Treasury increased more than $147,000,000," Cleveland noted in Aug. 8, 1893, message calling for repeal, adding:

> Unless Government bonds are to be constantly issued and sold to replenish our exhausted gold, only to be again exhausted, it is apparent that the operation of the silver-purchase law now in force leads in the direction of the entire substitution of silver for the gold in the Government Treasury, and that this must be followed by the payment of all Government obligations in depreciated silver.[31]

On Nov. 1, 1893, Congress repealed the act. The following year the gold reserves sank to nearly $60 million, and the depression, which had swallowed up railroads and several hundred banks in the process, fostered civil unrest. Jacob S. Coxey led his "Coxey's Army" of the unemployed in a march on Washington, D.C., and a strike at the Pullman Palace Car Company in Illinois, by the 150,000-member strong American Railway Union, headed by

The Morgan dollar series includes a number of dates and mints that are extreme rarities in upper mint-state grades, including the 1893-S and the 1901.

The 1895 Morgan dollar is known only in proof.

Eugene V. Debs, turned violent. Cleveland was forced to call in federal troops. In June 1894, William Jennings Bryan, the "Boy Orator of the Platte," addressed a silver convention in Omaha, Nebraska, made up of silver Democrats. In calling for the reinstatement of the free coinage of silver at a 16 to 1 ratio, the convention platform, written by Bryan, declared:

> We indorse the language used by Hon. John G. Carlisle in 1878, when he denounced the 'conspiracy' to destroy silver money as 'the most gigantic crime of this or any other age,' and we agree with him that 'the consummation of such a scheme would ultimately entail more misery upon the human race than all the wars, pestilences and famines that ever occurred in the history of the world.' We are not willing to be parties to such a crime, and in order to undo the wrong already done, and to prevent the further

Coinage of the Morgan dollar stopped in 1904 and did not resume until 1921. During the intervening time, the 1918 Pittman Act authorized the melting of 270 million silver dollars.

appreciation of money, we favor the immediate restoration of the free and unlimited coinage of gold and silver at the present ratio of 16 to 1, without waiting for the aid or consent of any other nation on earth.

We regard the right to issue money as an attribute of sovereignty and believe that all money needed to supplement the gold and silver coinage of the Constitution, and to make the dollar so stable in its purchasing power that it will defraud neither debtor nor creditor, should be issued by the general Government, as the greenbacks were issued; that such money should be redeemable in coin, the Government to exercise the option by redeeming in gold or silver, whichever is more convenient for the Government. We believe that all money issued by the Government, whether gold, silver, or paper, should be made a full legal tender for all debts, public and private, and that no citizen should be permitted to demonetize by contract that which the Government makes money by law.[32]

In 1895, with the economy still in a state of havoc, Cleveland, in one of a series of attempts to restore the gold reserve through bond sales, made a deal to float a bond issue, with the help of August Belmont & Co., J.P. Morgan & Co., and N.M. Rothschild & Sons of London. The syndicate agreed to deliver 3.5 million ounces of gold to restore the Treasury reserves in return for 30-year bonds at 4 percent interest. Another bond issue the following year, the fourth since the depression began, was released, with reserves below $80 million.

Despite the repeals of the silver purchase provisions of both acts, the government could not halt the progress of the Free Silver Movement. The final chapter will explore, briefly, the rise of Populism and William Jennings Bryan's unsuccessful bid for the presidency in 1896 (which spawned its own series of fascinating collectibles). It was the pinnacle for free silver and the beginning of the end for the Morgan silver dollar.

Peace dollar coinage began in 1921 and continued into 1935.

Collecting Morgan Dollars

In all, 378.1 million Morgan dollars (named by collectors after their designer, George T. Morgan) were minted under the auspices of the 1878 Bland-Allison and 1890 Sherman Silver Purchase acts. Minting continued unabated until 1904. Under terms of the 1918 Pittman Act, more than 270 million Treasury-stored silver dollars were melted. Coinage resumed in 1921, at first with the Morgan dollar design and then with the Peace dollar motif by Anthony de Francisci. Coinage of the silver dollar ended in 1935. In 1964, a few hundred thousand silver dollars bearing the Peace dollar design were minted but were never released to circulation. Other than the current production of one-ounce silver American Eagle bullion coins, bearing a $1 face value, and commemorative issues, coinage of the silver dollar has become a thing of the past.

Over the years of its mintage, Morgan dollars were struck at five mints—Philadelphia (no mintmark), Denver (D mintmark, 1921 only), San Francisco (S mintmark), Carson City (CC mintmark) and New Orleans (O mintmark). The mintmark, if there is one, is located on the coin's reverse, below the eagle.

Pricing—Prices given here are current *retail* prices at the time of publication as compiled and used in Krause Publications' *Coin Prices* magazine. All prices are approximates of the price you can expect to pay a dealer to obtain one of the coins (they are not offers to buy or sell) and may vary with subsequent upward or downward movements in a particular series or the coin market as a whole. They can and do vary from dealer to dealer as well.

Grading—Caution is given that, before spending large sums of money on collectible coins, you should take the time to learn coin grading. There are a number of good reference works that can help in this regard, including *The Official American Numismatic Association Grading Standards for United States Coins*, edited by Ken Bressett and Abe Kosoff; *the Official Guide to Coin Grading and Counterfeit Detection*, by John W. Dannreuther, edited by Scott A. Travers; and *Photograde*, by James Ruddy. All of these references provide photographs of coins in various states of preservation to assist in learning how to grade.

Slight differences in grade can mean thousands of dollars in value. Among adjective grades, grading is broken down into coins ranging from about good to uncirculated. Suffice it to say though, that the term "good" in numismatic terminology is used for a coin that is heavily worn. A coin without any wear is generally described as uncirculated. Even in uncirculated, a coin can show several marks from contact with other coins (termed "bagmarks"), therefore, grading of such coins is broken down even further, most often into brilliant uncirculated, choice brilliant uncirculated or gem brilliant uncirculated.

In the numerical grading system, Mint State-70 is perfect and almost never encountered. The difference in price between an MS-60 coin and an MS-63 can be considerable. The same is true between MS-63 and MS-65 and other number variances. The only way to really understand this seeming minutia is by looking at a number of coins and, through time, learning what makes a coin an MS-63, and MS-64 or an MS-65, etc. It is important to go slow and be careful so you're not disappointed when it comes time to sell.

Informed buying—Besides learning to grade, an important element of becoming a proficient collector is to learn as much as possible about the history and characteristics of a coin before making a purchase. Knowledge is the key to building a collection that will bring you enjoyment and will have the potential for future appreciation in value.

There are several excellent books related to Morgan and Peace silver dollars as well as the earlier series of U.S. silver dollars that can provide tremendous insight into survival levels of the various coins, along with factors such as "eye appeal" and strike that can make a coin infinitely more or less salable. These sources often offer tips on how to spot altered or spurious coins as well.

Good examples in this regard for Trade, Morgan and Peace dollars include Q. David Bowers' *Silver Dollars & Trade Dollars of the United States: A Complete Encyclopedia*, and Wayne Miller's *The Morgan and Peace Dollar Textbook*. The aforementioned books, along with such works as *What Every Silver Dollar Buyer Should Know*, by Steve Ivy and Ron Howard, *The Comprehensive U.S. Silver Dollar Encyclopedia*, by John W. Highfill, and a host of others too numerous to mention here, provide in-depth analysis of the likely number of coins extant in various grades as well as strike characteristics for each date. For the earliest U.S. silver dollars, *The United States Early Silver Dollars, 1794 to 1803*, by Jules Reiver, is a good reference.

Coin dealers, who often times specialize in one series or another, can also be good sources of information, for they will have a feel for how many specimens of a certain coin regularly appear on the market and in what grades. They can also guide you in building a collection.

Mintages—Mintages are important in determining a coin's value, but they are not the sole consideration. Many high-mintage coins, for one reason or another, suffered heavy degrees of melting, were lost due to the passage of time, or were not saved in high states of preservation. A low-mintage does not guaranty rarity either, particularly if much of this mintage never made it into circulation. This can be because the coins were not released at the time of issue (such as many of the Carson City Morgan dollars) or, more commonly, because large numbers were set aside by collectors or the general public at the time of their release. Mintages given here are for regular-issue coins, not proofs.

Coin Grading

Careful consideration must be given to the condition of a coin before arriving at its value, since a minor difference in grading can mean a substantial difference in price. There are several factors to keep in mind when attributing varying grades of preservation. Determining the condition of a coin is both an exact science and a subjective judgement call. Complete agreement on the exact qualities that constitute a grade of condition does not always occur between two individuals.

The following chart, which appears in *Coin Prices* magazine, is a consensus based on the 10 most frequently encountered coins commanding premium values in circulated condition. The descriptive grading can be applied to other issues. Qualities described are based on the standards developed and adopted by the American Numismatic Association.

MS-65 (uncirculated)—MS stands for mint state, which refers to a coin that has never been placed in circulation. An MS-65 is a superior mint-state example. It will be sharply struck with full mint luster. There will be no distracting marks in the field or on the raised areas of the design. The coin may be brilliant or naturally toned, but it must have superior "eye appeal" to qualify as an MS-65.

MS-64 (uncirculated) —May have light scattered contact marks. Luster will be at least average.

MS-63 (uncirculated)—May have some distracting marks in prime focal areas with a few scattered hairlines. Coins in this grade will generally have a pleasing appearance.

MS-60 (uncirculated)—The typical quality encountered in coins struck for circulation. No wear will be evident, but a number of bag marks, nicks, or other abrasions will be present. Surfaces could be dull or spotted.

AU-50 (about uncirculated)—Just a light amount of wear from brief exposure to circulation or light rubbing from mishandling may be found on the elevated design areas. Those imperfections may appear as scratches or dull spots, along with bag marks or edge nicks. At least half of the original mint luster will usually be present.

XF-40 (extremely fine)—Coins must show only slight evidence of wear on the highest points of the design, particularly in the hairlines of the portrait on the obverse and the eagle's feathers and wreath found on most U.S. coins. A trace of luster may show in protected areas of the coin's surface.

VF-20 (very fine)—Coins reflect noticeable wear at the fine points in the design, though they may remain sharp overall. Although the details will be slightly smoothed, all lettering and major features must remain sharp.

F-12 (fine)—This is the most widely collected condition. Coins show evidence of moderate to considerable but generally even wear on all high points, though all elements of the design and lettering remain bold. Where "Liberty" appears on a headband it must be fully visible. The rim must be fully raised and sharp on 20th century coins.

VG-8 (very good)—Coins show considerable wear, with most of the points of detail worn nearly smooth. At least three letters must show where "Liberty" appears in a headband. On 20th century coinage, the rim is starting to merge with the lettering.

G-4 (good)—In this condition, only the basic design remains distinguishable in outline form, with all points of detail being worn smooth. "Liberty" has disappeared, and rims are nearly merging with the lettering.

About good or fair—A coin identifiable by date and mint but otherwise badly worn, with only parts of the lettering showing. Such coins are of value to collectors only as space fillers and command a significant premium only in case of extreme scarcity.

Proof—Created as collector coins, proof specimens are struck on specially selected planchets with highly polished dies and generally display a mirror-like finish, sometimes featuring frosted highlight areas.

Prooflike and deep-mirror prooflike—These terms describe the degree of reflectiveness and cameo contrast on well-struck Morgan dollars. A DMPL coin may appear to be a proof at first glance, and a prooflike specimen has a lesser (but still considerable) degree of flash. Bag marks are more noticeable on PL and DMPL Morgans. Some common dates are scarce in this condition.

Rarity—Because of the generally high mintages for Morgan dollars, many dates and mints in this series are common, even into the lower ranges of mint state. For example, the 1881-S, with a mintage of 12,760,000, can be purchased for around $30 in MS-60 and is currently bringing a little more than $100 in MS-65. The Morgan dollar series does, however, have its share of coins that are either rare due to low mintages, low survival or by condition. Sometimes it is a combination of all of these factors. Examples include the 1889-CC, which retails above $200, even in Very Good-8; the 1893-S, a $1,000-plus coin in VG-8; and the 1895-S, a $200 coin in Fine. The popularity of the Morgan dollar series has led to extremely high prices for some dates in MS-65, including the 1884-S, 1886-O, 1889-CC, 1892-S, 1893-O, 1893-S, 1895-O, 1896-O, and the 1901—all of which list near, or well above, $100,000 in that grade.

Varieties—The Morgan dollar series also features a number of a fascinating minting varieties (a few of which are shown here), ranging from overdates and overmintmarks to doubled dies. The standard reference in this regard is *The Comprehensive Catalogue and Encyclopedia of U.S. Morgan and Peace Silver Dollars*, by Leroy C. Van Allen and A. George Mallis, which provides illustrations, rarity ratings, and a "VAM" numbering system in regular use today for identification.

1878 7/8 tail feathers

1890-CC tail bar

1882-O/S mintmark

1888-O "hot lips" doubled profile

1900-O/CC

The Morgan dollar series includes a number of minting varieties, a few of which are shown here.

MORGAN DOLLAR PROFILE

1878

Mints: Philadelphia (10,509,550), Carson City (2,212,000), San Francisco (9,774,000). **Notes:** 1878—Comes in several varieties based on the number of tail feathers on the eagle, the shape of the eagle's breast, and the design of the top arrow feather. The best known of these is the so-called 1878 7/8 tail feathers. 1878-CC—Part of the GSA sales, which offered 60,993 coins of this date in uncirculated. 1878-S—A fairly common Morgan dollar. **Timeline:** The Bland-Allison Silver Purchase Act, pushed through by supporters of free silver, is passed over President Hayes' veto. It requires the government to purchase $2 million to $4 million in silver each month to be coined into silver dollars. The Greenback Labor Party organizes in Ohio, joining the Greenback and National parties in advocating the free coinage of silver. A yellow fever epidemic sweeps through the South. New Orleans is the hardest hit. Fourteen thousand succumb to the disease nationwide. First commercial telephone exchange established in New Haven, Conn. Edison Electric Light Co. is formed, and inventor Thomas Edison receives a patent for a sound-recording device called the phonograph. First U.S.-manufactured bicycles debut. California Sen. Aaron A. Sargent introduces women's suffrage amendment to the Constitution. Same amendment finally passes in 1919. Regular coinage of the Trade dollar ends. **Average commercial ratio of silver to gold:** 17.92 to 1. **Average value of silver in 412 1/2-grain dollar:** 89 cents.

Date	VG-8	F-12	VF-20	XF-40	AU-50	MS-60	MS-63	MS-64	MS-65	65DMPL	Prf-60	Prf-63	Prf-65
1878 8 tail feathers	15.00	17.00	20.00	25.00	39.00	88.00	135.	300.	1450.	6300.	925.	1650.	6250.
1878 7 tail feathers, reverse of 1878	12.50	13.00	15.00	20.00	25.00	45.00	76.00	300.	1500.	6300.	1000.	2400.	5350.
1878 7 tail feathers, reverse of 1879	12.50	13.00	15.00	20.00	25.00	40.00	135.	315.	2600.	8800.	-	-	55,000.
1878 7 over 8 tail feathers	13.00	15.00	22.00	30.00	48.00	115.	145.	330.	2650.	14,500.	-	-	-
1878CC	38.00	42.00	44.00	48.00	80.00	150.	180.	300.	1250.	3150.	-	-	-
1878S	12.50	13.50	16.00	18.00	22.00	38.00	49.00	70.00	225.	2250.	-	-	-

1879

Mints: Philadelphia (14,807,100), Carson City (756,000), New Orleans (2,887,000), San Francisco (9,110,000). **Notes:** 1879—Scarce in higher mint state. Otherwise common. 1879-CC—A scarce Carson City issue that brings premiums even in lower grades. 1879-O—Moderately priced up to lower mint-state grades. 1879-S—Two reverse varieties: The "Reverse of 1878," with a parallel top arrow feather and a concave eagle's breast, and "Reverse of 1879," with a slanting top arrow feather and a rounded eagle's breast. **Timeline:** Specie payments resume. Payments had been suspended in 1861. California adopts a state constitutional provision forbidding employment of Chinese, in response to growing anti-Chinese sentiment resulting from the high unemployment caused by the Panic of 1873. Frank W. Woolworth and W.H. Moore open the first "five-cent" store, in New York. George B. Seldon applies for a patent on his horseless carriage. Thomas A. Edison demonstrates, in public, his new incandescent lamp. First electric street lighting system installed in Cleveland. **Average commercial ratio of silver to gold:** 18.39 to 1. **Average value of silver in 412 1/2-grain dollar:** 86.9 cents.

Date	VG-8	F-12	VF-20	XF-40	AU-50	MS-60	MS-63	MS-64	MS-65	65DMPL	Prf-60	Prf-63	Prf-65
1879	12.00	12.50	13.00	14.00	18.00	28.00	58.00	140.	1000.	6950.	1450.	5000.	5500.
1879CC	48.00	78.00	145.	400.	790.	1600.	3550.	5350.	17,500.	50,000.	-		-
1879O	12.00	12.50	13.00	17.00	21.00	63.00	130.	320.	3300.	16,500.	-		-
1879S reverse of 1878	12.00	13.50	15.00	20.00	33.00	90.00	360.	1500.	7250.	22,000.	-		-
1879S reverse of 1879	12.00	12.50	13.50	14.00	19.00	28.00	35.00	51.00	105.	450.	-		-

1880 **Mints:** Philadelphia (12,601,355), Carson City (591,000), New Orleans (5,305,000), San Francisco (8,900,000). **Notes:** 1880—Fairly common, except in MS-65 or better. 1880-CC—Another GSA hoard coin, with more than 131,000 of its low mintage offered in uncirculated. Comes in "Reverse of 1878" and "Reverse of 1879" varieties. Minted from overdated dies. 1880-O—Common in lower grades, with many AU examples existing. A high-ticket coin in upper mint-state grades. 1880-S—Readily available in all grades. **Timeline:** Republicans nominate James A. Garfield for president. The Democrats select Winfield S. Hancock. Garfield wins, with Chester A. Arthur as vice president. Metropolitan Museum of Art opens in New York. *Ben-Hur*, by Lew Wallace, is published. Thomas Edison receives a patent for incandescent electric lamp. Salvation Army, first established in London, comes to Philadelphia. **Average commercial ratio of silver to gold:** 18.05 to 1**. Average value of silver in 412 1/2-grain dollar:** 88.6 cents.

Date	VG-8	F-12	VF-20	XF-40	AU-50	MS-60	MS-63	MS-64	MS-65	65DMPL	Prf-60	Prf-63	Prf-65
1880	12.00	12.50	13.50	14.00	18.00	24.00	50.00	100.	900.	3450.	1450.	5000.	5500.
1880 CC reverse of 1878	53.00	63.00	76.00	110.	190.	300.	325.	700.	2250.	11,000.	-	-	
1880 CC reverse of 1879	53.00	63.00	76.00	110.	190.	270.	300.	375.	900.	3150.	-	-	
1880O	12.00	12.50	13.00	17.00	20.00	43.00	285.	1500.	14,500.	70,000.	-	-	
1880S	12.00	12.50	13.50	15.00	18.00	26.00	35.00	51.00	105.	410.	-	-	

1881 **Mints:** Philadelphia (9,163,984), Carson City (296,000), New Orleans (5,708,000), San Francisco (12,760,000). **Notes**: 1881—Readily available. 1881-CC—Nearly 50 percent of the original mintage was part of the GSA sales. 1881-O—Readily available in circulated grades. Scarce in higher mint state. 1881-S—Usually well struck. Considered one of the most common Morgan dates, even in high grade. **Timeline:** Newly elected President James A. Garfield is fatally wounded by Charles J. Guiteau while waiting for a train in Washington, D.C. Following Garfield's death, Vice President Chester A. Arthur is sworn in as the nation's 21st President. American branch of the Red Cross established. Sioux chief Sitting Bull surrenders to Federal troops, having been a fugitive since the Battle of the Little Bighorn in 1876. **Average commercial ratio of silver to gold:** 18.25 to 1**. Average value of silver in 412 1/2-grain dollar:** 87.6 cents.

Date	VG-8	F-12	VF-20	XF-40	AU-50	MS-60	MS-63	MS-64	MS-65	65DMPL	Prf-60	Prf-63	Prf-65
1881	12.00	12.50	13.00	13.50	19.00	27.00	46.00	100.	900.	13,750.	750.	1450.	5500.
1881CC	110.	120.	130.	140.	190.	265.	295.	325.	650.	1450.	-		-
1881O	12.00	12.50	13.00	13.50	18.00	24.00	40.00	125.	1950.	15,000.	-		-
1881S	12.00	14.00	15.00	16.00	18.00	26.00	35.00	51.00	105.	460.	-		-

1882 **Mints:** Philadelphia (11,101,100), Carson City (1,133,000), New Orleans (6,090,000), San Francisco (9,250,000). **Notes**; 1882—Another common date, even into lower mint state. 1882-CC—More than 605,000 were sold in mint state as part of the GSA sales. 1882-O—Common in all grades. 1882-S—Generally a strong strike. A common date. **Timeline:** Geneva Convention of 1864, regarding the care of war wounded, is ratified by the U.S. Senate. The Knights of Columbus is founded in Connecticut. John L. Sullivan wins the bare-knuckle heavyweight championship title. The first major league baseball doubleheader is played. Notorious bandit and bank robber Jesse James is killed by Robert Ford in St. Joseph, Mo. The nation's first hydroelectric plant is built in Appleton, Wis. **Average commercial ratio of silver to gold:** 18.20 to 1**. Average value of silver in 412 1/2-grain dollar:** 87.8 cents.

Date	VG-8	F-12	VF-20	XF-40	AU-50	MS-60	MS-63	MS-64	MS-65	65DMPL	Prf-60	Prf-63	Prf-65
1882	12.00	12.50	13.00	13.50	18.00	24.00	39.00	55.00	480.	4100.	750.	1450.	5500.
1882CC	38.00	39.00	41.00	52.00	53.00	95.00	120.	150.	410.	825.	-		-
1882O	12.00	12.50	13.00	13.50	18.00	24.00	32.00	65.00	850.	4200.	-		-
1882S	12.00	12.50	13.00	14.00	18.00	26.00	35.00	51.00	105.	1100.	-		-

1883

Mints: Philadelphia (12,291,039), Carson City (1,204,000), New Orleans (8,725,000), San Francisco (6,250,000). **Notes**: 1883—A fairly common date. 1883-CC—Large numbers of mint-state specimens sold in GSA sales, 62.75 percent of the original mintage. 1883-O—A common O-mint dollar even into higher mint-state grades. 1883-S—Common in lower grades but a premium coin in upper circulated. Recognized as being scarce in mint state. **Timeline:** The spoils system of filling Federal jobs is taken to task by the creation of the Civil Service Commission, establishing examinations and rules for filling jobs. The Brooklyn Bridge is officially opened in New York. Long distance telephone service begins operation between New York City and Chicago. Standard time zones are established for the United States. **Average commercial ratio of silver to gold:** 18.64 to 1. **Average value of silver in 412-1/2 grain dollar:** 85.8 cents.

Date	VG-8	F-12	VF-20	XF-40	AU-50	MS-60	MS-63	MS-64	MS-65	65DMPL	Prf-60	Prf-63	Prf-65
1883	12.00	12.50	13.00	14.00	18.00	26.00	32.00	55.00	140.	760.	750.	1450.	5500.
1883CC	38.00	41.00	44.00	47.00	50.00	95.00	120.	135.	340.	690.	-		-
1883O	12.00	12.50	13.00	13.50	18.00	24.00	35.00	51.00	105.	575.	-		-
1883S	12.00	13.50	18.00	26.00	150.	425.	1600.	5000.	26,500.	94,500.	-		-

1884

Mints: Philadelphia (14,070,875), Carson City (1,136,000), New Orleans (9,730,000), San Francisco (3,200,000). **Notes**: 1884—Readily available in all grades. 1884-CC—A staggering 84.74 percent of original mintage was part of GSA sales in 1970s and 1980s. 1884-O—Readily available even in mint state. 1884-S—A classic series rarity in higher mint state. **Timeline:** Grover Cleveland is elected president, defeating James G. Blaine. Mark Twain's *Huckleberry Finn* is published. Knights of Labor designate the first Monday in September as Labor Day, to be celebrated annually. The cornerstone for the pedestal of the Statue of Liberty is laid in New York Harbor. **Average commercial ratio of silver to gold:** 18.61 to 1. **Average value of silver in 412 1/2-grain dollar:** 85.9 cents.

Date	VG-8	F-12	VF-20	XF-40	AU-50	MS-60	MS-63	MS-64	MS-65	65DMPL	Prf-60	Prf-63	Prf-65
1884	12.00	12.50	13.00	13.50	18.00	24.00	35.00	55.00	270.	2200.	750.	1450.	5500.
1884CC	47.00	50.00	55.00	63.00	68.00	95.00	120.	135.	340.	760.	-		-
1884O	12.00	12.50	13.00	13.50	18.00	24.00	35.00	51.00	105.	670.	-		-
1884S	12.00	14.00	19.00	36.00	220.	3800.	30,000.	90,000.	150,000.	220,000.	-		-

1885

Mints: Philadelphia (17,787,930), Carson City (228,000), New Orleans (9,185,000), San Francisco (1,497,000). **Notes**: 1885—A common date in all grades. 1885-CC—Readily available in mint state. GSA sales offered 148,285 of the original mintage. 1885-O—Common in all grades. 1885-S—Scarce in higher grades. Strike varies. **Timeline:** Special delivery postal service begun by the U.S. Post Office Department. Scot Joplin introduces ragtime to St. Louis with his arrival in that city. The Washington Monument is dedicated. It would open to the public three years later. The Statue of Liberty, a gift from France, arrives in New York City. The first electric streetcar service begins operation in Baltimore. In his annual message to Congress, President Grover Cleveland calls for repeal of the Bland-Allison Act, requiring coinage of silver into silver dollars, fearing a continued drain on the nation's gold reserves. **Average commercial ratio of silver to gold:** 19.41 to 1. **Average value of silver in 412 1/2-grain dollar:** 82.4 cents.

Date	VG-8	F-12	VF-20	XF-40	AU-50	MS-60	MS-63	MS-64	MS-65	65DMPL	Prf-60	Prf-63	Prf-65
1885	12.00	12.50	13.00	13.50	18.00	24.00	35.00	51.00	115.	570.	750.	1450.	5500.
1885CC	170.	190.	200.	210.	225.	275.	310.	340.	800.	1600.	-		-
1885O	12.00	12.50	13.00	13.50	18.00	24.00	35.00	51.00	105.	490.	-		-
1885S	12.00	13.50	17.00	21.00	46.00	115.	200.	400.	2500.	16,500.	-		-

1886

Mints: Philadelphia (19,963,886), New Orleans (10,710,000), San Francisco (750,000). **Notes**: 1886—Common in all grades. 1886-O—A condition rarity. Common in circulated grades but an extreme rarity in higher mint-state grades as marked by its price. 1886-S—Common date. Commands strong price in MS-65 and above. **Timeline:** The Haymarket Riot in Chicago leads to the death of seven police officers and the wounding of 60 civilians when a bomb explodes. Apache chief Geronimo surrenders to Gen. Nelson A. Miles in Arizona. The Statue of Liberty is unveiled and dedicated by President Grover Cleveland. The American Federation of Labor is organized in Ohio. Samuel Gompers serves as first AFL president. Charles Martin Hall is credited with developing a cheap method of extracting aluminum from ore. First Tournament of Roses held in Pasadena, Calif. **Average commercial ratio of silver to gold:** 20.78 to 1. **Average value of silver in 412 1/2-grain dollar:** 76.9 cents.

Date	VG-8	F-12	VF-20	XF-40	AU-50	MS-60	MS-63	MS-64	MS-65	65DMPL	Prf-60	Prf-63	Prf-65
1886	12.00	12.50	13.00	13.50	18.00	24.00	35.00	51.00	105.	575.	750.	1450.	5500.
1886O	12.00	12.50	15.00	18.00	76.00	325.	3000.	10,000.	235,000.	283,500.	-		-
1886S	22.00	26.00	37.00	47.00	70.00	170.	240.	550.	3650.	16,500.	-		-

1887

Mints: Philadelphia (20,290,710), New Orleans (11,550,000), San Francisco (1,771,000). **Notes**: 1887—Common in all grades. 1887-O—Common in lower grades. Full strike MS-65s are rare. 1887-S—Tough in MS-65, otherwise available. **Timeline:** The Interstate Commerce Commission, the first regulatory commission in U.S. history, is established as a result of growing complaints from farmers and others over excessive rail rates. Free delivery of mail provided to all communities with a population over 10,000. Henry Ward Beecher, advocate of abolition, dies at age 74. **Average commercial ratio of silver to gold:** 21.10 to 1. **Average value of silver in 412 1/2-grain dollar:** 75.8 cents.

Date	VG-8	F-12	VF-20	XF-40	AU-50	MS-60	MS-63	MS-64	MS-65	65DMPL	Prf-60	Prf-63	Prf-65
1887	12.00	12.50	13.00	13.50	18.00	24.00	35.00	51.00	115.	530.	750.	1450.	5500.
1887O	12.00	12.50	13.00	17.00	24.00	41.00	95.00	330.	5500.	8500.	-		-
1887S	12.00	13.50	15.00	20.00	37.00	70.00	150.	500.	3800.	27,000.	-		-

1888

Mints: Philadelphia (19,183,832), New Orleans (12,150,000), San Francisco (657,000). **Notes**: 1888—A relatively common date in all grades. 1888-O—Common date but often found flatly struck. 1888-S—A scarce coin in circulated grades and tougher than some in higher mint state. **Timeline:** Benjamin Harrison is elected President of the United States, defeating Grover Cleveland, who is attempting to gain a second term. George Eastman introduces the first Kodak, a square box camera. A yellow fever epidemic breaks out in Jacksonville, Fla., killing at least 400. A major snowstorm, the "blizzard of '88," sacks the eastern United States in March, leading to some 400 deaths. **Average commercial ratio of silver to gold:** 22 to 1. **Average value of silver in 412 1/2-grain dollar:** 72.7 cents.

Date	VG-8	F-12	VF-20	XF-40	AU-50	MS-60	MS-63	MS-64	MS-65	65DMPL	Prf-60	Prf-63	Prf-65
1888	12.00	12.50	13.00	13.50	18.00	24.00	35.00	53.00	190.	2350.	750.	1450.	5500.
1888O	12.00	12.50	13.00	13.50	22.00	26.00	39.00	75.00	550.	1600.	-		-
1888S	26.00	32.00	35.00	41.00	85.00	165.	235.	550.	4400.	10,500.	-		-

1889

Mints: Philadelphia (21,726,811), Carson City (350,000), New Orleans (11,875,000), San Francisco (700,000). **Notes**: 1889—Readily available in all grades. 1889-CC—A rare Carson City strike that brings hundreds of dollars in any grade. An extreme rarity in MS-65. 1889-O—Scarce in MS-65, otherwise available. 1889-S Readily available into mint state. **Timeline:** Land in Indian Territory, which would become Oklahoma Territory, is opened to white settlement, beginning the Oklahoma land rush. A devastating flood, caused by a dam breaking, nearly destroys Johnstown, Penn., costing more than 2,000 lives. John L. Sullivan wins the last professional heavyweight U.S. bare-knuckle fight in a 75 rounder. North Dakota and South Dakota are admitted to the Union. At a meeting in St. Louis of major farm and labor organizations, the groups establish a platform calling for the free coinage of silver. Singer Manufacturing Company produces the first electric sewing machine in the U.S. **Average commercial ratio of silver to gold:** 22.1 to 1. **Average value of silver in 412 1/2-grain dollar:** 72.3 cents.

Date	VG-8	F-12	VF-20	XF-40	AU-50	MS-60	MS-63	MS-64	MS-65	65DMPL	Prf-60	Prf-63	Prf-65
1889	12.00	12.50	13.00	13.50	18.00	24.00	35.00	51.00	350.	2950.	750.	1450.	5500.
1889CC	225.	290.	500.	1200.	2900.	7000.	19,000.	35,000.	280,000.	296,000.	-		-
1889O	12.00	12.50	13.00	18.00	31.00	100.	265.	625.	5650.	14,500.	-		-
1889S	21.00	26.00	31.00	39.00	65.00	135.	195.	375.	2000.	7550.	-		-

1890

Mints: Philadelphia (16,802,590), Carson City (2,309,041), New Orleans (10,701,000), San Francisco (8,230,373). **Notes**: 1890—Relatively common into lower mint-state grades. 1890-CC—Brings premium in circulated grades as a Carson City coin. Scarce in higher mint state. Often weakly struck. 1890-O—Readily available up to lower mint state. 1890-S—Readily available. **Timeline:** Growth of industrial trusts results in passage of the Sherman Antitrust Act. Sioux Chief Sitting Bull is killed by U.S. soldiers at the Pine Ridge Agency in South Dakota. U.S. population has doubled since the Civil War. Farmers, however, continue to face depressed prices, and interest rates on borrowing remain high. William Jennings Bryan is elected to Congress. Oklahoma Territory is formed out of western half of Indian Territory. Sherman Silver Purchase Act passed. First Army-Navy football game is played at West Point, N.Y. Navy wins 24-0. The Supreme Council of the Southern Alliance, a farm organization, meets in Florida and proclaims for cheap money. **Average commercial ratio of silver to gold:** 19.75 to 1. **Average value of silver in 412 1/2-grain dollar:** 80.9 cents.

Date	VG-8	F-12	VF-20	XF-40	AU-50	MS-60	MS-63	MS-64	MS-65	65DMPL	Prf-60	Prf-63	Prf-65
1890	12.00	12.50	13.00	13.50	18.00	24.00	35.00	140.	3400.	12,500.	750.	1450.	5500.
1890CC	38.00	39.00	44.00	55.00	110.	295.	355.	875.	7900.	9750.	-		-
1890CC tail bar	43.00	50.00	60.00	90.00	150.	390.	475.	1200.	8050.	9750.	-		-
1890O	12.00	12.50	13.00	18.00	23.00	37.00	85.00	200.	2450.	7550.	-		-
1890S	12.00	13.50	14.00	17.00	21.00	42.00	91.00	200.	900.	8200.	-		-

1891

Mints: Philadelphia (8,694,206), Carson City (1,618,000), New Orleans (7,954,529), San Francisco (5,296,000). **Notes**: 1891—Common into lower mint-state grades. 1891-CC—Brings premium in circulated grades as Carson City coin. Readily available up to lower mint state. 1891-O—Readily available up to lower mint state. Noted for being flatly struck—lacking eagle breast feathers and hair above Liberty's ear. 1891-S—Readily available. **Timeline:** The word "Populist" is coined for the political movement that has been gaining strength through various farmer and labor alliances. The Populist Party holds a convention in May in Ohio. Its plank continues the popular call for free coinage of silver. Thomas Alva Edison applies for a patent on a moving-picture camera. The game of basketball is invented by physical education instructor James Naismith in Massachusetts. **Average commercial ratio of silver to gold:** 20.92 to 1. **Average value of silver in 412 1/2-grain dollar:** 76.4 cents.

Date	VG-8	F-12	VF-20	XF-40	AU-50	MS-60	MS-63	MS-64	MS-65	65DMPL	Prf-60	Prf-63	Prf-65
1891	12.00	12.50	13.00	18.00	23.00	40.00	135.	590.	8200.	25,000.	750.	1450.	5500.
1891CC	38.00	40.00	46.00	58.00	120.	295.	350.	700.	3150.	20,000.	-		-
1891O	12.00	12.50	13.00	17.00	33.00	89.00	220.	650.	7000.	21,500.	-		-
1891S	12.00	13.50	15.00	17.00	24.00	42.00	100.	250.	1700.	7250.	-		-

1892

Mints: Philadelphia (1,037,245), Carson City (1,352,000), New Orleans (2,744,000), San Francisco (1,200,000). **Notes**: 1892—Readily available in lower grades. Higher mint-state pieces are tough. 1892-CC—Popularity of CC mintmark makes this a premium coin in any grade. Scarce in gem. 1892-O—Common to lower mint state. Notorious for weak strikes. 1892-S—Common in lower grades; a real rarity in mint state. **Timeline:** Ellis Island becomes the receiving station for immigrants. Grover Cleveland wins a second term as President, over incumbent President Benjamin Harrison. Arthur Conan Doyle's *The Adventures of Sherlock Holmes* is published. Labor and capitol clash as the Homestead Strike occurs. Lizzie Borden is charged with murdering her father and mother in Massachusetts. George Ferris designs the Ferris Wheel. Gentleman Jim Corbett knocks out John L. Sullivan in the 21st round of the first match to use boxing gloves. The People's Party is formally organized. **Average commercial ratio of silver and gold:** 23.72 to 1. **Average value of silver in 412 1/2-grain dollar:** 67.4 cents.

Date	VG-8	F-12	VF-20	XF-40	AU-50	MS-60	MS-63	MS-64	MS-65	65DMPL	Prf-60	Prf-63	Prf-65
1892	12.00	12.50	19.00	26.00	66.00	150.	325.	660.	3800.	15,750.	750.	1450.	5500.
1892CC	46.00	56.00	80.00	125.	225.	450.	850.	1400.	8200.	19,000.	-		-
1892O	12.00	12.50	20.00	23.00	66.00	110.	225.	625.	7300.	27,000.	-		-
1892S	18.00	20.00	43.00	170.	2150.	18,000.	51,500.	85,000.	94,500.	157,500.	-		-

1893

Mints: Philadelphia (378,792), Carson City (677,000), New Orleans (300,000), San Francisco (100,000). **Notes:** 1893—Low-mintage, scarce favorite. A great rarity in mint state. 1893-CC—Low mintage and scarce in all grades. 1893-O—Scarce in any grade. A great rarity in MS-65. 1893-S—A series key. Rare and desirable in all grades. Gem specimens are major auction highlights. **Timeline:** The Philadelphia and Reading Railroad files for bankruptcy as the economy begins to falter. Pressure applied on President Cleveland to repeal Sherman Silver Purchase Act, fearing it will force U.S. off the gold standard by draining its reserves. Panic begins in May, with bank collapses, as the nation drifts into depression. The Sherman Silver Purchase Act is repealed in October, but the depression has spread worldwide. Thomas A. Edison sets up a motion-picture lot in New Jersey. The World's Columbian Exposition is officially opened in Chicago. **Average commercial ratio of silver to gold:** 26.49 to 1. **Average value of silver in 412 1/2-grain dollar:** 60.3 cents.

Date	VG-8	F-12	VF-20	XF-40	AU-50	MS-60	MS-63	MS-64	MS-65	65DMPL	Prf-60	Prf-63	Prf-65
1893	69.00	79.00	89.00	160.	215.	400.	825.	1400.	7600.	38,000.	750.	1450.	5500.
1893CC	100.	120.	230.	550.	750.	1400.	4650.	7950.	53,500.	88,000.	-		-
1893O	77.00	120.	150.	220.	600.	1400.	6500.	14,500.	195,000.	201,500.	-		-
1893S	1100.	1300.	2200.	5000.	13,500.	47,000.	90,000.	155,000.	285,000.	315,000.	-		-

1894

Mints: Philadelphia (110,972), New Orleans (1,723,000), San Francisco (1,260,000). **Notes:** 1894—Low-mintage Philadelphia issue. Desirable in all grades. 1894-O—Rare in MS-65. 1894-S—Scarce in most grades. Brings good premiums in higher circulated grades and above. **Timeline:** Unemployed workers, calling themselves "Coxey's Army," after their leader, Jacob S. Coxey, march on Washington, D.C. A large portion of the World's Columbian Exposition grounds are destroyed by fire. William Jennings Bryan leads a Democratic Silver Convention in Omaha, calling for free coinage of silver. William "Coin" Harvey publishes *Coin's Financial School*. The depression deepens. Gold continues to drain from reserves, and a large number of banks fail. Thomas Alva Edison gives a public demonstration of his moving-picture camera. The Federal Government offers two bond issues, each of $50 million, to make up for gold reserve losses. **Average commercial ratio of silver to gold:** 32.56 to 1. **Average value of silver in 412 1/2-grain dollar:** 49.1 cents.

Date	VG-8	F-12	VF-20	XF-40	AU-50	MS-60	MS-63	MS-64	MS-65	65DMPL	Prf-60	Prf-63	Prf-65
1894	300.	350.	400.	450.	600.	900.	4300.	5650.	18,500.	44,000.	1050.	1500.	5500.
1894O	22.00	25.00	35.00	50.00	160.	550.	3800.	7500.	45,500.	56,500.	-		-
1894S	30.00	42.00	63.00	110.	250.	450.	800.	1600.	5850.	19,000.	-		-

1895

Mints: Philadelphia (12,880), New Orleans (450,000), San Francisco (400,000). **Notes:** 1895—Often referred to as the "King of Morgan dollars." Known only in proof. 1895-O—A premium piece in any grade. A well-known rarity in mint state. 1895-S—A scarce, premium issue. **Timeline:** Gettysburg National Military Park is established. Free silver advocates hold a convention in Salt Lake City, Utah Territory. Charles E. Duryea receives a patent on an automobile. The first professional football game is played. President Cleveland floats a third bond issue, which, with the help of August Belmont, J.P. Morgan and the Rothschild interests, provides 3.5 million ounces of gold to replenish reserves. **Average commercial ratio of silver to gold:** 31.6 to 1. **Average value of silver in 412 1/2-grain dollar:** 50.6 cents.

Date	VG-8	F-12	VF-20	XF-40	AU-50	MS-60	MS-63	MS-64	MS-65	65DMPL	Prf-60	Prf-63	Prf-65
1895	Proof only	11,250.	13,750.	16,500.	18,500.	-	-	-	-	-	19,000.	24,500.	32,000.
1895O	105.	140.	190.	275.	800.	10,750.	36,500.	80,000.	215,000.	-	-		-
1895S	160.	200.	230.	460.	825.	1600.	3800.	6500.	17,500.	40,500.	-		-

1896

Mints: Philadelphia (9,976,762), New Orleans (4,900,000), San Francisco (5,000,000). **Notes:** 1896—Readily available in all grades. 1896-O—Common in circulated grades but a rarity when it comes to pieces in upper mint-state grades. 1896-S—Common in lower circulated grades. Scarce and priced as such in grades Very Fine and up. **Timeline:** William McKinley, supporting a hard money plank, defeats free silver supporter William Jennings Bryan for the presidency. The comic strip is developed with the first appearance of "The Yellow Kid" by Richard F. Outcault. The first Ford automobile is assembled in Detroit. Gold is discovered on the Klondike River in Canada. First modern Olympic Games are played in Athens, Greece. Utah is admitted as the 45th state. Government floats fourth bond issue to help shore up still falling gold reserve. **Average commercial ratio of silver to gold:** 30.59 to 1. **Average value of silver in 412 1/2-grain dollar:** 52.3 cents.

Date	VG-8	F-12	VF-20	XF-40	AU-50	MS-60	MS-63	MS-64	MS-65	65DMPL	Prf-60	Prf-63	Prf-65
1896	12.00	12.50	13.00	13.50	18.00	24.00	35.00	53.00	160.	975.	750.	1450.	5500.
1896O	12.00	12.50	17.00	20.00	120.	800.	7700.	41,000.	138,500.	170,000.	-		-
1896S	13.00	24.00	45.00	165.	410.	725.	1600.	2950.	11,000.	25,000.	-		-

1897

Mints: Philadelphia (2,822,731), New Orleans (4,004,000), San Francisco (5,825,000). **Notes:** 1897—Readily available in all grades. 1897-O—Common in circulated grades up to AU. A rarity in higher mint-state grades. 1897-S—Readily available in all grades. **Timeline:** Economy begins to recover. National Congress of Mothers, which in the mid-1920s becomes the National Congress of Parents and Teachers (PTA), is founded in Washington, D.C. A shipment of $750,000 in gold arrives in San Francisco from the Klondike. National Monetary Conference meets in Indianapolis and endorses the gold standard. A coal miners' strike shuts down mines in Pennsylvania, Ohio, and West Virginia. Bob Fitzsimmons takes the heavyweight boxing title from James J. "Gentleman Jim" Corbett in a 14-round bout at Carson City, Nev. The Stanley Steamer is invented. **Average commercial ratio of silver to gold:** 34.2 to 1. **Average value of silver in 412 1/2-grain dollar:** 46.7 cents.

Date	VG-8	F-12	VF-20	XF-40	AU-50	MS-60	MS-63	MS-64	MS-65	65DMPL	Prf-60	Prf-63	Prf-65
1897	12.00	12.50	13.00	13.50	18.00	27.00	35.00	53.00	250.	2900.	750.	1450.	5500.
1897O	12.00	12.50	14.00	22.00	105.	600.	4900.	19,500.	49,000.	56,500.	-		-
1897S	12.00	12.50	14.00	18.00	22.00	42.00	81.00	125.	630.	1700	-		-

1898

Mints: Philadelphia (5,884,735), New Orleans (4,440,000), San Francisco (4,102,000). **Notes:** 1898—Readily available in all grades. 1898-O—Readily available in all grades. One of the Treasury's Department's 1962 surprise releases. 1898-S—Readily available up to lower mint-state grades. **Timeline:** The U.S. battleship *Maine* explodes in Havana Harbor, leads country into Spanish-American War. Treaty of Paris, ending war, cedes Guam and Porto Rico to the United States and establishes sovereignty of Cuba. Philippine Islands also formally ceded to United States. Annexation of Hawaii approved. Theodore Roosevelt, who led the Rough Riders up San Juan Hill during the Spanish-American War, is nominated by the Republican Party for governor of New York. **Average commercial ratio of silver to gold:** 35.03 to 1. **Average value of silver in 412 1/2-grain dollar:** 45.6 cents.

Date	VG-8	F-12	VF-20	XF-40	AU-50	MS-60	MS-63	MS-64	MS-65	65DMPL	Prf-60	Prf-63	Prf-65
1898	12.00	12.50	14.00	15.00	18.00	24.00	35.00	53.00	220.	1075.	750.	1450.	5500.
1898O	13.50	14.00	14.50	15.00	27.00	29.00	35.00	51.00	110.	510.	-	-	
1898S	13.00	14.00	15.00	28.00	65.00	175.	250.	500.	2400.	11,250.	-	-	

1899

Mints: Philadelphia (330,846), New Orleans (12,290,000), San Francisco (2,562,000). **Notes:** 1899 Low-mintage date carrying a premium even in lower grades. 1899-O Readily available in all grades. 1899-S—Scarce in higher mint state. **Timeline:** Philippine guerrillas fire on American forces at Manila. Congress authorizes use of voting machines for federal elections. U.S. officially establishes jurisdiction over Guam, and the Treaty of Paris is ratified by the Senate. James J. Jeffries wins the heavyweight title by knocking out Bob Fitzsimmons in the 11th round of a fight at Coney Island, N.Y. **Average commercial ratio of silver to gold:** 34.36 to 1. **Average value of silver in 412 1/2-grain dollar:** 46.6 cents.

Date	VG-8	F-12	VF-20	XF-40	AU-50	MS-60	MS-63	MS-64	MS-65	65DMPL	Prf-60	Prf-63	Prf-65
1899	25.00	30.00	44.00	48.00	77.00	100.	135.	200.	650.	2250.	750.	1450.	5500.
1899O	12.00	12.50	13.00	13.50	27.00	31.00	37.00	53.00	120.	825.	-	-	
1899S	12.00	18.00	22.00	30.00	90.00	190.	200.	500.	2100.	8600.	-	-	

1900

Mints: Philadelphia (8,830,912), New Orleans (12,590,000), San Francisco (3,540,000). **Notes:** 1900—Readily available in all grades. 1900-O—Another Treasury-release date. Readily available. 1900-S—Readily available up to higher mint state. **Timeline:** The Gold Standard Act is passed by Congress. William McKinley is reelected president over Democratic candidate William Jennings Bryan. Theodore Roosevelt serves as McKinley's vice president. *The Wonderful Wizard of Oz*, by L. Frank Baum, is published. A hurricane kills 6,000 in Galveston, Texas. Eastman Kodak introduces its Brownie Box Camera. The American League is formed in Chicago. **Average commercial ratio of silver and gold:** 33.3 to 1. **Average value of silver in 412 1/2-grain dollar:** 48 cents.

Date	VG-8	F-12	VF-20	XF-40	AU-50	MS-60	MS-63	MS-64	MS-65	65DMPL	Prf-60	Prf-63	Prf-65
1900	12.00	12.50	13.00	13.50	18.00	30.00	36.00	55.00	160.	11,000.	750.	1450.	5500.
1900O	12.00	13.00	14.00	15.00	29.00	38.00	40.00	60.00	130.	3000.	-		-
1900O/CC	22.00	27.00	38.00	49.00	120.	200.	340.	550.	1640.	19,000.	-		-
1900S	14.00	19.00	21.00	35.00	77.00	180.	220.	350.	925.	9450.	-		-

1901

Mints: Philadelphia (6,962,813), New Orleans (13,320,000), San Francisco (2,284,000). **Notes:** 1901—A rarity in mint state. Available in lower grades. 1901-O—A 1960s Treasury release coin, making it readily available. Often weakly struck. Tough in MS-65 or better. 1901-S—Fairly scarce. Brings good premiums in AU and above. **Timeline:** President William McKinley is assassinated while attending the Pan-American Exposition in Buffalo, N.Y. Theodore Roosevelt takes over as president. The Socialist Party is formed. United States Steel, the nation's first billion-dollar corporation, is organized. First big oil gusher tapped into in Texas. **Average commercial ratio of silver to gold:** 34.68 to 1. **Average value of silver in 412 1/2-grain dollar:** 46.1 cents.

Date	VG-8	F-12	VF-20	XF-40	AU-50	MS-60	MS-63	MS-64	MS-65	65DMPL	Prf-60	Prf-63	Prf-65
1901	15.00	22.00	33.00	60.00	230.	1500.	18,000.	61,000.	189,000.	220K	950.	1900.	8100.
1901O	12.00	12.50	13.00	13.50	27.00	30.00	35.00	53.00	170.	3800.	-		-
1901S	15.00	18.00	27.00	50.00	165.	265.	525.	850.	5350.	12,500.	-		-

1902

Mints: Philadelphia (7,994,777), New Orleans (8,636,000), San Francisco (1,530,000). **Notes:** 1902—Readily available up to higher mint-state grades. 1902-O—Another heavy Treasury release. Readily available in mint state. Often flatly struck. 1902-S—A scarce coin in all grades. **Timeline:** Isthmian Canal Act is passed, authorizing funding and building of a canal across the Isthmus of Panama. The Philippine Government Act is passed by Congress setting up civil government in the Philippines under the supervision of the United States. Cuba gains its independence from the United States. First Tournament of Roses football game played in Pasadena, Calif. Michigan beats Stanford 49-0. **Average commercial ratio of silver to gold:** 39.15 to 1. **Average value of silver in 412 1/2-grain dollar:** 40.8 cents.

Date	VG-8	F-12	VF-20	XF-40	AU-50	MS-60	MS-63	MS-64	MS-65	65DMPL	Prf-60	Prf-63	Prf-65
1902	12.00	12.50	13.00	19.00	22.00	34.00	90.00	135.	460.	15,750.	750.	1450.	5750.
1902O	12.00	12.50	13.00	13.50	23.00	25.00	35.00	51.00	140.	3600.	-		-
1902S	27.00	37.00	80.00	105.	130.	210.	310.	625.	3700.	15,000.	-		-

1903

Mints: Philadelphia (4,652,755), New Orleans (4,450,000), San Francisco (1,241,000). **Notes:** 1903—Readily available in all grades. 1903-O—Legendary Treasury release coin. Before 1962 thought to be a great rarity. Now readily available in mint state. Circulated pieces are rare and bring strong prices. 1903-S—Scarce in all grades, especially so in mint state. **Timeline:** A treaty between the United States and Panama provides the United States with control over a 10-mile strip of land on which to construct the Panama Canal. Orville and Wilbur Wright make successful manned flights of their airplane at Kitty Hawk, N.C. The *Great Train Robbery* is filmed. The first World Series baseball games are played. The Boston Red Sox beat the Pittsburgh Pirates, five games to three, in a best-of-nine series. **Average commercial ratio of silver to gold:** 38.1 to 1. **Average value of silver in 412 1/2-grain dollar:** 42 cents.

Date	VG-8	F-12	VF-20	XF-40	AU-50	MS-60	MS-63	MS-64	MS-65	65DMPL	Prf-60	Prf-63	Prf-65
1903	12.50	14.00	15.00	21.00	24.00	34.00	57.00	65.00	180.	9150.	750.	1450.	5500.
1903O	125.	150.	170.	180.	200.	240.	275.	300.	460.	4650.	-		-
1903S	22.00	27.00	77.00	250.	1100.	2900.	4500.	5250.	7450.	35,000.	-		-

1904

Mints: Philadelphia (2,788,650), New Orleans (3,720,000), San Francisco (2,304,000). **Notes:** 1904—Scarce in higher mint-state grades. 1904-O—Treasury Department 1960s release. Readily available in mint state. 1904-S—Scarce above Very Fine and rare in higher mint state. **Timeline:** Socialist National Convention nominates Eugene V. Debs for president. Debs receives 402,460 votes but is far outpaced by the Democratic (Alton B. Parker) and Republican (incumbent Theodore Roosevelt) candidates. Roosevelt is reelected. First perfect baseball game, pitched by Cy Young of the Boston Americans, who win 3-0 over Philadelphia. United States plays host to its first Olympic Games, as part of the St. Louis Exposition. Following ratification of Hay-Bunau-Varilla Treaty (providing land for a canal in Panama), Roosevelt appoints a seven-man board to oversee construction of the Panama Canal. **Average commercial ratio of silver to gold:** 35.70 to 1. **Average value of silver in 412 1/2-grain dollar:** 44.8 cents.

Date	VG-8	F-12	VF-20	XF-40	AU-50	MS-60	MS-63	MS-64	MS-65	65DMPL	Prf-60	Prf-63	Prf-65
1904	12.00	12.50	13.00	18.00	31.00	60.00	170.	560.	4400.	38,000.	750.	1450.	5500.
1904O	12.00	12.50	13.00	14.00	21.00	24.00	35.00	51.00	105.	550.	-		-
1904S	16.00	25.00	42.00	185.	520.	950.	2100.	2750.	6550.	19,000.	-		-

1921

Mints: Philadelphia (44,690,000), Denver (20,345,000), San Francisco (21,695,000). **Notes:** 1921—High mintage, readily available. 1921-D—Only Denver Mint Morgan dollar. Readily available. 1921-S—Readily available up to higher mint-state grades. **Timeline:** End of war with Germany officially declared by a joint resolution of Congress. Margaret Gorman of Washington, D.C., is crowned as the first Miss America. Warren G. Harding is inaugurated president. Nicola Sacco and Bartolomeo Santo are convicted of murder. Gen. William "Billy" Mitchell demonstrates the superiority of planes over ships with aerial bombardment tests. The first play-by-play description of a World Series game is broadcast by WJZ, Newark, N.J. First Armistice Day declared by President Woodrow Wilson. Coinage of the Peace silver dollar begins. **Average commercial ratio of silver to gold:** 32.75 to 1. **Average value of silver in 412 1/2-grain dollar:** 48.8 cents.

Date	VG-8	F-12	VF-20	XF-40	AU-50	MS-60	MS-63	MS-64	MS-65	65DMPL	Prf-60	Prf-63	Prf-65
1921	11.00	11.50	12.00	13.00	14.00	18.00	23.00	35.00	150.	8800.	-		-
1921D	11.00	11.50	12.00	13.00	15.00	32.00	37.00	70.00	300.	15,000.	-		-
1921S	11.00	11.50	12.00	13.00	16.00	26.00	53.00	150.	1850.	22,000.	-		

Chapter 24

A COMSTOCK LEGACY

Nothing, other than perhaps the melting of 270 million silver dollars under auspices of the 1918 Pittman Act, showcases the lack of demand for silver dollars in commerce during the late 19th century more than the early 1970s sales by the General Services Administration of nearly 3 million silver dollars, most of which were from the Carson City Mint. The idea of a branch mint in Nevada sprang out of a desire to find an inexpensive means for the Comstock ore to be transported from mine to mint. Costs and risks of moving the ore to California were substantial. Those who proposed the new western mint believed it would not only benefit Comstock miners, by cutting the cost of shipping bullion to the U.S. Mint, but also the government, by keeping the nation's precious metals from being shipped overseas, as was happening with much of the bullion sent on to San Francisco.

On March 3, 1863, a bill establishing a branch mint in Nevada, recommended for consideration by Treasury Secretary Salmon P. Chase, was reported out of the House Ways and Means Committee without objection. It passed the Senate the same day. In July, Chase commissioned Rep. Hiram P. Bennet of the Territory of Colorado to investigate a site in Carson City.

Established in 1858 by Abraham Curry, a converted easterner who had found California property values too rich for his tastes, Carson City would soon become an important freight area, pro-

With its location near the Comstock, the Carson City Mint was expected to be of great service to the processing of the nation's mineral wealth.

viding finished boards for the mines, harvested from timber in the Lake Tahoe basin. With the completion of the Virginia and Truckee Railroad in 1869, it held an all-important direct link to Virginia City and the lode. Rapidly expanding in population, under the influence of the nearby silver discoveries, it became the territory's capital in 1861 and the state capital three years later.

By the time Rep. Bennet arrived in September 1863, Carson City was the second largest town in the area, with some 2,500 inhabitants and potential for additional growth. In a letter to Treasury Secretary Chase, written shortly after his arrival in Carson City, Bennet enthusiastically described the 70-square-foot site for the mint, located a short distance from the courthouse, noting that the site, though larger than the secretary's instructions, was available to the government free of charge.

The Civil War would intervene, however, and it was not until February 1865 that Congress authorized the purchase of the site. A commission led by Curry, Henry C. Rice and John H. Mills, would receive final authorization from the East to begin construction of the mint. On Sept. 24, 1866, the first cornerstone was laid, using stone quarried by prison inmates from a site owned by Curry. Two years later the building was completed and machinery received.

In his Sept. 27, 1869, *Report of the Director of the Mint*, Mint Director James Pollock recorded that the branch mint in Carson City was rapidly approaching completion:

> The machinery is nearly all in place, and operations will soon be commenced. Orders were issued to complete and put into operation as promptly as possible the assay department. This will be done. The superintendent of this branch reports that they will be ready to open early in September; and this will probably be the case so far as the general operations are concerned; but the more complicated details in reference to the furnaces, assay apparatus, &c., will require some weeks longer. From the peculiar character of the bullion that will be deposited for fine bars or coinage, the operative officers of this branch should be practical, experienced and scientific men. The deposits will be generally of mixed bullion with a gold fineness of two and one-half to forty thousandths; silver, nine hundred and forty to nine hundred and sixty, and a small percentage of base metals, lead, &c. This bullion, whether deposited for fine bars or coinage, must be refined, or refined and parted, according to the condition of the deposit. It does not seem likely that much, if any, parting will be done at Carson. The bars of mixed bullion being officially stamped with both gold and silver proportions, will be as salable in that form as if they were parted. Quotations are constantly made in the London market for silver bars containing gold and selling accordingly. The operations of this branch will, in all probability, culminate in commercial bars, as *coin* already abounds in that region so extensively that their papers express alarm as to the prospect of a redundancy. Practically it will be much more an assay office than a mint, and as such, fully meet the wants of the district. The power to make coin may be of occasional benefit; perhaps, in the future, of much advantage.[1]

The new mint officially opened for business in January 1870. According to numismatic writer Pete Smith, the first items struck at the mint were not coins but silver napkin rings. The first coinage, Smith notes, was of Seated Liberty dollars—the first, second and third examples of these given to President Ulysses S. Grant, Nevada Gov. Lewis Bradley and Curry, respectively. Striking of gold coins began a month later with gold eagles.[2]

Curry would serve as the mint's first superintendent, stepping down in September 1870 to pursue an unsuccessful bid to become Nevada's lieutenant governor. Rice succeeded him, holding the post until 1873. In all, the mint would have nine superintendents and strike dollars, half dollars, quarter dollars, 20-cent pieces, and dimes in silver, and double eagles, eagles and half eagles in gold. Low mintages were the norm, rather than the exception, at this facility.

The *Report of the Director of the Mint* for the fiscal year ending June 30, 1871, observed that gold and silver deposits at the new mint had exceeded the prior year by $2 million, rising to $2.94 million. But despite the optimism, benefits of shipping silver and gold to California (regardless of the higher expenses and risks) continued to outweigh those offered by the Carson City facility. These included California's superior private and government facilities for parting and refining, and a ready outlet for silver bars. San Francisco's direct link to the Pacific Ocean, and the healthy market for trade with the Orient, helped siphon off the production of the big mines, limiting coinage at the Carson City facility largely to what was needed for local coinage and "the assaying and stamping of unparted gold and silver bars."[3]

By the 1880s, the Comstock Lode had been gutted of its wealth, and the draw off of precious metals to San Francisco began to flag itself in the annual Mint director reports of the late 1870s and early 1880s. The report for the fiscal year 1875, for example, recorded deposits of just over $5.57 million in gold and silver bullion at Carson City, as compared to more than five times that amount—$31.489 million—at San Francisco. By the following year's report, the Carson City totals had risen to $8.2 million, as compared to San Francisco at $36.8 million, but over the next few years Carson City's share of the nation's precious metals wealth declined: $5.1 million in 1877, $3.1 million in 1878, and $1.34 million in 1879. As the amount of bullion waned, so did the amount of work being done at the mint. In his report for fiscal year 1879, Mint Director Horatio C. Burchard said of Carson City:

> This mint accomplished but little coinage during the year, and for several months was comparatively idle. The receipts of gold have at one time been great and almost entirely of the production of the State of Nevada. The records show that of all gold deposited at this mint during the last seven years, less than $100,000 was produced by other States and Territories.
>
> Although situated in close proximity to a large silver-producing section of [the] country, owners of silver bullion have been demanding a higher price for delivery at Carson than silver could be procured for at Philadelphia or San Francisco.[4]

By 1880, the Carson City bullion deposit totals had fallen below the $1 million mark for the first time, while San Francisco still boasted a healthy

Minting At Carson City

Once the silver bars from the Comstock Lode were delivered to the Carson City Mint, they needed to go through a number of processes, including refining, rolling, planchet cutting and upsetting, before arriving in the press room for transformation into CC-mint-marked coins. This last step, the striking of the coins, was performed on this storied 12,000-pound press, which was at Carson City through much of the facility's tenure as a U.S. branch mint. In 1899, following Carson City's reduction to the status of an assay office, the big press was dismantled and shipped to Philadelphia. There it was remodeled to run by electricity and, in 1945, shipped to the San Francisco Mint, where it served until the close of that facility in 1955.

It was saved from the scrap heap in 1958 and returned to the Nevada State Museum for display. During the coinage shortage of the early 1960s, the well-traveled press was sent to the Denver Mint. In 1976 it was used to strike Nevada's official Bicentennial medal. Today it resides in its own room in the museum, near the museum's display of CC coins, and is still used to strike medals.

The coinage press at right is on display at the Nevada State Museum. It was built at the Virginia and Truckee Railroad shop for use at the Carson City Mint. It continues to be used to strike medals, such as the one above.

First-year coinages at the Carson City Mint were low. Minting began with the Seated Liberty silver dollar.

$39.27 million. Mint Director Burchard explained that the high price of silver in San Francisco, along with lower domestic production, led to the suspension of coinage at the Carson City Mint from Nov. 1, 1879, through May 1, 1880. He wrote:

> The superior facilities at San Francisco for filling with dispatch orders for speedy delivery of silver bullion to China, and the diminished production of silver in the States and Territories contiguous to the Pacific coast, have frequently operated to carry the price of silver bullion at San Francisco above the prices at New York and London, and to render it difficult at times to purchase at market rates silver bullion for delivery at the Pacific Coast Mints. During the year the department was able to procure for those mints bullion only sufficient to coin 8,318,000 standard silver dollars. This inability compelled the suspension of coinage at the Carson Mint from November 1, 1879 to May 1, 1880, the stock of silver bullion at the former date having been reduced to 12,342.41 standard ounces. The purchase and reception of silver bullion was, however, in the mean time continued, and a stock accumulated by the 16th of April, 1880, of 227,087.54 standard ounces. This amount, with the prospect of additional supplies, justified the resumption of coinage, but the whole

With a mintage of just 3,789, the 1870-CC $20 gold piece is a high-priced rarity, listing at $80,000 in AU-50.

amount of silver bullion obtained for the Carson Mint during the year amounted at its coining value to $597,624.28 only.[5]

In March 1885, Carson City Mint Superintendent James Crawford died, and the mint closed, pending the naming of a new superintendent. It would not reopen until late in 1886 and then only for assay purposes. With the growing demand for silver coinage brought on by the strengthening Free Silver Movement, the Carson City Mint gained new life in 1889, with coinage beginning in October of that year. Passage of the Sherman Silver Purchase Act in 1890 and the requirements for increased coinages of standard silver dollars would help keep it in operation until 1893. After that, it served only as an assay office.

The building being put up for sale in 1933, it was purchased by the State of Nevada for use as a museum and art center, opening to the public in that capacity on Oct. 31, 1941. Today it houses a nearly complete collection of Carson City gold and silver coins.

Until recently, the collection, displayed since 1989, was on loan from First Interstate Bank. In 1999 (in a ceremony that included the arrival of Nevada Gov. Kenny Guinn and bank officials aboard a Wells Fargo & Co. stagecoach drawn by four horses), official transfer of the collection to the museum ownership was made by Wells Fargo to mark its merger with Norwest Bank, which had previously merged with First Interstate Bank.[6]

The GSA Silver Dollar Sales

Despite the beliefs of 19th century political activists, who forever tagged the Coinage Act of 1873 as a crime against the common man (demanding the free and unlimited coinage of silver dollars), this bulky coin was never well accepted by the public, and only held limited favor in the West. Hundreds of millions of Morgan and Peace dollars remained in Treasury hands after coinage of the silver dollar ended in 1935. Over the next few decades, the Treasury piecemealed the coins out into the channels of trade. In fiscal year 1962, for example, the Treasury shipped 33 million of the 102 million silver dollars it still retained, getting ready, as Mint Director Eva Adams put it, for the coins to turn up as traditional Christmas stocking stuffers.

Among this dispersal by merrymaking Treasury elves were some coins believed for years by coin collectors to be excessively rare, including several New Orleans dates, chief among which was the 1903-O. Up until the Treasury's release of heretofore unknown bag quantities of this date and mint combination, rarely encountered uncirculated specimens of the 1903-O Morgan dollar were trading at $1,500 a coin. Within weeks of the Treasury's release its retail value had plummeted to under $50.

It is the kind of thing that sends shivers down the spine of any collector—the thought that shortly after they purchased a coin, large quantities of it would appear on the market, driving prices downward. Yet that was not the end of the Treasury's

Less than two dozen examples of the 1876-CC 20-cent pieces are known to exist.

A cancelled 1884-CC Carson City Morgan dollar die. Courtesy of the Nevada State Museum Photograph Collection.

holdings or its surprises. A 1964 audit of remaining silver dollar supplies revealed the existence of millions of uncirculated low-mintage Carson City dollars that had languished in the Treasury's vaults for decades. The news cast yet another shroud over the silver dollar market until they were finally dispersed in a series of five sales beginning in 1972 and two additional sales in 1980.

Two years before the first sale of this impressive silver dollar hoard, largely populated by uncirculated coins with full mint bloom, Congress passed provisions authorizing the transfer of the nearly 3 million silver dollars (all but about 100,000 of which were from the Carson City Mint) from Treasury control to the General Services Administration. The GSA was then mandated to conduct sales and dispose of the government's remaining stock of silver dollars.

In 1971, Congress appropriated funds and formal transfer from the Treasury to the GSA took place in December of that year, with the physical movement of the 77 tons of silver dollars, still in their original canvas bags, from Treasury Department vaults in Washington, D.C., to the United States Bullion Depository in West Point, N.Y., via two heavily insured truck shipments.[7]

A distinguished hobby panel—including John Jay Pittman, president of the American Numismatic Association; Amon Carter Jr., collector and a member of the Joint Commission on the Coinage (which formulated recommendations that ultimately placed the coins in the GSA's hands); Henry Grunthal, curator of European and modern coins for the American Numismatic Society; Clifford Mishler, editor of *Numismatic News*; and Margo Russell, editor of *Coin World*—was selected to provide advice to the GSA on how to grade, package and dispose of the coins. At a special examination of a portion of the hoard, held on March 10, 1972, at GSA headquarters in Washington reviews as to the condition of the coins by the numismatic experts present were encouraging. "While nearly all of the dollars displayed abrasions, as was anticipated when consideration is given to the fact that they have been moved in and out of several government depositories in bulk over the past 90-odd years, many still possess proof-like surface qualities," the March 28, 1972,

Many collectors are drawn to Carson City dollars by the coin's famous "CC" mintmark. It was just such an attraction that the General Services Administration hoped would make disposing of its nearly 3 million silver dollars an easy task.

A ton of Comstock silver bars await shipment to the Carson City Mint in this circa 1880 photograph taken outside of the Wells Fargo express office in Virginia City. Courtesy of Joe Curtis, Mark Twain's Book Store, Virginia City, Nev.

issue of *Numismatic News*, a weekly newspaper for coin collectors, reported.[8]

The panel estimated that at least 95 percent of the coins would qualify for sale as uncirculated. "We were surprised and pleased with the condition of the coins we saw today," Pittman said in an interview on behalf of the panel. "They are in better condition than we had expected. Many were in beautiful condition and some had almost proof-like quality."[9] Many, it would also be learned, were valuable minting varieties—doubled dates and mintmarks and various forms of

The 1903-O Morgan dollar was considered a great rarity until the Treasury released bag quantities in the early 1960s.

Government employees inspect and sort the CC silver dollars at the U.S. Bullion Depository in West Point, N.Y., in this 1973 GSA photograph.

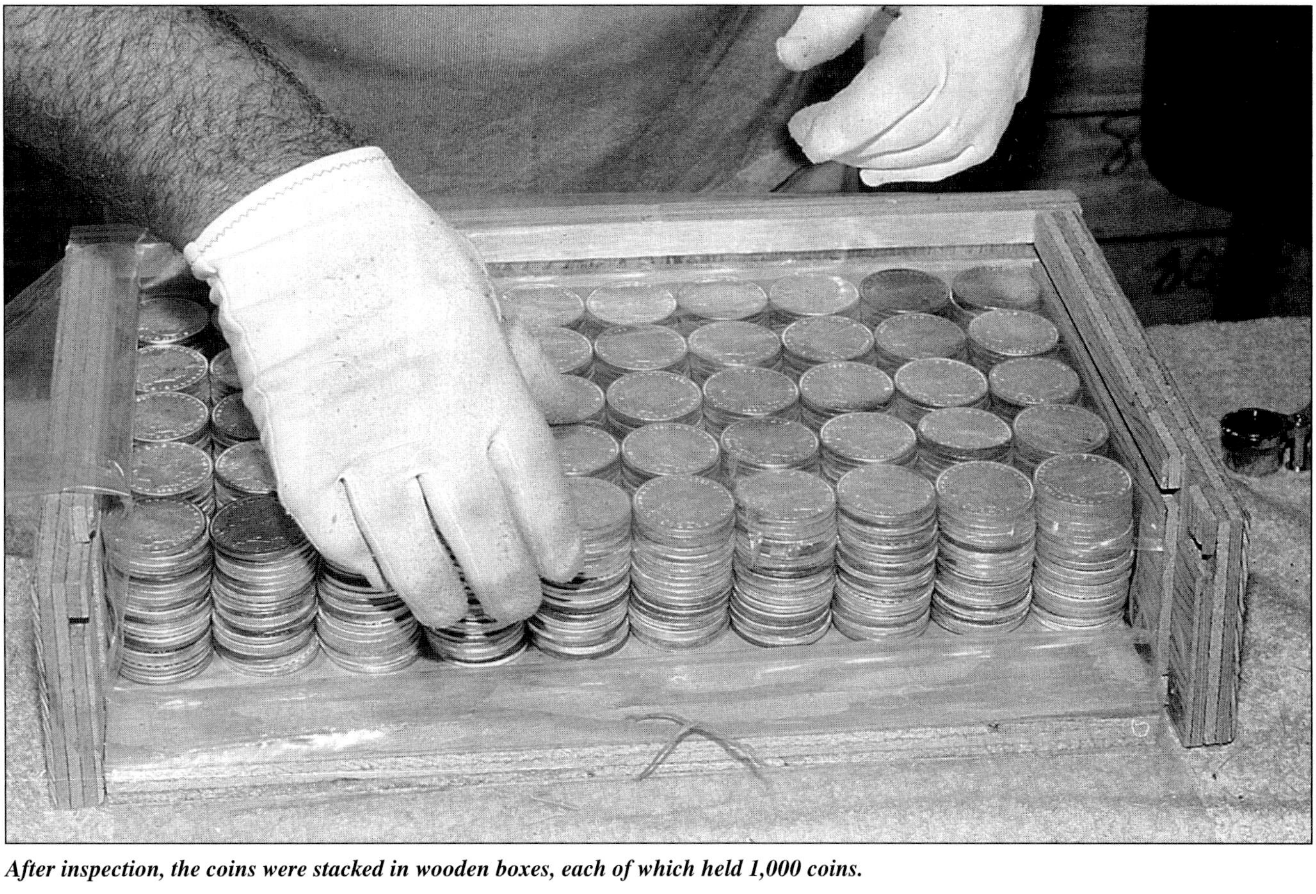

After inspection, the coins were stacked in wooden boxes, each of which held 1,000 coins.

misstruck coins, some of which were unknown to collectors.

Following the arrival of the dollars at the United States Bullion Depository, the first task for government employees was to sort and stack the coins in wooden trays. The coins were then individually graded by white-gloved inspectors, using two groups of CC dollars (one group of 28 coins judged by the numismatic panel to be uncirculated and one group of 22 coins found not to meet that criteria) as guides to further separation. Those that did not make the grade would be sold as circulated or, if they were too tarnished, nicked or otherwise damaged, withdrawn from the sale entirely.

Included in the Treasury hoard, according to Van Allen-Mallis, were the following dates and totals:

1878-CC....................60,993
1879-CC....................4,123
1880-CC....................131,529
1881-CC....................147,485
1882-CC....................605,029
1882-CC....................755,518
1884-CC....................962,638
1885-CC....................148,285
1890-CC....................3,949
1891-CC....................5,687

Also included were solitary examples of the rare 1889-CC, 1892-CC, and 1893-CC; 27,980 mixed uncirculated Philadelphia, New Orleans and San Francisco dollars; 84,165 coins placed in a mixed circulated category; and 311 dollars judged unfit for sale.[10]

These figures become more dramatic for 1880-1885 Carson City coins in the hoard when compared to original mintages. Provided below are the mintage figures along with the percentage of the original coinage still held by the GSA into the early 1970s:

1880-CC (591,000)....................22.6%
1881-CC (296,000)....................49.83%
1882-CC (1,133,000)....................53.40%
1883-CC (1,204,000)....................62.75%
1884-CC (1,136,000)....................84.74%
1885-CC (228,000)....................65.04%

A GSA promotional photograph from the filming of .900 Fine, a 30-minute film promoting the sales.

Ultimately the coins were sorted into five categories for the upcoming sales—(1.) uncirculated CC dollars, (2.) mixed CC dollars (which included dollars that were tarnished or scratched and the hoard's single examples of the 1889-CC, 1892-CC and 1893-CC), (3.) mixed circulated, (4.) mixed uncirculated dollars of other mints, and (5.) coins that were judged unsalable.[11] Market values, at the time, for these coins in uncirculated ranged from $14 for the 1878-CC to $200 for the 1879-CC.

"The Great Silver Sale" Oct. 31, 1972, to Jan. 31, 1973

The GSA announced that the first sale, open to all U.S. citizens living at home and abroad, would offer 381,000 1882-CC dollars, 523,000 1883-CC dollars, and 788,000 1884-CC dollars. It also set a minimum bid of $30 per coin, a figure somewhat below the then prevalent retail value of the coins involved. A widespread media blitz followed, which included the distribution of order forms, brochures and posters to 100,000 post offices, banks, federal information centers and other venues around the nation. A 28-minute movie, titled *.900 Fine*, narrated by actor Burgess Meredith, was produced and distributed. The film opened with scenes of a crate of silver dollars being moved, under armed guard, from deep in the Treasury to a Brink's truck for shipment to New York. Milking the appeal of the old west, it then segued to the story of silver's discovery on the Comstock, describing the lode as a "coquette," who for years teased miners as to her true wealth and Virginia City as "the gaudiest, wealthiest, go-to-hell town the West had ever seen."

Despite the GSA's enthusiasm for these pristine relics of the past and its heavy promotion of "The Great Silver Sale," the coin-buying public did not respond as the agency had anticipated. By mid-January 1973, with sales lagging behind department expectations, the GSA placed advertisements in 30 key newspapers across the nation and sent reminder cards to everyone on the mint's mailing list. These efforts were of minimal help. Only about 700,000 coins of the 1,692,000 up for bid were purchased.[12] The large quantities of each of the dates being offered along with a general disdain by some over the GSA's touting the coins as investments, as well as uncertainty as to the future market value and true grade of the coins, likely dissuading large-scale collector commitment. Non-collectors, as well as collectors, likely also balked at the $30 price tag, near the current market value and well above the coin's bullion value.

Mailing of successful bidders began on Feb. 1, 1973, with *Numismatic News* reporting that Arthur B. Coltman of Philadelphia received the first coin. A rare 20-percent off-center dollar, valued at around $1,000, was also part of this first shipment. It went out randomly to Tom Reneke of Astoria, Ore., a non-collector who in later interviews was noticeably nonplused by his good fortune.[13]

The GSA sale included high percentages of the original mintages of some of the Carson City Morgans. Of 1,136,000 1884-CC silver dollars minted, the GSA sale offered 84.74 percent of the original mintage (962,638 coins).

"The Great Silver Sale" extension Feb. 15, 1973, to April 30, 1973

A second bidding period for the remaining nearly 1 million 1882, 1883 and 1884 coins began on Feb. 15, 1973. In announcing the Great Silver Sale's extension, the GSA blamed the poor response to the prior order period to "the limited time we had to inform people of the initial sale," though many in the hobby suspected the agency was smarting a bit from the lack of collector participation.[14] Those who had criticized the agency's sales tactics reveled in the GSA's misfortune, while those who bid in the first order period also got a bit of good news. Because of the poor performance, all of those who had bid at least the $30 minimum would receive the coins for that price and be issued refunds for any excess they had submitted.

Rules for the extension were the same as for the first offering. The minimum was again $30. However, those who had received coins in the first order period were ineligible to bid on a duplicate of the same date. The extension's sales results were even more disappointing, with only a little more than 100,000 additional coins sold by the time bidding closed on April 30,1973.

"The Coins Jesse James Never Got!" June 1, 1973, to July 31, 1973

Not discouraged, the GSA organized a second sale, which ran from June 1, 1973, to July 31, 1973. The sale's promotional material again played the western theme to the hilt, telling American families that they could "Get one of the coins Jesses James never got."[15]

For this sale, the selection of coins being offered was changed, as were rules of participation and the means of publicizing their availability. The silver dollars being offered would include circulated and uncirculated specimens from the GSA

For its June 1 to July 31, 1973, sale, the GSA promoted the coins as ones Jesse James never got.

hoard, some of which required only $3 minimum bids, and examples of the CC dates from 1878-1885 and 1890-1891. Order blanks and pamphlets, which had previously been available at public locations across the nation, would now only be sent to those who participated in the prior sales, plus the 3 million names on the U.S. Mint's mailing list.

The dollars were divided into nine sales categories, grouped under four general headings, each requiring a separate order blank. The order blanks were color-coded (green, yellow, red and white) with each blank corresponding to two or more "selections" of coins. The first selection, part of "The Potluck!" grouping (which, as its name suggests, allowed no choice of date or mint), consisted of 95,000 circulated Morgan and Peace dollars from various mints. The coins were housed in Mylar display packets enclosed in a carrying envelope and required a $3 minimum bid. Selection two, rounding out "The Potluck!" group, featured 28,000 uncirculated Morgan and Peace dollars from various mints, excluding Carson City. Housed in similar packaging, these coins were offered at a minimum bid of $5.

For the third selection, under "The Silver Bonanza!" heading, the GSA offered bidders 690,000 mixed CC dollars—1878-1885, 1890, and 1891. The GSA order form explained that these were coins that were uncirculated but were kept out of the uncirculated category because of nicks or tarnish. Each was packaged in a boxed presentation case, with minimum bid set at $15. The fourth selection, also part of "The Silver Bonanza!", presented 50,000 1878-CC dollars. These were housed in the same manner as the mixed CC dollars, with a minimum bid of $15.

Selections five and six, "The Carson City '90/'84!", featured 3,700 1890-CC dollars, with a minimum bid of $30, and 525,000 1884-CC dollars, with a minimum bid of $30. Both were packaged in presentation cases.

The final three selections were grouped under the heading "CC Triple Choice!" and included uncirculated CC dollars date 1891 (5,000), 1882 (95,000), and 1883 (270,000), all with minimum bids of $30.[16]

Under the GSA rules, a bidder could bid on one coin from each of the nine categories, but no collector could bid on more than nine coins. If a group sold out, the coins would go to the highest bidders. Bidders were also given a second-chance feature. By ticking a box on the order form, they could automatically have their bid applied to another category, should their first choice result in an unsuccessful bid. As in the previous sale, bidders were not supposed to get duplicates of any coin they already obtained from the GSA.

The GSA received a bit of a promotional boost prior to the opening of this sale by allowing noted numismatists and error/variety specialists Leroy C. Van Allen and A. George Mallis (authors of a standard collector's guide to Morgan and Peace silver dollars) to visit the U.S. Bullion Depository, in May 1973, and closely examine a representative grouping of all of the dates in the GSA holdings. To the joy of collectors, they reported on a vast number of minting varieties among the silver dollars. Some of these varieties were previously unknown to the collecting community, and, Van Allen and Mallis predicted, would make future sales "turn out to be an old-fashioned treasure hunt."[17] Among their findings was that most of the 1880-CC dollars in the GSA hoard would likely be worth additional premiums to error collectors.

"Virtually all of the 115,000 uncirculated coins of this year are varieties with a possible 30 per cent of these being the more visible overdates that have, in the past, commanded prices of $150 to over $400 each," their summary statement in the July 24, 1973, issue of *Numismatic News* related. "In fact some years consisted almost entirely of varieties which should make coin collectors happy. In addition to finding known varieties, many new or previously unknown varieties were found. Some of these varieties are quite prominent and would tend to make the coins command a premium price."[18] Their date-by-date breakdown was as follows:

1878-CC—70 percent of the 47,500 coins were of eight minting varieties, including a new mintmark variety.

1882-CC—90 percent of the 383,000 uncirculated coins were all of one variety with a slight doubling of the tops of "82" in the date.

1883-CC—About 40 percent of 524,000 uncirculated coins were of three then-known types and approximately 20 percent were of a "spectacular doubled date" in which all of the date digits were doubled at the top.

1884-CC—About 75 percent of 788,600 uncirculated coins were varieties of seven different types including doubled dates and mintmarks along with four previously unseen varieties.

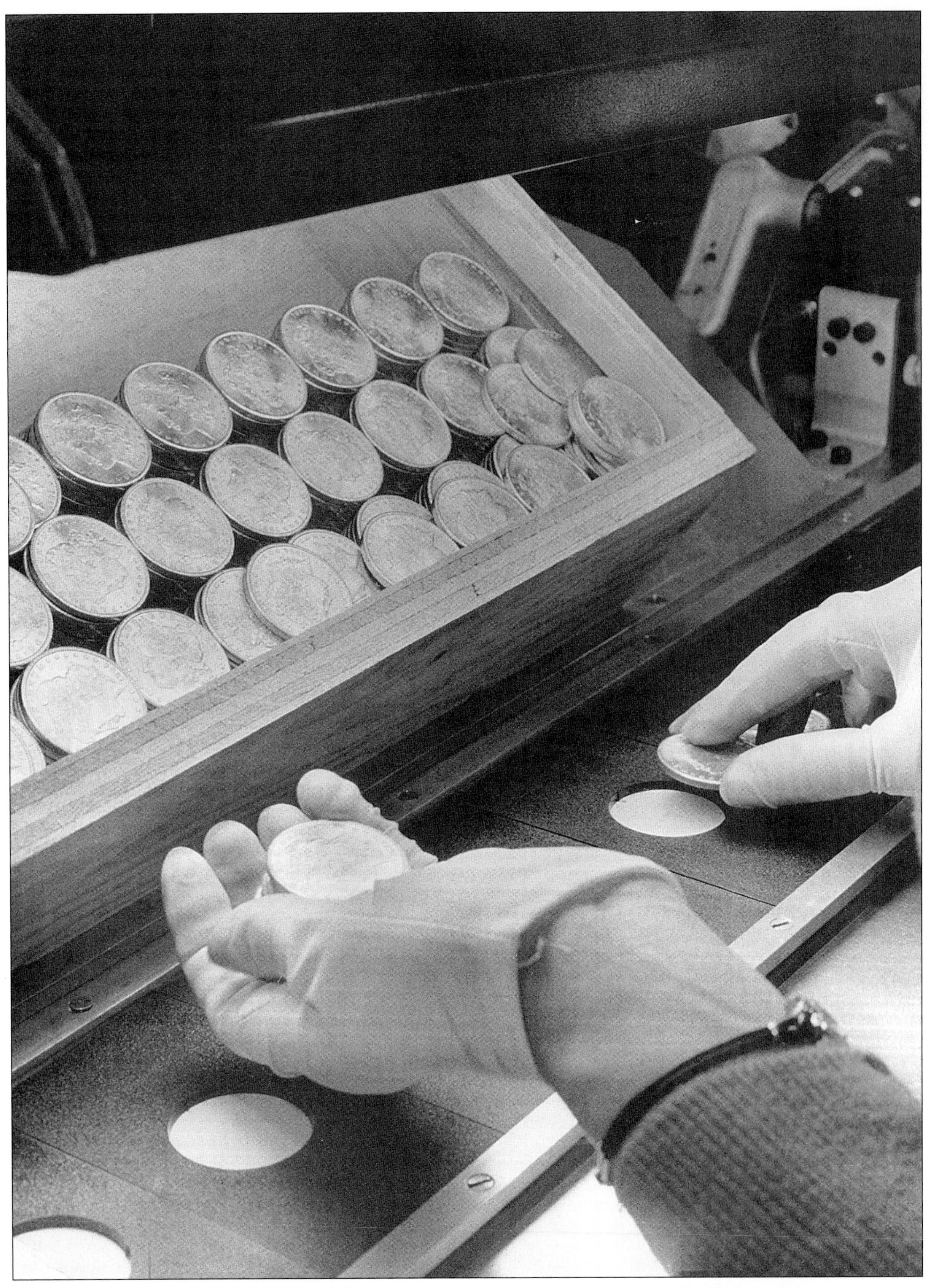

A GSA worker inserts uncirculated Morgans into the hard plastic holders in which they were sold. Photo by Larry Stevens.

1890-CC—About 10 percent of 3,600 uncirculated coins were of a new variety with a doubled "18."

1891-CC—About 60 percent of 4,700 uncirculated coins were of a known doubled mintmark variety.[19]

This sale drew a wider response than the first two. With some 1 million bids received, the agency disposed of another 453,000 coins. Five categories sold out, including mixed circulated Morgan and Peace dollars, uncirculated Morgan and Peace dollars, 1878-CC, 1890-CC and 1891-CC, drawing the total number of coins remaining to around 1,761,000.[20]

The most popular categories were those with the lowest minimum bids. For example, the offering of mixed circulated Morgan and Peace dollars and uncirculated coins from various mints (under the group heading "The Potluck!") received 500,000 bids. The average bid for the $3 minimum grouping of circulated Morgan and Peace dollars was $3.90 while the average bid for the uncirculated Morgan and Peace dollars was $7.66. The latter received bids ranging from $6 to $200.[21]

Categories with large quantities of coins available were not so successful, likely a continuing collector wariness of coins in which the majority of the original mintage was known to be in uncirculated. Approximately 521,000 1884-CC were offered with only 51,500 bids. Of the 91,405 1882-CC dollars on hand, 42,900 were bid on. In the case of the 1883-CC, 266,445 were available and only 34,900 bids were received.[22]

30-day Surplus Dollar Sale
Oct. 1, 1973, to Oct. 31, 1973

The third sale featured three scarcer dates. For this sale, with a higher minimum, the GSA opted not to send out order forms to those on the mint's mailing list and cut back on its print advertisements. Rather it sent out order forms to anyone who had bid $15 or more on a coin in a prior sale. Offered were the 1880-CC (114,982), 1881-CC (122,698) and 1885-CC (130,807) dollars with a minimum bid set at $60 for each date. Final sales figures showed that 213,189 coins were sold, including 74,070 1880-CC dollars, 71,099 1881-CC dollars and 68,020 1885-CC dollars. The average bid was $67.

"The 1879-cc Silver Dollars"
Feb. 1, 1974, to Feb. 28, 1974

For the Feb 1, 1974, launch of the fourth sale, which featured 3,609 1879-CC dollars (retailing for $485 each), the GSA expected only serious collectors to participate and curtailed its mailing of order forms. Minimum bid was set at $300 for the sale, which ended Feb. 28, 1974. These coins sold out quickly with most bids coming in at the $300 level but some as high as $1,525.

"The Last of a Legacy"
April 1, 1974, to June 30, 1974

A fifth sale was held from April 1, 1974, to June 30, 1974, for the remaining 1,391,056 coins. Included were seven categories—1880-1885 CC dollars, plus more than 500,000 mixed uncirculated CC dollars. Minimum bids were set at $15 on the mixed uncirculated dollars; $30 on the 1882 (35,700), 1883 (226,052), and 1884 (456,520) coins; and $60 on the 1880 (40,847) 1881 (51,587) and 1885 (62,781) dollars.[23] Some 87,000 distribution points were engaged throughout the country, including banks, savings and loans, post offices, credit unions and federal information centers where order forms could be obtained. A nationwide advertising campaign on CBS and NBC radio, along with advertising in general interest and trade publications, was employed.[24]

Promoted under the heading "The Last of a Legacy," more than 416,000 silver dollars were sold during this sale. Only the 1882-CC category sold out.

"90% Silver, 100% History"
Feb. 8, 1980, to April 8, 1980

With about $53 million obtained from the first five sales, less than 1 million coins remained in storage, until new laws enacted by Congress mandated the GSA to complete its dispersal. This time, however, there would not be any restriction against buying duplicate dates or the number of coins that could be ordered. Also, bidding was out and a fixed price schedule was in.

Fortunately for the GSA and not so fortunately for those who bought coins in this sale, silver and gold bullion markets were just coming off all-time highs. The Jan. 19, 1980, issue of *Numismatic News* recorded silver at a spot price of $36.80 an ounce and gold at $634. Realizing that the bullion market was volatile, the GSA decided not to set final fixed prices on the remaining groups of silver dollars (which besides any numismatic value, each contained nearly an ounce of meltable silver) until just before the sale opened on Feb. 8, 1980. A GSA spokesman even suggested that it might be necessary "to send order forms with blank spaces where the customers can write in the quoted prices when they are announced."[25]

Offered were 195,745 1883-CC dollars, 428,152 1884-CC dollars, plus 299,390 mixed CC uncirculated coins. The "Mixed Years-CC" category, which encompassed coins from 1878-1885 and 1889-1893, was further described as "A potpourri of uncirculated 'CC' dollars...most culled from inventory for failing to meet high sorting standards...others added because small quantities prevented offering them separately."[26]

Originally the GSA planned to sell the 1883 and 1884 at $42 and $40, respectively, and the mixed CC uncirculated coins at $20. However, a sudden surge in the price of silver pushed the bullion value of the mixed CC coins above the original sale price. Final prices were set at $65 for the 1883-CC, $60 for the 1884-CC, and $45 for the mixed CC coins.

As with most of the earlier sales, the GSA again conducted a massive media campaign. This time the headline read "90% Silver, 100% History," with another widespread mailing of order forms to potential customers. It also placed order forms in about 50 daily newspapers, including the *Wall Street Journal* and the *New York Times*.

Unlike the early 1970s sales, this sale at first allowed bidders to order as many coins as they liked. Though, if their orders exceeded 500 coins from any or all of the categories, any number in excess 500 would not be filled until the close of the sale, in order of which they were received, should coins still be available.

The strong bullion market, which saw millions of U.S. coins melted, generated high public awareness of the value of all U.S. coins and helped flood the GSA with so many orders that it sold out within the first 10 days. The GSA was then forced to cut its previously announced order limits to assure a wider distribution of the coins and less unhappy customers. Following the sellout, the agency announced that it would fill each winning order with up to 10 coins in the 1883-CC category, 20 in the 1884-CC and five in the mixed CC category. The move angered those who had already placed large orders and now had their money tied up with the GSA. Further complicating matters was the collapse of the bullion markets. By mid-March, silver and gold prices had begun a serious decline. Silver, which peaked in London at $50 in early January, fell to $20.65 by March 18. On March 24, 1980, Nelson Bunker Hunt, who had been attempting to corner the silver market, failed to make a $100 million margin call. In response, bullion traders began dumping silver. The price of silver plummeted from $21.25 on March 24 to $10.80 on March 27. Ironically, one day later, the

For its sale of scarce 1879-CC silver dollars, the GSA set a minimum bid of $300. Today the coin retails for $1,600 in MS-60.

GSA began shipments of its coins to the successful and now largely disgruntled bidders.[27]

Defending the GSA's decision to cut order limits and raise prices, a somewhat beleaguered Roy Markon, commissioner of the GSA's Federal Property Resources Service, appeared before a July 12, 1980, gathering of collectors. "As expected, reaction to the limits was loud and vocal, especially from customers who had placed large orders," Markon told students attending the ANA's annual Summer Seminar. "They had large sums of money tied up, would lose substantial interest income on their funds and would end up with a handful of coins. What began with loud shouts of anger in February and most of March faded to a whimper when silver bullion prices plummeted in late March. In protest, many of these customers placed 'stop payments' on their checks and withdrew from the sale."[28] Of the fall in silver prices and customers' reactions, he said:

> In March, just about the time the first shipment of coins was going into the mails, silver bullion prices bottomed out. As if on cue, a chorus of customers—obviously not numismatists—developed the following logic: If you raised the price of the coins because the price of silver bullion went up, you should lower the price of the coins now that the silver bullion price has gone down.[29]

Not so, said Markon, the price had been based on the going retail of the coins in early February, just before the sale, and, by law, the GSA could not sell government property for anything less than it was worth. Fortunately for the GSA, unfilled orders were waiting in line to absorb the rejected coins.

"The Last of the Carson City Dollars" July 1, 1980, to July 31, 1980

For the final sale of the remaining 54,820 coins, tagged as "The Last of the Carson City Dollars," the GSA went back to setting minimum bids. Included were 4,281 1880-CC, 18,975 1881-CC, and 31,564 1885-CC silver dollars offered at minimums of $180. At the time these coins were selling at around $200 retail. The 1880-CC and 1881-CC sold out quickly. Only the 1885-CC failed to be fully dispersed.

The GSA reported that it took a bid of at least $210 to win an 1880-CC dollar, with one bidder paying $925. For the 1881-CC, bids ranged from $185 to $1,000. For the 1885-CC, some lucky bidders received coins at the $180 minimum with successful bids in this category running as high as $925. Only 455 1885-CC dollars remained at the sale's close. These were awarded to the unfilled bids that came in after the noon July 31 sale deadline but were still postmarked by that date.[30]

Today the mystique of the last of the great GSA silver dollar sales lives on. Despite any concerns voiced by collectors, the market readily absorbed the coins. All of the CC dates that were sold in individual categories for minimum bids or at fixed prices in the 1970s retail for multiples of those figures in Mint State-60. Those who purchased GSA coins in the 1980s did not fare as well. Price comparisons here are for the 1970s offerings. The 1879-CC (minimum bid $300) today sells for $1,600 in MS-60, the 1880-CC ($60) brings $300, 1881-CC ($60) $265, 1882-CC ($30) $95, 1883-CC ($30) $95, 1884-CC ($30) $95, 1885-CC ($60) $275, 1890-CC ($30) $295 and the 1891-CC ($30) $295. The individual examples of the 1889-CC, 1892-CC, and 1893-CC retail in that grade at $7,000, $450 and $1,400, respectively.

In 1999, Littleton Rare Coin Company, Littleton, New Hampshire, announced its acquisition of a minihoard of 8,000 GSA coins still in their original holders, purchased from a Georgia business executive who became fixated with owning GSA coins. The majority of the CC coins were dated 1882, 1883 and 1884. He apparently liked the fact that the coins came directly from government vaults and probably enjoyed the thought they truly were coins that Jesses James never got.

Chapter 25

THE FINAL BATTLE

The great appeal of the Free Silver Movement, which enjoyed a tremendous momentum in the 1890s when another miserable depression engulfed the nation, had its origins in the Panic of 1873, as has been shown, and the hotbed of agrarian unrest following the Civil War. The period after the war witnessed the opening of the West to settlement and the industrial revolution, both of which would have a lasting effect on agriculture in the United States. The settlement of the West created more tillable farmland, which, in turn, brought an increase in farm surplus, thus helping to lower prices, while the industrial revolution changed the methods of farming forever.

Before the Civil War, farming had been mainly a subsistence venture. Farmers had relied on their own skills in manufacturing household goods and in making their own clothing. The industrial revolution brought with it factories, which were controlled by organized trusts, and expansion of the railroads, which held a monopolistic control over the movement of farm produce to market. Farmers found that they now had to contend with business organizations in order to make a living. The farmer became acutely aware that these additional restrictions on his freedom were also impinging on his profits.

Agrarians viewed the low prices for their produce as the result of under consumption, not overproduction. To the farmer, the urban masses appeared to be undernourished, and the only things keeping farm produce from market were such artificial restrictions as railroad rates and bank credit. It seemed to the farmer that the harder he worked, the more prices for his produce dropped. Wheat, for example, which in 1881 sold at $1.10 a bushel, by 1890 was trading at only 40 cents. Corn prices also declined, dropping from 63 cents to 26 cents by 1890. Along with the fall in market prices came a simultaneous decrease in farmland value.[1]

To the nation's agrarians, there were a number of enemies working in league to prevent their return to prosperity. Particularly offensive were the railroads, trusts, bankers and eastern capitalists on Wall Street. Another of their foes seemed to lie in the country's system of currency and credit. Farmers noted that, whenever they borrowed money, wild fluctuations in currency values made them pay their debt back in depreciated money, thus they ended up paying back more than they had borrowed. Conversely, while prices on machinery, clothes and other necessities continued to rise, crop prices continued to fall.

Out of this unrest, along with factory workers and small businessmen, the People's (Populist) Party, was formed in 1892—the party being an aggregate of several different interest groups including the Knights of Labor, prohibitionists, greenbackers and various farmer alliances. It held its first national presidential convention in July of that year, at which the Populists nominated James B. Weaver, a greenbacker and former Union general, for president, along with James G. Field, a former Confederate general, for his running mate. Working off a platform written by former greenbacker Ignatius Donnelly, calling for the return of the government "into the hands of 'the plain people,'" its most unifying plank was its cry for the free and unlimited coinage of silver at a ratio of 16 to 1.[2] Other of its reform planks, which would get washed under in the mania associated with free silver, looked for an alliance between farmers and laborers, whose enemies were believed to be the same; a graduated income tax; the establishment of postal savings banks; federal ownership and operation of telephone and telegraph; nationalization of the railroads, government reclamation of all railroad and corporation lands for settlers; and recognition of the eight-hour work day. The Populists enjoyed great success in the election. Weaver, though losing, attracted more than 1 million votes, and at least a dozen of its leaders were sent to Congress, setting the stage for the 1896 campaign and a renewed cry for free silver.

But free silver was not an issue that appealed strictly along party lines. By the 1890s, it had grown into a social movement with its own ideology that spread beyond party affiliations, uniting

Populists, Democrats, Republicans, former greenbackers and various splinter groups, under its proud banner of justice for the common man. Like any such movement, it provided a set doctrine for its followers and unifying trappings, including songs, parades, badges and pins and battle cries, that enraged and inspired the faithful. It also had a bible, *Coin's Financial School*, written by William H. "Coin" Harvey, which could easily explain the complex money question to those who did not understand it—and their numbers were legion—while pointing its fleshy literary finger at those who had destroyed the nation in the name of greed.

Its author, Harvey, an incurable entrepreneur, whose wanderlust drove him from one grandiose scheme to another, was born in 1852, in the village of Buffalo, located in the western part of Virginia. Harvey's unyielding quest for wealth, interrupted from time to time by his pursuit of a law career, drew him to the mine fields of Colorado in the early 1880s. It was there that he became acutely aware of the plight in store for the white metal that would later bring him fame. In 1893, after discovering that increased production costs, coupled with the ever-waning value of silver, had destroyed his chance at wealth through the physical mining of silver, Harvey turned to the written pursuit of the precious metal, establishing his own free silver publishing company in Chicago, the Midwestern heart of the Free Silver Movement.[3]

William H. "Coin" Harvey.

One year later, in June 1894, he released *Coin's Financial School,* which clearly enjoyed a widespread popularity, due to Harvey's ability to reduce the complex money question to a level that was readily understood by the masses and his fictional setting for the discussion of the money question, a setting that carried such an air of reality that many of his readers accepted his work as a recapitulation of an actual event. Harvey's fictional classic portrayed leading newspaper editors, businessmen, politicians, and financiers attending a series of six lectures on the money question held at the Art Institute in Chicago in May 1894—lessons that were taught by a precocious youth named "Coin." Through these lectures, ably directed by young Coin, who readily rebuts questions from his influential pro-gold audience, such real-life luminaries as Lyman J. Gage (who later served as the Secretary of the Treasury under President William McKinley), J. Laurence Laughlin (a professor of economics at the University of Chicago), and wealthy merchants Philip D. Armour and Marshall Field are drawn away from their misguided support of the gold standard.[4]

Harvey's unflattering portrayal of actual gold standard advocates angered several of those whom he named as his misguided lecture participants, including Prof. Laughlin. Incensed by the unauthorized inclusion of his name in Harvey's *Coin's Financial School*, Laughlin lashed out at Harvey's work in an article titled, "'Coin's' Food for the Gullible," printed in the July 1895 issue of *The Forum*, retorting:

> The style of the book is ingeniously contrived to carry out its purpose. The dapper but mythical youth, who is supposed to have lectured in the Art Institute at Chicago in May, 1894, of course never existed. The author has cleverly used this device as a means of exposition and of entertaining his impressionable readers. Moreover, the author has shrewdly counted on the gullibility of three-quarters of his readers who have honestly supposed that the mythical lectures really took place, and that the persons mentioned therein, as having asked questions and having been refuted, were really present. That the lectures never took place, and, therefore, that the persons mentioned therein never could have made any such remarks as those assigned to them, is little understood by thousands who believe

WILL HE BE BUNCOED?

IT WAS GREENBACKS; IT IS NOW SILVER; AND ALWAYS FIAT MONEY.

***William Harvey's Coin's Financial School is lampooned in this May 25, 1895, cartoon from* Harper's Weekly.**

> that the school actually existed. The impression of deceit and unreality in the exposition of a difficult subject by a small boy who refutes experts and authorities would at least have seemed to make a widespread belief in the book impossible; but a willingness to believe that a person of standing had been 'floored' and demolished by a youth who taught views which seem to reflect upon the fortunate classes, have been cleverly satisfied.[5]

Willard Fisher, a reviewer, who found Harvey's work to be of little economic use and highly dangerous, claimed in his article, "'Coin' and his Critics," for the January 1896 issue of the *Quarterly Journal of Economics* that:

> The book will, therefore, be of no value to those who have been trained to think about monetary problems. Indeed, to such people it will seem strange that so crude a product could have created so great a sensation. But we must remember that the great mass of the people are quite incompetent to judge the worth of such a book, and that upon these a great impression may be made by skillful sophistry. And in this dangerous art Mr. Harvey has great proficiency.[6]

That the critics disagreed with the findings of *Coin's Financial School* did not matter to Harvey, for he believed it to be one of the greatest economic works of all time and of unequaled importance to the welfare of the country. Harvey did not stop with *Coin's Financial School*; as the economic champion of the burgeoning Free Silver Movement, he eagerly agreed to debate anyone who was willing to challenge the economic teachings of Coin. In May 1895, he accepted the invitations of the Illinois Club to debate Prof. Laughlin on the money question, an event which he saw as of the utmost importance to his righteous cause and glowingly recorded as part of his ever-growing *Coin's Financial Series* under the title, *The Crime of 1873 and the Harvey-Laughlin Joint Debate*.

The debate took place before a packed hall on May 17, 1895. According to Harvey's illustrious account, the hall selected for the confrontation, which was able to seat a meager 500 people, was not nearly large enough to accommodate the throng of people who wished to view the disputants. Even a hall that was capable of seating 3,000 onlookers would have been only half as large as was necessary, Harvey declared.

The mere fact such a debate could take place in Chicago signaled a victory for bimetallism, as Harvey explained, for now "COIN'S FINANCIAL SCHOOL had at least gotten under Chicago," and "in this city that had so long turned a deaf ear to the truths of bimetallism, COIN was to meet the champion of the gold standard forces."[7] Harvey exalted:

> Before the disputants sat probably the most intelligent audience ever assembled in the hall. Every seat was taken, even including those in the little gallery or box in the corner of the room. Wherever the eye ranged over the throng it rested on men who were the bone and sinew of the community, and the wisest business men of the city. It was an audience so experienced and critical that it might well abash any but the most accomplished expert in political economy.[8]

Although arguably the most popular of all of Harvey's writings, selling (by his wife's estimate) some 1.5 million copies, *Coin's Financial School* was not his only effort in regard to free silver. His more colorful *A Tale of Two Nations* employed a fictitious meeting in Great Britain between a naive, corrupt U.S. senator (John Sherman) and Baron von Rothschild, where a plan was hatched to bring about the demonetization of silver in the United States in 1873 and, thereby, allow England to bring the United States under its domination. Harvey would later release, *Coin's Financial School Up to Date* and others works within this vein.

While Harvey's *Coin's Financial School* ranks as the most popular and widely read free silver tract, Harvey devoted only a small portion of this classic piece of free silver fiction to a discussion of the conspiratorial aspects of the so-called Crime of 1873. Preferring to use his fictional educational forum on

A William Jennings Bryan campaign badge.

the money question to focus on the need for the restoration of the free and unlimited coinage of silver, Harvey, through his main character Coin, stressed that the silver dollar (of 371 1/4 grains pure silver) had constituted the unit of value since the formation of the government in 1792, until the Coinage Act of 1873 demonetized it and, thereby, eliminated one half of the nation's supply of hard money. The demonetization of silver, Coin declared, led to hardship and misery. He informed his celebrated lecture participants that the act had come to be known as:

> A crime, because it has confiscated millions of dollars worth of property. A crime, because it has made thousands of paupers. A crime, because it has made tens of thousands of tramps. A crime because it has made thousands of suicides. A crime, because it has brought tears to strong men's eyes, and hunger and pinching want to widows and orphans. A crime, because it is destroying the honest yeomanry of the land, the bulwark of the nation. A crime, because it has brought this once great republic to the verge of ruin, where it is now in imminent danger of tottering to its fall.[9]

The popularity of *Harvey's Coin's Financial School* also spawned a plethora of pro-gold pastiches such as John F. Cargill's *A Freak of Finance*, published in 1896.[10] In direct parody of "Coin" Harvey's work, Cargill's fictitious characters included Professor Mabie C. Goldwin (probably Laughlin), who journeyed to New York on business related to a prominent educational institution in Chicago, with which he is connected. Other recognizable characters are Mr. Silver Coin, the twin brother of the gentleman of the same family, who recently appeared in a book on finance, and Mr. Justus I. Hope, president of a leading Chicago bank.

Other gold standard authors who parodied Harvey's work included Cotton M. Barley's, *The Financial School at Farmerville*; H.L. Bliss' *Coin's Financial Fraud*; Stanley Waterloo's *Honest Money: 'Coin's' Fallacies Exposed*; Stanley Wood's *Answer to Coin's Financial School*; and L.G. Powers' *Farmer Hayseed in Town: or The Closing Days of Coin's Financial School*.

Official notification to William Jennings Bryan of his nomination as candidate for the presidency of the National Free Silver Party, Lincoln, Neb., Sept. 8, 1896. Bryan is at center, holding an umbrella. Courtesy of the Nebraska State Historical Society.

By the election year of 1896, through the spread of the teachings of Harvey and others of his ilk, several free silver groups had come into existence, including the American Bimetallic League, formed in 1892. There was also a motley mix of special interest groups, who, though they had varied agendas, had adopted free silver as a plank. What was needed, if there was to be any success for the cause in the political realm, was someone who could bring these divergent interests together as a unified force. William Jennings Bryan, who was born on March 19, 1860, in Salem, Ill., and would become the Free Silver Movement's greatest orator, hoped to achieved such a fusion.

Bryan was an experienced speaker and a longtime supporter of free silver within the Democratic Party. In 1890, he had won election to the U.S. Congress as a representative from Nebraska on a plank he wrote declaring: "We demand the free coinage of silver on equal terms with gold and silver and denounce the effort of the Republican party to serve the interests of Wall Street as against the rights of the people."[11] Bryan served two terms in the House, from 1891-1895, during which time he continued to make waves as a champion of the free silver cause, attending state conventions, where he helped institute resolutions calling for its free and unlimited coinage.

When a bill was introduce to repeal the Sherman Silver Purchase Act, Bryan served as a free silver leader in the 1893 debate he termed "the most important economic discussion which ever took place in our Congress."[12] In an impassioned speech, Bryan flayed:

> I have read with care the message sent to us last week, and have considered it in the light of every reasonable construction of which it is capable. If I am able to understand its language it points to the burial of silver, with no promise of resurrection. Its reasoning is in the direction of a single standard. It leads irresistibly to universal gold monometallism—to a realm over whose door is written: 'Abandon hope, all ye who enter here!' Before that door I stop, appalled. Have gentlemen considered the effect of a single gold standard universally adopted? Let us not deceive ourselves with the hope that we can discard silver for gold, and that other nations will take it up and keep it as a part of the world's currency....Is it not more reasonable to suppose that a further fall in the bullion value of silver will be followed by a demand for a limitation of the legal tender qualities of the silver already in existence? That is already being urged by some. Is it not reasonable to suppose that our hostile action will lead to hostile action on the part of other nations? Every country must have money for its people, and if silver is abandoned and gold substituted it must be drawn from the world's already scanty supply. We hear much about a 'stable currency' and an 'honest dollar.' It is a significant fact that those who have spoken in favor of unconditional repeal have for the most part avoided a discussion of the effect of an appreciating standard. They take it for granted that a gold standard is not only an honest standard, but the only stable standard. I denounce that child of ignorance and avarice, the gold dollar under a universal gold standard, as the most dishonest dollar which we could employ.[13]

In 1894, Bryan declined renomination for another term in the House and, instead, ran unsuccessfully for a Senate seat, crisscrossing Nebraska, giving speeches and instituting the same robust campaign style he would adopt two years later in his first bid for the presidency. On July 7, 1896, the Democratic National Convention opened in Chicago with the party split between delegates who favored a return to bimetallism and those who wanted to retain the gold standard. The following day, platform debates having ended, Bryan rose to deliver the closing argument in favor of the platform decided upon. "You come to us and tell us that the great cities are in favor of the gold standard; we reply that the great cities rest upon our broad and fertile prairies," Bryan ranted. "Burn down your cities and leave our farms, and your cities will spring up again as if by magic; but destroy our farms and the grass will grow in every city of the country."[14] With a chilling closing metaphor that will echo throughout political history, Bryan declared:

> Therefore, we care not upon what lines the battle is fought. If they say bimetallism is good, but that we cannot have it until other nations help us, we reply that, instead of having a gold standard because England has, we will restore bimetallism, and then let England have bimetallism because the United States has it. If they dare to come out in the open field and defend the gold standard as a good thing, we will fight them to the uttermost. Having behind us the producing masses of this nation and the world, supported by the commercial interests, the laboring interests, and the toilers everywhere, we will answer their demand for a gold standard by saying to them: You shall not press down upon the brow of labor this crown of thorns, you shall not crucify mankind upon a cross of gold.[15]

Bryan's pro-silver tirade brought about wild demonstrations in the packed hall. It also swept him to the forefront of his party as its candidate for president of the United States. Bryan would win out, over Richard P. Bland, for the nomination of the Democratic Party after five ballots. By the end of the party conventions of 1896, Bryan had won the nomination for president from the Populists, Democrats, National Silver Party, and several

Bryan was a tireless campaigner. He is shown here at a whistlestop during the 1896 presidential campaign. Courtesy of the Nebraska State Historical Society.

minor parties, such as the single taxers, Christian Socialists and the Broad-Gauge prohibitionists. The free silver issue also enjoyed support among a Republican Party faction.

While most platforms, including that of the Democratic Party, called for the restoration of free and unlimited coinage of silver at 16 to 1 ratio, not all party faithfuls agreed with the silver issue. Shortly after the close of the Democratic convention, Sound Money leagues or Honest Money democracy clubs sprang up throughout the Midwest and the East, populated by disenchanted Democrats and others who supported the gold standard. These groups later met in Indianapolis to form the National Democratic Party, which nominated Sen. John M. Palmer, of Illinois, to the presidency.

After winning the nomination, Bryan, displaying considerable zeal and dedication, set out on the first of four cross-country "whistle stop" campaign trips, rolling out of Chicago by train. Often he would speak from its back platform to save time, in an effort to meet with as many voters as possible. Many times forced to buy his own train tickets, meals and tote his own luggage, the baggy pants orator from Nebraska took his campaign through 29 states and delivered more than 600 speeches to an estimated 5 million people.

Bryan traveled mainly through rural areas, where support for the Free Silver Movement was the strongest. He generally drew large and enthusiastic crowds, who would arrive for his speeches decked out in the full panoply of the campaign, including the familiar hats, buttons and signs. Besides the normal campaign trappings, Bryan was frequently greeted by various representations of the bimetallic standard, such as a carriage drawn by 16 white horses and one yellow one, 16 young ladies dressed in white gowns and one in yellow, or by the gift of 16 white chrysanthemums and a yellow one. He also received thousands of gifts including gold canes, thorn canes, lucky coins, lucky stones and a silver Waterbury pocket watch. The watch was presented to him by a Connecticut supporter who thought it was embarrassing for Bryan to carry a gold pocket watch while giving a speech in favor of silver.

Meanwhile, the pro-gold Republican nominee, Gov. William McKinley, ran his own well-financed but dull "front porch" campaign from his home in Ohio. McKinley and his "gold bug" supporters feared that an independent return to bimetallism by the United States, at a time when most countries adhered to a gold standard, would drain the country of its gold reserves, flood it with silver and ruin the purchasing power of the dollar. It was not surprising, therefore, that the Republicans launched an all-out attack on Bryan's integrity and on the Free Silver Movement. Besides labeling Bryan a demagogue and a traitor to the nation, gold advocates circulated metal tokens in order to enlighten the voters on the dangers of free silver.

The most authoritative study to date on these tokens, many new varieties of which have been discovered since its publication, is Farran Zerbe's article, "Bryan Money. Tokens of the Presidential Campaigns of 1896 and 1900—Comparative and Satirical." It was first printed in the July 1926 issue of the American Numismatic Association's monthly journal, *The Numismatist.*

Zerbe divided the tokens into comparative and satirical categories. By relying on information

"United Snakes of America" reads the legend on this piece of Bryan Money.

"In God We Trust For The Other 47 CTS" reads this satirical piece of Bryan Money.

compiled from major collections, including his own and that of Howland Wood, Zerbe was able to identify 141 varieties.

One of the more common pieces (Zerbe-6) carries the legend "A Government Dollar Contains 412 1/2 Grains Coin Silver 900-1000 Fine" and "This Piece Contains 823 Grains Coin Silver In Value The Equivalent Of One Gold Dollar Sept. 16, 1896."

The reverse depicted a cartwheel of Morgan dollar size and contained the legend "Size Of The Government Dollar Containing 412 1/2 Grains Of Silver 900-1000 Fine."

In contrast to the comparative tokens, the satirical Bryan Money was generally of much poorer quality and composition. These pieces, many of which were privately made, were generally cast of base metals such as lead, pewter, iron, nickel and white metal.

This piece of Bryan Money, struck in coin silver, displayed the size of 412 1/2-grain silver dollar against the size it would need to be to contain a dollar's worth of silver.

According to the November 1987 catalog for the Ebenezer Milton Sanders Collection, sold by Auctions by Bowers and Merena, Wolfeboro, New Hampshire, the dollar-sized satirical pieces were made in Wisconsin and New York City. Dime-size tokens were produced in San Francisco, Cleveland, Chicago and Pittsburgh.

A five-cent denomination is also cataloged by Zerbe, along with various forms of Bryan Money and pieces from the presidential campaign in 1900.

The dollar tokens carry a rather amateurish design resembling the Morgan dollar. They range in size from 3.5 to five inches. The largest of these were sometimes known variously as stove griddles, whales or pie plates and weighed up to a hefty 28 ounces.

The satirical Bryan Money is known for its humorous and sarcastic legends. Popular quips were "In Bryan We Trust For The Other 47CTS"; "From The Silver Mines Of the Bunco State"; and "In McKinley We Trust, In Bryan We Bust."

One of the most creative pieces in the series is a dime token, which carries as the central device a donkey-headed goose with "POP" on its body. It symbolized the unity between the Democrats and the Populists and was surrounded by the legend "United Snakes Of America."

Another interesting piece, a mechanical token (Z-134) that can still be readily located, shows an eagle on the obverse with outstretched wings and its head to the right. Above is the legend "I'm All Right." When a ring, located a the top of the piece, is moved to the right, the eagle's head and right wing droop and the legend changes to "Where Am I At?"

When the ring is in the upright position the legend on the reverse reads "Sound Money Means A Dollar Worth 100 Cents" and across the bottom "McKinley,

The comparative pieces came in a variety of styles and sizes.

While Bryan traveled the country searching for votes, William McKinley ran a more subdued campaign. He was assassinated in 1901 while attending the Pan-American Exposition in Buffalo, N.Y.

Large-size pieces of Bryan Money (running around 85mm in diameter) were made in base metal and depicted crude representations of the Morgan dollar.

Hobart And Prosperity." When it is moved to the right, it reads "Free Silver Means A Dollar Worth 50 Cents" and across the bottom "Bryan, Sewall And Adversity."

After 14 weeks of exhaustive campaigning, Bryan returned to his home in Nebraska to recuperate and await the outcome of the election. The election results were not favorable to Bryan, as he lost to McKinley by a popular vote of 7,035,638 to 6,467,946. The Electoral College vote ran 271 for McKinley to 176 for Bryan. It was the most votes ever awarded to any previous losing presidential candidate, however, even though he won the six mountain states, he was unable to obtain the vote of any of the industrial states. Bryan is quoted as having said, "the campaign of 1896 was a memorable one whether we measure it by the magnitude of the issues involved or by the depth of interest aroused."[16]

The 1896 balloting proved to be the closest Bryan ever came to being elected president. It also sounded the death knell for the Free Silver Movement. The ghost of free silver, once again championed by Bryan, but only half-heartedly supported by the Democratic Party, made one last belabored appearance in 1900, but it was only a faint shadow of its former self. Celebrating its removal as a political force, on Nov. 4, 1896, one day after Bryan's defeat, the *New York Tribune* bid "good riddance" to the movement observing that, "Not since the fall of Richmond have patriotic Americans had so much cause for rejoicing."[17]

For his part, Bryan, after his failed 1896 bid, licked his wounds by writing, *The First Battle*, an epic dedicated to the continuation of the movement, at the end of which he reproduced a poem called "An Inspiration," written by Ella Wheeler Wilcox:

I.

However the battle is ended,
Though proudly the victor comes
With fluttering flags and prancing nags
And echoing roll of drums,
Still truth proclaims this motto
In letters of living light,—
No question is ever settled
Until it is settled right.

II.

Though the heel of the strong oppressor
May grind the weak in the dust,
And the voices of fame with one acclaim
May call him great and just,
Let those who applaud take warning,
And keep this motto in sight,—
No question is ever settled
Until it is settled right.

III.

Let those who have failed take courage;
Tho' the enemy seems to have won,
Tho' his ranks are strong, if he be in the wrong
The battle is not yet done;
For, sure as the morning follows
The darkest hour of the night,
No question is ever settled
Until it is settled right.

IV.

O man bowed down with labor!
O woman young, yet old!
O heart oppressed in the toiler's breast
And crushed by the power of gold!
Keep on with your weary battle
Against triumphant might;
No question is ever settled
Until it is settled right.[18]

A crudely designed piece of Bryan Money. Zerbe lists it has having been produced in various metals, including lead, white metal and aluminum.

However, the silver issue was all but dead. The economy began to recover, produce prices improved, and new gold discoveries, along with development of more efficient refining processes, caused the stock of gold to expand. In the wake of the economic recovery and an increase in the money supply, support for free silver weakened. In 1900, Congress passed an act that placed the United States officially on a gold standard and directed the Treasury secretary "to maintain all forms of money in parity with this standard."

Despite three attempts, Bryan never gained the nation's highest office. From 1913-1915 he served as Secretary of State under Woodrow Wilson. In 1925, he again earned notoriety as one of the prosecutors arguing against evolution in the famed Scopes "monkey trial." He died a few days after the trial closed.

For his part, William H. "Coin" Harvey held faith long after the silver issue had faded. In the 1920s, he could be found planning the construction of a great pyramid in which to permanently preserve copies of his own books, for the time when civilization collapsed under the weight of the gold standard. According to Richard Hofstadter, in his introduction to the Harvard reprint of *Coin's Financial School*, Harvey's pyramid was to have been 40 feet square at its base and rise some 130 feet in height. It would have borne a plaque instructing: "When this can be read go below and find the cause of the death of a former Civilization."[19] His pyramid, and thereby his world, would live on past the fall of Civilization and would leave any new generation, rising from the ashes of destruction, a clear record of what had happened and why it happened.

Harvey began construction, but ran out of money before the pyramid was finished. The site, Hofstadter says, did serve as a tourist attraction, where lectures were freely given and copies of Harvey's various books were sold. In 1931, Harvey ran for president, as the candidate of the Liberty Party. He died five years later at the age of 84. His beloved cause had been laid to rest long before.

For his part, William C. Ralston, who had gone for a fatal swim on a steamy August day in 1875, left behind a group of incriminating letters Dr. Henry R. Linderman probably would have wished had long since been destroyed—letters that would serve to illustrate the true story of the Crime of 1873, the Free Silver Movement and America's beloved and berated silver dollar.

Appendix A

The Coinage Act of 1873

ACT OF FEBRUARY 12, 1873.

An act revising and amending the laws relative to the Mint, assay-offices, and coinage of the United States.

Be it enacted by the Senate and House of Representatives of the United States of America in Congress assembled, That the Mint of the United States is hereby established as a Bureau of the Treasury Department, embracing in its organization and under its control all mints for the manufacture of coin, and all assay-offices for the stamping of bars, which are now, or which may be hereafter, authorized by law. The chief officer of the said Bureau shall be denominated the Director of the Mint, and shall be under the general direction of the Secretary of the Treasury. He shall be appointed by the President, by and with the advice and consent of the Senate, and shall hold his office for the term of five years, unless sooner removed by the President, upon reasons to be communicated by him to the Senate.

SEC. 2. That the Director of the Mint shall have the general supervision of all mints and assay-offices, and shall make an annual report to the Secretary of the Treasury of their operations, at the close of each fiscal year, and from time to time such additional reports, setting forth the operations and condition of such institutions, as the Secretary of the Treasury shall require, and shall lay before him the annual estimates for their support. And the Secretary of the Treasury shall appoint the number of clerks, classified according to law, necessary to discharge the duties of said Bureau.

SEC. 3. Specifies the officers of each mint. Reproduced in Revised Statutes, section 3496.

SEC. 4. Defines powers and duties of superintendents of mints. Reproduced in Revised Statutes, sections 3503, 3504, 3505, and 3506.

SEC. 5. Defines duties of assayers. Reproduced in Revised Statutes, section 3507.

SEC. 6. Defines duties of melter and refiner. Reproduced in Revised Statutes, section 3508.

SEC. 7. Defines the duty of the coiner and is reproduced in Revised Statutes, section 3509.

SEC. 8. Defines the duties of the engraver and is reproduced in Revised Statutes, section 3510.

SEC. 9. Prescribes how temporary vacancies from sickness or otherwise may be filled by the superintendent and is reproduced in Revised Statutes, section 3502.

SEC. 10. Prescribes the oath of officers, assistant clerks and employés, and is reproduced in Revised Statutes, section 3500.

SEC. 11. Prescribes the bond of superintendent and other officers and is reproduced in Revised Statutes, section 3501.

SEC. 12. Prescribes the salaries of the different officers and that they shall be payable monthly, and is reproduced in Revised Statutes, sections 3498 and 3499.

SEC. 13. Fixes the standard of fineness of gold and silver coins and is reproduced in Revised Statutes, section 3514.

SEC. 14. That the gold coins of the United States shall be a one-dollar piece, which, at the standard weight of twenty-five and eight-tenths grains, shall be the unit of value; a quarter-eagle, or two-and-a-half dollar piece; a three-dollar piece; a half eagle, or five-dollar piece; an eagle, or ten-dollar piece; and a double-eagle, or twenty-dollar piece. And the standard weight of the gold dollar shall be twenty-five and eight-tenths grains; of the quarter-eagle, or two-and-a-half dollar piece, sixty-four and a-half grains; of the three-dollar piece, seventy-seven and four-tenths grains; of the half-eagle or five-dollar piece, one hundred and twenty-nine grains; of the eagle or ten-dollar piece, two hundred and fifty-eight grains; of the double-eagle, or twenty-dollar piece, five hundred and sixteen grains; which coins shall be a legal tender in all payments at their nominal value when not below the standard weight and limit of tolerance provided in this act for the single piece, and when reduced in weight, below said standard and tolerance, shall be a legal tender at valuation in proportion of their actual weight; and any gold coin of the United States, if reduced in weight by natural abrasion not more than one-half of one percentum below the standard weight prescribed by law, after a circulation of twenty years, as shown by its date of coinage, and at a ratable proportion for any period less than twenty years, shall be received at their nominal value by the United States Treasury and its offices, under such regulations as the Secretary of the Treasury may prescribe for the protection of the Government against fraudulent abrasion or other practices; and any gold coins in the Treasury of the United States reduced in weight below this limit of abrasion shall be recoined.

SEC. 15. Describes the silver coins of the United States, prescribes their weight, legal tender quality, etc., and is reproduced in Revised Statutes, sections 3513 and 3586.

SEC. 16. Describes the minor coins of the United States and their alloy, fixes their weight and legal tender quality, and is reproduced in Revised Statutes, sections 3515 and 3587.

SEC. 17. Prohibits the issue of any other coins that those set forth and is reproduced in Revised Statutes, section 3516.

SEC. 18. That upon the coins of the United States there shall be the following devices and legends: Upon one side there shall be an impression emblematic of liberty, with an inscription of the word "Liberty" and the year of the coin age, and upon the reverse shall be the figure or representation of an eagle, with the inscriptions "United States of America" and "E Pluribus Unum," and a designation of the value of the coin; but on the gold dollar and three-dollar piece, the dime, five, three, and one cent piece the figure of the eagle shall be omitted; and on the reverse of the silver trade-dollar the weight and the fineness of the coin shall be inscribed; and the Director of the Mint, with the approval of the Secretary of the Treasury, may cause the motto "In God We Trust" to be inscribed upon such coins as shall admit of such motto; and any one of the foregoing inscriptions may be on the rim of the gold and silver coins.

SEC. 19. Authorizes the casting and stamping of gold or silver bars and is reproduced in Revised Statutes, section 3518.

SEC. 20. Provides for deposits of gold bullion for coinage and is reproduced in Revised Statutes, section 3519.

SEC. 21. Provides for deposits of silver bullion, casting into bars or coining into trade dollars, and is reproduced in Revised Statutes, section 3520.

SEC. 22. Provides for the weighing of bullion and determining its fitness and mode of melting, and is reproduced in revised Statutes, section 3521.

SEC. 23. Provides for the assay of bullion and is reproduced in Revised Statutes, section 3522.

SEC. 24. Provides for a report by the assayer and is reproduced in Revised Statutes, section 3523.

SEC. 25. Provides for charges for converting bullion into coin and the preparation of bars, and is reproduced in Revised Statutes, section 3524.

SEC. 26. Provides for verification of calculations of superintendent by the assayer and his countersigning certificate, and is reproduced in Revised Statutes, section 3525.

SEC. 27. Provides for the purchase of bullion for silver coinage and for the disposition of seigniorage, and is reproduced in Revised Statutes, section 3526.

SEC. 28. Provides how silver coins shall be paid out, where and for what, and is reproduced in Revised Statutes, section 3527.

SEC. 29. Provides for the purchase of metal for the minor coinage and is reproduced in Revised Statutes, section 3528.

SEC. 30. Provides for methods of exchanging minor coins and limits the legal tender thereof, and is reproduced in Revised Statutes, section 3529.

SEC. 31. Provides for melting and refining of bullion and coinage into ingots, and is reproduced in Revised Statutes, section 3530.

SEC. 32. Provides for the assaying and giving of certificates in regard to ingots, and is reproduced in Revised Statutes, section 3531.

SEC. 33. Provides for the coinage of ingots and prescribes deviation for legal standard, reproduced in Revised Statutes, section 3533.

SEC. 34. Provides for bars for payment of deposits, for ascertaining fineness, etc., and is reproduced in Revised Statutes, section 3534.

SEC. 35. Relates to ingots for coinage and their delivery to the coiner, and is reproduced in Revised Statutes, section 3532.

SEC. 36. Provides for deviations of weight of gold coins and the limitations, and is reproduced in Revised Statutes, section 3535.

SEC. 37. Provides for the deviations of weight in silver coins, and is reproduced in Revised Statutes, section 3536.

SEC. 38. Provides for the adjustment of weight of the minor coinage, and is reproduced in Revised Statutes, section 3537.

SEC. 39. Provides for the delivery by the coiner to the superintendent of coins for assay, and is reproduced in Revised Statutes, section 3538.

SEC. 40. Prescribes the mode of delivery of such coins by the coiner to the Superintendent, and is reproduced in Revised Statutes, section 3539.

SEC. 41. Provides for the disposition of clippings of bullion, etc., and is reproduced in Revised Statutes, section 3540.

SEC. 42. Provides with what the coiner shall be charged and credited as to the character of accounts to be rendered, and is reproduced in Revised Statutes, section 3541.

SEC. 43. Provides for the examination of the accounts, by the superintendent, of the coiner and melter and refiner, and what amount will be allowed for wastage, and is reproduced in Revised Statutes, section 3542.

SEC. 44. Provides for a balance sheet reported to the Director of the Mint and also an expense account, and is reproduced in Revised Statutes, section 3543.

SEC. 45. Provides for the payment of coins or bars to depositors, and is reproduced in Revised Statutes, section 3544.

SEC. 46. Provides for the exchange of unparted bullion and a charge for parting, and is reproduced in Revised Statutes, section 3546.

SEC. 47. Provides for speedy returns by the Secretary of the Treasury to depositors of bullion, and is reproduced in Revised Statutes, section 3545.

SEC. 48. Provides for the annual test of weight of coins by an assay commission, specifies where it shall take place, etc., and is reproduced in Revised Statutes, section 3547.

SEC. 49. Provides for a standard troy pound of the Mint of the United States, and is reproduced in Revised Statutes, section 3548.

SEC. 50. Provides a standard weight of each mint and assay office and regulates the testing thereof annually, and is reproduced in Revised Statutes, section 3549.

SEC. 51. Provides for the destruction of obverse working dies, and is reproduced in Revised Statutes, section 3550.

SEC. 52. Provides that dies of a national character and medals may be made at the Mint at Philadelphia, and is reproduced in Revised Statutes, section 3551.

SEC. 53. Provides that all receipts for charges and deductions, etc., shall be covered into the Treasury of the United States and that no expenditures shall be made for salaries other than by appropriations, and is reproduced in Revised Statutes, section 3552.

SEC. 54. Provides for the officers of the assay office at New York and their appointment, defines the business of the assay office, and is reproduced in Revised Statutes, section 3553.

SEC. 55. That the duties of the superintendent, assayer, and melter and refiner of said office shall correspond to those of superintendents, assayers, and melters and refiners of mints; and all parts of this act relating to mints and their officers, the duties and responsibilities of such officers, and others employed therein, the oath to be taken, and the bonds and sureties to be given by them, (as far as the same may be applicable,) shall extend to the assay-office at New York, and to its officers, assistants, clerks, workmen, and others employed therein.

SEC. 56. Defines the salaries of superintendent, etc., and is reproduced in Revised Statutes, section 3556 and 3557.

SEC. 57. That the business at the branch mint at Denver, while conducted as an assay-office, and of the assay-office at Boise City, Idaho, and all other assay-offices hereafter to be established, shall be confined to the receipt of gold and silver bullion, for melting and assaying, to be returned to depositors of the same, in bars, with the weight and fineness stamped thereon; and the officers of assay-offices, when their services are necessary, shall consist of an assayer, who shall have charge thereof, and a melter, to be appointed by the President, by and with the advice and consent of the Senate; and the assayer may employ as many clerks, workmen, and laborers, under the direction of the Director of the Mint, as may be provided for by law. The salaries of said officers shall not exceed the sum of two thousand five hundred dollars to the assayer and melter, one thousand eight hundred dollars each to the clerks, and the workmen and laborers shall receive such wages as are customary according to their respective stations and occupations.

SEC. 58. That each officer and clerk to be appointed at such assay-offices, before entering upon the execution of his office shall take an oath or affirmation before some judge of the United States, or of the Supreme Court, as prescribed by the act of July second, eighteen hundred and sixty-two and each become bound to the United States of America, with one or more sureties, to the satisfaction of the Director of the Mint or of one of the judges of the supreme court of the State or Territory in which the same may be located, and of the Secretary of the Treasury, conditioned for the faithful performance of the duties of their offices; and the said assayers shall discharge the duties of disbursing agents for the payment of the expenses of their respective assay-offices.

SEC. 59. That the general direction of the business of assay-offices of the United States shall be under the control and regulation of the Director of the Mint, subject to the approbation of the Secretary of the Treasury; and for that purpose it shall be the duty of the said Director to prescribe such regulations and to require such returns periodically and occasionally, and to establish such charges for melting, parting, assaying, and stamping bullion as shall appear to him to be necessary for the purpose of carrying into effect the intention of this act.

SEC. 60. That all the provisions of this act for the regulation of the mints of the United States, and for the government of the officers and persons employed therein, and for the punishment of all offenses connected with the mints or coinage of the United States, shall be, and they are hereby declared to be, in full force in relation to the assay-offices, as far as the same may be applicable thereto.

SEC. 61. That if any person or persons shall falsely make, forge, or counterfeit, or cause or procure to be falsely made, forged, or counterfeited, or willingly aid or assist in falsely making, forging, or counterfeiting, any coin or bars in resemblance or similitude of the gold or silver coins or bars, which have been, or hereafter may be, coined or stamped at the mints and assay-offices of the United States, or in resemblance or similitude of any foreign gold or silver coin which by law is, or hereafter may be made, current in the United States, or are in actual use and circulation as money within the United States, or shall pass, utter, publish, or sell, or attempt to pass, utter, publish, or sell, or bring into the United States from any foreign place, or have in his possession, any such false, forged, or counterfeited coin or bars, knowing the same to be false, forged, or counterfeited, every person so offending shall be deemed guilty of felony, and shall, on conviction thereof, be punished by fine not exceeding five thousand dollars, and by imprisonment and confinement at hard labor not exceeding ten years, according to the aggravation of the offense.

SEC. 62. That if any person or persons shall falsely make, forge, or counterfeit, or cause or procure to be falsely made, forged, or counterfeited, or willingly aid or assist in falsely making, forging, or counterfeiting any coin in the resemblance or similitude of any of the minor coinage which has been, or hereafter may be, coined at the mints of the United States; or shall pass, utter, publish, or sell, or bring into the United States from any foreign place, or have in his possession, any such false, forged, or counterfeited coin, with intent to defraud any body politic or corporation, or any person or persons whatsoever, every person so offending shall be deemed guilty of felony, and shall, on conviction thereof, be punished by fine not exceeding one thousand dollars and by imprisonment and confinement at hard labor not exceeding three years.

SEC. 63. That if any person shall fraudulently, by any art, way, or means whatsoever, deface, mutilate, impair, diminish, falsify, scale, or lighten the gold or silver coins which have been, or which shall hereafter be, coined at the mints of the United States, or any foreign gold or silver coins which are by law made current, or are in actual use and circulation as money within the United States, every person so offending shall be deemed guilty of a high misdemeanor, and shall be imprisoned not exceeding two years, and fined not exceeding two thousand dollars.

SEC. 64. That if any of the gold or silver coins which shall be struck or coined at any of the mints of the United States shall be debased, or made worse as to the proportion of fine gold or fine silver therein contained; or shall be of less weight or value than the same ought to be, pursuant to the several acts relative thereto; or if any of the weights used at any of the mints or assay-offices of the United States shall be defaced, increased, or diminished through the fault or connivance of any of the officers or persons who shall be employed at the said mints or assay-offices, with a fraudulent intent; and if any of the said officers or persons shall embezzle any of the metals which shall at any time be committed to their charge for the purpose of being coined, or any of the coins which shall be struck or coined at the said mints, or any medals, coins, or other moneys of said mints or assay-offices at any time committed to their charge, or of which they may have assumed the charge, every such officer or person who shall commit any or either of the said offenses shall be deemed guilty of felony, and shall be imprisoned at hard labor for a term not less than one year nor more than ten years, and shall be fined in a sum not exceeding ten thousand dollars.

SEC. 65. That this act shall take effect on the first day of April, eighteen hundred and seventy-three, when the offices of the treasurer of the mints in Philadelphia, San Francisco, and New Orleans shall be vacated, and the assistant treasurer at New York shall cease to perform the duties of treasurer of the assay-office. The other officers and employés of the mints and assay-offices now appointed shall continue to hold their respective offices, they having first given the necessary bonds, until further appointments may be required, the Director of the Mint at Philadelphia being styled and acting as superintendent thereof. The duties of the treasurers shall devolve as herein provided upon the superintendents, and said treasurers shall act only as assistant treasurers of the United States: *Provided,* That the salaries heretofore paid to the treasurers of the mints at Philadelphia, San Francisco, and New Orleans, acting as assistant treasurers, shall hereafter be paid to them as "assistant Treasurers of the United States," and that the salary of the assistant treasurer at New York shall not be diminished by the vacation of his office as treasurer of the assay-office.

SEC. 66. That the different mints and assay-offices authorized by this act shall be known as "the mint of the United States at Philadelphia," "the mint of the United States at San Francisco," "the mint of the United States at Carson," "the mint of the United States at Denver," "the United States assay-office at New York," and "the United States assay-office at Boise City, Idaho," "the United States assay-office at Charlotte, North Carolina;" and all unexpended appropriations heretofore authorized by law for the use of the mint of the United States at Philadelphia, the branch-mint of the United States at California, the branch-mint of the United States at Denver, the United States assay-office in New York, the United States assay-office in Charlotte, North Carolina, and the United States assay-office in Boise City, Idaho, are hereby authorized to be transferred for the account and use of the institutions established and located respectively at the places designated by this act.

SEC. 67. That this act shall be known as the "Coinage act of eighteen hundred and seventy-three;" and all other acts and parts of acts pertaining to the mints, assay-offices, and coinage of the United States inconsistent with the provisions of this act are hereby repealed: *Provided,* That this act shall not be construed to affect any act done, right accrued, or penalty incurred, under former acts, but every such right is hereby saved; and all suits and prosecutions for acts already done in violation of any former act or acts of Congress relating to the subjects embraced in this act may be begun or proceeded with in like manner as if this act had not been passed; and all penal clauses and provisions in existing laws relating to the subjects embraced in this act shall be deemed applicable thereto: *And provided further,* That so much of the first section of "An act making appropriations for sundry civil expenses of the Government for the year ending June thirty, eighteen hundred and seventy-one, and for other purposes," approved July fifteen, eighteen hundred and seventy, as provides that until after the completion and occupation of the branch-mint building in San Francisco, it shall be lawful to exchange, at any mint or branch-mint of the United States, unrefined or unparted bullion, whenever, in the opinion of the Secretary of the Treasury, it can be done with advantage to the Government, is hereby repealed.

Appendix B

The Revised Statutes of 1874

ACT OF JUNE 22, 1874.

Sections relating to coinage.

SEC. 3495. The different mints and assay-offices shall be known as-
First. The mint of the United States at Philadelphia.
Second. The mint of the United States at San Francisco.
Third. The mint of the United States at New Orleans.
Fourth. The mint of the United States at Carson.
Fifth. The mint of the United States at Denver.
Sixth. The United States assay-office at New York.
Seventh. The United States assay-office at Boise City, Idaho.
Eighth. The United States assay-office at Charlotte, North Carolina.

SEC. 3496. The officers of each mint shall be a superintendent, an assayer, a melter and refiner, and a coiner and, for the mint at Philadelphia, an engraver; all to be appointed by the President, by and with the advice and consent of the Senate.

SEC. 3497. The superintendent of the mints at Philadelphia, San Francisco, and New Orleans shall be, and perform the duties of, treasurers of said mints respectively.

SEC. 3498. The officers of the several mints shall be entitled to the following salaries, to be paid monthly:
First. The superintendents of the mints at Philadelphia and San Francisco, to four thousand five hundred dollars a year each.
Second. The assayers, melters and refiners, and the coiners to those mints, to three thousand dollars a year each.
Third. The engraver of the mint at Philadelphia, to three thousand dollars a year.
Fourth. The superintendent of the mint at Carson City to three thousand dollars a year.
Fifth. The assayer, the melter and refiner, and the coiner of the mint at Carson City, to two thousand five hundred dollars a year each.

SEC. 3499. There shall be allowed to the assistants and clerks of the several mints such annual salaries as the Director of the Mint may, with the approbation of the Secretary of the Treasury, determine, and to the workmen reasonable according to their respective stations and occupations, to be determined by the superintendent, and approved by the Director of the Mint. The salaries provided for in this and the preceding section, and the wages of workmen permanently engaged, shall be payable in monthly installments.

SEC. 3500. Every officer, assistant, and clerk appointed for any mint shall, before he enters upon the execution of his office, take an oath before some judge of the United States, or judge of some court of record of the State in which such mint is located, faithfully and diligently to perform the duties thereof; in addition to other official oaths prescribed by law, such oath, duly certified, shall be transmitted to the Secretary of the Treasury. The superintendent of each mint may require such oath from any of the employés of the mint.

SEC. 3501. The superintendent, the assayer, the melter and refiner, and the coiner of each mint, before entering upon the execution of their respective offices, shall become bound to the United States, with one or more sureties, approved by the Secretary of the Treasury, in the sum of not less than ten nor more than fifty thousand dollars, with condition for the faithful and diligent performance of the duties of his office. Similar bonds may be required of the assistants and clerks, in such sums as the superintendent shall determine, with the approbation of the Director of the Mint; but the same shall not be construed to relieve the superintendent or other officers from liability to the United States for acts, omissions, or negligence of their subordinates or employés; and the Secretary of the Treasury may, at his discretion, increase the bonds of the superintendents.

SEC. 3502. Whenever any officer of a mint or assay-office shall be temporarily absent, on account of sickness or any other cause, it shall be lawful for the superintendent, with the consent of such officer, to appoint some person attached to the mint to act in the place of such officer during his absence; but all such appointments shall be forthwith reported to the Director of the Mint for his approval; and in all cases whatsoever the principal shall be responsible for the acts of his representative. In case of the temporary absence of the superintendent, the chief clerk shall act in his place; in case of the temporary absence of the Director of the Mint the Secretary of the Treasury may designate some one to act in his place.

SEC. 3503. The superintendent of each mint shall have the control thereof, the superintendence of the officers and persons employed therein, and the supervision of the business thereof, subject to the approval of the Director of the Mint. He shall make reports to the Director of the Mint at such times and according to such forms as the Director may prescribe; which shall exhibit in detail, and under appropriate heads, the deposits of bullion, the amount of gold, silver, and minor coinage, and the amount of unparted, standard, and refined bars issued, and such other statistics and information as may be required.

SEC. 3504. He shall keep and render, quarter-yearly, to the Director of the Mint, for the purpose of adjustment according to such forms as may be prescribed by the Secretary of the Treasury, regular and faithful accounts of his transactions with the other officers of the Mint and the depositors; and shall also render to him a monthly statement of the ordinary expenses of the mint or assay-office under his charge. He shall also appoint all assistants, clerks, one of whom shall be designated "chief clerk," and workmen employed under his superintendence; but no person shall be appointed to employment in the office of the assayer, melter and refiner, coiner, and engraver, except on the recommendation and nomination in writing of those officers, respectively. He shall forth with report to the Director of the Mint the names of all persons appointed by him the duties to be performed, the rate of compensation, the appropriation from which compensation is to be made, and the grounds of the appointment; and if the Director of the Mint shall disapprove the same, the appointment shall be vacated.

SEC. 3505. Any gold coins of the United States, if reduced in weight by natural abrasion not more than one-half of one per centum below the standard weight prescribed by law, after a circulation of twenty years, as shown by the date of coinage, and at a ratable proportion for any period less than twenty years, shall be received at their nominal value by the United States Treasury and its offices, under such regulations as the Secretary of the Treasury may prescribe for the protection of the Government against fraudulent abrasion or other practices.

SEC. 3506. The superintendent of each mint shall receive and safely keep, until legally withdrawn, all moneys or bullion which shall be for the use or the expenses of the mint. He shall receive all bullion brought to the mint for assay or coinage; shall be the keeper of all bullion or coin in the mint, except while the same is legally in the hands of other officers; and shall deliver all coins struck at the mint to the persons to whom they shall be legally payable. From the report of the assayer and the weight of the bullion, he shall compute the value of each deposit, and also the amount of the charges or deductions, if any, of all which he shall give a detailed memorandum to the depositor; and he shall also give at the same time, under his hand, a certificate of the net amount of the deposit, to be paid in coins or bars of the same species of bullion as that deposited, the correctness of which certificate shall be verified by the assayer, who shall countersign the same, and in all cases of transfer of coin or bullion, shall give and receive vouchers, stating the amount and character of such coin and bullion.

SEC. 3507. The assayer shall assay all metals and bullion, whenever such assays are required in the operations of the mint; and shall make assays of coin or samples of bullion whenever required by the superintendent.

SEC. 3508. The melter and refiner shall execute all the operations which are necessary in order to form ingots of standard silver or gold, and alloys for minor coinage, suitable for the coiner, from the metals legally delivered to him for that purpose; and shall also execute all the operations which are necessary in order to form bars conformable in all respects to the law, from the gold and silver bullion delivered to him for that purpose. He shall keep a careful record of all transactions with the superintendent, noting the weight and character of the bullion, and shall be responsible for all bullion delivered to him until the same is returned to the superintendent and the proper vouchers obtained.

SEC. 3509. The coiner shall execute all the operations which are necessary in order to form coins, conformable in all respects to the law, from the standard gold and silver ingots, and alloys for minor coinage, legally delivered to him for that purpose; and shall be responsible for all bullion delivered to him, until the same is returned to the superintendent and the proper vouchers obtained.

SEC. 3510. The engraver shall prepare from the original dies already authorized all the working-dies required for use in the coinage of the several mints, and, when new coins or devices are authorized, shall, if required by the Director of the Mint, prepare the devices, models, molds, and matrices, or original dies, for the same; but the Director of the Mint shall nevertheless have power, with the approval of the Secretary of the Treasury, to engage temporarily for this purpose the services of one or more artists, distinguished in their respective departments of art, who shall be paid for such service from the contingent appropriation for the mint at Philadelphia.

SEC. 3511. The gold coins of the United States shall be a one-dollar piece, which, at the standard weight of twenty-five and eight-tenths grains, shall be the unit of value; a quarter-eagle, or two and a half dollar piece; a three-dollar piece; a half-eagle, or five-dollar piece; an eagle, or ten-dollar piece; and a double-eagle, or twenty-dollar piece. And the standard weight of the gold dollar shall be twenty-five and eight-tenths grains; of the quarter-eagle, or two and a half dollar piece, sixty-four and a half grains; of the three-dollar piece, seventy-seven and four-tenths grains; of the half-eagle, or five-dollar piece, one hundred and twenty-nine grains; of the eagle, or ten-dollar piece, two hundred and fifty-eight grains; of the double-eagle, or twenty-dollar piece, five hundred and sixteen grains.

SEC. 3512. Any gold coins in the Treasury of the United States, when reduced in weight by natural abrasion more than one-half of one per centum below the standard weight prescribed by law, shall be recoined.

SEC. 3513. The silver coins of the United States shall be a trade dollar, a half-dollar, or fifty-cent piece, a quarter-dollar, or twenty-five cent piece, a dime, or ten-cent piece; and the weight of the trade-dollar shall be four hundred and twenty grains troy; the weight of the half-dollar shall be twelve grams and one-half of a gram; the quarter-dollar and the dime shall be, respectively, one-half and one-fifth of the weight of said half dollar.

SEC. 3514. The standard for both gold and silver coins of the United States shall be such that of one thousand parts by weight nine hundred shall be of pure metal and one hundred of alloy. The alloy of the silver coins shall be of copper. The alloy of gold coins shall be of copper, or of copper and silver; but the silver shall in no case exceed one-tenth of the whole alloy.

SEC. 3515. The minor coins of the United States shall be a five-cent piece, a three-cent piece, and a one-cent piece. The alloy for the five and three cent pieces shall be of copper and nickel, to be composed of three-fourths copper and one-fourth nickel. The alloy of the one-cent piece shall be ninety-five per centum of copper and five per centum of tin and zinc, in such proportions as shall be determined by the Director of the Mint. The weight of the piece of five cents shall be seventy-seven and sixteen-hundredths grains troy; of the three-cent piece; thirty grains; and of the one-cent piece, forty-eight grains.

SEC. 3516. No coins, either of gold, silver, or minor coinage, shall hereafter be issued from the Mint other than those of the denominations, standards, and weights set forth in this Title.

SEC. 3517. Upon the coins there shall be the following devices and legends: Upon one side there shall be an impression emblematic of liberty, with an inscription of the word "Liberty" and the year of the coinage, and upon the reverse shall be the figure or representation of an eagle, with the inscriptions "United States of America" and "E Pluribus Unum," and the designation of the value of the coin; but on the gold dollar and three-dollar piece, the dime, five, three, and one cent piece, the figure of the eagle shall be omitted; and on the reverse of the silver trade-dollar the weight and the fineness of the coin shall be inscribed.

SEC. 3518. At the option of the owner gold or silver may be cast into bars of fine metal, or of standard fineness, or unparted, as he may prefer, with a stamp upon the same designating the weight and fineness, and with such devices impressed thereon as may be deemed expedient to prevent fraudulent imitation, and no such bars shall be issued of a less weight than five ounces.

SEC. 3519. Any owner of gold bullion may deposit the same at any mint, to be formed into coin or bars for his benefit. It shall be lawful, however, to refuse any deposit of less value than one hundred dollars, or any bullion so base as to be unsuitable for the operations of the Mint. In case where gold and silver are combined, if either metal be in such small proportion that it cannot be separated advantageously, no allowance shall be made to the depositor for its value.

SEC. 3520. Any owner of silver bullion may deposit the same at any mint, to be formed into bars, or into dollars of the weight of four hundred and twenty grains troy, designated in this Title as trade-dollars, and no deposit of silver for other coinage shall be received. Silver bullion contained in gold deposits, and separated therefrom, may, however, be paid for in silver coin, at such valuations as may be, from time to time, established by the Director of the Mint.

SEC. 3521. When bullion is deposited in any of the mints, it shall be weighed by the superintendent, and when practicable, in the presence of the depositor, to whom a receipt shall be given, which shall state the description and weight of the bullion. When, however, the bullion is in such a state as to require melting, or the removal of base metals, before its value can be ascertained, the weight, after such operation, shall be considered as the true weight of the bullion deposited. The fitness of the bullion to be received shall be determined by the assayer, and the mode of melting by the melter and refiner.

SEC. 3522. From every parcel of bullion deposited for coinage or bars, the superintendent shall deliver to the assayer a sufficient portion for the purpose of being assayed. The bullion remaining from the operations of the assay shall be returned to the superintendent by the assayer.

SEC. 3523. The assayer shall report to the superintendent the quality or fineness of the bullion assayed by him, and such information as will enable him to compute the amount of the charges hereinafter provided for, to be made to the depositor.

SEC. 3524. The charge for converting standard gold bullion into coin shall be one-fifth of one per centum. The charges for converting standard silver into trade-dollars for melting and refining when bullion is below standard, for toughening when metals are contained in it which render it unfit for coinage, for copper used for alloy when the bullion is above standard, for separating the gold and silver when these metals exist together in the bullion, and for the preparation of bars, shall be fixed, from time to time, by the Director, with the concurrence of the Secretary of the Treasury, so as to equal but not exceed, in their judgment, the actual average cost to each mint and assay-office of the material, labor, wastage, and use of machinery employed in each of the cases aforementioned.

SEC. 3525. The assayer shall verify all calculations made by the superintendent of the value of deposits, and, if satisfied of the correctness thereof, shall countersign the certificate required to be given by the superintendent to the depositor.

SEC. 3526. In order to procure bullion for the silver coinage authorized by this title, the superintendents, with the approval of the Director of the Mint, as to price, terms, and quantity, shall purchase such bullion with the bullion-fund. The gain arising from the coinage of such silver bullion into coin of a nominal value exceeding the cost thereof shall be credited to a special fund denominated the silver-profit fund. This fund shall be charged with the wastage incurred in the silver coinage, and with the expense of distributing such silver coins as hereinafter provided. The balance to the credit of this fund shall be from time to time, and at least twice a year, paid into the Treasury of the United States.

SEC. 3527. Silver coins other than the trade-dollar shall be paid out at the several mints, and at the assay-office in New York City, in exchange for gold coins at par, in sums not less than on hundred dollars. It shall be lawful, also, to transmit parcels of the same, from time to time, to the assistant treasurers, depositaries, and other officers of the United States, under general regulations proposed by the Director of the Mint, and approved by the Secretary of the Treasury. Nothing herein contained shall, however, prevent the payment of silver coins, at their nominal value, for silver parted from gold, as provided in this Title, or for change less than one dollar in settlement for gold deposits. But for two years after the twelfth day of February, eighteen hundred and seventy-three, silver coins shall be paid at the mint in Philadelphia, and the assay-office in New York City, for silver bullion purchased for coinage, under such regulations as may be prescribed by the Director of the Mint and approved by the Secretary of the Treasury.

SEC. 3528. For the purchase of metal for the minor coinage authorized by this Title, a sum not exceeding fifty thousand dollars in lawful money of the United States shall be transferred by the Secretary of the Treasury to the credit of the superintendent of the mint at Philadelphia, at which establishment only, until otherwise provided by law, such coinage shall be carried on. The superintendent, with the approval of the Director of the Mint as to price, terms, and quantity, shall purchase the metal required for such coinage by public advertisement, and the lowest and best bid shall be accepted, the fineness of the metals to be determined on the mint assay. The gain arising from the coinage of such metals into coin of a nominal value, exceeding the cost thereof, shall be credited to the special fund denominated the minor-coinage profit fund; and this fund shall be charged with the wastage incurred in such coinage, and with the cost of distributing said coins as hereinafter provided. The balance remaining to the credit of this fund, and any balance of profits accrued from minor coinage under former acts, shall be, from time to time, and at least twice a year, covered into the Treasury.

SEC. 3529. The minor coins authorized by this Title may, at the direction of the Director of the Mint, be delivered in any of the principal cities and towns of the United States, at the cost of the Mint, for transportation, and shall be exchangeable at par at the mint in Philadelphia, at the discretion of the superintendent, for any other coin of copper, bronze, or copper-nickel heretofore authorized by law. It shall be lawful for the Treasurer and the several assistant treasurers and depositaries of the United States to redeem, in lawful money, under such rules as may be prescribed by the Secretary of the Treasury, all copper, bronze, and copper-nickel coins authorized by law when presented in sums of not less than twenty dollars. Whenever, under this authority, these coins are presented for redemption in such quantity as to show the amount outstanding to be redundant, the Secretary of the Treasury is authorized and required to direct that such coinage shall cease until otherwise ordered by him.

SEC. 3530. Parcels of bullion shall be, from time to time, transferred by the superintendent to the melter and refiner. A careful record of these transfers, noting the weight and character of the bullion, shall be kept, and vouchers shall be taken for the delivery of the same, duly receipted by the melter and refiner. The bullion thus placed in the hands of the melter and refiner shall be subjected to the several processes which may be necessary to form it into ingots of the legal standard, and of a quality suitable for coinage.

SEC. 3531. The ingots so prepared shall be assayed. If they prove to be within the limits allowed for deviation from the standard, the assayer shall certify the fact to the superintendent, who shall thereupon receipt for the same, and transfer them to the coiner.

SEC. 3532. The superintendent shall, from time to time, deliver to the coiner ingots for the purpose of coinage. A careful record of these transfers, noting the weight and character of the bullion shall be kept, and vouchers shall be taken for the delivery of the same, duly receipted by the coiner. The ingots thus placed in the hands of the coiner shall be subjected to the several processes necessary to make from them coins in all respects conformable to law.

SEC. 3533. No ingots shall be used for coinage which differ from the legal standard more than the following proportions, namely: In gold ingots, one thousandth; in silver ingots, three thousandths; in minor-coinage alloys, twenty-five thousandths, in the proportion of nickel.

SEC. 3534. The melter and refiner shall prepare all bars required for the payment of deposits; but the fineness thereof shall be ascertained and stamped thereon by the assayer. The melter and refiner shall deliver such bars to the superintendent, who shall receipt for the same.

SEC. 3535. In adjusting the weights of the gold coins, the following deviations shall not be exceeded in any single piece: In the double-eagle and the eagle, one-half of a grain; in the half-eagle, the three-dollar piece, the quarter-eagle, and the one-dollar piece, one-fourth of a grain. And in weighing a number of pieces together, when delivered by the coiner to the superintendent, and by the superintendent to the depositor, the deviation from the standard weight shall not exceed one hundredth of an ounce in five thousand dollars in double-eagles, eagles, half-eagles, or quarter-eagles, in one thousand three-dollar pieces, and in one thousand one-dollar pieces.

SEC. 3536. In adjusting the weight of the silver coins the following deviations shall not be exceeded in any single piece: In the dollar, the half and quarter dollar, and in the dime, one and one-half grains. And in weighing large number of pieces together, when delivered by the coiner to the superintendent, and by the superintendent to the depositor, the deviations from the standard weight shall not exceed two-hundredths of an ounce in one thousand dollars, half-dollars, or quarter-dollars, and one-hundredth of an ounce in one thousand dimes.

SEC. 3537. In adjusting the weight of the minor coins provided by this Title, there shall be no greater deviation allowed than three grains for the five-cent piece and two grains for the three and one cent pieces.

SEC. 3538. The coiner shall, from time to time, as coins are prepared, deliver them to the superintendent, who shall receipt for the same, and who shall keep a careful record of their kind, number, and actual weight. In receiving coins it shall be the duty of the superintendent to ascertain, by the trial of a number of single pieces separately, whether the coins of that delivery are within the legal limits of the standard weight; and if his trials for this purpose shall not prove satisfactory, he shall cause all the coins of such delivery to be weighed separately, and such as are not of legal weight shall be defaced and delivered to the melter and refiner as standard bullion, to be again formed into ingots and recoined; or the whole delivery may, if more convenient, be remelted.

SEC. 3539. At every delivery of coins made by the coiner to a superintendent, it shall be the duty of such superintendent, in the presence of the assayer, to take indiscriminately a certain number of pieces of each variety for the annual trial of coins, the number for gold coins being not less than one piece for each one thousand pieces or any fractional part of one thousand pieces delivered; and for silver coins one piece for each two thousand pieces or any fractional part of two thousand pieces delivered.

The pieces so taken shall be carefully sealed up in an envelope, properly labeled, stating the date of the delivery, the number and denomination of the pieces inclosed, and the amount of the delivery from which they were taken. These sealed parcels containing the reserved pieces shall be deposited in a pyx, designated for the purpose at each mint, which shall be kept under the joint care of the superintendent and assayer, and be so secured that neither can have access to its contents without the presence of the other, and the reserved pieces in their sealed envelopes from the coinage of each mint shall be transmitted quarterly to the mint in Philadelphia. A record shall also be kept at the same time of the number and denomination of the pieces so taken for the annual trial of coins, and of the number and denominations of the pieces represented by them and so delivered, a copy of which record shall be transmitted quarterly to the Director of the Mint. Other pieces may, at any time, be taken for such tests as the Director of the Mint shall prescribe.

SEC. 3540. The coiner shall, from time to time, deliver to the superintendent the clippings and other portions of bullion remaining after the process of coining; and the superintendent shall receipt for the same and keep a careful record of their weight and character.

SEC. 3541. The superintendent shall debit the coiner with the amount in weight of standard metal of all the bullion placed in his hands, and credit him with the amount in weight of all the coins, clippings, and other bullion returned by him to the superintendent. Once at least in every year, and at such time as the Director of the Mint shall appoint, there shall be an accurate and full settlement of the accounts of the coiner, and the melter and refiner, at which time those officer shall deliver up to the superintendent all the coins, clippings, and other bullion in their possession, respectively, accompanied by statements of all the bullion delivered to them since the last annual settlement, and all the bullion returned by them during the same period, including the amount returned for the purpose of settlement.

SEC. 3542. When all the coins, clippings, and other bullion have been delivered to the superintendent, it shall be his duty to examine the accounts and statements rendered by the coiner and the melter and refiner. The difference between the amount charged and credited to each officer shall be allowed as necessary wastage, if the superintendent shall be satisfied that there has been a bona-fide waste of the precious metals, and if the amount shall not exceed, in the case of the melter and refiner, one thousandth of the whole amount of gold, and one and one-half thousandths of the whole amount of silver delivered to him since the last annual settlement, and in the case of the coiner, one-thousandth of the whole amount of silver, and one-half thousandth of the whole amount of gold that has been delivered to him by the superintendent. All copper used in the alloy of gold and silver bullion shall be separately charged to the melter and refiner, and accounted for by him.

SEC. 3543. It shall also be the duty of the superintendent to forward a correct statement of his balance-sheet, at the close of such settlement, to the Director of the Mint; who shall compare the total amount of gold and silver bullion and coin on hand with the total liabilities of the mint. At the same time a statement of the ordinary expense account, and the moneys therein, shall also be made by the superintendent.

SEC. 3544. When the coins or bars which are the equivalent to any deposit of bullion are ready for delivery, they shall be paid to the depositor, or his order, by the superintendent; and the payments shall be made, if demanded, in the order in which the bullion shall have been brought to the mint. In cases, however, where there is delay in manipulating a refractory deposit, or for any other unavoidable cause, the payment of subsequent deposits, the value of which is known, shall not be delayed thereby. In the denominations of coin delivered, the superintendent shall comply with the wishes of the depositor, except when impracticable or inconvenient to do so.

SEC 3545. For the purpose of enabling the mints and the assay-office in New York to make returns to depositors with as little delay as possible, it shall be the duty of the Secretary of the Treasury to keep in such mints and assay-office, when the state of the Treasury will admit thereof, such an amount of public money, or bullion procured for the purpose, as he shall judge convenient and necessary, out of which those who bring bullion to the said mints and assay-office may be paid the value thereof, in coin or bars, as soon as practicable after the value has been ascertained. On payment thereof being made, the bullion so deposited shall become the property of the United States. The Secretary of the Treasury may, however, at any time withdraw the fund, or any portion thereof.

SEC. 3546. Unparted bullion may be exchanged at any of the mints for fine bars, on such terms and conditions as may be prescribed by the Director of the Mint, with the approval of the Secretary of the Treasury. The fineness, weight, and value of the bullion received and given in exchange shall in all cases be determined by the Mint assay. The charge to the depositor for refining or parting shall not exceed that allowed and deducted for the same operation in the exchange of unrefined for refined bullion.

SEC. 3547. To secure a due conformity in the gold and silver coins to their respective standards of fineness and weight, the judge of the district court for the eastern district of Pennsylvania, the Comptroller of the Currency, the assayer of the assay-office at New York, and such other persons as the President shall, from time to time, designate, shall meet as assay-commissioners, at the mint in Philadelphia, to examine and test, in the presence of the Director of the Mint, the fineness and weight of the coins reserved by the several mints for this purpose, on the second Wednesday in February, annually, and may continue their meeting by adjournment, if necessary. If a majority of the commissioners fail to attend at any time appointed for their meeting, the Director of the Mint shall call a meeting of the commissioners at such other time as he may deem convenient. If it appears by such examination and test that these coins do not differ from the standard fineness and weight by a greater quantity than is allowed by law, the trial shall be considered and reported as satisfactory. If, however, any greater deviation from the legal standard or weight appears, this fact shall be certified to the President; and if, on a view of the circumstances of the case, he shall so decide, the officers implicated in the error shall be thenceforward disqualified from holding their respective offices.

SEC. 3548. For the purpose of securing a due conformity in weight of the coins of the United States to the provisions of this Title, the brass troy-pound weight procured by the minister of the United States at London, in the year eighteen hundred and twenty-seven, for the use of the Mint, and now in the custody of the mint in Philadelphia, shall be the standard troy pound of the Mint of the United States, conformably to which the coinage thereof shall be regulated.

SEC. 3549. It shall be the duty of the Director of the Mint to procure for each mint and assay-office, to be kept safely thereat, a series of standard weights corresponding to the standard troy pound of the Mint of the United States, consisting of a one-pound weight and the requisite subdivisions and multiples thereof, from the hundredth part of a grain to twenty-five pounds. The troy weight ordinarily employed in the transaction of such mints and assay-offices shall be regulated according to the above standards at least once in every year, under the inspection of the superintendent and assayer; and the accuracy of those used a the mint at Philadelphia shall be tested annually, in the presence of the assay-commissioners, at the time of the annual examination and test of coins.

SEC. 3550. The obverse working dies at each mint shall, at the end of each calendar year, be defaced and destroyed by the coiner in the presence of the superintendent and assayer.

SEC. 3551. Dies of a national character may be executed by the engraver, and national and other medals struck by the coiner of the mint at Philadelphia, under such regulations as the superintendent, with the approval of the Director of the Mint, may prescribe. Such work shall not, however, interfere with the regular coinage operations, and no private medal dies shall be prepared at any mint, or the machinery or apparatus thereof be used for that purpose.

SEC. 3552. The moneys arising from all charges and deductions on and from gold and silver bullion and the manufacture of medals, and from all other sources, except as provided by this Title, shall, from time to time, be covered into the Treasury, and no part of such deductions or metal charges, or profit on silver or minor coinage, shall be expended in salaries or wages. All expenditures of the mints and assay-offices, not herein otherwise provided for, shall be paid from appropriations made by law on estimates furnished by the Secretary of the Treasury.

SEC. 3553. The business of the United States assay-office at New York shall be in all respects similar to that of the mints, except that bars only, and not coin, shall be manufactured therein; and no metals shall be purchased for minor coinage. All bullion intended by the depositor to be converted into coins, of the United States, and silver bullion purchased for coinage, when assayed, parted, and refined, and its net value certified, shall be transferred to the mint at Philadelphia, under such directions as shall be made by the Secretary of the Treasury, at the expense of the contingent fund of the Mint, and shall be there coined, and the proceeds returned to the assay-office. And the Secretary of the Treasury is hereby authorized to make the necessary arrangements for the adjustment of the accounts upon such transfers between the respective offices.

SEC. 3554. The officers of the assay-office at New York shall be a superintendent, an assayer, and a melter and refiner; each of whom shall be appointed by the President, by and with the advice and consent of the Senate.

SEC. 3555. The duties of the superintendent, the assayer, and the melter and refiner of the assay-office at New York shall correspond to those of superintendents, assayers, and melters and refiners of mints; and all the provisions of this Title relating to mints and their officers, the duties and responsibilities of such officers, and others employed therein, the oaths to be taken, and the bonds and sureties to be given by them, shall extend, as far as the same may be applicable, to the assay-office at New York, and to its officers, clerks, and employés.

SEC. 3556. The officers of the assay-office at New York shall be entitled to the following salaries:

First. The superintendent, to four thousand five hundred dollars a year.

Second. The assayer, to three thousand dollars a year.

Third. The melter and refiner, to three thousand dollars.

SEC. 3557. The appointment and compensation of assistants, clerks, and workmen in the assay-office at New York shall be regulated in the same manner as is prescribed in regard to mints.

SEC. 3558. The business of the mint of the United States at Denver, while conducted as an assay-office, that of the United States assay-office at Boise City, and that of any other assay-offices hereafter established, shall be confined to the receipt of gold and silver bullion, for melting and assaying, to be returned to depositors of the same, in bars, with the weight and fineness stamped thereon.

SEC. 3559. The officers of the assay-offices embraced by the preceding section shall be, when their respective services are required, an assayer and a melter; each of whom shall be appointed by the President, by and with the advice and consent of the Senate. Their salaries shall not exceed two thousand five hundred dollars a year each.

SEC. 3560. The assayer at each of the assay-offices embraced by section thirty-five hundred and fifty-eight, shall have general charge of the office; and may employ, under the direction of the Director of the Mint, such clerks, workmen, and laborers as may be authorized therefore by law; and shall discharge the duties of disbursing agent for the expenses of the office under his charge. The salaries paid to clerks shall not exceed one thousand eight hundred dollars a year each. Workmen and laborers shall receive such wages as are customary according to their respective stations and occupations.

SEC. 3561. Each officer and clerk appointed at either of the assay-offices embraced by section thirty-five hundred and fifty-eight shall, before entering upon the duties of his office, take an oath pursuant to the provisions of Title XIX, "PROVISIONS APPLYING TO SEVERAL CLASSES OF OFFICERS," and shall give a bond to the United States, with one or more sureties, satisfactory to the Director of the Mint or to one of the judges of the supreme court of the State or Territory in which the office to which he is appointed is located, conditioned for the faithful performance of his duties.

SEC. 3562. All provisions of law for the regulation of mints, the government of officers and persons employed therein, and for the punishment of all offenses connected with mints or coinage, shall extend to all assay-offices as far as applicable.

SEC. 3563. The money of account of the United States shall be expressed in dollars or units, dimes or tenths, cents, or hundredths, and mills or thousandths, a dime being the tenth part of a dollar, a cent the hundredth part of a dollar, a mill the thousandth part of a dollar; and all accounts in the public offices and all proceedings in the courts shall be kept and had in conformity to this regulation.

SEC. 3564. The value of foreign coin as expressed in the money of account of the United States shall be that of the pure metal of such coin of standard value; and the values of the standard coins in circulation of the various nations of the world shall be estimated annually by the Director of the Mint, and be proclaimed on the first day of January by the Secretary of the Treasury.

SEC. 3565. In all payments by or to the Treasury, whether made here or in foreign countries, where it becomes necessary to compute the value of the sovereign or pound sterling, it shall be deemed equal to four dollars eighty-six cents and six and one-half mills, and the same rule shall be applied in appraising merchandise imported where the value is, by the invoice, in sovereigns or pounds sterling, and in the construction of contracts payable in sovereigns or pounds sterling; and this valuation shall be the par of exchange between Great Britain and the United States; and all contracts made after the first day of January, eighteen hundred and seventy-four, based on an assumed par of exchange with Great Britain of fifty-four pence to the dollar, or four dollars forty-four and four-ninths cents to the sovereign or pound sterling, shall be null and void.

SEC. 3566. All foreign gold and silver coins received in payment for moneys due to the United States shall, before being issued in circulation, be coined anew.

SEC. 3567. The pieces commonly known as the quarter, eighth, and sixteenth of the Spanish pillar dollar, and of the Mexican dollar, shall be receivable at the Treasury of the United States, and its several offices, and at the several post-offices and land-offices, at the rates of valuation following: the fourth of a dollar, or piece of two reals, at twenty cents; the eighth of a dollar, or piece of one real, at ten cents; and the sixteenth of a dollar, or half-real, at five cents.

SEC. 3568. The Director of the Mint, with the approval of the Secretary of the Treasury, may prescribe such regulations as are necessary and proper, to secure the transmission of the coins mentioned in the preceding section to the mint for recoinage, and the * (re)turn or distribution of the proceeds thereof, when deemed expedient, and may prescribe such forms of account as are appropriate and applicable to the circumstances. The expenses incident to such transmission or distribution, and of recoinage, shall be charged against the account of silver profit and loss, and the net profits, if any, shall be paid, from time to time, into the Treasury.

COUNTERFEITING COIN.

SEC. 5457. Every person who falsely makes, forges, or counterfeits, or causes, or procures to be falsely made, forge, or counterfeited, or willingly aids, or assists in falsely making, forging, or counterfeiting any coin or bars in resemblance or similitude of the gold or silver coins or bars which have been, or hereafter may be, coined or stamped at the mints and assay-offices of the United States, or in resemblance or similitude of any foreign gold or silver coin which by law is, or hereafter may be made, current in the United States, or are in actual use and circulation as money within the United States, or who passes, utters, publishes, or sells, or attempts to pass, utter, publish, or sell, or bring into the United States from any foreign place, or has in his possession, any such false, forged, or counterfeited coin or bars, knowing the same to be false, forged, or counterfeited shall be punished by a fine or not more than five thousand dollars and by imprisonment at hard labor not more than ten years.

SEC. 5458. Every person who falsely makes, forges, or counterfeits, or causes, or procures to be falsely made, forged, or counterfeited, or willingly aids, or assists in falsely making, forging, or counterfeiting, any coin in the resemblance or similitude of any of the minor coinage which has been, or hereafter may be, coined at the mints of the United States; or who passes, utters, publishes, or sells, or brings into the United States from any foreign place, or has in his possession, any such false, forged, or counterfeited coin, with intent to defraud any person whatsoever, shall be punished by a fine of not more than one thousand dollars and by imprisonment at hard labor not more than three years.

SEC. 5459. Every person who fraudulently, by any art, way, or means, defaces, mutilates, impairs, diminishes, falsifies, scales, or lightens the gold and silver coins which have been, or which may hereafter be, coined at the mints of the United States, or any foreign gold or silver coins which are by law made current or are in actual use and circulation as money within the United States, shall be imprisoned not more than two years and fined not more than two thousand dollars.

SEC. 5460. If any of the gold or silver coins struck or coined at any of the mints of the United States shall be debased, or made worse as to the proportion of fine gold or fine silver therein contained; or shall be of less weight or value than the same ought to be, pursuant to law; or if any of the weights used at any of the mints or assay-offices of the United States shall be defaced, increased, or diminished through the fault or connivance of any of the officers or persons who are employed at the said mints or assay-offices, with a fraudulent intent; and if any of the said officers or persons shall embezzle any of the metals at any time committed to their charge for the purpose of being coined, or any of the coins struck or coined at the said mints, or any medals, coins, or other moneys of said mints or assay-offices at any time committed to their charge, or of which they may have assumed the charge, every such officer or person who commits any or either of the said offenses shall be imprisoned at hard labor for a term not less than one year nor more than ten years, and shall be fined in a sum not more than ten thousand dollars.

SEC. 5461. Every person who, except as authorized by law, makes, or causes to be made, or utters or passes, or attempts to utter or pass, any coins of gold or silver or other metal, or alloys of metals, intended for the use and purpose of current money, whether in the resemblance of coins of the United States or of foreign countries, or of original design, shall be punished by fine of not more than three thousand dollars, or by imprisonment not more than five years, or both.

SEC. 5462. Every person not lawfully authorized, who makes, issues, or passes, or causes to be made, issued, or passed, any coin, card, token or device in metal or its compounds, which may be intended to be used as money for any one-cent, two-cent, three-cent, or five-cent piece, now or hereafter authorized by law, or for coins of equal value, shall be punished by a fine of not more than one thousand dollars and by imprisonment not more than five years.

PAYMENTS BY OR TO THE UNITED STATES.

SEC. 3473. All duties on imports shall be paid in gold and silver coin only, or in demand Treasury notes, issued under the authority of the acts of July seventeen, eighteen hundred and sixty-one, chapter five; and February twelve, eighteen hundred and sixty-two, chapter twenty; and all taxes and all other debts and demands than duties on imports, accruing or becoming due to the United States, shall be paid in gold and silver coin, Treasury notes, United States notes, or notes of national banks; and upon every such payment credit shall be given for the amount of principal and interest due on any Treasury note not received in payment on the day when the same are received.

SEC. 3474. No gold or silver other than coin of standard fineness of the United States, shall be receivable in payment of dues to the United States, except as provided in section twenty-three hundred and sixty-six, Title "Public Lands," and in section thirty-five hundred and sixty-seven, Title "Coinage, Weights, and Measures."

LEGAL TENDER.

SEC. 3584. No foreign gold or silver coins shall be a legal tender in payment of debts.

SEC. 3585. The gold coins of the United States shall be a legal tender in all payments at their nominal value when not below the standard weight and limit of tolerance provided by law for the single piece, and, when reduced in weight below such standard and tolerance, shall be a legal tender at valuation in proportion to their actual weight.

SEC. 3586. The silver coins of the United States shall be a legal tender at their nominal value for any amount not exceeding five dollars in any one payment.

SEC. 3587. The minor coins of the United States shall be a legal tender at their nominal value for any amount not exceeding twenty-five cents in any one payment.

SEC. 3700. The Secretary of the Treasury may purchase coin with any of the bonds or notes of the United States, authorized by law, at such rates and upon such terms as he may deem most advantageous to the public interest.

NOTES

Chapter 1. Rush To Washoe

1. Eliot Lord, *Comstock Mining and Miners* (Washington, DC: Government Printing Office, 1883; reprint ed., Berkeley, CA: Howell-North Press, 1959), p. 12
2. Dan De Quille, *The Big Bonanza: An Authentic Account of the Discovery, History, and Working of the World-Renowned Comstock Lode of Nevada Including the Present Condition of the Various Mines Situated Thereon—Sketches of the Most Prominent Men Interested in Them—Incidents and Adventures Connected With Mining, the Indians, and the Country—Amusing Stories, Experiences, Anecdotes, etc., etc. and a Full Exposition of the Production of Pure Silver* (Hartford, CT: American Publishing Co., 1876; reprint ed., New York: Apollo Editions, 1969), p. 10.
3. See Lord, *Comstock Mining and Miners*, p. 26 and De Quille, *The Big Bonanza*, p. 14. Lord places the Grosh brothers crossing the Sierra Nevada in 1853. De Quille, who gives their name as Grosch, has them crossing the year prior.
4. Lord, *Comstock Mining and Miners*, p. 27. The letters were published by Lord in his 1883 work prepared as part of a series of monographs for the U.S. Geological Survey.
5. Ibid., pp. 27-28.
6. Ibid., p. 31.
7. De Quille, *The Big Bonanza*, p. 19. Some historians have argued that the silver the ill-fated brothers discovered was not connected to the main body of the Comstock but, rather, with a low-grade ore vein around Silver City. Yet, these discoveries pointed to what lie ahead—the true outcroppings of the now fabled lode.
8. Lord, *Comstock Mining and Miners*, p. 24. Lord provides a table of average earnings for the period.
9. De Quille, *The Big Bonanza*, p. 23.
10. Ibid., p. 27.
11. De Quille estimated that the take was as much as $1,000 per day, with a single pan, in some spots, bringing in $50 to $150. Because of its adulteration with silver, the gold was worth in the range of $11 an ounce. See De Quille, *The Big Bonanza*, p. 30.
12. In return for the arrastras, Osborn and Winters received a two-sixth interest in the Comstock partners' original 1,400 feet that had been split between Comstock, Penrod, O'Riley and McLaughlin. Lord, *Comstock Mining and Miners*, p. 55.
13. Although some historians have disputed the figures, the assayer later claimed that the ore assayed at $3,876 to a ton—three-quarters silver and one-quarter gold. See Grant H. Smith, *The History of the Comstock Lode*, for example. Lord, in *Comstock Mining and Miners*, breaks it down as $3,000 in silver and $876 in gold per ton.
14. Lord, *Comstock Mining and Miners*, p. 71.
15. J. Ross Browne, *Crusoe's Island: Ramble in the footsteps of Alexander Selkirk. With Sketches of Adventure in California and Washoe.* (New York: Harper Brothers, 1864), p. 390.
16. Ibid., p. 370.
17. Ibid.
18. De Quille, *The Big Bonanza*, p. 34.
19. Lord, *Comstock Mining and Miners*, pp. 56-57.
20. Browne, pp. 372-374.
21. Ibid., pp. 377-378.

Chapter 2. Heady Times

1. Eliot Lord, *Comstock Mining and Miners* (Washington, DC: Government Printing Office, 1883; reprint ed., Berkeley, CA: Howell-North Press, 1959), p. 62.
2. Ibid.
3. Grant H. Smith, *The History of the Comstock Lode* (Reno, NV: University of Nevada Press, 1943; reprint ed., Reno, NV: University of Nevada Press, 1998), p.16.
4. Dan De Quille, *The Big Bonanza: An Authentic Account of the Discovery, History, and Working of the World-Renowned Comstock Lode of Nevada Including the Present Condition of the Various Mines Situated Thereon—Sketches of the Most Prominent Men Interested in Them—Incidents and Adventures Connected With Mining, the Indians, and the Country—Amusing Stories, Experiences, Anecdotes, etc., etc. and a Full Exposition of the Production of Pure Silver* (Hartford, CT: American Publishing Co., 1876; reprint ed., New York: Apollo Editions, 1969), p. 90.
5. Rodman Paul, *Mining Frontiers of the Far West 1848-1880* (New York: Holt, Rinehart and Winston, 1963), p. 66.
6. De Quille, *The Big Bonanza*, p. 92.
7. T.A. Rickard, *A History of American Mining* (New York: McGraw-Hill Book Co. Inc., 1932), p. 102. The Feb. 6, 1875, *Alta California* gives a good indication of the waste associated with milling. In referring to a new amalgamation process invented by Abel Patchen of San Francisco, which was tested at the San Francisco Assaying and Refining Company,

company manager Louis A. Garnett related that with the new process, 95 percent of all of the gold and silver in the ore was saved, whereas, by the ordinary process, just 70 percent would have been realized. The article added: "The reports of the Hale and Norcross mine show that in eight years 299,000 tons were milled and only $25 16 were obtained from each ton on an average, though the assay value was $38 27. The yield was less than 66 per cent. of the assay value." See, "The New Amalgamating Process," *Alta California*, 6 February 1875.

8. Ira B. Cross, *Financing an Empire: History of Banking in California* (New York: S.J. Clarke Publishing Co., 1927), vol. 1, p. 238.
9. J. Wells Kelly, ed., *First Directory of Nevada Territory Containing the Names of Residents in the Principal Towns; A Historical Sketch, the Organic Act, and Other Political Matters of Interest; Together with a Description of all the Quartz Mills; Reduction Works, and all Other Industrial Establishments in the Territory; of the Leading Mining Claims, and Various Mineral Discoveries, Works of Internal Improvement, et with a Table of Distances, Lists of Public Officers and Other Useful Information* (San Francisco: Valentine & Co., 1862; reprint ed., The Talisman Press, 1962.), pp. 14-15.
10. Cross, *Financing,* p. 238.
11. Ibid.
12. Mark Twain, *Roughing It* (Hartford, CT: American Publishing Co., 1891), p. 193.
13. Ibid., pp. 238-239, quoting T.R. Jones, "What Was in California Fifty Years Ago," *Grizzly Bear*, vol. XIII-XIV, p. 4.
14. Joseph L. King, *History of the San Francisco Stock and Exchange Board* (San Francisco: By the author, 1910), pp. 245-248.
15. De Quille, *The Big Bonanza,* p. 115.
16. Hubert H. Bancroft, *The Works of Hubert Howe Bancroft*, vol. 25: *History of Nevada, Colorado, and Wyoming*, 1540-1888 (History Company Publishers, 1890), p. 671.
17. De Quille, *The Big Bonanza*, p. 115; Bancroft, *History of Nevada*, p. 672.
18. Lord, *Comstock Mining and Miners*, p. 428; Smith, *The History*, pp. 132-133. Smith claims the stock boom started with Alvinza Hayward, who, Smith says, deliberately drove up Savage stock, dragging the 150 other stocks on board with it, partly to help out the Senatorial bid of his partner, John P. Jones. The so-called "Boom of 1872," Smith says, broke in May 1872 when William Sharon, who was running against Jones for the Senate, floated a false story that Jones had started the deadly fire at the Yellow Jacket mine in April 1869 to force stock prices down. See Smith, *The History*, pp. 132-133.
19. King, *The History of San Francisco Stock and Exchange Board,* p. 200.
20. Lord, *Comstock Mining and Miners,* p. 289.
21. Ibid.
22. "Mining Intelligence," *Virginia City Territorial Enterprise*, 16 February 1869.
23. "Mining Intelligence," *Virginia City Territorial Enterprise*, 18 February 1869.
24. Lord, *Comstock Mining and Miners*, p. 290.
25. Ibid., pp. 290-291.
26. According to Rodman Paul, half of the total production of the Comstock came from two pair of adjacent mines that also produced four-fifths of the dividends—the Crown Point and Belcher, and the Consolidated Virginia and California. See Paul, *Mining Frontiers*, p. 62.
27. See "Production of Comstock Mines from 1859 to January 1, 1882," Smith, *The History*, pp. 310-311.

The $40,000 Shave

1. Joseph L. King, *History of the San Francisco Stock and Exchange Board* (San Francisco: By the author, 1910), pp. 131-132.
2. Ibid., pp. 135-136.

Chapter 3. Dangers Below

1. *Virginia City Territorial Enterprise,* 6 July 1882.
2. *Virginia City Territorial Enterprise,* 13 August 1882.
3. Eliot Lord, *Comstock Mining and Miners* (Washington, DC: Government Printing Office, 1883; reprint ed., Berkeley, CA: Howell-North Press, 1959), p. 404.
4. T.H. Watkins, *Gold and Silver in the West* (New York: Bonanza Books, 1971), p. 209.
5. Grant H. Smith, *The History of the Comstock Lode* (Reno, NV: University of Nevada Press, 1943; reprint ed, Reno, NV.: University of Nevada Press, 1998), p. 75.
6. *Virginia City Territorial Enterprise,* 25 November 1882.
7. Lord, *Comstock Mining and Miners*, p. 394.
8. *Virginia City Territorial Enterprise,* 6 January 1882.
9. Ibid.
10. *Virginia City Territorial Enterprise,* 3 February 1882.
11. Dan De Quille, *The Big Bonanza: An Authentic Account of the Discovery, History, and Working of the World-Renowned Comstock Lode of Nevada Including the Present Condition of the Various Mines Situated Thereon—Sketches of the Most Prominent Men Interested in Them—Incidents and Adventures Connected With Mining, the Indians, and the Country—Amusing Stories, Experiences, Anecdotes, etc., etc. and a Full Exposition of the Production of Pure Silver* (Hartford, CT: American Publishing Co., 1876; reprint ed., New York: Apollo Editions, 1969), pp. 146-147.

12. Joseph L. King, *History of the San Francisco Stock and Exchange Board* (San Francisco: By the author, 1910), p. 192.
13. *Virginia City Territorial Enterprise,* 25 February 1882.
14. Ibid.
15. Lord, *Comstock Mining and Miners*, p. 394.
16. Smith, *The History*, pp. 230-231.
17. Ibid., p. 235.

Chapter 4. Awful Calamity

1. "Awful Calamity," *Virginia City Territorial Enterprise,* 8 April 1869.
2. "An Awful Calamity in Our Mines," *Virginia City Territorial Enterprise*, 8 April 1869.
3. Ibid.
4. Ibid.
5. Ibid.
6. "The Gold Hill Calamity," *Virginia City Territorial Enterprise,* 10 April 1869.
7. "The Gold Hill Disaster," *Virginia City Territorial Enterprise,* 17 April 1869.
8. "Awful Calamity in Our Mines," *Virginia City Territorial Enterprise,* 8 April 1869.
9. Ibid. The April 8 issue of the *Virginia City Territorial Enterprise* gives the last names of the three brothers as Bicknell. John is identified as James there, as well. The use of "Bickle" and "John" are based on subsequent editions, including accounts of the coroner's inquest and funeral.
10. Ibid.
11. Ibid.
12. "The Gold Hill Mining Calamity," *Virginia City Territorial Enterprise,* 9 April 1869.
13. Ibid.
14. "The Gold Hill Calamity," *Virginia City Territorial Enterprise,* 10 April 1869.
15. "The Gold Hill Calamity," *Virginia City Territorial Enterprise,* 11 April 1869.
16. "The Yellow Jacket Mine," *Virginia City Territorial Enterprise,* 20 April 1869.
17. "The Burning Mines in Gold Hill," *Virginia City Territorial Enterprise,* 14 April 1869.
18. "Malicious Rumors," *Virginia City Territorial Enterprise,* 13 April 1869.
19. "Yellow Jacket Election," *Virginia City Territorial Enterprise,* 20 April 1869.

Chapter 5. Sutro's Tunnel

1. Eliot Lord, *Comstock Mining and Miners* (Washington, DC: Government Printing Office, 1883; reprint ed., Berkeley, CA: Howell-North Press, 1959), p. 233.
2. Sutro Tunnel advertisement, *Virginia City Territorial Enterprise*, 3 September 1869.
3. Ibid.
4. "Speech of Adolph Sutro," *Virginia City Territorial Enterprise*, 23 September 1869.
5. Lord, *Comstock Mining and Miners*, p. 232.
6. "Speech of Adolph Sutro," *Virginia City Territorial Enterprise*, 23 September 1869.
7. Lord, *Comstock Mining and Miners*, p. 236.
8. "Speech of Adolph Sutro," *Virginia City Territorial Enterprise*, 23 September 1869.
9. Lord, *Comstock Mining and Miners*, p. 236.
10. David Lavender, *Nothing Seemed Impossible: William C. Ralston and Early San Francisco* (Palo Alta, CA: American West Publishing Co., 1975), p. 233.
11. Ibid.
12. "Speech of Adolph Sutro," *Virginia City Territorial Enterprise*, 23 September 1869.
13. Ibid.
14. Ibid.
15. Lord, *Comstock Mining and Miners*, p. 298.
16. Grant H. Smith, *The History of the Comstock Lode* (Reno, NV: University of Nevada Press, 1943; reprint ed, Reno, NV: University of Nevada Press, 1998), p. 110.
17. "Speech of Adolph Sutro," *Virginia City Territorial Enterprise*, 23 September 1869.
18. Ibid.
19. Ibid.
20. Ibid.
21. "A Few Words of Comment," *Virginia City Territorial Enterprise*, 23 September 1869.
22. Smith, *The History*, p. 111.
23. Ibid.
24. Ibid.

Chapter 6. The Crookedest Road

1. David Lavender, *Nothing Seemed Impossible: William C. Ralston and Early San Francisco* (Palo Alto, CA: American West Publishing Co., 1975), p. 269.

2. Grant H. Smith, *The History of the Comstock Lode* (Reno, NV: University of Nevada Press, 1943; reprint ed., Reno, NV: University of Nevada Press, 1998), p. 123. Smith put the cost of hauling the ore by wagon at $4 per ton.
3. Cecil G. Tilton, *William Chapman: Courageous Builder* (Boston: The Christopher Publishing House, 1935), p.149.
4. *Virginia City Territorial Enterprise*, 20 February 1869.
5. Eliot Lord, *Comstock Mining and Miners* (Washington, DC: Government Printing Office, 1883; reprint ed., Berkeley, CA: Howell-North Press, 1959), p. 251.
6. George Lyman, *Ralston's Ring: California Plunders the Comstock Lode* (New York: Charles Scribner's Sons, 1937), p. 338. He quotes from *Gold Hill News*, 13 November 1869.
7. Dan De Quille, *The Big Bonanza: An Authentic Account of the Discovery, History, and Working of the World-Renowned Comstock Lode of Nevada Including the Present Condition of the Various Mines Situated Thereon—Sketches of the Most Prominent Men Interested in Them—Incidents and Adventures Connected With Mining, the Indians, and the Country—Amusing Stories, Experiences, Anecdotes, etc., etc. and a Full Exposition of the Production of Pure Silver* (Hartford, CT: American Publishing Co., 1876; reprint ed., New York: Apollo Editions, 1969), pp.165-166.
8. *Virginia City Territorial Enterprise*, 19 October 1869.
9. Lord, *Comstock Mining and Miners*, p. 255.

Chapter 7. Empire Builder

1. David Lavender, *Nothing Seemed Impossible: William C. Ralston and Early San Francisco* (Palo Alto, CA: American West Publishing Co., 1975), p. 62.
2. Julian Dana, *The Man Who Built San Francisco: A Study of Ralston's Journey with Banners* (New York: Macmillan Co., 1936), p. 50.
3. Ibid., p. 74.
4. Ibid., p. 87. Others claim similar amounts. Lavender, however, gives the total in gold on board the ship at much higher, $462,770.31, but does not provide a source for this figure.
5. The *Brother Jonathan* was another ill-fated steamer. It would sink a little more than a decade later with more than 230 passengers and a golden cargo on board. For a lengthy and well-researched account of the *Yankee Blade*, including subsequent attempts to recover its valuable cargo, see Q. David Bower's *American Coin Treasures and Hoards*. The *Brother Jonathan's* loss and its cargo of rare gold bars are recounted in another work by this prolific numismatic author, *The Treasure Ship S.S. Brother Jonathan: Her Life and Loss 1850-1865*.
6. Lavender, *Nothing Seemed Impossible*, p. 128.
7. Ibid., p. 203.
8. Cecil G. Tilton, *William Chapman: Courageous Builder* (Boston: The Christopher Publishing House, 1935), p. 145. Tilton details the various mills that came under the bank's control. His top figure is a $225,000 cost on the Real Del Monte, a 30-stamp mill.
9. Lavender, *Nothing Seemed Impossible*, p. 233.
10. Ibid., p. 187. Lavender notes that the Yellow Jacket made $6 million over three years but that, strangely, only $320,000 of this sum was ever distributed as dividends, while $300,000 was levied in assessments to make capital improvements. He credited the lack of dividends to Sharon's manipulation of the stock market, by declaring small dividends or assessments to eke the market in the direction he wanted, at the expense of investors.
11. Dana, *The Man*, p. 149.
12. Lavender, *Nothing Seemed Impossible*, p. 325.
13. Hirobumi Ito was also in the United States as part of the delegation that visited Belmont in January 1872. Lavender suggests it was at that time that Ito was shown the coinage bill by Ralston, discussing with Ralston his ideas for changing to a metric system based on the gold yen. However, by 1872, the first yen had been produced and the Japanese had already established a gold standard. It is likely Lavender became slightly confused as to the time periods involved, after viewing reference to Ito's visit in the 1964 work by T.F.M Adams and Awao Hoshii, *A Financial History of Modern Japan*, to which Lavender footnotes. Ito had been sent to the United States in 1870 to study Western currency systems. Following his return to Japan, he was named head of Japan's National Mint. See Adams and Hoshii, *A Financial History* (Tokyo: Thomas Francis Morton Adams Research, 1964), p. 5.
14. Lavender, p. 326-327.

Chapter 8. Origins of a Crime

1. U.S. Congress, House, *Report of the Secretary of the Treasury on the State of the Finances for the Year 1869*, H.R. Exec. Doc. 2, 41st Cong., 2d sess., 1869, p. IX.
2. U.S. Congress, Senate, *Report of John Jay Knox in Relation to a Revision of the Laws Pertaining to the Mint and Coinage of United States*, S. Misc. Doc. 132, 1870, p. 3.
3. Ibid.
4. Ibid.
5. Ibid., p. 12.
6. U.S., Congress, House, *Report of the Director of the Mint*, 40th Cong., 2d sess., 1867, p. 9.
7. U.S., Congress, House, 41st Cong., pt. 7, appendix, 13 April 1870, *Congressional Globe*, p. 610.

8. U.S., Congress, Senate, *Report of John Jay Knox in Relation to a Revision of the Laws Pertaining to the Mint and Coinage of the United States*, S. Misc. Doc. 132, 41st Cong., 2d sess., 1870, p. 12.
9. Ibid., pp. 30-31.
10. U.S., Congress, House, *Correspondence Pertaining*, pp. 30-31.
11. Ibid., p. 11.
12. U.S., Congress, House, *Report of the Director of the Mint*, H.R. Exec. Doc. 2, 41st Cong., 2d sess., 1869, p. 348.
13. U.S., Congress, House, *Correspondence Pertaining*, p. 19.
14. Ibid., p. 38.
15. Ibid., p. 51.
16. Ibid., p. 78.
17. Ibid., pp. 53-54.
18. U.S., Congress, Senate, *Report of John Jay Knox*, p. 11.

Chapter 9. The Perfect Ally

1. *Dictionary of American Biography* (New York: Charles Scribner's Sons, 1933), vol. VI, p. 273.
2. John M. Willem, Jr., *The United States Trade Dollar: America's Only Unwanted, Unhonored Coin* (New York: By the author, 1959), pp. 60-61; Q. David Bowers, *The Rare Silver Dollars Dated 1804 and the Exciting Adventures of Edmund Roberts* (Wolfeboro, NH: Bowers and Merena Galleries, Inc., 1999), p. 408.
3. See Henry R. Linderman to William C. Ralston, 26 March 1871; Henry R. Linderman to William C. Ralston, 19 May 1872; and William C. Ralston to Henry R. Linderman, 5 April 1871; William Chapman Ralston Papers (77/88c), The Bancroft Library, University of California, Berkeley.
4. See U.S. Congress, Senate, 40th Cong., 1st sess., 23 March 1867, *Congressional Globe*, p. 292; and U.S. Congress, Senate, Exec. Doc. 11, 40th Cong., 1st sess., 1867.
5. *Virginia City Territorial Enterprise*, 21 May 1869.
6. Also, as senators who were familiar with the bullion trade testified during the debate in Congress in early January 1871, the value of gold, whether it be in bar or coin form, was always regulated in the marketplace by its coinage value. Removing the coinage charge would effectively raise the value of all gold bullion domestically, whether or not it ended up in coinage or remained in bar form.
7. In a letter written at John Jay Knox's request, submitted to Congress in March 1867, San Francisco Assaying and Refining Company manager Louis A. Garnett argued for removal of the coinage charge and private refining of government bullion, claiming this would help keep bullion at home and greatly aid California by relieving it "of those constantly recurring periods of stringency in the money matters growing out of the demand for, and shipment abroad of, our bullion." He further told Knox, "During your sojourn here you doubtless learned enough of our peculiar system of exchange with the interior to understand that while the coinage of about $20,000,000 per annum seems to answer all of our wants as a circulating medium, yet nearly our entire product is made to answer the purpose of coin, being remitted from the interior in payment of merchandise sold by our merchants." See U.S. Congress, Senate Exec. Doc. 11, 40th Cong. 1st. sess., p. 4.
8. David Lavender, *Nothing Seemed Impossible: William C. Ralston and Early San Francisco* (Palo Alta, CA: American West Publishing Co., 1975), p. 284.
9. Ibid., p. 282.
10. U.S. Congress, Senate, S. Rept. 47, 41st Cong., 2d sess., 1870, pp. 276-277.
11. Ira B. Cross, *Financing an Empire: History of Banking in California* (New York: S.J. Clarke Publishing Co., 1927), vol. 1, p. 285.
12. U.S. Congress, Senate, *Report of John Jay Knox in Relation to a Revision of the Laws Pertaining to the Mint and Coinage of United States*, S. Misc. Doc. 132, 1870, p. 6.
13. Ibid.
14. Ibid., pp. 6-7.
15. Ibid., p. 6.
16. Ibid.
17. See U.S., Congress, House, *Correspondence Pertaining to the Proposed Revision of the Mint and Coinage Laws of the United States*, H.R. Exec. Doc. 307, 41st Cong., 2d sess., 1870.
18. Ibid., pp. 52-53.
19. Ibid., p. 54.

Chapter 10. Free Gold

1. U.S., Congress, Senate, 41st Cong., 3d sess., pt. 1, 9 January 1871, *Congressional Globe*, p. 368.
2. Ibid.
3. Ibid.
4. Ibid.
5. Ibid. p.370.
6. Ibid.
7. Ira B. Cross, *Financing an Empire: History of Banking in California* (New York: S.J. Clarke Publishing Co., 1927), vol. 1, pp. 258-259.

8. U.S., Congress, Senate, 41st Cong., 3d sess., pt. 1, 9 January 1871, *Congressional Globe,* p. 371.
9. Ibid., p. 374.
10. Ibid., p. 376.
11. Ibid., p. 372
12. Ibid., p.377.
13. Ibid.
14. Ibid.
15. Ibid.
16. Ibid.
17. Ibid., p. 368.
18. Ibid.
19. Ibid., p. 373.
20. Ibid., p. 372.
21. U.S., Congress, Senate, 41st Cong., 3d sess., pt. 1, 10 January 1871, *Congressional Globe*, p.394.
22. Ibid.
23. Ibid., p.396.
24. Ibid.

Chapter 11. Mr. Guyescutes

1. Letter, 14 January 1870 [sic, 1871], "Guyescutes" to William C. Ralston, William Chapman Ralston Papers (77/88c), The Bancroft Library, University of California, Berkeley.
2. Handwriting comparison of the "Guyescutes" letter with the next letter from Henry R. Linderman to William C. Ralston shows that both were written by the same person. References by Guyescutes to a cabinet position change and an updating on this change by Linderman in his Feb. 3, 1871, letter add weight to this conclusion. The mint bill was not introduced into Congress until April 1870. There were no such pending measures on Jan. 14, 1870. However, as of Jan. 14, 1871, the mint bill was in House committee, as referred to by Guyescutes. Linderman made a similar early-year dating mistake in a January 1875 letter, correcting the 1874 to 1875 before posting it.
3. David Lavender, *Nothing Seemed Impossible: William C. Ralston and Early San Francisco* (Palo Alta, CA: American West Publishing Co., 1975), p. 287.
4. Guyescutes to Ralston, 14 January 1871.
5. Ibid.
6. Ibid.
7. Ibid.
8. Linderman mentions attending such meetings in other letters as well. See, for example, Henry R. Linderman to William C. Ralston, 3 February 1871, William Chapman Ralston Papers (77/88c), The Bancroft Library, University of California, Berkeley.
9. Guyescutes to Ralston, 14 January 1871.
10. Ibid.
11. See John M. Willem, Jr., *The United States Trade Dollar: America's Only Unwanted, Unhonored Coin* (New York: By the author, 1959). Considering Linderman's little-known paid employment by Ralston, it is likely that he had a greater impact on the mint bill than heretofore imagined. Ralston was certainly content with his work, agreeing in his April 5, 1871, letter to Linderman to grant the $5,000 Linderman requested for his continued allegiance to the cause.
12. Letter, Henry R. Linderman to William C. Ralston, 3 February 1871, William Chapman Ralston Papers (77/88c), The Bancroft Library, University of California, Berkeley.
13. Letter, Henry R. Linderman to William C. Ralston, 8 February 1871, William Chapman Ralston Papers (77/88c), The Bancroft Library, University of California, Berkeley.
14. Ibid.
15. Ibid.
16. Letter, Henry R. Linderman to William C. Ralston, 26 March 1871, William Chapman Ralston Papers (77/88c), The Bancroft Library, University of California, Berkeley. The name of the person who made the complaint is illegible.
17. Ibid.
18. Ibid. However, a few days later, Linderman apparently changed his mind about waiting for the mint bill's passage to obtain a free coinage. In his March 30, 1871, letter to Ralston, Linderman wrote, "I am remaining here still in the hope that we may be able to attach an amendment, repealing the coinage charge, to the deficiency appropriations Bill. We must not accept anything but a free gold coinage—which we can certainly carry, as an important feature of the Mint Bill, next session." This effort also apparently failed. See Henry R. Linderman to William C. Ralston, 30 March 1871, William Chapman Ralston Papers (77/88c), The Bancroft Library, University of California, Berkeley.
19. Ibid.
20. Ibid. Ralston's attempt to secure the contract and a monopoly over refining of bullion for the San Francisco Mint raised a storm of controversy in the late 1860s and had only gained some credibility through the passage of an amendment to an appropriations measure in July 1870, while the mint bill was in the Senate Finance Committee.
21. Ibid. Linderman placed an asterisk directly after the sentence: "The Secretary, strongly favors a free coinage, and is well

pleased with the results of the present refining system." It referred to his margin note, which read: "At the proper time the savings of expenses effected [on refining] should be prepared for the Secretary's report after June 20 I think will be best."

22. Rep. Clarkson Potter, in a reference perhaps directed at Linderman, complained during the April 9, 1872, House debate over the mint bill about the new Director of the Bureau of the Mint position:

    In the first place, it is proposed by this bill to change the whole system of officers of the Mint. The bill provides for a Director of the Mint. Now, while I do not know a great deal about these matters, I have not been able to resist the conviction that the bill is designed to make a place for a particular person. I find that the Director of the Mint at Philadelphia, whose report to the Secretary of the Treasury I have before me, condemns the proposed change as unwise and unnecessary; and other experts with whom I have personally consulted have agreed with him in that regard.

    U.S., Congress, House, 42d Cong., 2d sess., pt. 3, 9 April 1872, *Congressional Globe*, p. 2310.
23. Henry R. Linderman to William C. Ralston, 26 March 1871, William Chapman Ralston Papers (77/88c), The Bancroft Library, University of California, Berkeley.
24. Ibid.
25. Ibid. Linderman's period of service is difficult to decipher. He mentions 13 months, apparently as taking him up to the end of the San Francisco Assaying and Refining Company's contract with the mint, which likely means that the $5,000 he requested would cover the period from September 1871 through September 1872.
26. Letter, William C. Ralston to Henry R. Linderman, 5 April 1871, William Chapman Ralston Papers (77/88c), The Bancroft Library, University of California, Berkeley.
27. See Henry R. Linderman to William C. Ralston, 9 March 1873, William Chapman Ralston Papers (77/88c), The Bancroft Library, University of California, Berkeley.
28. Letter, Henry R. Linderman to William C. Ralston, 19 August 1871, William Chapman Ralston Papers (77/88c), The Bancroft Library, University of California, Berkeley.
29. Ibid.
30. Linderman to Ralston, 26 March 1871.

Chapter 12. Refined Monopoly

1. David Lavender, *Nothing Seemed Impossible: William C. Ralston and Early San Francisco* (Palo Alta, CA: American West Publishing Co., 1975), p. 282.
2. See *San Francisco Chronicle*, 8 July 1869, and Lavender, *Nothing Seemed Impossible*, pp. 282-283.
3. Roy Hill, "History of San Francisco Mint," *Money Talks: A Numismatic Anthology Selected from the CalCoin News* (Irvine, CA: California State Numismatic Association, 1970), pp. 3-11; Donald Kagin, *Private Gold Coins and Patterns of the United States* (New York: Arco Publishing Co., 1981), p. 163. Kagin's book is the definitive work on Territorial gold coins, outlining the backgrounds of many of Ralston's contemporaries.
4. Kagin, *Private Gold Coins*, pp. 166-167.
5. John C. Hewston Jr. to William C. Ralston, 25 June 1868, William Chapman Ralston Papers (77/88c), The Bancroft Library, University of California, Berkeley.
6. See Hewston to Ralston, 25 June 1868, and Lavender, *Nothing Seemed Impossible*.
7. Hewston to Ralston, 25 June 1868.
8. Ibid.
9. U.S., Congress, Senate, S. Rept. 47, 41st Cong., 2d sess., 1870, p. 267.
10. See U.S., Congress, Senate, 40th Cong., 2d sess., 13 July 1868, *Congressional Globe*, p. 4001.
11. U.S., Congress, Senate, 40th Cong., 2d sess, 16 July 1868, *Congressional Globe,* p. 4093.
12. U.S., Congress, Appendix, 40th Cong., 2d sess., 20 July 1868, *Congressional Globe*, p. 524.
13. Boutwell expressed his support for the measure and that of Mint Director Pollock's in this letter. Boutwell wrote, "The views presented by the director of the mint relative to receiving deposits of refined bullion suitable for coinage and paying the depositor thereof in unparted bars, meets my approval, and I have no doubt if the proposed bill shall become law, and the discretion in this particular left to the officers of the mint, subject to the approval of the Secretary, that the interests of all parties will be protected and a considerable amount saved to the government at present lost from the wastage and expense of refining gold and silver bullion. See U.S., Congress, Senate, S. Doc. 30, 40th Cong., 2d sess., 1869.
14. "Washington Intelligence," *Virginia City Territorial Enterprise*, 16 February 1869. For the refinery's stance on the protest against their contract, see Louis A. Garnett's Sept. 4, 1869, testimony before the Joint Select Committee on Retrenchment. Garnett charged that all of those who signed the objection to private refining were representatives of foreign banks and local assayers:

    When this proposition of exchanging fine gold for unrefined bullion at the mint was made, there was quite an earnest protest against it, which was signed exclusively by foreign bankers, who come here and sell exchange against produce abroad, buy up our bullion and export it out of the country to cover the exchange, and by private assayers. Assayers and refiners are two distinct things. Private assayers simply melt the crude bullion as it comes from the mines into bars, and stamp its value for export, unrefined. The refiner also does that same sort of work, and at the same time, when deposits are made for that purpose, refines it. You will see at once that if we make the minting value of gold here greater than abroad, it will all seek our mints instead of being exported, and consequently foreign bankers will not buy it for export, nor will private assayers get the bars to make, and they, therefore, joined the protest, assigning that this would lead to a monopoly of the bullion on the part of the refinery, and consequently to the detriment of commerce; also that it would be a means of the private refiner raising his charges.

As to the protest's charges that the Treasury's contract with the San Francisco Assaying and Refining Company gave undo control over the mint to one refiner, Garnett said:

It cannot possibly lead to any monopoly, because the refiner as well as the assayer is simply the bailee of the depositor. There is another thing in regard to exchange in the mint. I say six millions go to the mint of our product. Assuming now that this law were passed, I could not control all that bullion in the mint without in advance going and putting a refined ounce in the place of each ounce I get. Therefore I do not control ultimately a single ounce that I do not already, for I have to surrender to the mint my refined ounce before the mint gives me its unrefined ounce; and hence it does not lead to the control of a single ounce on the part of the refiner more than he would otherwise have; nor, as I have already explained, can he raise his price, because at once it goes off abroad. So the objections have no foundation whatever, and, as I say, spring entirely from interested motives. Assayers understanding that if by low rates of charge for refining we made gold more valuable for coin than for export, their business would be broken up, oppose the plan, and so do the foreign bankers.

Senate, 41st Cong., 2d sess., S. Rept. 47, 1870, p. 279.

15. Letter, Donohoe, Kelly and Co., Bankers, et al, 20 January 1869, William Chapman Ralston Papers (77/88c), The Bancroft Library, University of California, Berkeley.
16. Ibid.
17. Ibid.
18. Letter, Eugene Kelly & Co. to Samuel S. Cox, 13 July 1870, William Chapman Ralston Papers (77/88c), The Bancroft Library, University of California, Berkeley.
19. It was originally planned that the new San Francisco Mint building would be able to employ the sulfuric acid process. However, upon measuring the space allowed for it, Prof. Rogers recommended the use of the nitric acid process in its stead. See Henry R. Linderman's *Report of the Director of the Mint* for 1875.
20. U.S., Congress, House, 42d Cong., 2d sess., pt. 3, 9 April 1872, *Congressional Globe*, p. 2310.
21. Ibid.
22. Ibid.
23. Ibid.
24. U.S., Congress, House, 42d Cong., 2d sess., pt. 3, 9 April 1872, *Congressional Globe*, p. 2313.
25. Ibid. Some idea of the amount of bullion making its way through the San Francisco Assaying and Refining Company can be gained from reports in the *Alta California*. The July 6, 1874, issue, for example, observing that most of the region's bullion went through the refinery for parting and refining, reported that for the first six months of 1874, the San Francisco Assay and Refining Company sent more than 486,000 ounces of gold and 30,000 ounces of silver to the San Francisco Mint. This amounted to $10 million in gold and $38,000 in silver. The refinery received eight cents an ounce for refining the 486,000 ounces of gold, providing a six-month gross of $38,880. "Financial and Commercial Statistics, for the Six Months Ending June 30, 1874," *Alta California*, 6 July 1874.
26. Considering he was fully aware of who was behind the provision, Wood was likely posturing. If he wasn't, a letter maintained in Ralston's correspondence file would have left no doubt as to the provision's source. In a July 30, 1870, letter from California Sen. Eugene Casserly, Casserly began by telling Ralston that he had received Ralston's letter on the "Mint-bullion matter," with its "last loud call to action." He added that he was aware that the plan was to "put the bill [authorizing the exchange of refined for unrefined bullion] on as an amendment to one of the money bills in the Senate" and "such was the course it finally took—but amended to secure its passage—so as to limit its operation until the completion of the new mint and not afterwards." See Eugene Casserly to William C. Ralston, 30 July 1870, William Chapman Ralston Papers (77/88c), The Bancroft Library, University of California, Berkeley.
27. U.S., Congress, House, 42d Cong., 2d sess., pt. 3, 9 April 1872, *Congressional Globe*, p. 2313.
28. That Linderman fully supported private refining can be ascertained from his 1869 report filed after his return from the Pacific coast, where he examined the branch mint in San Francisco. Linderman wrote, "There are now in operation two large and complete private refineries, which do almost the exclusive refining of silver and the greater portion of the gold operated on for fine bars for export or coinage at the Mint. These refineries are the principal depositories of fine gold at the branch mint, and as their charges are much lower than the government, the true policy would be to allow them, or others that may be established hereafter, to do all the refining under such regulations, and upon such terms as would at all times insure the government against risk or loss, and at the lowest possible rate of cost." Linderman's arguments took on the distinct tone of Louis A. Garnett, who was in regular contact with Washington urging his views, and apparently had significant influence on Linderman long before the first payment was made. Linderman wrote, in his Oct. 8, 1869, report, "It may be asked why the Mint cannot use the same process [sulfuric acid, which was cheaper]. The reason seems to be that the sulphuric-acid process is too offensive to be maintained in the heart of a city where it is necessary that the mint should be located for convenience and safety. Moreover, it requires much more space than the nitric-acid process, or than can be afforded in such institutions." For his part, Garnett had argued in an 1867 letter to John Jay Knox, "The government uses the tedious and expensive process of refining by nitric acid, (which alone can be used in the heart of the city,) while private refiners employ the more expeditious and commercial sulphuric acid." For Linderman's report see U.S., Congress, Senate, S. Exec. Doc. 51, 41st Cong., 2d sess., 1870, pp. 4-5. Linderman's report had been referred to the Senate Committee on Finance. Also included with this is Linderman's report, written along with

Knox, dated Feb. 7, 1870, on "Refining and Parting of Precious Metals at the United States Assay Office, New York," in which they similarly said:

> The sulphuric-acid process has also been adopted and brought to great perfection by private enterprise on the Pacific Coast, where it became a necessity, in consequence of the large production of silver containing gold, in Nevada, and as a means of preventing the product (gold and silver) of that section of our country from shipment abroad in an unparted condition, on account of much cheaper parting in France, and elsewhere in Europe, compared with the cost at the San Francisco branch mint.
>
> The successful introduction of this process on the Pacific Coast has resulted very beneficially to our country by furnishing fine gold and silver bars, which could not otherwise have been prepared at sufficiently low rates for our important and growing trade with China. It also enables the bullion dealers of San Francisco to furnish standard bullion to some of the South American mints for coinage.

See U.S., Congress, Senate, S. Exec. Doc. 51, 41st Cong., 2d sess., 1870, p. 9. For Garnett's comments on this and the region's concerns over the coinage charge, see U.S., Congress, Senate, S. Exec. Doc. 11, 40th Cong., 1st sess, 1867, p. 4.

29. Letter, Henry R. Linderman to William C. Ralston, 3 February 1871, William Chapman Ralston Papers (77/88c), The Bancroft Library, University of California, Berkeley.
30. Letter, Henry R. Linderman to William C. Ralston, 8 February 1871, William Chapman Ralston Papers (77/88c), The Bancroft Library, University of California, Berkeley. See also *New York Times*, 6 February 1871.
31. *New York Times*, 6 February 1871.
32. Ibid.
33. Letter, Henry R. Linderman to William C. Ralston, 8 February 1871, William Chapman Ralston Papers (77/88c), The Bancroft Library, University of California, Berkeley.
34. U.S., Congress, House, 42d Cong., 2d sess., 9 April 1872, *Congressional Globe*, p. 2315.
35. Letter, Henry R. Linderman to William C. Ralston, 19 May 1872, William Chapman Ralston Papers (77/88c), The Bancroft Library, University of California, Berkeley.
36. Ibid.
37. Ibid.

The Granite Lady

1. *Alta California*, 29 October 1874.
2. "The New Mint," *Alta California*, 6 November 1874.
3. Ibid.
4. Ibid.
5. Ibid.

Chapter 13. Gold Standard Secured

1. U.S., Congress, House, *Report of the Secretary of the Treasury on the State of the Finances for the Year 1871*, H.R. Exec. Doc. 2, 42d Cong., 2d sess., 1871, p. XV.
2. For example, see National Executive Silver Committee, *Silver in the Fifty-First Congress* (Washington, DC: George R. Gray, Printer, 1890), p. 21, in which the committee claimed that, "on the 9th of April the bill was called up, and a long explanatory speech made on it by Mr. Hooper, to which, it would seem from subsequent events, no one listened and which no one understood."
3. U.S., Congress, House, 42d Cong., 2d sess., pt. 3, 9 April 1872, *Congressional Globe*, p. 2305.
4. Ibid.
5. Ibid.
6. Ibid., p. 2306.
7. Ibid., p. 2308.
8. Ibid., p. 2310.
9. Ibid., p. 2316.
10. Ibid.
11. Ibid.
12. Ibid.
13. Ibid.
14. Ibid.
15. Ibid., p. 2311.
16. U.S. Congress, Senate, 42d Cong., 3d sess., pt. 1, 17 January 1873, *Congressional Globe*, p. 672.
17. Ibid.
18. Ibid., p. 673.

Chapter 14. The Good Fight

1. *Washington Star*, 12 February 1873.

2. *Washington Star*, 13 February 1873.
3. Letter, Henry R. Linderman to William C. Ralston, 9 March 1873, William Chapman Ralston Papers (77/88c), The Bancroft Library, University of California, Berkeley.
4. Ibid.
5. Ibid.
6. Ibid.
7. Ibid.
8. Ibid.
9. Ibid.
10. U.S., Congress, House, *Report of the Director of the Mint*, House Exec. Doc. 2, 43d Cong., 1st sess,, 1873, p. 477.
11. For the latter argument see Neil Carothers, *Fractional Money: A History of the Small Coins and Fractional Paper Currency of the United States*. New York: John Wiley & Sons, 1930.
12. See Paul M. O'Leary, "The Scene of the Crime of 1873 Revisited: A Note," *Journal of Political Economy* 69 (August 1960) and Allen Weinstein, "Was There a 'Crime of 1873'? The Case of the Demonetized Dollar," *The Journal of American History* 54 (September 1967). O'Leary, who accepted the theory that the silver-producing interests were indifferent to the bill's contents in 1871 and 1872 and were not paying attention in early 1873 when it passed, charged that Linderman purposely concealed his specialized knowledge of the bleak future for silver from Congress, as part of a what O'Leary termed was "a calculated hostility to silver," aimed at placing the United States on a gold standard before silver advocates could awaken to the possibility of a resumption of specie payments on a silver basis. Weinstein claimed that O'Leary was basically correct, that government officials in the Treasury and Congress, aware that silver would soon fall in value, worked to secure passage of the bill before monetary inflationists learned what was ahead for this metal. Weinstein also attempted to implicate Treasury Secretary George S. Boutwell and Sen. John Sherman in the cover-up. By Weinstein's account, they worked to revise the measure in December 1872, removing the 385-grain subsidiary dollar and substituting the Trade dollar without explaining to Congress their primary reason for doing—the expected downturn in the value of silver.
13. Linderman's report was published by the Government Printing Office. A synopsis of the report appeared on Feb. 10, 1873, in the *Alta California*, just prior to the bill's passage, under the heading "The Branch Mints of the Pacific Coast." The *Alta* claimed to have learned of the report from the Philadelphia press. It also appeared in the March 1873 issue of *Bankers' Magazine and Statistical Register.* Treasury Secretary Boutwell's report was written on Dec. 2, 1872, the day of the opening of the third session of the 42nd Congress, in which the Trade dollar amendment first appeared.
14. Letter, Henry R. Linderman to William C. Ralston, 19 May 1872, William Chapman Ralston Papers (77/88c), The Bancroft Library, University of California, Berkeley.
15. Ibid.
16. Ibid.
17. In March 1873, after taking over as Mint director, Linderman hinted to Ralston that he would leave the matter of additional compensation up to Ralston. It is likely, considering the importance of the measure to Ralston, that Linderman's employment with Ralston ran through final passage of the bill in early 1873.
18. Linderman had earlier published a pamphlet, titled "Free Coinage of Gold," in which he also mentioned the new German coinage law. Rep. Hooper related during the April 9, 1872, debate over the mint bill that:

    The following statement is taken from the pamphlet of Dr. Linderman, on the 'Free Coinage of Gold:'

    > 'The seigniorage on silver varies in different countries, and also with the price of silver bullion. In the United States it is four per cent.; in Great Britain about ten per cent.; in France, Belgium, Italy, and Spain, about seven and a half per cent.; in Sweden, over twelve per cent.
    >
    > 'The coinage bill recently brought forward by the German empire adopts gold as the sole standard of value, and demonetizes silver as to coinage; but the particulars are not at hand to show the extent of the seigniorage on silver.
    >
    > 'If the United States were to exact the same rate of seigniorage as Great Britain, silver coin and United States notes would circulate concurrently at the present premium on gold as compared with paper money.'

    See U.S., Congress, House, 42d Cong., 2d sess., pt. 3, *Congressional Globe*, p. 2309.
19. In his March 1917 article, "History of the Trade Dollar," for *American Economic Review*, Porter Garnett claimed that it was during this meeting that his father, Louis A. Garnett, provided Linderman with the specifications for the new dollar coin.
20. Letter, John Robertson to William C. Ralston, 7 November 1872, William Chapman Ralston Papers (77/88c), The Bancroft Library, University of California, Berkeley.
21. Henry R. Linderman and John Torrey, "The Production of Gold and Silver," from 19 November 1872, Treasury Department *Special Report of Examination of Branch Mints on the Pacific Coast*; reprinted in *Bankers' Magazine and Statistical Register* 7, 3d series (March 1873): 710.
22. Ibid.
23. Ibid.
24. Ibid., p. 711.

25. Ibid.
26. Ibid.
27. Ibid.
28. Ibid., p. 712.
29. Ibid.
30. U.S., Congress, House, *Report of the Secretary of the Treasury on the State of the Finances for the Year 1872*, H.R. Exec. Doc. 1, pt. 7, 42d Cong., 3d sess., 1872, p. XII.
31. Ibid.

Chapter 15. Ralston Dollars

1. Porter Garnett, "History of the Trade Dollar," *American Economic Review* 7 (March 1917): 91.
2. Ibid., p. 95.
3. Conrad Weigand, "Discount on Silver Bars," *Virginia City Territorial Enterprise*, 4 February 1873.
4. Ibid.
5. See William Chapman Ralston Papers (77/88c), The Bancroft Library, University of California, Berkeley.
6. "Origins of the Trade Dollar," *Virginia City Territorial Enterprise*, 28 March 1876.
7. *Alta California*, 21 November 1874.
8. Ibid.
9. Ibid.
10. U.S., Congress, Senate, *Report of the United States Monetary Commission*, S. Rept. 703, 44th Cong., 2d sess., 1877, vol. 2, p. 200.
11. U.S., Congress, Senate *Report of John Jay Knox in Relation to a Revision of the Laws Pertaining to the Mint and Coinage of the United States*, S. Misc. Doc. 132, 41st Cong., 2d sess., 1870, p. 11.
12. U.S., Congress, House, *Correspondence Pertaining to the Proposed Revision of the Mint and Coinage Laws of the United States*, H.R. Exec. Doc. 307, 41st Cong., 2d sess., 1870, p. 71.
13. The appearance of the weight and fineness on the reverse of the Commercial dollar patterns might derive from a combination of the ideas of a trade coinage and an international coinage. D.G. Briton Thompson, in *Ruggles of New York: A Life of Samuel Ruggles*, wrote that, following the passage of a Senate Finance Committee resolution, on Feb. 8, 1870, calling for the President to invite correspondence with Great Britain and other foreign powers "to promote the adoption...of a common unit and standard of an international gold coinage...," Secretary of State Hamilton Fish sent a circular letter to the American legations in Europe. It called for the adoption of gold and favored Rep. William D. Kelley's so-called German or dollar scheme, which would have made for a unit metrically oriented to the German crown. However, if nothing else was accomplished, Fish suggested that it would be well for nations to adjust their gold coinage to the nearest decigram and stamp the weight on the coins. Late in 1872, while the mint bill was before the Senate, Dr. Henry R. Linderman also pushed for the inclusion of weight and fineness on the reverse of nation's subsidiary silver coins, to help promote an international coinage. U.S., Congress, Senate, 41st Cong., 2d sess., pt. 2, 8 February 1870, *Congressional Globe*, p. 1097; D.G. Briton Thompson, *Ruggles of New York: A Life of Samuel Ruggles*, Studies in History, Economics and Public Law, ed. Faculty of Political Science of Columbia University, no. 524 (New York: Columbia University Press, 1946), p. 157.
14. David Lavender, *Nothing Seemed Impossible: William C. Ralston and Early San Francisco* (Palo Alta, CA: American West Publishing Co., 1975), p. 257.
15. Ira B. Cross, *Financing an Empire: History of Banking in California* (New York: S.J. Clarke Publishing Co., 1927), vol. 1, pp. 257-259. According to the Oct. 12, 1864, issue of the *Evening Bulletin*, quoted by Cross, "at the time they [the British banks] were confining themselves to the purchase of bullion for shipment to oriental markets to be paid for out of the proceeds of bills of exchange which they sold on London." Of this, the *Bulletin* complained, the rates offered on sterling were so low as to make it impossible for local California banks to compete.
16. *Alta California*, 5 August 1869. In the same issue of the *Alta California*, under the heading "Shipment of Treasure for China and Japan," the treasure total for the Bank of California, apparently via the same steamer, the *Oregonian*, was given at a higher level of $108,300, exceeded only by the Bank of British North America, at $265,203.93.
17. "Trade with China," *Virginia City Territorial Enterprise*, 11 August 1869.
18. *Virginia City Territorial Enterprise*, 14 May 1869.
19. Ibid.
20. Ibid.
21. Ibid.
22. A portion of Bailey's letter appeared in the Feb. 10, 1873, *Alta California* under the heading "American Finance and the East." More complete coverage, however, was provided in the Feb. 6, 1873, issue of the *New York Tribune*.
23. David A. Bailey, "A Letter from Council at Hong Kong," *New York Tribune*, 6 February 1873.
24. Ibid.
25. Ibid.
26. Ibid.
27. Letter, John Robertson to William C. Ralston, 8 September 1873, William Chapman Ralston Papers (77/88c), The Bancroft Library, University of California, Berkeley.

28. John Robertson to William C. Ralston, 8 October 1873, William Chapman Ralston Papers (77/88c), The Bancroft Library, University of California, Berkeley. In this same letter, Robertson informed Ralston that after seeing the American Trade dollars, the Japanese might follow Ralston's example. Indeed, in 1875, the Japanese issued a trade coin in the same weight and fineness as the U.S. Trade dollar. It, like the American version, was a failure.
29. Robertson to Ralston, 8 September 1873, William Chapman Ralston Papers (77/88c), The Bancroft Library, University of California, Berkeley.
30. John Robertson to William C. Ralston, 29 September 1874, William Chapman Ralston Papers (77/88c), The Bancroft Library, University of California, Berkeley.
31. John Robertson to William C. Ralston, 21 December 1874, William Chapman Ralston Papers (77/88c), The Bancroft Library, University of California, Berkeley.
32. See Henry R. Linderman to William C. Ralston, 13 February 1875 and 18 February 1875, William Chapman Ralston Papers (77/88c), The Bancroft Library, University of California, Berkeley.
33. U.S., Congress, Senate, 42d Cong., 3d sess., pt. 1, 17 January 1873, *Congressional Globe*, p. 672.
34. Letter, Henry R. Linderman to William C. Ralston, 19 May 1872, William Chapman Ralston Papers (77/88c), The Bancroft Library, University of California, Berkeley.

Chapter 16. Worthy Reasons

1. George S. Boutwell, *Mr. Boutwell's Speech on the Mint Bill of 1873 Delivered before the Twentieth Century Club*, Boston, Oct. 14, 1896 (Boston: Beacon Press, 1896), pp. 11-12.
2. Conrad Weigand, "Discount on Silver Bars," *Virginia City Territorial Enterprise*, 4 February 1873.
3. U.S., Congress, House, *Correspondence Pertaining to the Proposed Revision of the Mint and Coinage Laws of the United States*, H..R. Exec. Doc. 307, 41st Cong., 2d sess., 1870, pp. 53-54.
4. Ibid., p. 38.
5. Mary Ellen Glass, *Silver and Politics in Nevada, 1892-1902*, the Lancetlead Series: Nevada and the West (Nevada: University of Nevada Press, 1969), p. 14.
6. R.W. Julian, "The Trade Dollar: America's Unloved Coin," *Coins* Magazine, June 1979, p. 84. Julian observed that as the San Francisco Mint struck very few dollars in the early 1870s and none at all in the 1860s, it "shows quite clearly that such coins were not wanted for the export trade to the Far East." Julian claimed the large coinages at the Philadelphia Mint between 1866-1873 "almost certainly were connected in some manner with the Central American and West Indies trade connection; it is possible that coined American dollars brought a premium in trading with that area."
7. Henry R. Linderman, in response to questioning before the United States Monetary Commission in 1876, observed that the Trade dollar was never intended to be a legal-tender coin and that the standard silver dollar was not able to compete with its Mexican rival in Far Eastern markets. He told the commission:

   > The trade dollar was a transaction by itself, and intended specifically as a medium of exchange in our relations with China. The old dollar would not have gone there. We tried that for eighty years. It was settled by experience. They were shipped there by Philadelphia merchants; and they would not take them. They considered them of less value than they really were. They are the most suspicious people in the world.

See U.S., Congress, Senate, *Report of the United States Monetary Commission*, S. Rept. 703, 44th Cong., 2d sess., 1877, vol. 2, p. 201.

8. "Real Money," *Alta California*, 25 December 1874.
9. Ibid.
10. U.S., Congress, Senate, 42d Cong., 3d sess., pt. 1, 17 January 1873, *Congressional Globe*, p. 671.
11. Ibid.
12. David Lavender, *Nothing Seemed Impossible: William C. Ralston and Early San Francisco* (Palo Alta, CA: American West Publishing Co., 1975), p. 332. Along these same lines, Joseph L. King provided some insight into the region's interest in the return to specie payments and its adherence to a gold standard. Explaining that gold payments had been suspended in 1861 when the war effort drained the Treasury of gold, California, King said, wasn't affected because of its distance. He wrote:

    > We were isolated in California. There being no railroad, it took 30 days for the news to come from the Eastern States, via Panama. Our business men, influenced by Banker William C. Ralston, determined to transact all of our business in gold as heretofore—and the California Legislature passed laws to that effect.
    >
    > And so arose the singular circumstance that in California we paid all of our bills in gold, the banks cashing checks, and the merchants keeping bank accounts in gold, while in the East legal tenders were used. The paper money of the Government depreciated so low that it sold at 35c on this Coast.

    Noting that Federal successes in 1864 at Vicksburg and Gettysburg helped raise the price of paper to beyond 60 cents, he explained:

    > All the Government employees on this Coast, including those serving here in the army and navy, were paid in Government paper, a great hardship to them, as, in order to pay their household expenses, they were compelled to exchange it for gold at a great loss. It would be a happy day for them when their pay in currency would have so increased in value as to be equal to gold—when the Government would resume the custom, in vogue before the war, of paying all of its debts in specie—that is gold.

> The gold is specie; the paper money is currency.
>
> The resumption of specie payments would mean that the Government would pay specie—that is gold—or its equivalent, for any and all of its debts.
>
> On a visit East in 1876 I found young relatives who had never seen gold, and on being shown a $20 piece, looked at it and handled it as they would those old, large copper cents in circulation at the time. I feel positive in this statement that if asked to give a $20 currency bill for one of those $20 gold pieces, they would have declined to do so. To young people at that time gold was an unknown quantity. So long as gold was at a premium in New York, so long as the currency—the money of the Government—was at a discount in San Francisco, just so long were the finances of the country unsettled.

Joseph L. King, *History of the San Francisco Stock and Exchange Board* (San Francisco: By the author, 1910), pp. 284-286.

13. Ibid.
14. Ibid.
15. "The New Mint," *Alta California*, 29 October 1874.

Chapter 17. Failed Experiment

1. Also, the implementation of the Specie Resumption Act released great numbers of subsidiary silver coins just at a time when silver's value had fallen enough to allow subsidiary coins that had been shipped to Canada and elsewhere to begin flowing back into the United States.
2. John M. Willem quotes from the Aug. 3, 1876, issue of the *Virginia City Territorial Enterprise* of a meeting by area saloon keepers, held at the Delta Saloon in Virginia City, to set prices at which they would accept the depreciated Trade dollars. Interestingly, besides the debate over how much of a discount would be placed on the coins, the *Territorial Enterprise* recorded that the Aug. 2, 1876, meeting had a low attendance, with only 24 saloons being represented, one-seventh of the number of such establishments in town! John M. Willem, Jr., *The United States Trade Dollar: America's Only Unwanted, Unhonored Coin* (New York: By the author, 1959), pp. 114-115.
3. As quoted in the *Virginia City Territorial Enterprise*, 16 April 1876.
4. Ibid.
5. U.S., Cong., House, *Report of the Director of the Mint*, H.R. Exec. Doc. 2, 45th Cong., 2d sess., 1877, p. 12.
6. Ibid.
7. Ibid., p. 50-51.
8. Ibid., p. 51.
9. Ibid.
10. U.S., Congress, House, *Report of the Secretary of the Treasury on State of the Finances for the Year 1877*, H.R. Exec. Doc. 2, 45th Cong., 2d sess., 1877, p. XX.
11. *Report of the Director of the Mint*, 1877, p. 13.
12. U.S., Cong., House, *Report of the Director of the Mint*, H.R. Exec. Doc. 2, 45th Cong., 2d sess., 1878, p. 10.
13. Ibid., p. 11.
14. Ibid., p. 39.
15. Ibid.
16. Ibid., p. 41.
17. Ibid., p. 42.
18. Ibid.
19. Ibid., p. 43.
20. Ibid.
21. Ibid., p. 12.
22. *New York Times*, 6 June 1883.
23. John M. Willem, Jr., *The United States Trade Dollar: America's Only Unwanted, Unhonored Coin*, p. 130. An 1884 House report had slightly different figures, although its total coinage figure probably did not include collector proofs. The report, submitted by Rep. Clement Dowd, a member of the House Committee on Coinage, Weights and Measures, found that:

    > The whole amount coined under the law [the Coinage Act of 1873] has been $35,959,360. The amount exported up to January 1, 1884, was about $27,089,817. Of the balance in this country a considerable quantity has been melted and used in the arts, and it is probable that of the amount exported a small portion has been returned to this country. The Director of the Mint estimates that there are about $7,000,000 now in this country.

    See U.S. Congress, House, *To Retire and Recoin the United States Trade Dollar*, H. Rept. 324, 48th Cong., 1st sess., 1884.
24. As cited in Don Taxay, *The U.S. Mint and Coinage: An Illustrated History from 1776 to the Present* (New York: Arco Publishing Co., 1969), p. 283.
25. Ben Perly Poore, ed., *Message from the President of the United States to the Two Houses of Congress at the Commencement of the Second Session of the Forty-Eighth Congress, with the Reports of the Heads of Departments and Selections from Accompanying Documents* (Washington, DC: Government Printing Office, 1884), p. 13.
26. U.S., Congress, House, *Report of the Secretary of the Treasury on State of the Finances for the Year 1884*, H.R. Exec. Doc.

2, 48th Cong., 2d sess., 1884, p. XXXVII.

Chapter 18. Saving Silver

1. Walter T.K. Nugent, *The Money Question During Reconstruction* (New York: W.W. Morton & Co., 1967), p. 28; John Jay Knox, *United States Notes: A History of the Various Issues of Paper Money by the Government of the United States* (London: T.F. Fisher Unwin, 1885; reprint ed., New York: Sanford J. Durst, 1978), pp. 139-140.
2. U.S., Congress, House, *Report of the Secretary of the Treasury on State of the Finances for the Year 1874*, H.R. Exec. Doc. 2, 43d Cong., 2d sess., 1874, p. 8.
3. U.S., Congress, House, *Report of the Comptroller of the Currency*, H.R. Exec. Doc. 2, 44th Cong., 1st sess., 1875, p. 199.
4. Nugent, *The Money Question*, p. 31.
5. U.S. Congress, Senate, *Report of John Jay Knox in Relation to a Revision of the Laws Pertaining to the Mint and Coinage of United States*, S. Misc. Doc. 132, 1870, p. 10.
6. U.S., Congress, House, 42d Cong., 2d sess., pt. 3, 9 April 1872, *Congressional Globe*, p. 2306.
7. Ibid.
8. Ibid., p. 2311.
9. Ibid.
10. Ibid.
11. U.S., Congress, House, *Report of the Secretary of the Treasury on State of the Finances for the Year 1873*, H.R. Exec. Doc. 2, 43d Cong., 1st sess.,1873, p. XXXIII.
12. See U.S., Congress, House, *Report of the Director of the Mint*, H.R. Exec. Doc. 2, 43d Cong., 1st sess., 1873, p. 478.
13. Ibid., pp. 478-479.
14. Ibid., p. 479.
15. "Silver for Change," *New York Times*, 29 October 1873.
16. "Resumption of Silver Payment," *New York Times*, 26 October 1873.
17. "Issue of Silver by the Treasury," *New York Times*, 26 October 1873.
18. George L. Anderson, "The Proposed Resumption of Silver Payments in 1873," *The Pacific Historical Review*, 8 (September 1939): 311.
19. Ibid., p. 312.
20. "Silver Payments at the Treasury," *New York Times*, 29 October 1873.
21. "Wall Street Topics," *New York Times*, 30 October 1873.
22. Neil Carothers, *Fractional Money: A History of the Small Coins and Fractional Paper Currency of the United States* (New York: John Wiley & Sons, 1930), p. 247.
23. *Alta California*, 26 December 1874; "Silver for Coinage," *San Francisco Chronicle*, 16 June 1875.
24. U.S., Congress, House, *Report of the Director of the Mint*, H.R. Exec. Doc. 2, 43d Cong., 2d sess., 1874, p. 200.
25. Ibid.
26. Ibid.
27. Ibid., p. 201.
28. U.S., Congress, House, *Coinage Laws of the United States, 1792-1894* (Washington, D.C.: Government Printing Office, 1894), p. 61.
29. *Report of the Director of the Mint*, 1874, p. 200.
30. Letter, "Old Man" to William C. Ralston, 7 January 1875, William Chapman Ralston Papers (77/88c), The Bancroft Library, University of California, Berkeley. In an interesting sidelight to this letter, Linderman told Ralston, "I believe my fights are about over although I will have to see this silver resumption business safely launched. After that I shall be compelled to retire and seek some private business. My salary is entirely too low."
31. Ibid.
32. Ibid.
33. Ibid.
34. *Alta California,* 26 December 1874.
35. "Old Man" to Ralston, 7 January 1875.
36. As reproduced in the *Alta California*, 19 January 1875.
37. Ibid.
38. U.S., Cong., House, *Report of the Director of the Mint*, H.R. Exec. Doc. 2, 44th Cong., 1st sess., 1875, p. 11.
39. "Silver for Coinage," *San Francisco Chronicle*, 16 June 1875.
40. Ibid.
41. U.S., Congress, House, 44th Cong., 1st sess., 16 March 1876, *Congressional Globe*, pp. 1764-1765.
42. Ibid., p. 1765.
43. U.S., Congress, House, *Coinage Laws of the United States, 1792-1894* (Washington, DC: Government Printing Office, 1894), p. 625.
44. Don Taxay, *The U.S. Mint and Coinage: An Illustrated History from 1776 to the Present* (New York: Arco Publishing Co., 1969), pp. 265-266, quoting from November 1878 *Bankers' Magazine and Statistical Register.*
45. Ironically, one year earlier, Treasury Secretary Sherman called for all restrictions to be removed from the issuance of subsidiary silver coins. Also, amazingly, Sherman decided additional subsidiary coins could be issued to account for any frac-

tional notes that may have been destroyed through use. "It was well known, however, that a very large amount of fractional currency issued had been destroyed, and could not be presented for redemption, and could hardly be held to be 'outstanding,'" Sherman wrote in his Dec. 3, 1877, *Report of the Treasury Secretary on the State of the Finances for 1877.* Therefore, Sherman related, in consultation with the Comptroller of the Currency and the Mint director, the amount either lost or destroyed was estimated to be $8,083,513, for which fractional coins were issued to meet this amount. The Treasury secretary then suggested:

> It is submitted that the limitation upon the amount of such fractional coin to be issued in exchange for United States notes should be repealed. This coin is readily taken, is in great favor with the people, its issue is profitable to the Government, and experience has shown that there is no difficulty in maintaining it at par with United States notes...The true limit of such coin is the demand that may be made for its issue, and if only issued in exchange for United States notes there is no danger of an excess being issued.

See U.S., Congress, House, *Report of the Secretary of the Treasury on State of the Finances for the Year 1877*, H.R. Exec. Doc. 2, 45th Cong., 2d sess., 1877, p. XIX.

46. U.S., Congress, House, *Report of the Secretary of the Treasury on State of the Finances for the Year 1899*, H.R. Exec. Doc. 1, 56th Cong., 1st sess., 1899, p. 12.
47. "Old Man" to William C. Ralston, 14 March 1875, William Chapman Ralston Papers (77/88c), The Bancroft Library, University of California, Berkeley.
48. Ibid.

Arrows and Rays

1. Ira B. Cross, *Financing an Empire: History of Banking in California* (Chicago: S.J. Clarke Publishing Co., 1927), vol. 1, p. 124, quoting from Harris Newmark's "Sixty Years in California."

Shortchanged

1. Dan De Quille, *The Big Bonanza: An Authentic Account of the Discovery, History, and Working of the World-Renowned Comstock Lode of Nevada Including the Present Condition of the Various Mines Situated Thereon—Sketches of the Most Prominent Men Interested in Them—Incidents and Adventures Connected With Mining, the Indians, and the Country—Amusing Stories, Experiences, Anecdotes, etc., etc. and a Full Exposition of the Production of Pure Silver* (Hartford, CT: American Publishing Co., 1876; reprint ed., New York, NY: Apollo Editions, 1969), p. 268.

Chapter 19. A Fateful Day

1. Letter, "Old Man" to William C. Ralston, 16 March 1875, William Chapman Ralston Papers (77/88c), The Bancroft Library, University of California, Berkeley.
2. Ibid.
3. Grant H. Smith, *The History of the Comstock Lode* (Reno, NV: University of Nevada Press, 1943; reprint ed., Reno, NV: University of Nevada Press, 1998), p. 116.
4. Julian Dana, *The Man Who Built San Francisco: A Study of Ralston's Journey with Banners* (New York: Macmillan Co., 1936), p. 301.
5. Smith, *The History of*, p. 151.
6. Dan De Quille, *The Big Bonanza: An Authentic Account of the Discovery, History, and Working of the World-Renowned Comstock Lode of Nevada Including the Present Condition of the Various Mines Situated Thereon—Sketches of the Most Prominent Men Interested in Them—Incidents and Adventures Connected With Mining, the Indians, and the Country—Amusing Stories, Experiences, Anecdotes, etc., etc. and a Full Exposition of the Production of Pure Silver* (Hartford, CT: American Publishing Co., 1876; reprint ed., New York: Apollo Editions, 1969), pp. 365-366.
7. Ibid., p. 372.
8. Eliot Lord, *Comstock Mining and Miners* (Washington, DC: Government Printing Office, 1883; reprint ed., Berkeley, CA: Howell-North Press, 1959), p. 314.
9. U.S., Congress, House, *Report of the Director of the Mint,* H.R. Exec. 2, 44th Cong., 1st sess., 1875, p. 83.
10. Smith, *History of*, pp. 167 and 310. Smith explained that the main body of ore was encountered at the 1,500- to 1,550-foot levels, where the ore existed in two large bodies, one in the Consolidated Virginia and the other extending into the California, divided by a sufficiently mineralized body of porphyry horse that the two bodies were eventually joined, creating a continuous body of ore that ran 900 feet. Its greatest width was 200 feet.
11. "Report on Mines," *New York Tribune*, 31 July 1875. By Linderman's later estimation, "the total production of all the mines on the Comstock may be safely estimated at not less than fifty million dollars per annum, about forty-five per cent. of which will be gold." See U.S. Congress, *Report of the Director of the Mint,* H.R. Exec. 2, 44th Cong., 1st sess., 1875, p. 20.
12. Dana, *The Man Who Built San Francisco*, p. 340.
13. David Lavender, *Nothing Seemed Impossible: William C. Ralston and Early San Francisco* (Palo Alta, CA: American West Publishing Co., 1975), p. 368.
14. Ibid.
15. Ibid., p. 356. Also see Ira B. Cross, *Financing an Empire: History of Banking in California* (New York: S.J. Clarke Pub-

lishing Co., 1927), vol. 1, p. 404.

16. In his March 16, 1875, letter (again signed as "Old Man," but this time on Director of the Mint stationary), Linderman told Ralston of a conversation he had with J. Pierpont Morgan of Drexel, Morgan & Company. Morgan believed that the current gold lock-up would likely continue at least until May. However, the break would not come.
17. Cross, *Financing an Empire*, p. 398.
18. Ibid.
19. "A Tight Money Market," *San Francisco Chronicle*, 26 August 1875.
20. "Retiring Capital for the New Bank," *San Francisco Chronicle*, 26 August 1875.
21. Lavender, *Nothing Seemed Impossible*, pp. 372 and 374.
22. *Alta California*, 26 August 1875.
23. Ibid.
24. Ibid.
25. Ibid.
26. "Relations Between Flood & O'Brien and the Bank," *Alta California*, 27 August 1875.
27. "Incidents," *Alta California*, 27 August 1875.
28. "Miscellaneous Incidents: A Crazy Female at the Bank Window," *San Francisco Chronicle*, 27 August 1875.
29. Ibid.
30. *Alta California*, 27 August 1875.
31. Ibid.
32. Ibid.
33. Ibid.
34. Ibid.
35. For more information on the sale, see "Palace Hotel," *San Francisco Chronicle*, 15 May 1875.
36. Lavender, *Nothing Seemed Impossible*, p. 374.
37. Joseph L. King, *History of the San Francisco Stock and Exchange Board* (San Francisco: By the author, 1910), pp. 103-104.
38. Cecil G. Tilton, *William Chapman: Courageous Builder* (Boston: The Christopher Publishing House, 1935), p. 340.
39. "The Crash," *San Francisco Chronicle*, 26 August 1875.
40. "The Financial Panic," *San Francisco Chronicle*, 27 August 1875.
41. Joseph L. King, *History of the San Francisco Stock and Exchange Board* (San Francisco: By the author, 1910), pp. 104-105.
42. Ibid., p. 102.
43. Ibid. The Aug. 27, 1875, *San Francisco Chronicle*, however, credits the closing of the Bank of California with saving King $30,000 in gold that was about to be deposited at the bank by one of King's clerks.
44. Lavender, *Nothing Seemed Impossible*, p. 345; Cross, *Financing an Empire*, p. 403.
45. Cross, *Financing an Empire*, p. 403.
46. *New York Tribune*, 27 August 1875.
47. Ibid.
48. *Alta California*, 27 August 1875
49. *Alta California*, 28 August 1875.
50. "William Sherman, U.S. Sub-Treasurer, Interviewed," *Alta California*, 28 August 1875.
51. Ibid.
52. "B.F. Sherwood," *Alta California*, 28 August 1875.
53. *Alta California*, 28 August 1875.
54. One of the more interesting suggested solutions to the money shortage came from San Francisco Sub-Treasury head William Sherman. In the Aug. 28, 1875, issue of the *Alta California*, Sherman advocated the use of Trade dollars as a temporary circulation substitute. "The bank of Government could furnish the Mint with additional funds and increase their bullion fund largely," Sherman told the *Alta* of his plan. "It would enable the Mint then to buy silver bullion or to coin it into trade dollars, which trade dollars could be used as a circulating medium for the time being." Asked if he had made any such proposition, Sherman replied that he suggested it "to one or two banks," who were then referred to Superintendent La Grange as to whether it was practicable. "You see readily the operation of that would be that a silver bar or silver bullion taken there, when its value was ascertained, the bullion fund allowing it, Superintendent La Grange would be authorized to pay its value the next day in trade dollars, provided he had enough on hand," Sherman told the *Alta*. Asked how many Trade dollars the Mint superintendent had on hand for this purpose, Sherman replied:

    > I do not know. He has a very large amount of subsidiary silver coined, and the way this might be, for the Secretary of the Treasury to put a million, or two million, in gold into the hands of the Superintendent by increasing the bullion fund, which would enable him to buy silver bullion, which the Government is ready to buy, and which they have been doing all along, in furtherance of the project to call in all the fractional currency.
55. *Alta California*, 30 August 1875.
56. Ibid.
57. "The Latest from San Francisco: Dr. Linderman Reports the National Gold Bank All Right," *New York Tribune*, 31 August 1875.

Chapter 20. Ralston's Demise

1. "Statements of Eye-Witnesses," *Alta California*, 28 August 1875.
2. "The Keeper's Story," *San Francisco Chronicle*, 28 August 1875.
3. *Alta California*, 28 August 1875.
4. Ibid.
5. *Alta California*, 29 August 1875.
6. Ibid.
7. *Alta California*, 28 August 1875.
8. Ibid.
9. Ibid.
10. Ibid.
11. *New York Tribune*, 28 August 1875.
12. "Apoplexy the Cause of Death," *Alta California*, 29 August 1875.
13. Ibid.
14. "Dead. William C. Ralston Drowned Off Black Point," *Alta California,* 28 August 1875.
15. "No Proof That Ralston's Death Was Suicidal," *Alta California*, 29 August 1875.
16. Ibid.
17. Ibid
18. "The Dead Banker," *Alta California,* 30 August 1875.
19. Ibid.
20. "Draped in Mourning," *Alta California,* 29 August 1875.
21. "Religious Services," *Alta California,* 31 August 1875.
22. Ibid.
23. "The Sermon," *San Francisco Chronicle*, 31 August 1875.
24. "The Cortege," *Alta California*, 31 August 1875.
25. Ibid.
26. "Voice of the People," *Alta California*, 29 August 1875.
27. Ibid.
28. Ibid.
29. Ibid.
30. Ibid.
31. Ibid.
32. "At the Churches," *Alta California*, 30 August 1875.
33. *Memorial to William C. Ralston*, San Francisco: *Alta California*, 1875, p. 12. See also, "How are the Mighty Fallen," *Alta California*, 30 August 1875.
34. *Memorial*, p. 25.
35. Ibid., p. 19.
36. Ibid., p. 27.

Chapter 21. Silver's Rebirth

1. *Alta California*, 14 December 1874.
2. J.S. Moore, "The Silver Question," *North American Review*, March 1877, p. 298.
3. Irwin Unger, *The Green Back Era: A Social and Political History of American Finance, 1865-1879* (Princeton: Princeton University Press, 1964), pp. 328-329. Edward Chester, in his *A Guide to Political Platforms*, observed, of the Greenback Party's 1876 platform (which called for an immediate and unconditional repeal of the Specie Resumption Act, and protested against the sale of government bonds to purchase silver to be used as currency), "to the true Greenbacker one must not forget, silver was as 'hard' as gold." Edward W. Chester, *A Guide to Political Platforms* (Hamden, CT: Shoe String Press, 1977), p. 98.
4. Ibid., pp. 332-333. The Public Credit Act of 1869 pledged repayment of the national debt in gold.
5. In 1878, George Melville Weston compiled his letters, submitted to the various newspapers, and, with supporting chapters, publishing them under the title *The Silver Question*, from which all subsequent references to Weston's writings are taken.
6. George Melville Weston, *The Silver Question* (New York: I.S. Homans, 1878), p. 105.
7. Ibid., p. 106.
8. Ibid.
9. Ibid., p. 109.
10. "The Gold Fraud," *New York Graphic*, 9 May 1876.
11. Ibid.
12. Ibid.
13. "The Finances of France and Germany," *Cincinnati Commercial*, 8 July 1876.
14. *Cincinnati Commercial*, 18 July 1876.

15. "Resuming the Old Standard," *Cincinnati Commercial*, 23 July 1876.
16. Weston, *The Silver Question*, p. 181.
17. Ibid., p. 182.
18. Ibid.
19. Ibid., p. 183.
20. Ibid., p. 184.
21. Ibid.
22. Ibid., p. 186.
23. U.S., Congress, Senate, *Report of the United States Monetary Commission*, S. Rept. 703, 44th Cong., 2d sess., 1877, vol. 1, p. 4.
24. Ibid., p. 89.
25. Ibid.
26. U.S., Congress, House, 45th Cong., 2d sess., pt. 2, 9 March 1878, *Congressional Record*, p. 1605.
27. U.S., Congress, House, 46th Cong., 1st sess., pt. 1, 10 May 1879, *Congressional Record*, p. 1231.

Chapter 22. Bloody Footprints

1. Horace White, "Silver as Legal-Tender," *The Public* 9 (March 1876): 198.
2. Ibid.
3. Ibid., p. 199.
4. Z.L.W., "Silver Inflation," *New York Tribune*, 24 July 1876.
5. Richard P. Bland and Henry V. Poor, "Debtor and Creditor," *North American Review* 127 (July-August 1878): 117-131. See also, Henry V. Poor, *Resumption and the Silver Question* (New York: J.J. Little & Co., 1878.)
6. Ibid., p. 131.
7. *The Silver Question. A Memorial to Congress (January 1878) by the Representatives of the Banks of New York, Boston, Philadelphia, and Baltimore to memorialize Congress against the passage of the pending silver bill* (New York: Bonnell Stationers and Printers, 1878), p. 12.
8. Ibid., pp. 12-13.
9. U.S. Congress, Senate, 51st Cong., 1st sess., pt. 6, 22 May 1890, *Congressional Record*, p. 5127.
10. William M. Stewart, *Silver and the Science of Money* (Washington, DC, 1894), p. 10.
11. Ibid.
12. Ibid.
13. Ibid.
14. Though Emery's development of the Ernest Seyd myth was widely observed, the origin of this free silver myth dates back to the beginning of the movement in 1876. The Seyd myth was regularly used by free silver authors, throughout the history of the movement, as evidence of a European conspiracy to demonetize silver in the United States.
15. Sarah E.V. Emery, *Seven Financial Conspiracies which have Enslaved the American People* (By the author, 1887; reprint ed., Westport, CT: Hyperion Press Reprint Series, *The Radical Tradition in America*, Hyperion Press, 1975), p. 52. The actual text of Rep. Samuel Hooper's statement reads, "Mr. Ernest Seyd of London, a distinguished writer, who has given great attention to the subject of mints and coinage, after examining the first draft of the bill, furnished many valuable suggestions which have been incorporated in this bill." See U.S. Congress, House, 42d Cong., 2d sess., pt. 3, 9 April 1872, *Congressional Globe*, pp. 2304-2305.
16. Gordon Clark, *Handbook of Money* (Chicago: Silver Knight Publishing Co., 1896), p. 190.
17. Ibid., pp. 190-191.
18. Ibid., p. 191.
19. Ibid.
20. Ibid., p. 192.
21. Ibid.
22. Ibid., pp. 192-193.
23. James Thomas McCleary, "The Crime of 1873," *Sound Currency* 3 (June 1896): 123.
24. Gordon Clark, *Handbook of Money* (Chicago: Silver Knight Publishing Co., 1896), p. 196.
25. McCleary, "The Crime of 1873," p. 122.
26. Ibid., p. 123.
27. Clark, *Handbook*, p. 202.
28. Ibid., p. 204.
29. Ibid., pp. 204-205.
30. Donnelly was also famous for his literary efforts at trying to prove the lost continent of Atlantis existed and for his mathematical formula that purported to show that the works of William Shakespeare contained a hidden message. The message was, according to Donnelly, that Sir Francis Bacon was their true author!
31. Ignatius Donnelly, *The American People's Money* (Chicago: Laird & Lee Publishers, 1895), p. 159.
32. Ibid., pp. 159-160.
33. Ibid., 160.

34. Roswell G. Horr and William Hope Harvey, *The Great Debate on the Financial Question between Hon. Roswell G. Horr of New York and William H. Harvey of Illinois* (Chicago: Debate Publishing Co., 1895).
35. E.J.. Farmer, *The Conspiracy Against Silver or a Plea for Bimetallism in the United States* (Hiles & Cagshall, 1886; reprint ed., New York: Greenwood Press, Publishers, 1969), pp. 7-8.

Chapter 23. Partial Victory

1. Louis W. Koenig, *Bryan: A Political Biography of William Jennings Bryan* (New York: G.P. Putnam's Sons, 1971), p. 170.
2. U.S., Congress, House, *Coinage Laws of the United States, 1792-1894* (Washington, DC: Government Printing Office, 1894), p. 64.
3. Ibid., p. 65.
4. Henry R. Linderman, *Money and Legal Tender in the United States* (New York: G.P. Putnam's Sons, 1877), p. 115.
5. Ibid., p. 116.
6. *Documentary History of Banking & Currency in the United States* (New York: Chelsea House Publishers, 1983), vol. 3, p. 78.
7. Ibid.
8. Ibid., p. 79.
9. Ibid., p. 80.
10. It would later be claimed that the silver interests, in this case the bonanza firm, were behind the move to reinstate unlimited coinage of the silver dollar. There is, however, some evidence to suggest otherwise. In its Jan. 9, 1878, issue, prior to the passage of the Bland-Allison Act, the *New York Tribune* reported, under the heading "A New Foe to the Sham Dollar," that:

    Advices received by Secretary Sherman and others, through trustworthy sources, are said to disprove the assumption that Bland's Silver Bill is supported by the great silver mine owners of the United States. Messrs. Flood & O'Brien and their associates of the Bank of Nevada, at San Francisco, who hold the controlling interest in nearly every successful silver producing mine in the country, unhesitatingly decline themselves against unlimited remonetization. They favor moderate coinage of silver dollars of such weight as will be appropriate in value to that of the gold dollar.
11. U.S., Congress, House, *Report of the Director of the Mint*, H.R. Exec. 2, 45th Cong., 3d sess., 1878, p. 7.
12. Ibid., p 8.
13. Ibid.
14. *New York Tribune*, 17 June 1878.
15. U.S., Congress, House, 16 March 1876, 44th Cong., 1st sess., 1876, *Congressional Globe*, p. 1769.
16. "Dr. Linderman Not Frightened," *New York Tribune*, 18 June 1878.
17. S.P. Dewey, T*he Bonanza Mines of Nevada: Gross Frauds in the Management Exposed, Reply of S.P. Dewey,* 1878; reprinted in *Gold: Historical and Economic Aspects*, Kenneth Carpenter, advisory ed. (New York: Arno Press, 1974), p. 10.
18. Ibid., p. 11.
19. Ibid.
20. Grant H. Smith, *The History of the Comstock Lode* (Reno, NV: University of Nevada Press, 1943; reprinted, Reno, NV: University of Nevada Press, 1998), p. 219.
21. Ibid., p. 220.
22. Ibid., p. 186.
23. *Dictionary of American Biography* (New York: Charles Scribner's Sons, 1933), p. 273.
24. *Report of the Director of the Min*t, 1878, p. 7.
25. *Coinage Laws of the United States*, p. 600.
26. Ibid.
27. Ibid.
28. Ibid., p. 70.
29. Ibid., p. 71.
30. Ibid., p. 110.
31. *Documentary History of Banking and Currency*, p. 115.
32. William Jennings Bryan, *The First Battle: A Story of the Campaign of 1896* (Chicago: W.B. Conkey Co. 1896), pp. 151-152.

The Linderman Collection

1. Q. David Bowers, *The Rare Silver Dollars Dated 1804 and the Exciting Adventures of Edmund Roberts* (Wolfeboro, NH: Bowers and Merena Galleries, Inc., 1999), p. 408.
2. "Note," *Catalogue of the Linderman Collection of United States Coins and Pattern Pieces*, Sale No. 17, Lyman H. Low & Co., 1887.
3. Eric P. Newman and Kenneth E. Bressett, *The Fantastic 1804 Dollar* (Racine, WI: Whitman Publishing Co., 1962), p.

141.
4. *Catalogue of a Valuable Collection*, p. 8.
5. Ibid., p. 9.
6. Andrew W. Pollock III, *United States Patterns and Related Issues* (Wolfeboro, NH: Bowers and Merena Galleries, Inc., 1994), p. 163.
7. *The Garrett Collection Sales*, Sale no. 1, Bowers and Ruddy Galleries, Inc., 28-29 November 1979, p. 79.
8. *Catalogue of the Linderman Collection*, p. 7.
9. Ibid.
10. "Note," *Linderman Collection of Coins*, Sale no. 84, Scott Stamp & Coin Co., Ltd., 28 February 1888.

A Pauper

1. "Petition of Emily Linderman Widow for Letter of Administration and Accent of Henry Linderman, son." D 250, filed Jan. 16, 1880, Supreme Court, District of Columbia.
2. Ibid.

Chapter 24. A Comstock Legacy

1. U.S., Congress, House, *Report of the Director of the Mint*, H.R. Exec. 2, 41st Cong., 2d sess., 1869, p. 346.
2. Pete Smith, "Curry and the Carson City Mint," *The Numismatist* 107 (January 1994), p. 76.
3. U.S., Congress, House, *Report of the Director of the Mint*, H.R. Exec. 2, 42d Cong., 2d sess., 1871, p. 429.
4. U.S., Congress, House, *Report of the Director of the Mint*, H.R. Exec. 2, 46th Cong., 2d sess., 1879, p. 13.
5. U.S., Congress, House, *Report of the Director of the Mint*, H.R. Exec. 2, 46th Cong., 3d sess., 1880, p. 6.
6. *Tahoe Daily Tribune*, 9 December 1999.
7. Leroy C. Van Allen and A. George Mallis, *Comprehensive Catalog and Encyclopedia of U.S. Morgan and Peace Silver Dollars* (New York: FCI Press-ARCO, 1976), p. 247.
8. "Carson City Silver Dollar Selection Underway at GSA," *Numismatic News*, 28 March 1972.
9. Ibid.
10. Totals are from Van Allen-Mallis, p. 249. Final figures provided by the GSA for the coins packaged for sale as published in *Numismatic News*, April 30, 1973, differ slightly from Van Allen-Mallis figures.
11. Ibid., p. 248.
12. "GSA Re-opening CC Dollar Ordering," *Numismatic News*, 13 February 1973.
13. "Bidding Resumes for CC Dollars; Outlook Clouded," *Numismatic News*, 20 February 1973.
14. Ibid.
15. *Numismatic News,* 17 July 1973.
16. "GSA Announces New Bid Period With New Dates," *Numismatic News*, 22 May 1973.
17. "Current CC Silver Dollar Sale Called Treasure Hunt," *Numismatic News,* 24 July 1973
18. Ibid.
19. Ibid.
20. "GSA Pleased With Sale of 215,000 CC Dollars," *Numismatic News*, 20 November 1973.
21. Ibid.
22. "Phase 3 Dollar Sale Brings Million Bids," *Numismatic News*, 28 August 1973.
23. "'79-CC Dollar Sale Starts Feb. 1; Minimum Bid $300," *Numismatic News*, 8 January 1974.
24. "GSA Recaps Third Sale; More CC Events in 1974," *Numismatic News,* 11 December 1973.
25. "GSA Changes Sales Methods for Disposal of CC Dollars," *Numismatic News*, 19 January 1980.
26. *Numismatic News*, 16 February 1980.
27. "Early May is Target Goal for Processing of CC $1," *Numismatic News*, 19 April 1980.
28. "Critics of GSA Dollar Sale Answered by Agency Leader," *Numismatic News*, 26 July 1980.
29. Ibid.
30. "End of an Era: Last of Carson City Dollars Shipped to Buyers by GSA," *Numismatic News*, 4 October 1980.

Chapter 25. The Final Battle

1. Louis W. Koenig, *Bryan: A Political Biography* (New York: G.P. Putnam's Sons, 1971), p. 83.
2. Edward W. Chester, *A Guide to Political Platforms* (Hamden, CT: Shoe String Press, 1977), p. 123.
3. Richard Hofstadter, "Free Silver and the Mind of 'Coin' Harvey," *The Paranoid Style in American Politics and Other Essays* (New York: Alfred Knopf, 1965): 249-250.
4. Another of Harvey's targets was Chicagoan Potter Palmer. This name should be familiar to numismatists, as it was socialite Mrs. Potter Palmer, of the Board of Lady Managers, who headed the drive behind the issuance of the 1893 Isabella quarter.

5. J. Laurence Laughlin, "'Coin's' Food for the Gullible," *The Forum* (July 1895): 576-577.
6. Willard Fisher, "'Coin' and His Critics," *Quarterly Journal of Economics* (January 1896): 192.
7. William Hope Harvey, *The Crime of 1873 and the Harvey-Laughlin Joint Debate*, Coin's Financial Series, No. 7 (Chicago: Coin Publishing Co., 1895), p. 55.
8. Ibid., pp. 54-55.
9. William Hope Harvey, *Coin's Financial School*, ed. Richard Hofstadter (Chicago: By the author, 1894; reprint ed., Cambridge, MA: Harvard University Press, Belknap Press, 1963), p. 204.
10. Full reference, John F. Cargill, *A Freak in Finance or the Boy Teacher Taught being a Reply to "Coin's Financial School," and containing an OUTLINE HISTORY of Bimetallism in the United States from 1792 to the Present Time also a brief statement of the theory of money and some other facts Curious and Interesting* (Chicago: Rand, McNally Co., Publishers, 1896).
11. William Jennings Bryan, *The First Battle: A Story of the Campaign of 1896* (Chicago: W.B. Conkey Co. 1896), p. 71.
12. Ibid., p. 77.
13. Ibid. pp. 79-80.
14. Ibid., p. 205.
15. Ibid., p. 206.
16. See Wayne C. Williams, *William Jennings Bryan* (New York: G.P. Putnam's Sons, 1936).
17. "Good Riddance," *New York Tribune*, 4 November 1896.
18. Bryan, *First Battle*, p. 629.
19. William Hope Harvey, *Coin's Financial School*, ed. Richard Hofstadter (Chicago: By the author, 1894; reprint ed., Cambridge: Harvard University Press, Belknap Press, 1963), p. 7.

BIBLIOGRAPHY

Books

Anderson, George L. "The Proposed Resumption of Specie Payments in 1873." *Pacific Review* 8 (September 1939): 301-316.

Adams, T.F.M. and Awaio Hoshii. *A Financial History of Modern Japan.* Tokyo: Thomas Francis Morton Adams Research, 1964.

Angel, Myron, ed. *History of Nevada.* Oakland, CA: Thompson and West, 1881.

Bancroft, Hubert H. *The Works of Hubert Howe Bancroft.* Vol. 25: *History of Nevada, Colorado, and Wyoming, 1540-1888.* San Francisco: History Company Publishers, 1890.

Boutwell, George S. *Mr. Boutwell's Speech on the Mint Bill of 1873 Delivered before the Twentieth Century Club, Boston, October 14, 1896.* Boston: Beacon Press, 1896.

Bowers, Q. David. *The Rare Silver Dollars Dated 1804 and the Exciting Adventures of Edmund Roberts.* Wolfeboro, NH: Bowers and Merena Galleries, Inc., 1999.

Browne, J. Ross. *Crusoe's Island: Ramble in the footsteps of Alexander Selkirk. With Sketches of Adventure in California and Washoe.* New York: Harper Brothers, 1864.

Bryan, William Jennings. *The First Battle: A Story of the Campaign of 1896.* Chicago: W.B. Conkey Co., 1896.

Bryan, William Jennings and Bryan, Mary Baird. *The Memoirs of William Jennings Bryan.* Philadelphia: John C. Winston Co., 1925.

Cargill, John F. *A Freak of Finance or the Boy Teacher Taught being a Reply to "Coin's Financial School," and containing an OUTLINE History of Bimetallism in the United States from 1792 to the Present Time also a brief statement of the theory of money and some other facts Curious and Interesting.* New York: Rand, McNally & Co., Publishers, 1896.

Carlson, Helen S. *Nevada Place Names: A Geographical Dictionary.* Reno, NV: University of Nevada Press, 1974.

Carothers, Neil. *Fractional Money: A History of the Small Coins and Fractional Paper Currency of the United States.* New York: John Wiley & Sons, 1930.

Chester, Edward W. *A Guide to Political Platforms.* Hamden, CT: Shoe String Press, 1977.

Clark, Gordon. *Handbook of Money.* Chicago: Silver Knight Publishing Co., 1896.

Cross, Ira B. *Financing an Empire: History of Banking in California.* 2 vols. Chicago: The S.J. Clarke Publishing Co., 1927.

Dana, Julian. *The Man Who Built San Francisco: A Study of Ralston's Journey with Banners.* New York: The Macmillan Co., 1936.

Del Mar, Alexander. *Story of the Gold Conspiracy as told at the Memphis Convention.* Chicago: Charles H. Kerr & Co., 1895.

Dewey, S.P. *The Bonanza Mines of Nevada: Gross Frauds in the Management Exposed, Reply of S.P. Dewey,* 1878. Reprinted in Carpenter, Kenneth, advisory ed. *Gold: Historical and Economic Aspects.* New York: Arno Press, 1974.

Dictionary of American Biography. New York: Charles Scribner's Sons, 1933, Vol. VI.

Donnelly, Ignatius. *The American People's Money.* Chicago: Laird & Lee Publishers, 1895.

Elliot, Russell R. *History of Nevada.* Lincoln, NE: University of Nebraska Press, 1973.

Emery, Sarah E.V. *Seven Financial Conspiracies which have Enslaved the American People.* By the author, 1887, reprint ed., Westport, CT: Hyperion Reprint Series, *The Radical Tradition in America,* Hyperion Press, 1955.

Farmer, E.J. *The Conspiracy against Silver or a Plea for Bimetallism in the United States.* Hiles & Cagshall, 1886; reprint ed., New York: Greenwood Press, Publishers, 1969.

Friedman, Milton, and Schwartz, Anna Jacobson. *Monetary History of the United States, 1867-1960.* Princeton: Princeton University Press, 1963.

Glass, Mary Ellen. *Silver and Politics in Nevada, 1892-1902.* The Lancetlead Series: *Nevada and the West.* Nevada: University of Nevada Press, 1969.

Harvey, William Hope. *Coin's Financial School.* Edited by Richard Hofstadter. Chicago: By the author, 1894; reprint ed., Cambridge, MA: Harvard University Press, Belknap Press, 1963.

——. *The Crime of 1873 and the Harvey-Laughlin Joint Debate.* Coin's Financial Series, no. 7. Chicago: Coin Publishing Co., 1895.

——. *A Tale of Two Nations.* Chicago: Coin Publishing Co., 1894.

Hofstadter, Richard. "Free Silver and the Mind of 'Coin' Harvey." *The Paranoid Style in American Politics and Other Essays,* pp. 238-315. New York: Alfred Knopf, 1965.

Horr, Roswell G., and Harvey, William Hope. *The Great Debate on the Financial Question between Hon. Roswell G. Horr of New York and William H. Harvey of Illinois*. Chicago: Debate Publishing Co., 1895.

Judd, J. Hewitt. *United States Patterns, Experimental and Trial Pieces*. Racine, WI: Western Publishing Co., 1959.

Kagin, Donald H. *Private Gold Coins and Patterns of the United States*. New York: Arco Publishing Co., 1981.

Kelly, J. Wells. *First Directory of Nevada Territory Containing the Names of Residents in the Principal Towns; A Historical Sketch, the Organic Act, and Other Political Matters of Interest; Together with a Description of all the Quartz Mills; Reduction Works, and all Other Industrial Establishments in the Territory; of the Leading Mining Claims, and Various Mineral Discoveries, Works of Internal Improvement, et with a Table of Distances, Lists of Public Officers and Other Useful Information.* San Francisco: Valentine & Co., 1862, reprint ed., The Talisman Press, 1962.

King, Joseph L. *History of the San Francisco Stock and Exchange Board*. San Francisco: By the author, 1910.

Knox, John Jay. *United States Notes: A History of the Various Issues of Paper Money by the Government of the United States*. London: T.F. Fisher Unwin, 1885; reprint ed., New York: Sanford J. Durst, 1978.

Koenig, Louis W. *Bryan: A Political Biography of William Jennings Bryan*. New York: G.P. Putnam's Sons, 1971.

Lavender, David. *Nothing Seemed Impossible: William C. Ralston and Early San Francisco.* Western Biographical Series. Palo Alto, CA: American West Publishing Co., 1975.

Linderman, Henry R. *Money and Legal Tender in the United States.* New York: G.P. Putnam's Sons, 1877.

Lord, Eliot. *Comstock Mining and Miners*. Washington, DC: Government Printing Office, 1883. Reprint ed. Berkeley, CA: Howell-North, 1959.

Lyman, George. *Ralston's Ring: California Plunders the Comstock.* New York: Charles Scribner's Sons, 1937.

Memorial to William C. Ralston. San Francisco: *Alta California*, 1875.

National Executive Silver Committee. *Silver in the Fifty-First Congress*. Washington, DC: George R. Gray, Printer, 1890.

Nugent, Walter T.K. *The Money Question During Reconstruction*. New York: W.W. Norton & Co., 1967.

Newman, Eric P. and Bressett, Kenneth E. *The Fantastic 1804 Dollar.* Racine, WI: Whitman Publishing Co., 1962.

Paul, Rodman. *Mining Frontiers of the Far West 1848-1880*. New York: Holt, Rinehart and Winston, 1963.

Pollock III, Andrew W. *United States Patterns and Related Issues*. Wolfeboro, NH: Bowers and Merena Galleries, Inc., 1994.

Poor, Henry Varnum. *Resumption and the Silver Question*. New York: J.J. Little & Co., 1878.

Poore, Ben Perly, ed. *Message from the President of the United States to the Two Houses of Congress at the Commencement of the Second Session of the Forty-Eighth Congress, with the Reports of the Heads of Departments and Selections from Accompanying Documents.* Washington, DC: Government Printing Office, 1884.

Rickard, T.A. *A History of American Mining*. New York: McGraw-Hill Book Co., Inc., 1932.

Shinn, Charles Howard. *The Story of the Mine: As Illustrated by the Great Comstock Lode of Nevada.* Story of the West Series. New York: D. Appleton, 1910; reprint ed., Reno, NV: University of Nevada Press, 1980. Vintage Nevada Series.

Smith, Grant H. *The History of the Comstock Lode*. Reno, NV: University of Nevada Press, 1943; reprint ed., with new material by Joseph V. Tingley, Reno, NV: University of Nevada Press, 1998.

Stevens, C.M. *Silver vs. Gold: Free Silver and the People—A Campaign Handbook for Struggling Millions against the Gold-Hoarding Millionaires*. New York: Tennyson Neely Publishers, 1896.

Stewart, William M. *Silver and the Science of Money.* Washington, DC: 1894.

The Silver Question. A Memorial to Congress (January 1878) by the Representatives of the Banks of New York, Boston, Philadelphia, and Baltimore to memorialize Congress against passage of the pending silver bill. New York: Bonnell Stationers and Printers, 1878.

Studenski, Paul, and Kroos, Herman E. *Financial History of the United States*, 2nd ed. New York: McGraw-Hill Book Co., 1963.

Taxay, Don. *The U.S. Mint and Coinage: An Illustrated History from 1776 to the Present.* New York: Arco Publishing Co., 1966.

Thompson, D.G. Brinton. *Ruggles of New York: A Life of Samuel B. Ruggles*. Studies in History, Economics, and Public Law, ed. Faculty of Political Science of Columbia University, no. 524. New York: Columbia University Press, 1946.

Tilton, Cecil G. *William Chapman Ralston: Courage Builder.* Boston: The Christopher Publishing Co., 1935.

Twain, Mark (Samuel Clemens). *Roughing It*. Hartford, CT: American Publishing Co, 1891.

Unger, Irwin. *The Greenback Era: A Social and Political History of American Finance, 1865-1879.* Princeton: Princeton University Press, 1964.

Young, Otis E. *An Informational Account of Precious-metals Prospecting, Placering, Lode Mining, and Milling on the American Frontier from Spanish Times to 1893.* Norman, OK: University of Oklahoma Press, 1970.

Watkins, T.H. *Gold and Silver in the West: The Illustrated History of an American Dream.* New York: American West Publishing Co., 1971.

Weinstein, Allen. *Prelude to Populism: Origins of the Silver Issue, 1867-1878.* New Haven, CT: Yale University Press, 1970.

Weston, George M. *The Silver Question.* New York: I.S. Homans, 1878.

White, Horace. *Money and Banking: An Illustrated by American History.* Boston: Gin & Co., 1896.

Willem, John M. Jr. *The United States Trade Dollar: America's Only Unwanted, Unhonored Coin.* New York: By the author, 1959.

William Wright (Dan De Quille pseud.) *The Big Bonanza.* Hartford, CT: American Publishing Co., 1876; reprint ed. New York: Alfred A. Knopf, 1953.

Journals and Magazines

Anderson, George L.. "The Proposed Resumption of Silver Payments in 1873." *Pacific Historical Review* 8 (September 1939): 301-316.

Bland, Richard P., and Poor, Henry V. "Debtor and Creditor." *North American Review* 127 (July-August 1878): 117-131.

Garnett, Porter. "History of the Trade Dollar." *American Economic Review* 7 (March 1917): 91-97.

Fisher, Willard. "'Coin' and His Critics." *Quarterly Journal of Economics* (January 1896): 187-208.

Hill, Roy. "History of San Francisco Mint," *Money Talks: A Numismatic Anthology Selected from the CALCOIN NEWS* (Irvine, CA: California State Numismatic Association, 1970): 3-11

Julian, R.W. "The Trade Dollar: America's Unloved Coin." *Coins* Magazine, June 1979, pp. 82-98.

Lalor, J.J. "Early and Recent Currency Legislation." *The Forum* 11 (18 September 1896): 117-128.

Laughlin, J. Laurence. "'Coin's' Food for the Gullible." *The Forum* 19 (July 1895): 573-585.

Linderman, Henry R., and Torrey, John. "The Production of Gold and Silver." From 19 November 1872 Treasury Department *Special Report of Examination of Branch Mints on the Pacific Coast*; reprinted in *Bankers' Magazine and Statistical Register* 7, 3rd series (March 1873): 710-716.

McCleary, James Thompson. "The Crime of 1873." *Sound Currency* 3 (1 June 1896): 116-130.

Moore, J.S. "The Silver Question." *North American Review* 124 (March 1877); 116-130.

O'Leary, Paul M. "The Scene of the Crime of 1873 Revisited: A Note." *Journal of Political Economy* 69 (August 1960): 288-392.

Smith, Pete. "Curry and the Carson City Mint." *The Numismatist* 107 (January 1994): 76-78.

Weinstein, Allen. "Was There a 'Crime of 1873'?: The Case of the Demonetized Dollar." *The Journal of American History* 54 (September 1967): 307-326.

White, Horace. "Silver as a Legal-Tender." *The Public* 9 (23 March 1876): 188-199.

Zerbe, Farran, "Bryan Money: Tokens of the Presidential Campaign of 1896 and 1900—Comparative and Satirical." *The Numismatist* 36 (July 1926): 313-376

Auction Catalogs

Auctions by Bowers and Merena. *Ebenezer Milton Sanders Collection*, 1987.

Bowers and Ruddy Galleries, Inc. *The Garrett Collection Sales*, Sale no. 1, Bowers and Ruddy Galleries, Inc., 1979.

Lyman H. Low & Co. *Catalogue of the Linderman Collection of United States Coins and Pattern Pieces*, Sale no. 17, 1887.

Scott Stamp & Coin Co., Ltd., *Linderman Collection of Coins*, Sale no. 84, 1888.

Newspapers and Magazines

Various issues of the following newspapers were used in preparation of the text. See Notes for exact citations.

Alta California.

Cincinnati Commercial.

New York Graphic.

New York Times.

New York Tribune.

Numismatic News.

Philadelphia North American and United States Gazette.

San Francisco Chronicle.

Tahoe Daily Tribune.

Virginia City Territorial Enterprise.

Unpublished Manuscripts/Letters

"Petition of Emily Linderman Widow for Letter of Administration and Accent of Henry Linderman, son." D 250, filed Jan. 16, 1880, Supreme Court, District of Columbia.

Van Ryzin, Robert R. "The Tainted History of the Crime of 1873," Master's thesis, University of Wisconsin-Oshkosh, 1986.

William Chapman Ralston Papers (77/88c), The Bancroft Library, University of California, Berkeley.

Congressional Documents

See citations in Notes for *Congressional Globe* and *Congressional Record* references.

U.S. Congress. House. *Coinage Laws of the United States, 1792-1894.* 4th ed. Washington, DC: Government Printing Office, 1894.

General References

Barley, Cotton M. (pseud.). *The Financial School at Farmerville*. Chicago: Currency Publishing House, 1895.

Barnett, Paul. "The Crime of 1873 Re-Examined." *Agricultural History* 38 (July 1964): 178-181.

Bliss, H.L. *Coin's Financial Fraud: A Complete and Comprehensive Treatise on the Currency Question, and an Answer to and Complete Refutation of the Advocates of the Free Coinage of Silver.* Chicago: Donohue, Henneberry & Co., 1895.

"The Coinage Act of 1873." *The Nation* (6 December 1877): 343-344.

"The Crime of 1873." *The Century* 52 (September 1896): 792-793.

Carter, Benjamin. "The Crime of 1873." *The Nation* (6 August 1891): 96.

"The Demonetization of Silver." *The Nation* (1 March 1900): 162.

"A Foretaste of Socialism." *The Nation* (21 September 1893): 206-207.

Garrett, L. Maury. "The Money Conspiracy." *Money* 3 (December 1899): 174-1777.

Henderson, John C. *Silver and Gold Money.* Montana: Inter Mountain Publishing Co., 1893.

Halstead, Murat. "A Silver Senator Reviewed." *North American Review* 154 (June 1892): 666-671.

Harrison, Benjamin. "Compulsory Dishonesty." *The Forum* 22 (October 1896): 129-135.

Harvey, William Hope. "Coin's Financial School and Its Censors." *North American Review* 161 (July 1895): 71-79.

———. "The Free Silver Argument." *The Forum* 19 (June 1895): 401-409.

Hayes, H. Gordon. "Bimetallism Before and After 1834." *American Economic Review* 23 (December 1933): 677-679.

Horton, S. Dana. *Silver and Gold and their Relation to the Problem of Resumption.* Cincinnati: Robert Clarke & Co., 1877.

Jevons, W. Stanley. "The Silver Question." *Journal of Social Science* 9 (January 1878): 14-20.

Johnston, Stephen. "Hon. Stephen Johnson Greenback Party Candidate for Governor of Ohio to John Sherman." *Anti-Monopolist* 27 (September 1877).

Laughlin, Laurence J. *The History of Bimetallism in the United States.* New York: D. Appleton & Co., 1897.

Leech, Edward O. "Silver Legislation and Its Results." *North American Review* 157 (July 1893): 43-51.

McPherson, Edward. *A Handbook of Politics for 1874: Being a Record of Important Political Action, National and State from July 15, 1872 to July 15, 1874.* 7th ed. Washington, DC: Solomon & Chapman, 1874.

Marble, Manton. "Currency Quacks, and the Silver Bill." *North American Review* 126 (January-February 1878): 156-170.

Nelson, Henry Loomis. "Bimetallism in History." *Sound Currency* 2 (1 January 1895): 174-186.

Powderly, T.V. "The Working Man and Free Silver." *North American Review* 153 (December 1891): 728-736.

"The President and the Silver Movement." *The Nation* (21 June 1877): 360-361.

Roberts, J.O. "The Awful 'Crime' of 1873." *Money* 3 (July 1899): 6-8.

Sherman, John. *Recollections of Forty Years in the House, Senate and Cabinet.* 2 vols. New York: Werner Co., 1895.

"The Silver Question." *The Graphic*, 14 March 1876.

Stewart, William M. "Silver, and the Need for More Money." *The Forum* 11 (June 1891): 429-437.

Upton, J.K. *Money in Politics*. Boston: D. Lothrop Co., 1895.

Walker, Francis A. "The Free Coinage of Silver." *The Journal of Political Economy* 1 (March 1893): 163-178.

———. "The Silver Monetary Conferences of 1867 and 1878, and the Future of Silver." *Princeton Review* (January 1879): 28-54.

Waterloo, Stanley. *Honest Money: 'Coin's' Fallacies Exposed.* Chicago: Equitable Publishing Co., 1895.

Wells, David A. *The Silver Question: The Dollar of the Fathers versus the Dollar of the Sons, Also an Extract from an Article in the North American Review, 1877, on the Unconstitutionality of the Repeal of the Obligations of the Resumption Act.* New York: G.P. Putnam's Sons, 1877.

———. "The Downfall of Certain Financial Fallacies." *The Forum* 16 (October 1893): 131-149.

White, Horace. "Coin's Financial Fool, a Reply to Coin's Financial School." *Sound Currency* 2 (1 May 1895): 406-424.

White, Trumbell, ed. *Silver and Gold, or Both Sides of the Shield: A symposium of the views of all parties on the Currency Question as expressed by their leading advocates: Thoroughly expounding the Doctrines of FREE SILVER, Monometallism and Bimetallism with all the arguments pro. and con!*. Publishers Union, 1895.

"Why the Demonetization of Silver did not attract Popular Attention." *The Nation* (20 December 1877): 377-378.

Wood, Stanley. *Answer to Coin's Financial School.* Chicago: A.B. Sherwood Publishing Co., 1895.

INDEX

D

E

F

G

H

P

R

S

T

U

Numismatic News

World Coin News

EXPERT NUMISMATIC INFORMATION

Numismatic News

The #1 source for numismatic information. Timely reports on market trends and news concerning collectible coins and paper money. Provides collectors with up-to-date, comprehensive pricing.

Weekly Publication
1 year (52 issues)
only
$32.00

World Coin News

The leading authority on world coins. Reports on new issues, market trends and other coin news from around the world. Each issue also provides a calendar of upcoming shows worldwide.

Monthly Publication
1 year (12 issues)
only
$25.98

Bank Note Reporter

Covers market trends, buying tips and historical perspectives on all aspects of numismatics. News section wraps up the latest happenings in numismatics. Calendar of upcoming shows nationwide.

Monthly Publication
1 year (12 issues)
only
$24.98

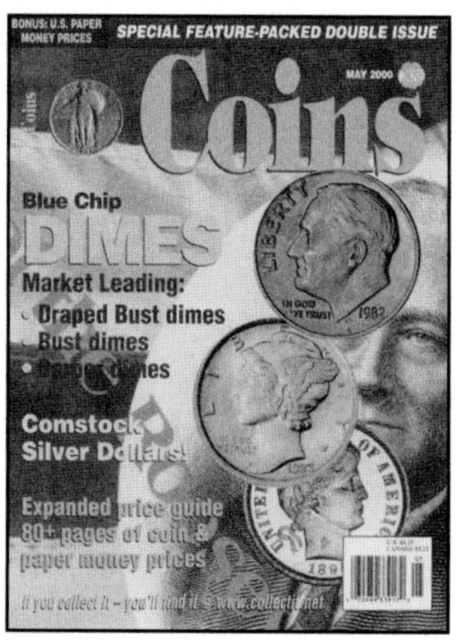

The finest publication for paper money collectors available. Contains news on market trends, up-to-date foreign exchange chart, price guide, world currency section, historical features and much more.

Monthly
Publication
1 year (12 issues)
only
$32.00

A complete guide to retail values for collectible U.S. coins. A market update section (value guide) begins each issue. A current coin show calendar, guide to grading U.S. coins and a collector Q&A..

Bi-monthly
Publication
1 year (6 issues)
only
$18.98

TO PLACE A CREDIT CARD ORDER CALL TOLL-FREE

800-258-0929

DEPT. ABAYI2

M-F, 7 AM - 8 PM · SAT, 8 AM - 2 PM, CST

OR SEND YOUR ORDER ON A 3X5 CARD WITH PAYMENT TO:

KRAUSE PUBLICATIONS, ABAYI2 · 700 E. STATE ST. · IOLA, WI 54990-0001